A Brief for Professional Education

ED SCHOOL

Geraldine Jonçich Clifford
James W. Guthrie

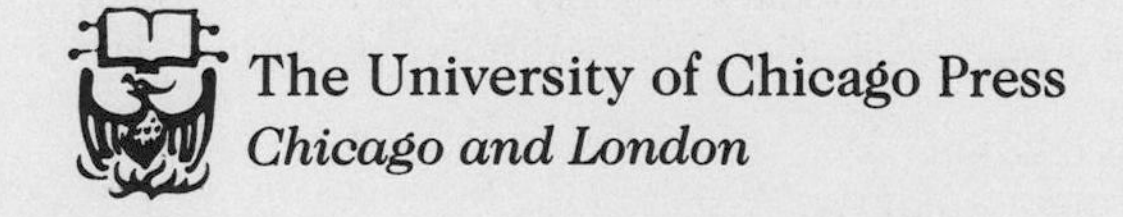

The University of Chicago Press
Chicago and London

The University of Chicago Press gratefully acknowledges the contribution of the Exxon Education Foundation toward the publication of this book.

The University of Chicago Press, Chicago 60637
The University of Chicago Press, Ltd., London

Paperback edition 1990
Printed in the United States of America

97 96 95 94 93 92 91 90 5432

LIBRARY OF CONGRESS CATALOGING-IN-PUBLICATION DATA

Clifford, Geraldine Jonçich.
Ed school : a brief for professional education /
Geraldine Jonçich Clifford and James W. Guthrie.
p. cm.
Bibliography: p.
Includes index.
ISBN 0-226-11017-6 (cloth)
ISBN 0-226-11016-8 (paper)
1. Teachers—Training of—United States—History. 2. Universities and colleges—United States—History. 3. Education—Study and teaching (Higher)—United States—History. I. Guthrie, James W. II. Title.
LB2165.C59 1988
370′.7′10973—dc19 87-30147
CIP

This book is printed on acid-free paper.

FOR PAULA AND BILL

Marriage is one long conversation, checkered by disputes.

—*Robert Louis Stevenson*

AND FOR DORIS HOWES CALLOWAY

A friend may well be reckoned the masterpiece of nature.

—*Ralph Waldo Emerson*

Contents

Preface

The genesis of this book lies in some routine summer housekeeping. James Guthrie, chairman of the Department of Education at Berkeley, was cleaning his office of files generated in the battles to maintain the School of Education. On August 23, 1982, he wrote to his predecessor, Geraldine Clifford, the following:

> Do you think the world would note or long remember a piece that the two of us might write about the last decade here at Berkeley's Graduate School of Education? I suppose such an article might range all the way from an extraordinarily bitter and cynical piece entitled something such as "How to Destroy a Professional School on a Prestigious Campus" to something more analytical, attempting to capture the tension on a Letters and Science–dominated campus between academic units and professional schools.

Were we, as participant observers, too close to events to be good historians or policy analysts? In the ensuing six months we tried to answer this question by writing a draft of the "Berkeley story." We sent it to some of our colleagues in the school, to select deans and professors in similar institutions, and to a few individuals who we thought would have a particular interest in our chronicle of those months and years when Berkeley's School of Education rode its own roller coaster of consoling hopes and wretched nightmares. Their responses ranged from enthusiastic encouragement to rush into print, to more measured suggestions about analysis and style, to straightforward advice not to publish the story. This last advice was based on perceptions that we were "too close to too-recent events" or on the belief that such an exposure would only rouse the opposition to education at Berkeley and make the job of the new dean more difficult. The essay was set aside.

Subsequently the director of Educational Studies at Oxford University, Harry Judge, published *American Graduate Schools of Education: A View from Abroad.* Judge had come to Berkeley in the course of his research. One of us talked at length with him about Berkeley and, in so doing, began to draw the contrast with UCLA which appears in this present book. We found Judge's work an important potential contribution to the emerging discussions going on in a few leading universities about reforming the triangular relationships between public school professionals, schools of education, and universities. What we thought was still lacking in these reconsiderations were historical perspective on the evolution of major schools of education as a generic type and case studies that might yield lessons by calling attention to the specific character of real (rather than Judge's composite) institutions—to their "culture," style, and idiosyncratic development. There was, then, more to be understood and written about the fit of this particular kind of institution in twentieth-century American higher education.

Our conversations with other European scholars who passed through Berkeley or those we met at professional meetings also revealed surprising similarities in the characteristics of foreign education schools and in their positions on their respective campuses. Witness Cambridge University's refusal to incorporate the Institute of Education into the university. This seemed to be part of the general perception abroad that departments of education are not genuine university departments.[1]

In the meantime, Berkeley's new dean of education, Bernard Gifford, encouraged us with the word that he had found our draft paper helpful in teaching him about the tasks before him. His telling of our Berkeley story aroused interest in a number of other institutions as well. An invitation to present an historical paper on education schools at the 1985 meetings of the American Educational Research Association caused us to consider resuming and somewhat recasting our project. The immediate task was to compare developments at the University of Chicago from 1900 to 1940 with those at four other schools

1. Boris Ford, "Schools of Education and Social Work," *The Idea of a New University: An Experiment in Sussex,* ed. David Daiches (Cambridge, Mass.: MIT Press, 1964), 135.

of education: at Berkeley, Harvard, Stanford, and Columbia. Before that work was finished, we decided to extend the comparison to ten institutions as a larger context for the Berkeley case study and to discuss present-day events in American education and in schools of education that seemed to us to argue for an unprecedented commitment by leading education schools to the full implications of being professional schools.

We wish to express our gratitude to those who have informed, advised, encouraged, and even discouraged us. Special thanks to Lawrence Cremin, Lee Shulman, and Gary Sykes for valuable suggestions on how to improve the manuscript. We have not acknowledged everyone we spoke with. Those who have been formally interviewed, however, and those who have read portions of the manuscript are cited in the notes. We hope that our labors will illuminate the important issues facing schools of education, higher education, and the professions of teaching and administering schools in the United States.

Why should not teachers be well provided for, to continue their whole in the schoole, as *Divines, Lawyers, Physicians* do in their several professions? I conclude, therefore, that this trade requireth a particular college for these four causes. First, for the subject, being the mean to make or mar the whole fry of our state. Secondly, for the number, whether of them that are to learn, or of them that are to teach. Thirdly, for the necessity of the profession, which may not be spared. Fourthly, for the matter of their study, which is comparable to the greatest possession, for language, for judgment, for skills how to train, for variety in all points of learning, wherein the framing of the mind and the exercising of the body craveth exquisite consideration, besides the staidness of the person.

Richard Mulcaster, *Positions, Wherein Those Primitive circumstances be Examined, Which Are Necessaire for the Training up of Children, either for Skill in Their Booke, or Health in Their Bodie* (1581)

1 Introduction

One Education, Educators, and Education Schools

The president of Harvard College, writing in 1865 as his institution was groping its way toward becoming a university, drew the common distinction between liberal education—"which may conduce to the general perfection and improvement of the pupil"—and professional education—"that culture and instruction which fits . . . for some chosen walk in life." He recommended against the "mere appointment of a Professor of Didactics in each college" because of the already overcrowded undergraduate curriculum and the insufficiency of time to do justice to the subject. "But the establishment of a Normal School in a University, and of a special course for Bachelors of Arts in a Normal School, would be steps calculated to raise the standard of excellence required of teachers, and would lift towards its proper dignity the high profession of teaching."[1]

This book is about those "normal schools in a university" in the United States: about their origins, historical evolution, continuing problems, and future prospects. Our thesis is that schools of education, particularly those located on the campuses of prestigious research universities, have become ensnared improvidently in the academic and political cultures of their institutions and have neglected their professional allegiances. They are like marginal men, aliens in their own worlds. They have seldom succeeded in satisfying the scholarly norms of their campus letters and science colleagues, and they are simultaneously estranged from their practicing professional peers.

1. Thomas Hill, "Remarks on the Study of Didactics in Colleges," *American Journal of Education* 15, no. 38 (March 1865): 179.

The more forcefully they have rowed toward the shores of scholarly research, the more distant they have become from the public schools they are duty bound to serve. Conversely, systematic efforts at addressing the applied problems of public schools have placed schools of education at risk on their own campuses.

While our focus is upon graduate schools and departments of education, this book is not about all such institutions. Rather, we have chosen to concentrate on a select few, those which are located on the campuses of the nation's most influential research universities. These institutions have traditionally prepared only a tiny fraction of the nation's teachers, and have vacillated about whether they should do even that much of this ill-regarded work. Nevertheless, they exert a disproportionate influence on all the rest. They may even claim that their teacher education programs are experimental models for others to emulate or that their graduates are destined to be the future teacher-leaders of the field, or that, by preparing teachers, they elevate the intellectual standing of the teaching profession. Through their advanced degree programs, they also train and certify most of the faculty who staff the schools of education which produce the majority of American teachers. As the nation's centers of educational research, they are likely to perform whatever systematic inquiry is conducted on teacher education or fed into the content of professional courses in teacher training programs throughout the system of schools of education.

As we will show, their influence has been neither consisent nor positive in the professionalization of teaching. Their deans are today attempting to exert the dominant influence over the restructuring of teaching, in ways that continue to celebrate researchers over teachers, educational science over eclectic craft knowledge.[2] Thus, though few in number, slender in resources, often insecure institutionally, and stubbornly patronizing, these elite schools of education have commonly exerted disproportionate influence over the remaining teacher training institutions throughout the nation. That is our justification for the comparisons and analyses we undertake in subsequent chapters.

This book concentrates on the internal cultures of the beacon

2. The irony of the Holmes Group of education school deans in identifying itself with Harvard's one-time dean, Henry W. Holmes, is discussed in William R. Johnson, "Empowering Practitioners: Holmes, Carnegie, and the Lessons of History," *History of Education Quarterly* 27, no. 2 (Summer 1987): 221–40.

schools of education and their interactions with their campuses on the one hand and with public schools on the other. However, schools of education cannot be fully understood without appreciating the position of education and schooling, particularly public schools, in American cultural and social life. Thus we delay for the moment pursuing our major thesis in order to describe the broader social context in which American education, educators, and schools of education are embedded.

Before beginning our description of the external social environment that shapes American schooling and educators, we wish to make clear that this book is intended for multiple audiences, not all of whom are likely to share a common understanding of present conditions or are necessarily interested in a common core of future solutions. Those readers who are already thoroughly informed regarding the conditions of schooling and school policy may wish to detour immediately to subsequent chapters which lay the historical groundwork for our thesis of schools of education as organizational chameleons, trapped regardless of the coloration they adopt. Those less familiar with the cultural context of American education will wish to continue this chapter to learn more about the forces which shape American schooling and the nature of the controversy over the professionalization of teaching and its relationship to schools of education.

Education in the United States is entangled in an untidy mix of cultural and personal values, public policy issues, and ambiguous professional self-perceptions. Nowhere is the fact more obvious or problematic than in the preparation of the nation's public school teachers. As has happened cyclically in its past, America, in approaching the end of the twentieth century, is again in need of larger numbers of teachers, and policymakers are unsure of how to satisfy that need. This section describes the situation and suggests that too many resources have already been committed to education for us to allow the problems to continue unresolved.

The Paradox of Public Values

Americans purport to, and probably do, believe deeply in schooling, and over time they have elevated its pursuit to the level of a secular religion. But education is valued most as an instrument, and not as an end in itself. Learning is, like teaching, distinct from and inferior to, doing. Writing of the "American," historian Henry Steele Commager observes, "Education was his religion, and to it he paid the tribute both of his money and his affection; yet, as he expected his religion to be practical and pay dividends, he expected education to prepare for life—by which he meant, increasingly, jobs and professions."[3]

Formal knowledge has increasingly been viewed as crucial for the fulfillment of individual goals as more and more occupations require extended schooling. The high school dropout, once the bulk of the blue- and white-collar classes, is now considered "damaged goods"—an economic and social problem to himself and to society. By law as well as social pressure students are compelled to attend school, admonished repeatedly not to drop out, and informed routinely of the relationship between school success and their own economic well being. Presidents, captains of industry, national heroes, and a seemingly endless stream of other luminaries provide unsolicited personal testimony regarding the virtues of education and the unhappy consequences of its neglect.

Not only do Americans accord formal education a high place in their pantheon of personal gods, but their spokesmen have also grown progressively more obsessed with the significance of schooling for nurturing society and promoting national purposes. Social cohesion, civic unity, national defense, personal health, family stability, economic vitality, racial harmony, and safe driving are some of the national agenda items that schools have been expected to promote and sustain. We may smile tolerantly at this list of goals, but to do so is sadly to underestimate both the extent of disagreement about priorities and the impossibility of ever satisfying America's desires with respect to education.

It seems as if there is seldom a public crisis for which schooling is not seen as at least a partial solution. The slogan of "open a school and close a prison" was employed in the nineteenth century to win the commitment of public opinion and especially tax-conscious businessmen to the cause of public-supported education. Although that simple faith has long since evaporated, one still hears that advice implied in the proposition that "It costs less to send a boy to Stanford than to San Quentin!" Protecting the environment, preventing teenage pregnancy, promoting racial harmony, encouraging world peace, ending world hunger, discouraging alcoholism and drug abuse are but a few of the campaigns currently assigned to schools. A list of previous assignments would include almost every major social problem or aspiration the nation has ever encountered. *The dangers of disillusionment as a*

3. Henry Steele Commager, *The American Mind* (New Haven, Conn.: Yale University Press, 1950), 10.

result of overpromising are great, and yet policy makers and even educators repeatedly succumb to the temptation to make such promises.

This predisposition of society toward formal education is reflected in the enormous resources invested in schooling, making teaching "the most political and most public of all the professions.[4] The sheer numbers connected with America's education system would dumbfound those who established the outlines of this system only a century ago. By the late twentieth century, for example, these facts obtained: One out of every four United States residents was enrolled in a school or college; educational institutions annually spent more than $400 billion; more than one out of every twenty dollars of the total value of all goods and services produced in the United States was being used for supporting schools; education consumed more tax revenues than any other public sector undertaking except defense, health services, and paying the annual interest on the national debt; more individuals in the United States were employed in education than either earned their livelihood directly from agriculture or served as uniformed personnel in the military. Thus, whether measured in terms of its prominent position in the consciousness of citizens or the magnitude of its involvement in public resources, education in America has become a central undertaking of the society.[5]

Yet despite the extensive commitments of attention and resources, Americans appear to be ambivalent about schooling. There is, for one thing, a streak of anti-intellectualism embedded in the national character, and that anti-intellectualism is itself a self-contradictory set of attitudes. It includes a distrust of experts that goes at least as far back as Andrew Jackson, if not to the Reformation's attack on the priestly class of the established Church of Rome. It esteems the common sense of the ordinary man as more reliable with fewer pretensions than the knowledge of persons educated in "mere theories." At the 1893 World's Fair in Chicago, forty acres were given to displaying the cattle breeder's art and two to the educational exhibit. "It is hard for Americans to understand that it is possible for men to be politically equal while intellectually unequal," wrote the

4. Martin Haberman, "Licensing Teachers: Lessons from Other Professions," *Phi Delta Kappan,* 67, no. 10 (June 1986): 719.

5. Moreover, every indicator suggests that education will increase its command of resources between now and the end of the twentieth century. Kindergarten through twelfth-grade enrollments, approximately 46 million in 1988, are growing and will continue upward for at least the remainder of this century.

historian Albert Bushnell Hart in 1938.[6] Mild and benign forms of anti-intellectualism, contends another historian, Richard Hofstadter, are widespread, and often they have been evoked around defensible causes: evangelical religion, greater humaneness in education, more democratic politics, a more just society. Finally, it also seems clear "that those who have some quarrel with intellect are almost always ambivalent about it: they mix respect and awe with suspicion and resentment."[7]

National ambivalence toward intellectual and academic matters spills over into views regarding schooling. Americans have consistently preferred "good character" to great scholarship. Cyclically, schools are looked to as national saviors and subsequently seen as failing to "pay off"—defrauding the public of its purchased benefits. For example, following the launching of the Soviet Union's Sputnik, the alleged absence of academic rigor in public schools was held to be the major explanation for Soviet technological superiority. Indeed, so badly had the schools let America down that George R. Price, a famous physicist of the day, stated in the 18 November 1957 issue of *Life* magazine that "few predictions seem more certain than this: Russia is going to surpass us in mathematics and the social sciences. . . . In short, unless we depart utterly from our present behavior, it is reasonable to expect that by no later than 1975 the United States will be a member of the Union of Soviet Socialist Republics." As a consequence of such professedly miserable past performance on the part of the nation's schools, in the subsequent year, 1958, Congress enacted the National Defense Education Act (NDEA). This legislation appropriated millions of dollars for intensified instruction in science, mathematics, and foreign languages.

Presumably, such policy action staved off, even if temporarily, the Soviet onslaught. Soon after, the United States successfully orbited an astronaut and ten years later landed a man on the moon. Some educators were quick to claim credit in behalf of the education system and to point out how responsive American schools could be when they were properly funded and had their communities behind them. Their triumph was only temporary. When, in 1987, American marines were indicted and convicted for complicity with Soviet spies, the former American ambassador to the United Nations attributed their miscon-

6. Albert Bushnell Hart, "The Teacher as a Professional Expert," *School Review* 1, no. 1 (Jan. 1938): 5, 7.

7. Richard Hofstadter, *Anti-Intellectualism in American Life* (New York: Random House, 1962), 21.

duct to the failure of schools to inculcate proper moral and political values.

Within this three-decade span, however, the competitive arena had enlarged to include international trade. Other nations were threatening America's technological superiority and economic well-being by superior invention and the inexpensive manufacture of consumer products. The United States was importing more than it was exporting and had evolved into the world's largest debtor nation, virtually overnight it seemed. Productivity grew at a lackluster pace. Annual trade deficits exceeded $170 billion. In this context, a blue-ribbon national commission on education was appointed by the United States Secretary of Education, Terrel Bell. It issued, in 1983, a well-publicized report asserting that the nation was again at risk. The recommended solution was to return rigor to American schooling.[8]

By the late 1980s, the link between education and national economic productivity that had first been articulated prominently in the 1840s, was reforged, and on these grounds American schools were brought into yet another intense period of reform.[9] Additional commissions, task forces, blue-ribbon panels, and study groups were busy at the national, state, and local level developing new education policy. Once again, the failures of schools were blamed for the nation's problems and yet their solution depended again on better schooling.[10]

There can be little doubt about the major costs involved in public schooling. Lower education (kindergarten through twelfth grade) alone absorbs approximately 5 percent of America's gross national product (GNP). This may explain the vigor with which periodic efforts are made to curtail schools' spending and improve their productivity. Not only are Americans ambivalent about the purposes and utility of schooling, they also exhibit cyclical distrust of the efficiency of school operations. In this regard they share the attitude of leading educationists early in this century, who turned much of the then-young science of education into a crusade for efficiency that promoted the bureaucratic, top-down controls that have limited teacher professionalism even as teachers acquired more formal preparation for their work.

8. National Commission on Excellence in Education, *A Nation at Risk* (Washington, D.C.: U.S. Government Printing Office, 1983).

9. Societal dynamics underlying this reform cycle are assessed in James W. Guthrie, "The Educational Policy Consequences of Economic Instability: The Emerging Political Economy of American Education," *Educational Evaluation and Policy Analysis* 7, no. 4 (Winter 1986): 319–32.

10. Congress responded, predictably, by enacting the Education for Economic Security Act, Public Law 98-377, U.S. Statutes at Large, Vol. 98, Part 2; Stat. 1267.

The decade of the 1970s, like the period 1900–1920, was characterized by a series of particularly intense efforts to render schools more efficient. As had been the case historically, proponents of productivity again diagnosed schools as poorly operated, and the injection of private-sector management techniques, described in bureaucratic babble, was the prescribed reform medicine.[11] School administrators were admonished, and in some instances mandated by state legislatures, to utilize program performance budgeting systems (PPBS), program evaluation review techniques (PERT), management by objectives (MBO), and other technocratic "remedies" derived from the private or defense sectors. Yet education does not meet most of the production assumptions upon which such technical management procedures are based. Hence, the accountability fad washed through the system, leaving virtually no residue. Not even performance-based teacher education (PBTE) systems, whatever they were intended to be, lasted.[12]

Proponents of heightened productivity next advocated expanded testing of students. The rationale was that educators could be pressured to perform more effectively if the system's "output," or student achievement, could be subjected to more intense public scrutiny. Thirty-five states responded during the 1970s to the call for standardized testing programs. Indeed, revisions of the late 1980s in the National Assessment of Education Progress (NAEP), to permit state-by-state comparisons, represent an unprecedented expansion of the strategy of accountability through testing—compromising the heretofore sacrosanct principle of local control of public education. This is a consequence of public distrust of student achievement which, as measured by the press's barometer, the Scholastic Aptitude Test scores, continued a nearly two-decade-long decline into the 1980s, followed by only small recoveries.

Frustration at the inability to gain increased educational productivity led fiscal guardians to propose limitations on school revenues

11. Historic efforts to instill private sector management techniques into schools are described in David Tyack, *The One Best System: A History of American Urban Education* (Cambridge, Mass.: Harvard University Press, 1974).

12. An analysis of the 1970s "accountability" movement and its weaknesses is provided in James W. Guthrie, "Social Science, Accountability, and the Political Economy of School Productivity," in *Indeterminacy in Education,* ed. John E. McDermott (Berkeley: McCutchan, 1976), 253–308. On PBTE, see N. L. Gage and Philip H. Winne, "Performance-Based Teacher Education," in *Teacher Education,* 74th Yearbook of the National Society for the Study of Education, part 2, ed. Kevin Ryan (Chicago: University of Chicago Press, 1975), 146–72.

and expenditures. The most dramatic displays in this regard were overall tax limitation initiatives such as California's Proposition 13, enacted in 1978, and Massachusetts' "Proposition 2½," passed by voters the following year. Capitalizing on taxpayer discontent, fifteen additional states passed legislation limiting school spending. The prevailing feeling seemed to be, "If we cannot make schools productive, then we can at least limit the amount of money educators waste."[13]

This latter strategy did have an effect. School purchasing power, besieged also by double-digit inflation and a subsequent recession, declined $7,000 per classroom between 1978 and 1983. By 1988, however, fueled by the previously described public fear of international competition, school spending had rebounded. Despite continued proposals to curb finances, school revenues climbed inexorably. Indeed, in constant 1940 dollars, United States' per-pupil spending will have increased by more than 500 percent in the half century between 1940 and 1990. It increased almost 30 percent from 1983 to 1987 alone.[14]

A Profession Unsure of Itself

Analagous to the inconsistent, topsy-turvy, love-hate relationship America has had with its schools is the paradox existing between the high regard for education and the low repute of the education profession—the intellectuals closest to the people. But the phenomenon is neither recent nor exclusively American. The sixteenth-century English educator, Richard Mulcaster, wrote mournfully, "Our calling creeps low and hath pain for companion, still thrust to the wall though still confessd good." Sir Thomas Elyot noted that many "well lerned" men would become teachers "if the name of a schole maister were not so moche had in contempte, and also if theyr labours with abvndant salaries mought be requited." The nineteenth-century farmers who controlled their local one-room schools in predominantly rural America had a profound distrust of professional educators. They wanted teacher qualifications which their own sons and daughters could readily obtain; the schools *belonged* to them, they reasoned, and their own

13. For additional information, see Mark Menchik et al., *Fiscal Restraint in Local Government: A Summary of Research Findings,* (Santa Monica: Rand Corporation, 1982).

14. Data derived from National Center for Education Statistics, *Projections of Educational Statistics to 1990–91* (Washington, D.C.: U.S. Department of Education, 1982) and Allan R. Odden "School Finance, 1983–87" (Paper presented at the annual meeting of the American Educational Research Association, Washington, D.C., April 1987).

standards should apply. If the new normal schools prevailed, some reasoned, there would be no way to compel their graduates to teach "unless it be for wages the public could not afford to pay."[15] Populism and penny-pinching combined with other conditions, such as the absence of a solid technological underpinning and the feminine nature of teaching over the past century, to perpetuate a workforce which appeared professionally insecure. This debilitation may well contribute to, and reinforce, those periodic outbreaks of public skepticism of education.[16]

From its high point after World War II, the percentage of undergraduates exhibiting a preference for teaching as a career has declined tremendously. A poll of 1984 high school graduates revealed that only 8 percent were "very interested in teaching as a career." Only 7.3 percent of college freshmen were planning to major in education according to a 1986 survey, but that was up from 6.2 percent in 1985.[17] This was at a time when employment opportunities for teachers were expanding substantially, and contrasts strongly with the fact that over 20 percent of undergraduates reported plans to major in education only a decade before. For a projected 171,000 new teachers needed in 1987, for example, only 142,000 teachers would be graduated from teacher training programs, and the demand-supply gap is expected to widen thereafter unless countermeasures are taken and a reserve pool of licensed but currently unemployed teachers is tapped. These figures may reverse themselves in the 1990s as prospective teachers respond to new labor-market signals, and the bloom fades from the MBA rose, particularly among young women now being diverted from teaching. It is too soon to predict, however. The point is that becoming a teacher appears to have but slight inherent professional appeal and is highly influenced, probably more than other professions, by economic con-

15. Samuel J. May to Horace Mann, 16 August 1839, Horace Mann Papers, Massachusetts Historical Society, Boston, Massachusetts.

16. Wayne E. Fuller, *The Old Country School: The Story of Rural Education in the Middle West* (Chicago: University of Chicago Press, 1982). See also George Gerbner, "Teacher Image and the Hidden Curriculum," *American Scholar* 42, no. 1 (Winter 1972–73): 66–92.

Haberman rightly notes ("Licensing Teachers," 720) that today, "The same public that demands higher-quality teachers in the abstract is also most pleased to have an untrained family member exploit the profession for a temporary job."

17. Richard E. Kemper and John N. Mangieri, "America's Future Teaching Force: Predictions and Recommendations, *Phi Delta Kappan* 68, no. 5 (Jan. 1987): 393–95; Robert Rothman, "More College Freshmen Note Interest in Teaching Career," *Education Week* 6, no. 16 (14 Jan. 1987): 12.

ditions. This flies in the face of nostalgic remembrances of underpaid-but-proud religio-teaching vocations.

By 1991, annual teacher demand is predicted to be 204,000. Under present licensing conditions new teacher hires are expected to fall 37,700 short of that number.[18] Given the shrinking pool, little wonder that teaching found itself unable to draw proportionately from the nation's supply of intellectual talent. Education majors were second to last in a list of thirteen college majors ranked in terms of mean Scholastic Aptitude Test (SAT) scores.[19] From 1973 until 1982 the gap between national average SAT scores and the mean for entering education majors increased from 54 to 80 points.[20]

College students planning to enter teaching have been facing increasingly skeptical parents as more attractive occupations became available to college graduates, especially young women. A 1984 opinion survey disclosed that the proportion of parents who approved of their child's entering teaching had declined from 40 percent in 1975 to 20 percent a decade later. Worse yet, almost half of practicing teachers reported that they would not enter teaching again; such teachers are not likely to encourage teaching choices by their students.[21] Matters have apparently worsened over time: in 1961, only 11 percent of teachers were so negatively disposed. Former teachers reported a continued interest in students and teaching, but specified that they were driven from the field by the lack of professional rewards, poor working conditions, and low public regard.

Such statistics regarding feelings are consistent with those describing job decisions. Out of every hundred beginning public school teachers, almost fifty have resigned their positions by the sixth or seventh year of teaching. There are so many former teachers, and those trained to teach but who never practiced, that teaching is second only to the military in having its "expertise" widely present in the general population. As Martin Haberman noted in 1986, this sharpens teaching's public character and vulnerability to criticism. For more than a generation, the popular view has been that those who leave

18. Carnegie Foundation for the Advancement of Teaching, "Future Teachers: Will There Be Enough Good Ones?" *Change* 18, no. 5 (Sept.–Oct., 1986): 27–30.

19. Phillip C. Schlechty and Victor S. Vance, "Recruitment, Selection, and Retention: The Shape of the Teaching Force," *Elementary School Journal* 83, no. 4 (1983): 469–87.

20. *Change*, 27.

21. Reported in *Conditions of Education* (Washington, D.C.: U.S. Department of Education, National Center for Educational Statistics, U.S. Government Printing Office, 1985), 168.

early or do not teach are disproportionately the most able and creative. Among those classroom teachers who remain in education, many of the most ambitious fall prey to the perverse incentive system which characterizes America's public schools. They follow the career pattern which, however informally presented, makes clear that the way to get ahead is to get out of the classroom. Hence, many will prepare themselves to become counselors, principals, central office administrators, superintendents, or other nonclassroom specialists. At each step up the career ladder they will receive higher pay, greater discretion over their time, more interaction with adults, and higher public regard. Probably no other major undertaking, with the possible exception of nursing, so systematically rewards its most productive employees for abandoning the institution's major purpose.

To equip themselves for more lucrative and prestigious roles, most former teachers enroll in schools of education. As it has for this entire century, graduate professional education prepares, socializes, and certifies the vast majority of the new recruits to a leadership of the education profession by those who have abandoned teaching. A measure of the comparative status of teachers and the institutions that prepare them is the language used to describe both. As Bernard Gifford has observed,

> Prospective lawyers as a group may be viewed as professionals responsible in good part for their own fortunes and performance, while prospective teachers are not afforded this measure of respect and are assumed to be a "product" turned out by their school. While the common term is "teacher training institution," the counterpart for the legal practitioner is not a "lawyer training institution."[22]

The cultural duplicity surrounding American education and the professional insecurity characterizing teaching in the United States are reflected even more intensely and consistently in the training and state licensing of teachers and among the faculty of schools of education. George Bernard Shaw asserted that "He who can, does. He who cannot, teaches." Some cynics elaborate the insult by adding, "He who cannot teach, teaches teachers to teach." In their usually unwittingly (we think) patronizing posture towards teachers, education faculty have undermined their own status as well.

22. Bernard R. Gifford, "Teacher Competency Testing and Its Effects on Minorities: Reflection and Recommendations," in *Educational Standards, Testing, and Access* (Princeton, N.J.: Educational Testing Service, 1985), 50–51.

Of Pedagogues and Public Policy

The view that teachers are less than fully able has found widespread expression in late twentieth-century policy efforts to professionalize teaching.[23] Originally this was expressed in the requirements that teachers have a general college education, a degree of professional preparation, and supervised experience as a teacher-in-training. By the second half of the twentieth century, most teachers fulfilled these requirements. Beginning in the early 1980s, the majority of states began promoting additional conditions for becoming and remaining a teacher. Among the many suggestions made to eliminate weaknesses and professionalize the craft are standardized admissions examinations for training programs, state-administered competency tests for renewing a license, additional training for full credentials, merit pay based on pupil achievement, restrictions on tenure systems, professional speciality boards for obtaining national standing as a teacher, and numerous plans for "career ladders."

By the late 1980s, the goal of professionalizing teaching was being given greater attention than perhaps at any other time in the history of education in this country. But the situation is not unclouded. Under pressure to solve the growing shortage of qualified teachers, many states were diluting entry-level standards with one hand while implementing new qualifications with the other. How could both actions rationally be pursued simultaneously?

This dimension of the public policy schizophrenia regarding education operates as follows. A state may establish more rigorous entry conditions requiring, for example, subject-matter competency examinations to gain a secondary teaching credential while permitting individuals applying in such shortage areas as mathematics and science to begin teaching with an "emergency credential." California is a case in point. A state which on many dimensions has led the charge to improve standards for teachers—having required for over a decade a fifth year of pedagogical training, preservice practice teaching, and a state-administered teacher examination—California nevertheless bowed to the exigencies of supply and demand by issuing literally tens of thousands of emergency credentials.[24] Whether the term is emergency, provisional, long-term substitute, teacher trainee, probationary,

23. See Bernard R. Gifford, "Prestige and Education: The Missing Link in School Reform," *Education Review* 10, no. 3 (Summer 1984): 186–98.

24. Between 1979 and 1984, low demand years for new teacher hires, California nevertheless issued more than 33,000 emergency credentials.

or some other label in common parlance throughout the United States, the effect is the same. Examples are legion. The city of Baltimore was one that decided to raise its teacher standards. A competency examination was required; many teacher applicants were barred from teaching for failing the test. Positions denied in August were, however, offered in September. A teacher shortage prompted officials to hire the failures, requiring them to take night courses to learn the skills they were teaching their students by day.[25]

Thus almost every state has a two-tiered teacher licensing system structuring this contradiction. There exists a high-status professional portal for becoming a teacher and a seldom publicized "peddler's entry" which bypasses the formal requirements. Public officials are able to issue prideful rhetorical claims based on the first, and to accommodate to the pressing realities of the labor market by means of the second. This stands in marked contrast to state-approved conditions for licensing other professionals such as attorneys, physicians, engineers, architects, and accountants.

This zany public policy regarding teacher training and employment not only reflects the ambivalent position of education in America's consciousness, but also the weak scientific base historically undergirding pedagogy. The ability to teach is often considered a "gift" or natural endowment. "Great teachers are born, not made," it is often said. Efforts of educators to claim a scientific basis for teaching are seldom persuasive to policy makers, in part because many academicians (untrained in pedagogy but themselves functioning as teachers) deny that there is more to teaching than knowledge of one's subject, experience, and, perhaps, some inborn character traits as a liking for young persons and endless patience.

No less influential an individual than the United States Secretary of Education, in addressing the National Governors' Association annual conference in January 1986, stated the characteristics that he thought teachers required: "Teachers should demonstrate competence in their subject area, have good character, and have the interest and ability to communicate with young people."[26] William Bennett's pronouncement contained no reference to pedagogy, supervised practice teaching, preservice training, or any other form of professional preparation. It is difficult to imagine the surgeon general issuing a similar manifesto regarding physicians or the attorney general asserting that lawyers need little or no specialized preparation. In the unlikely event

25. This example is courtesy of Julia Koppich, correspondence with authors.

26. Quoted in *Education Week* 5, no. 6 (12 March 1986): 15.

that such luminaries advocated abolition of professional preparation in their respective fields, practicing physicians and attorneys would be quick to discredit the statements and disassociate themselves from the speakers. The days are long past when physicians were selected for being "natural healers" or lawyers "natural persuaders."

Ironically, some teachers probably concur with Secretary Bennett and, even more, are themselves among the harshest critics of their pedagogical training. Stranger yet, school of education faculty often are also highly critical of their own profession—or, at least, of their colleagues' performance of it. A midwest professor of education wrote the following in a letter to the *Wall Street Journal:*

> Most of my students are education majors, at both graduate and undergraduate levels. In general they cannot write a simple declarative sentence, they cannot spell, and they cannot read with discernment. But as a group they are neither dumb nor incompetent. They are the end product of a mindless system designed by schools of education in universities and colleges. Now that competency tests for teachers are such a big flap, guess who will test the teachers? Right! The same professors of education who designed the Mickey Mouse system in the first place. The inmates are in charge of the asylum.[27]

America's Teacher Workforce

Before reviewing the condition of the education schools which prepare teachers and other professionals for education, it is useful to consider the occupation on which they are built: teaching in the nation's public and private schools. The position of the teacher workforce in the United States in the final two decades of the twentieth century can be used to illustrate two dimensions of the subject. First, it reminds us of certain historical, recurring issues such as the size of the enterprise which necessitated a feminization of teaching and the upsetting cycles of teacher supply and demand. Second, it permits us to probe the effects of various policy options which have figured in our past and from which future policy makers will likely choose.

Figure 1 displays the historic growth of the teacher workforce of the United States. Here can be seen the steady accretion throughout the nineteenth and early twentieth centuries, the plateau during the Great Depression, and the explosive expansion following World War II. Enrollments of prospective teachers peaked in 1971, however, and the

27. Letters to the Editor, *Wall Street Journal,* 11 July 1986, p. 21.

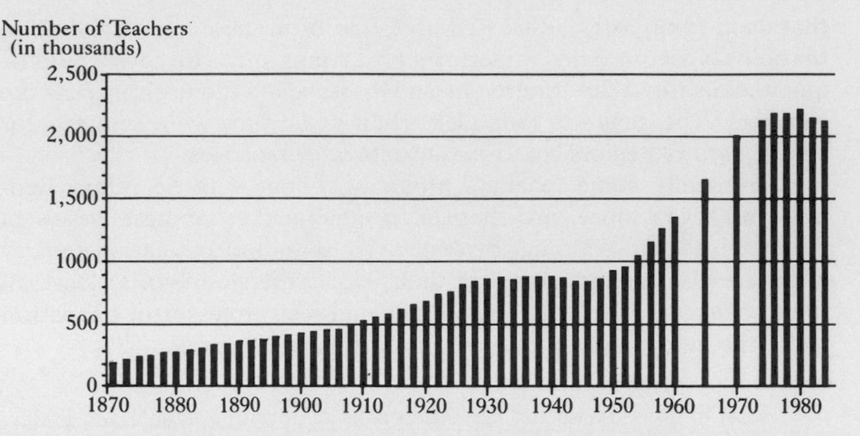

Fig. 1 Teachers in the Workforce from 1960 on, numbers are for full-time employees. Statistics from the Bureau of the Census and the National Education Association

growth of the workforce slowed; for a momentary period it even declined slightly. Not reflected in the figure is the fact that by the late 1980s, however, elementary school enrollments were again increasing, and teacher hirings began to climb once more.

In 1987, America's public schools were estimated to employ almost 3.5 million persons, of whom more than 2.5 million were professional licensed educators.[28] More than 80 percent of these, some 2.39 million, were classroom teachers.[29] The remainder were nonteaching personnel such as principals, librarians, counselors, and school district administrators. To get a sense of how large these figures are, contrast them with the nation's 465,000 lawyers, its 480,000 medical doctors and osteopaths, 1.2 million engineers, 84,000 registered architects.[30] Teaching is one of the nation's largest occupational categories. It is certainly the largest of the occupations which some sociologists label as "semi-professions."[31] Table 1 displays various summary statistics for the 1980s' teacher workforce. Here it can be seen

28. The remainder were so-called classified staff: custodians, cafeteria workers, clerks, etc.

29. Additionally, 354,000 instructors were employed by private schools. While these schools are not statutorily required by most states to employ credentialed teachers, many do.

30. Bureau of Labor Statistics, *Occupational Outlook Handbook, 1984–85 Edition* (Washington, D.C.: U.S. Department of Labor, 1984).

31. Amitai Etzioni, ed., *The Semi-Professions and Their Organizations: Teachers, Nurses, Social Workers*(New York: Free Press, 1969).

that teachers are still mostly women, a pattern that was established in the nineteenth century.[32]

The centrality of teaching to the career plans of college-educated women can be deduced from the fact that, in the mid-1960s, for example, 43 percent of all professionally employed women were teachers.[33] Women outnumbered men in this field two to one, and had been increasing their advantage over the two previous decades even though strenuous efforts had been made to recruit more men to teaching. While secondary school staffs were almost balanced with regard to gender, almost 90 percent of elementary teachers were women. Teaching is now a feminine occupation, and the consequences of this for its place among professions and among professional schools in universities are problematic, as we will discuss in subsequent chapters.

The teacher workforce has also been aging. In 1976 the age of the average teacher was thirty-three; in 1986 it was forty and 21 percent were fifty or older. Seventeen percent had taught for twenty years or longer. Their retirements plus the previously mentioned attrition will trigger a replacement of almost half the nation's 1985 teaching force by the year 1992. These shifts have important implications not only for future employment but also for schools of education, a topic to which we will return. Although the student population of the public schools became increasingly nonwhite, most of America's teachers were white. Less than 12 percent of the total teaching force was composed of teachers from minority races. These racial proportions had changed little from the previous two decades.

More than 99 percent of 1986 teachers held a bachelor of arts or higher degree. More than 50 percent held a master's degree or had at least six years of college education. This contrasted with the situation in the early 1960s when almost 15 percent of America's teachers had not graduated from college and less than a quarter of the total had any

32. This has been true for more than a century in most regions of the United States. See Myra H. Strober and Audri Gordon Lanford, "The Percentage of Women in Public School Teaching: Cross-Sectional Analysis, 1850–1880" (School of Education, Stanford University, Institute for Research on Educational Finance and Governance, Program Report Number 84-B11, Nov. 1984). See also Willard S. Elsbree, *The American Teacher: Evolution of a Profession in a Democracy* (New York: American Book Co., 1939), especially chap. 17.

33. In contrast, nurses were 20 percent of all professionally employed women workers, while lawyers (and judges) and physicians were under 1 percent each of all professionally employed women. In U.S. Department of Labor, *Job Horizons for College Women,* Bulletin 288, rev. (Washington, D.C.: U.S. Government Printing Office, 1967), 70.

graduate preparation. Thus, if education level or degrees held is associated with workforce improvement, there have been significant gains for teachers over a brief quarter century.

Another condition which changed dramatically over the same period was the unionization and politicization of teachers. The National Education Association (NEA) remained the largest teacher union, with almost 1.5 million members in 1988. The American Fed-

Table 1 Selected Characteristics of Public School Teachers in the United States, 1961–86

Item	1961	1966	1971	1976	1981	1986
Median age (years):						
All teachers	41	36	35	33	37	40
Men	34	33	33	33	38	41
Women	46	40	37	33	36	39
Age Distribution (%)						
Under age 30	NA	33.9	37.1	37.1	18.7	11
Age 30–39	NA	22.8	22.8	28.3	38.8	37.7
Age 40–49	NA	17.5	17.8	19.1	23.1	30.1
Age 50 and over	NA	25.8	22.3	15.5	19.4	21.2
Gender (%):						
Elementary						
Men	12.2	10.2	16	12.8	17.7	13.8
Women	87.8	89.8	84	87.2	82.3	86.2
Secondary						
Men	56.8	54.2	54.5	52.2	46.9	50.4
Women	43.2	45.7	45.4	47.8	53.1	49.6
Teaching Experience (%)						
1–2 years	14.3	18.4	16.8	11.3	5.3	4.6
3–4 years	13.2	14.4	15.6	16	8.2	4.8
5–14 years	34.5	35.9	39.6	46.2	49.2	40
15–19 years	10.4	9.8	9.7	12.5	15.4	23.1
20 or more years	27.6	21.4	18.3	14.1	21.9	27.5
Median years experience	11	8	8	8	12	15
Highest degree held (%):						
Less than bachelor's	14.6	7	2.9	0.9	0.4	0.3
Bachelor's	61.9	69.6	69.6	61.6	50.1	48.3
Master's or 6 years	23.1	23.2	27.1	37.1	49.3	50.7
Doctor's	0.4	0.1	0.4	0.4	0.3	0.7

Source: National Education Association, *Status of the American Public School Teacher, 1985–86* (Washington, D.C., 1987).

eration of Teachers (AFT) had in excess of 600,000 teachers members. The AFT's membership strength tended to be located in large city school districts, while NEA membership was better represented in suburban and rural districts. Both unions, however, contributed substantial amounts of money and members' time to state, federal, and sometimes local political campaigns. Their increasing militancy and self-consciousness also held implications for schools of education, as we will discuss in chapter 5.

Projecting the Future: The Race for Talent

Expanding enrollments and increasing teacher attrition began to create a renewed demand for educators in the United States by 1980. Table 2 displays projected summary employment statistics for classroom teachers. Here it can be seen that from 1988 to 1993, the United States is predicted to need between 140,000 and 215,000 additional public school teachers every year. Meanwhile, private schools are projected to employ an additional 22,000 to 36,000 teachers a year over the same period. Because private schools are not uniformly required by law to hire credentialed personnel, the precise nature of the labor market competition between them and public schools is not known. Nevertheless, it stands to reason that some degree of market overlap for new teachers exists. While adding these two sets of figures may not give an absolutely accurate picture of the competitive bidding for licensed teachers, nevertheless the sum of the two suggests the order of magnitude for total labor market demand for teachers.

As the century draws toward its end, the annual demand for new teachers amounts to approximately 20 percent of the total of United States college graduates.[34] This is an impressive figure; unless schooling modes are altered dramatically each year between 1988 and 1993, and perhaps thereafter, one out of every five U.S. college graduates will be needed simply to staff the nation's schools, precipitating a tense race for talent—especially given the expectation that college graduating classes will be smaller than in the previous three decades. It is unrealistic to imagine that such a large proportion of college cohorts will indeed enter teaching. More likely the gap will be filled partially by drawing on a reserve pool of prior graduates. Still, these persons must be attracted from their current employment into teaching. There will likely be strong competition. Can schools compete? If history is any guide, shortages will be accompanied by *both* large increases in

34. *Conditions of Education,* table 2.9, p. 124.

Table 2 Trends in the Demand for Classroom Teachers in the United States, 1980–93 (in thousands)

Year	Total Estimated Teacher Demand	Estimated Demand for Additional Teachers: Total	Public	Private	Elementary	Secondary	Estimated Supply of New Teacher Graduates[a]	New Supply as Percent of Demand for Additional Teachers
1980	2,463	134	110	24	76	58	144	107.5
1981	2,430	115	85	30	71	44	141	122.6
1982	2,445	161	130	31	107	54	143	88.8
1983	2,462	164	132	32	98	66	146	89.0
				Projected[b]				
1984	2,457	143	120	23	84	59	146	102.1
1985	2,467	158	134	24	96	62	146	92.4
1986	2,483	165	139	26	109	56	144	87.3
1987	2,505	171	144	27	125	46	142	83.0
1988	2,517	162	140	22	124	38	139	85.8
1989	2,543	177	146	31	130	47	139	78.5
1990	2,580	188	160	28	136	52	139	73.9
1991	2,630	204	176	28	138	66	138	67.6
1992	2,687	215	181	34	135	80	137	63.7
1993	2,737	211	175	36	125	86	133	63.0

[a]Estimates for 1980 and 1981 are from National Education Association, *Teacher Supply and Demand in Public Schools, 1981–82,* 1983. Other estimates developed by the National Center for Education Statistics.

[b]For methodological details, see *Projections of Education Statistics to 1992–93,* 1985.

Source: U.S. Department of Education, National Center for Education Statistics, *Projections of Education Statistics to 1992–93,* 1985, and unpublished tabulations (January 1985); and National Education Association, *Teacher Supply and Demand in Public Schools, 1981–82,* 1983, copyrighted.

salary and higher legislated standards for regular entry into teaching.[35] It is typically the case that the new higher standards are compromised by the local districts that do the actual hiring.

The supply side of the supply/demand equation for teachers is ordinarily remarkably sensitive both to salaries and to state-legislated minimum entry standards. Consequently, it is not easy to predict how many "qualified" individuals will be *available* for employment. However, after acknowledging substantial uncertainty, policy makers were

35. Michael Sedlak and Steven Schlossman, *Who Will Teach? Historical Perspectives on the Changing Appeal of the Teaching Profession* (Santa Monica, Calif.: Rand Corporation, Nov. 1986).

concluding that there would nationwide be an average shortage of approximately 50,000 teachers annually. Specialists in subject matter areas such as mathematics, science, foreign language, bilingual education, and special education are predicted to be in particularly short supply.[36] Also, after 1990, secondary school enrollments will begin to increase again, possibly triggering intensified demands in subject-matter specialities.

An anticipated average annual shortfall of 50,000 teachers nationally is not so large as to precipitate a crisis. When spread throughout many states, this level of added demand can be met by reasonable policies. Thus, it is important that public officials not overreact to a perception of teacher shortage and enact policies which, while addressing the problem in the short run, impose long-run damage on the educational system and the teaching profession—as has happened previously.[37]

The Range of "Solutions"

In a competitive economy there exist three fundamental strategies for resolving imbalances between labor supply and demand:

- enlarging prospective employee pools by simplifying work tasks or downgrading entry-level employment standards;
- increasing compensation or enhancing working conditions so as to render an occupation relatively more attractive;
- enhancing worker productivity, either through technology or training.

The kaleidoscopic policies that characterize American education typically employ only two of these strategies: decreasing standards and increasing salaries. Frequently, both occur at the same time and in the same state. The third strategy, enhancing workforce productivity, is seldom successfully implemented. Indeed, it can be argued that over the last half century educational productivity, at least in terms of labor output, has actually declined. The first two of these strategies and their probable effects are discussed below. The third will be discussed later in the chapter.

36. *Conditions of Education*, Table 3.2, p. 146.

37. See Emily C. Feistritzer, *The Making of a Teacher: A Report on Teacher Education and Certification* (Washington, D.C.: National Center for Educational Information, 1984).

Simplifying Work Tasks and Downgrading Entry Standards. It is logical that the pool of qualified prospective teachers could be expanded by simplifying instructional tasks, thereby rendering teaching easier so that more individuals would be able to perform. To date, however, the available science of instruction has not been translated sufficiently into practice to facilitate a reduction in task complexity. If anything, teaching has become more complex because of added societal expectations imposed upon schools and simultaneous changes in family and community conditions that are believed to be undermining the effectiveness of schooling. There has occurred a modest degree of technical specialization through the creation of such positions as counselors, librarians, and school psychologists. These have resulted, however, from added functions, not because of task simplification. Indeed, these specialties generally require more training than that expected of classroom teachers. Their training has caused a proliferation of graduate programs in schools of education and of advanced credentials imposed by state education officials.[38]

Lowering entry-level standards, as was discussed at the beginning of this chapter, has been a conventional policy response to teacher shortages. When elementary school class size grows and secondary students do not have instructors in academic specialities, school administrators find themselves subjected to parental pressure for additional hiring. These demands may eventually be converted by the political process into even more relaxed licensing standards and further "eased entry" into teaching.[39] This is a tempting strategy and allows resources to be shifted to more powerful groups. Sociologist Theodore Caplow points out, for example, that professions in male career fields require more years of costly preparation than do those in women's fields.[40]

The results for teaching are diluted academic criteria for entering schools of education, truncated requirements for pedagogical training, reduced practice teaching, and lowered professional thresholds for passing competency tests—along with the devaluing of teach-

38. Nor do these added specialists deserve uniform praise. In 1987 Secretary of Education William Bennett referred to the category of nonclassroom educators as "the blob . . . sucking up more and more resources while adding little, if anything, to student achievement"; quoted in *Education Week* 6, no. 21 (18 Feb. 1987): 18.

39. "Eased entry" is the term Lortie employs to describe the relative low entry-level qualifications for teaching in the United States. See Dan C. Lortie, *Schoolteacher: A Sociological Study* (Chicago: University of Chicago Press, 1975).

40. Theodore Caplow, *The Sociology of Work* (Minneapolis: University of Minnesota Press, 1954), 236–45.

ing because the goal is so easily achieved. The easiest means to accomplish this is to rely upon the previously described shadow world of emergency credentials. A common pretext is to claim that professional training offends the intellectual tastes of the graduates of prestigious (and expensive) colleges and universities, and that these "bright and creative" persons will be lost to teaching unless they can short-circuit the usual system for certification.

Such dilutions do succeed in redefining and expanding the pool of eligible prospective teachers in the short run. (They also undermine beginning teacher wage demands.) Beginning in 1984, thirty-one states either had already reduced or were planning to reduce teacher credentialing standards by such methods. A 1986 report by the American Association of Colleges for Teacher Education (AACTE) stated that two-thirds of the states had raised legal standards for teacher training and certification, but in the time since 1984, half the states permitted the hiring of teachers who bypassed state requirements.[41]

Proponents of alternative routes to the classroom are well placed in policy-making positions. Moreover, the absence of widely accepted pertinent research findings makes it relatively easy for them to dilute entry-level standards. Even obtaining high scores on subject-matter proficiency examinations has not been systematically related to effective classroom performance. There is no evidence that high professional-school grades predict good teachers—or successful doctors, engineers, clergymen, or businessmen, for that matter.[42] Education courses have always been fair game for skeptics, with practicing teachers among their most intense critics. Everywhere there is anecdotal evidence about heroic instructors who were thrown, "sink or swim," into the turbulence of teaching without benefit of formal training or practice teaching, and who survived to brag about it. That society condones such "practicing on the patients" may be testimony of how little, in fact, it regards children—at least other people's children.

The policy of relaxing requirements can expand the pool of employable teachers, and the risks to productivity, if any, appear low. Given such arguments, policy makers may well ask: "Why adhere to falsely high standards?" The democratic ethos can be invoked when politicians contend that restricting entry into teaching only plays into the self-serving hands of union activists attempting to elevate teacher

41. American Association of Colleges for Teacher Education (AACTE), *Teacher Education Policy in the States: A Fifty-State Survey* (Washington, D.C.: AACTE, 1986).

42. Christopher Jencks and David Riesman, *The Academic Revolution* (Garden City, N.Y.: Doubleday, 1968), 205.

salaries or teacher educators seeking a captive audience. After all, they may inquire, did not this strategy assist the nation admirably in a prior time of dramatic teacher shortages, the post–World War II baby-boom years?

The 1950s represent an analogous situation: rapid enrollment increases and concomitantly elevated teacher demand. It is unlikely that the overall quality of the teacher workforce was greatly diluted by recruitment strategies used to meet postwar demand.[43] A reservoir of educated, but under- or unemployed housewives did then exist, and many women were induced to enter teaching. All that was necessary was to elevate salaries sufficiently to recruit such individuals into the labor force for work that was considered compatible with women's family responsibilities.[44] Salaries did not have to be as high as later would be required because labor-market competition for these women's skills was then low and most were not expected to become heads of households. Under present circumstances, a similar strategy is unlikely to be as effective.[45]

In many states, the reserve pool of educated housewives has been drawn down. More than 70 percent of women between the ages of twenty-five and sixty-five are already employed outside the household. Not many of the remaining 25 to 30 percent are likely to be qualified for and interested in teaching. Moreover, the social economy of the American family has altered sufficiently to cause many married or formerly married women to make occupational decisions on primarily economic grounds, even if their family responsibilities eventually force them to compromise their career choices.[46]

43. It can be argued, however, that the prolonged Depression of the 1930s caused teaching to attract and retain an unprecedentedly able and talented corps of professionals and that those who joined or replaced them after World War II could not match them given the booming economy which diverted talent to other fields. If so, then this may help explain the widely held perception that the teaching profession, especially in urban areas, indeed became less able, committed, and professional than it had been for a brief period in the nation's earlier history.

44. A study of the attitudes of women enrolled in professional school programs at Yale University in the 1960s reveals the differing intentions between those in the prevailingly men's and women's professions on issues of reconciling home and work lives. See Adeline Gordon Levine, "Marital and Occupational Plans of Women in Professional Schools: Law, Medicine, Nursing, and Teaching" (Doctoral diss., Yale University, 1968).

45. Lynn Olson, "Study Examines 'Appeal' of Teaching" *Education Week* 6, no. 17 (21 Jan. 1987); 5.

46. A survey of 1,039 women who received master of business administration degrees from the leading business schools found that women were leaving the manage-

Surveys of former teachers yield findings similar to those regarding the reserve pool. Former teachers specified that they still reflected fondly upon students and teaching, but that they were unlikely to return to teaching unless salaries and working conditions improved appreciably. Moreover, in instances where former teachers are willing to reenter the profession, their geographic mobility is often restricted.[47] Thus, while reducing professional requirements and relying upon the reserve pool was previously a successful strategy, it is unlikely to prove equally productive again. The reserve pool is unlikely to meet the growing demand for fully qualified U.S. teachers. Moreover, reducing professional standards is likely merely to decrease further the quality of those entering teaching. As we will describe subsequently, the academic standing of teaching recruits is already disproportionately low, and diluting current entry standards risks creating a downwardly spiraling condition.

Improving Working Conditions and Increasing Salaries. Polls of both current and former teachers repeatedly reveal the distressing effect of poor working conditions upon their morale and professional outlook. Arguably, teachers have the least comfortable environmental surroundings of any professional group, save possibly journalists. The absence of privacy and restricted access to telephones, copy machines, secretarial assistance, and up-to-date instructional supplies and materials are annoying conditions to which teachers frequently refer. Ironically, the costs to elevate standards on this dimension would seem relatively low, at least when compared to the alternative of raising salaries. The costs of providing teachers with clean, safe, and attractive conditions of work may actually be higher, however, given the physical condition into which many schools and their neighborhoods have been allowed to lapse.

Improved working conditions might assist in retaining a significant proportion of the large numbers of teachers who annually leave the field feeling frustrated and unappreciated. This strategy is unlikely, however, to contribute greatly to recruiting larger numbers of able new

---

rial workforce in high numbers, many to devote more time to their families. "Women have given up the goal of being superwomen because it is impossible." From Alex Taylor, "Why Women Managers Are Bailing Out," *Fortune* 114, no. 4 (18 Aug. 1986): 16–23.

47. Julia Koppich and William Gerritz, *The California Teacher* (Analysis of a survey conducted by Louis Harris Associates for Metropolitan Life Insurance Company; Berkeley: Policy Analysis for California Education, 1986).

individuals into teaching. Successful recruiting is likely to depend more upon salaries than working conditions.

A conventional contention is that teaching is a calling. Consequently, teachers' pay, like that of clerics, can be held down because of altruism and emotional zeal. This view is at least partially reinforced by survey results which show that many have entered teaching for reasons other than material reward.[48] However, another aphorism, "You generally get what you pay for," also has a ring of reality. The growing labor problems of Catholic schools as their teacher workforce changed from primarily members of religious orders—with their vows of poverty and obedience—to lay men and women is instructive.

Economic research suggests that remuneration is significant in attracting large numbers of talented individuals into teaching. After summarizing related research, Ferris and Winkler assert that, in addition to being easy to implement, changes in compensation quickly and significantly improve teacher supply.[49] Three dimensions of salary appear significant for enhancing the supply of teachers: (1) relative purchasing power at time of entry, (2) career earning potential, and (3) favorable comparisons with other occupations. In periods of shortages, the status of teachers improves on the first dimension, relative purchasing power.[50] It is on the other two dimensions, career earning potential and earning power relative to other occupations, that America's teaching force compares poorly.[51]

Salaries and Shortages

Average teacher salaries over time compared with school enrollments are shown in figure 2. What is readily apparent is that teacher salaries respond strongly to fluctuations in demand. Student enrollments peaked nationwide in 1971; this was also the peak period for the

48. Ward Mason, *The Beginning Teacher: Status and Career Orientations* (Washington, D.C.: U.S. Government Printing Office, 1961).

49. James Ferris and Donald Winkler, "Compensation and the Supply of Teachers," (Paper prepared for the California Commission on the Teaching Profession, Sacramento, April 1985), 11.

50. See Dwayne Ward, "Labor Market Adjustments in Elementary and Secondary Teaching: The Reaction to the 'Teacher Surplus,'" *Teachers College Record* 77, no. 2 (Dec. 1975): 189–218; and Linda Darling-Hammond, "Teacher Supply and Demand: A Structural Perspective" (Paper prepared for the annual meeting of the American Educational Research Association, San Francisco, April 1986).

51. Added perspective on teacher pay is provided by David S. Stern, "Compensation for Teachers," *Review of Research in Education* 13 (1986): 285–316.

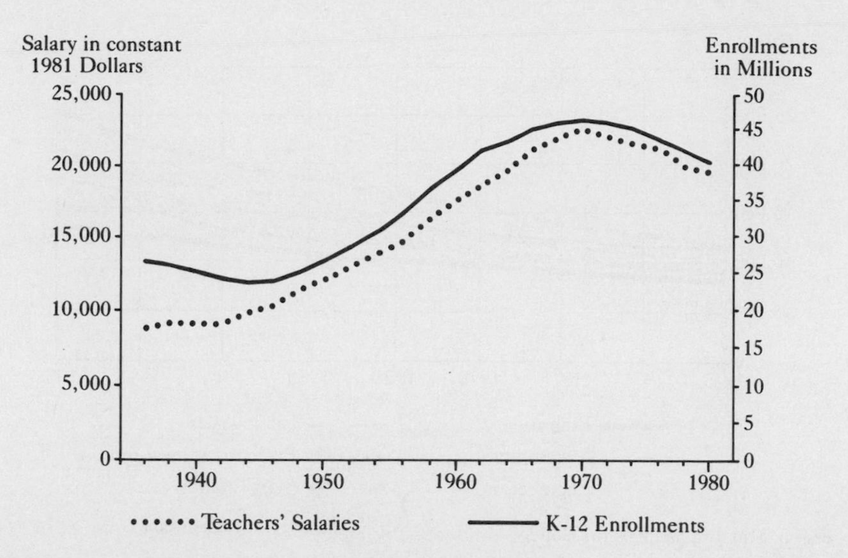

Fig. 2 Teacher Salaries and K–12 Enrollments, 1936–82

purchasing power of teachers' wages. During the subsequent decade, when enrollments were declining and the teacher labor pool contained many available and qualified individuals, purchasing power (teacher salaries in constant 1981 dollars) decreased 14 percent. Beginners' salaries particularly were affected negatively. The relationship between teacher supply and pay is most pronounced when the focus is on entry-level salaries. In 1975, beginning teacher salaries were $2,000 lower than entry-level salaries for all college graduates as a group (see fig. 3). By 1983, beginning teacher salaries were $6,000 lower than the average entry earning for all college graduates. In comparative terms, the beginning teacher's salary was slightly over half the median entering wage of the electrical engineer.

Career Earning Prospects. Few school districts in the United States relate an individual's compensation to instructional ability or teacher productivity.[52] Rather, teacher remuneration is linked almost exclusively to length of service and level of academic preparation. School districts generally rely upon a uniform salary schedule with specified yearly increments of employment on the vertical axis and coursework

52. For more on the topic of productivity pay for teachers, see Harry P. Hatry and John M. Greiner, *Teacher Incentive Plans* (Washington, D.C.: Urban Institute Press, 1985).

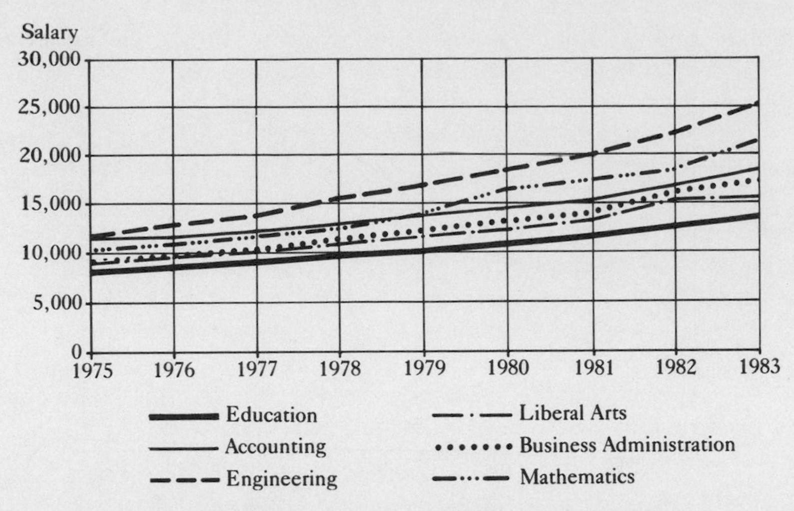

Fig. 3 Starting Salaries for College Graduates by Field of Study, 1975–83

unit increments beyond the bachelor's degree on the horizontal axis. The dollar spread between beginning teacher salary in the upper left-hand salary schedule quadrant and the maximum salary in the lower righthand quadrant averages 200 percent. This means that the teacher at the highest pay rung on the schedule can earn twice as much as one's entry-level counterpart. Movement across and down the schedule typically takes twelve or thirteen years, after which a teacher can expect only whatever cost-of-living salary increases are bargained for collectively.

In effect, by his or her mid-thirties a classroom teacher's earning power has peaked. In 1987, the mean maximum salary for United States teachers approximated $34,000. In contrast, a successful medical, legal, or technical professional's salary begins to escalate rapidly at this career juncture. Small wonder that many of the most ambitious teachers, sensing this salary ceiling, either leave education altogether or pursue previously described organizational incentives to leave the classroom for more lucrative opportunities in education.

Comparative Pay. Society expects teachers to perform like professionals, but be rewarded like missionaries. Figure 3 displays, in constant dollars, starting teacher salaries relative to beginning salaries for other professional and occupational undertakings. Two important features are presented here for the period from 1975 to 1983. First, teacher starting pay lagged behind most other occupations requiring comparable training. Hence, education starts the competition for talent at a deficit position. Also, these data make it plain that salaries in other fields far more effectively matched inflation over the eight-year period involved in this analysis than did compensation for entry-level teachers.

International Comparisons. U.S. teacher salaries compare unfavorably with those of employees and teachers in other nations. When adjustments are made for currencies and purchasing power, U.S. teachers are paid less than teachers in all comparison nations except Austria, Belgium, Finland, and France, as shown in table 3. In table 4, one can see that U.S. teachers generally are paid less relative to other occupations than teachers in other nations.

Table 3 Primary School Teachers' Salaries as a Percentage of Private Consumption per Head in U.S. Dollars, 1982 and 1985

	Private Consumption per Head		Salary as % of PC/Head	
Country	1982	1985	1982	1985
United States	8,743	10,214	263	241
Canada	7,488	8,484	339	357
Japan	5,957	6,744	335	339
Austria	5,720	6,490	214	210
Belgium	7,099	7,637	245	236
Denmark	6,064	6,842	284	293
Finland	5,554	6,287	231	231
France	7,373	8,009	185	172
Germany	6,561	7,274	302	288
Greece	3,754	4,089	277	355
Ireland	4,180	4,338	398	464
Italy	5,724	6,251	205	258
Luxembourg	7,763	8,540	335	345
Netherlands	6,773	7,270	276	250
Norway	5,994	6,624	258	276
Portugal	3,002	3,076	N/A	392
Spain	5,110	5,456	288	362
United Kingdom	5,733	6,535	268	279
Average	6,033	6,675	277	297

Note: Latest data available. Comparable data for Australia, Sweden, Switzerland, and Turkey are not available.

Sources: Salary data from Table 1. Personal consumption per head in U.S. dollars using current purchasing power parity (PPPs) for 1982 and 1985 are adapted from Stephen B. Lawton, "Teachers' Salaries: An International Perspective," Occasional Paper, Ontario Institute for Educational Studies, Ontario, Canada, 1987.

The good news is that entry-level pay for teachers does respond to market conditions; salaries do increase during times of shortage. The bad news is that teaching is not particularly remunerative either in terms of future pay or alternative occupations. What does this signify? If salaries are sufficient to attract all the labor needed, is that not sufficient? *This question suggests that problems of teacher quantity almost always become issues of teacher quality.*

Improving the Quality of America's Teachers

The variations in skill found in America's teachers reflect several interrelated factors. One is the person's inherent ability. Another is the quality of resources teachers have to work with. A third is the quality of training teachers receive, including their general education, their subject-matter preparation, and their professional training both before and after employment.

The Pool of Talent

According to analyses conducted by Schlechty and Vance, teaching has conventionally attracted 7 percent of the individuals from the top ability quintile of college graduates and 13 percent from the second quintile. (Ability was measured by the Scholastic Aptitude Test scores when persons identified as prospective teachers were high school seniors.)[53] It is encouraging that teaching can attract 20 percent of the total college graduate population in the top two quintiles of intellectual ability. On the other hand, teachers attracted from the top quintiles are the ones most likely to abandon the field; indeed, 85 percent of those recruited from the topmost quintile leave teaching after relatively brief careers. Equally distressing, teaching also draws heavily from the bottom quintiles of quality. Almost 50 percent of the individuals in the lowest two ability quintiles measured by Schlechty and Vance in North Carolina identified teaching as their intended ca-

53. Schlechty and Vance, "Recruitment, Selection, and Retention." Statistics are from the chapter by Judith E. Lanier and Judith W. Little, "Research on Teacher Education," in *Handbook of Research on Teaching,* ed. Merlin C. Wittrock, 3d ed. (New York: Macmillan, 1986), 540. Data must be interpreted carefully because they refer to career choices by high school seniors, not those entering teacher training or teaching itself. Also, these data are not disaggregated in a manner that renders it possible to distinguish among those entering distinct teaching fields, e.g., physical education as opposed to English or science.

Table 4 Teachers' Salaries Relative to Salaries in Other Occupations in OECD Countries, 1985

Country	Sales	Average Wage	Construction Worker	Bus Driver	Tool Maker	Electrical Engineer	Manager
United States	52	73	95	97	120	146	204
Canada	46	60	83	78	85	124	159
Japan	59	69	69	104	94	130	248
Austria	63	82	89	119	125	225	226
Belgium	70	69	91	101	95	158	155
Denmark	79	70	92	93	108	142	195
Finland	64	62	97	98	98	154	224
France	61	78	57	119	113	309	305
Germany	45	68	66	98	95	137	180
Greece	55	55	71	112	104	136	180
Ireland	60	65	53	65	81	132	170
Italy	88	83	75	106	94	174	159
Luxembourg	37	58	41	80	79	141	158
Netherlands	70	73	80	98	97	152	231
Norway	68	81	124	105	101	138	132
Portugal	50	NA	50	78	73	155	175
Spain	46	51	48	64	83	174	127
United Kingdom	53	74	76	81	94	159	138
Average	59	69	75	94	97	160	160

Source: Adapted from Stephen B. Lawton, who used data from Union Bank of Switzerland (1985) and International Labour Office (Geneva, 1985).

Note: Teachers' salary in each country = 100; salaries for other occupations are expressed as a percentage of the teachers' salary in that country. Position descriptions as follows: sales clerk employed in ladies' wear department of a large department store; received some training but not especially in selling with several years of selling experience (about 20–24 years old, single; average industrial wage, annualized pay based on 5–day week, 48–week year, using data on hourly wages and hours worked per week or month; construction worker, unskilled or semi-skilled laborer (about 25 years old, single); bus driver employed by municipal system, about 10 years driving experience (about 35 years old, married, two children); toolmakers/lathe operators, skilled mechanic with vocational training and about 10 years experience with a large company in the metal working industry (about 35 years old, married, two children); electrical engineer employed by an industrial firm in the machinery or electrical equipment industry, electric power company, or similar; completed university studies (college, technical institute or institute of higher technical education) with at least 5 years of practical experience (about 35 years old, married, no children); technical department manager of a production department (more than 100 employees) in a sizable company of the metal working industry; completed professional training with many years of experience in the field (about 40 years old, married, no children).

reer. Furthermore, lower-ability individuals are those most likely to remain in teaching as a career.[54]

The sheer size of the United States teaching force and the political forces that control the certification, selection, and retention of teachers ensure that teachers will remain a variable pool even when better measures are employed. Efforts to expand the pool of prospective teachers by diluting standards, however, will necessarily increase the percentage of individuals drawn from lower-ability quintiles. The dilution of standards also may well make it a less attractive occupation for individuals from high-ability groupings. Finally, as low-ability individuals are apparently the ones most likely to make a long career of teaching, it is not difficult to see that the effects of such a policy can operate for decades.

We can draw two conclusions from the analysis thus far. Raising salaries and decreasing entry-level standards will increase the *quantity* of prospective teachers. However, given the low pay scales, such strategies typically do *not* succeed in elevating the *quality* of candidates. With poor working conditions and attractive alternative occupations, it is difficult for the field of education to attract qualified professionals. Is it possible, then, for improvements in technology and training to enhance the producitity of the available talent?

The Promise of Technology

One reason that the quality of persons recruited to teaching is a serious concern is that teaching is a labor intensive occupation. Furthermore, it has resisted efforts to substitute capital for labor. The teacher/pupil ratio has dropped dramatically over the last half century. In 1930, the United States had on average one teacher for every thirty students; by 1985, the comparable ratio was one to eighteen. If the same trend persists, fifty years from now the United States might have one teacher for every eleven students. Contrast this situation with that of American agriculture, where startling gains in productivity have been made. According to the *Statistical Abstract of the United States* (1985), one farmer produces food for forty other people; fifty years ago it took ten farmers to accomplish the same task. In education, however, the only major effect of the technological revolution has been in

54. For more about the qualifications and career behavior of the low-ability group, see Lanier and Little, "Research on Teacher Education," 540.

the application to school systems of management principles developed initially for large business and industrial concerns.[55]

There is no technology on the immediate horizon that promises to have any important effect in reducing the amount of teacher time required.[56] The capability of computers has expanded and their costs have plummeted. Whereas computers may enhance the teacher's ability to cater to students' individual needs in some areas, there is no suggestion to date that they have eroded the numerical need for teachers. This could change, but given the pace of educational progress it seems unlikely that any breakthroughs will occur in sufficient time to solve current needs. Moreover, technological innovations, like other "reform" agendas, are typically introduced in ignorance of the complex structural and psychological realities of the teaching-learning process.[57] The result has been a history of failure, dashed hopes, and increased teacher cynicism about the political and intellectual systems that control the schools.

The Responsibilities of Training

Pedagogy is still far from a useful, much less a precise science.[58] For most of its relatively brief history, educational research has concentrated upon students rather than teachers, upon learning rather than teaching. Research has also employed a narrowly conceived methodology derived from experimental psychology, often focusing upon individuals asked to perform isolatable and measurable tasks bearing little resemblance to the world of the classroom. Greater attention has been given in many studies to issues of research design and descriptive statistics than to conceptualizing problems in terms of functional issues in education.

A repudiation of these old habits, as well as of massive empirical surveys, has been evident in educational research in the 1980s. In

55. Geraldine Jonçich Clifford, "The Impact of Technology on Education in the United States," in *Technology, the Economy, and Society: The American Experience*, ed. Stuart Bruchey and Joel Colton (New York: Columbia University Press, 1987), 251–77.

56. Larry Cuban, *Teachers and Machines: The Classroom Use of Technology since 1920* (New York: Teachers College Press, 1986).

57. Larry Cuban, *How Teachers Taught: Constancy and Change in American Classrooms, 1890–1980* (New York: Longman, 1984).

58. See, for example, Philip W. Jackson, "Facing Our Ignorance," *Teachers College Record* 88, no. 3 (Spring 1987): 384–89.

various Western nations, small-scale ethnographic studies in schools have become increasingly popular.[59] Research practitioners now contend that much that is useful is being discovered. One cannot help but be struck when reading a volume such as *The Handbook of Research on Teaching* (1986), by the wide range of instructional tactics whose efficacy is now supported by research. This information includes dimensions such as the appropriate sequence in which to present subject matter; effective means for specifying student performance expectations, asking questions, criticizing, and providing praise and other rewards; strategies for maintaining students on task; the appropriateness of small versus large group instruction; and the use of homework to complement in-class assignments.[60]

Yet, as a solution to the problem of teacher shortages, more effective training is much like hard technology: it is not a labor-saving strategy. Added capital investment in this sphere might well render teachers more effective with individual students, but it is unlikely to reduce the overall numbers of needed teachers. The teaching force in the United States deserves better training than it has received, and more flexible arrangements than the invariable one-teacher-per-classroom could make better use of the strengths of individual teachers. *But the nation's demand for competent, confident, and respected teacher professionals will challenge the creativity and determination of educators and public policy makers alike.*

For one thing, the declining social value of a teaching position combined with skepticism about the value of professional knowledge increase the resistance of practitioners to the training that is offered and to efforts to upgrade it. "If the linkage between a credential and a valued position is tight enough, there is less interest in the so-called 'relevance' of the educational processes that lead to the credential"; not so when the linkage is weak and the position devalued, as is the present case in teaching.[61] Today's more rebellious teachers, frustrated with their working conditions and discouraged by limited prospects of moving upward and outward from the classroom, even with advanced degrees in education that once promised such mobility, are

59. Lawrence A. Cremin, "The Problematics of Education in the 1980s: Some Reflections on the Oxford Workshop," *Oxford Review of Education* 9, no. 1 (1983): 14.

60. For an excellent review of effective instructional techniques, see Jere E. Brophy and Thomas L. Good, "Teacher Behavior and Student Achievement," in *Handbook of Research on Teaching,* 3d ed.

61. William Taylor, "The Crisis of Confidence in Teacher Education: An International Perspective," *Oxford Review of Education* 9, no. 1 (1983): 47.

more attentive to technique than to credential, "to the acquisition of skills and knowledge that will be of use in the classroom, that will permit more job satisfaction to be obtained, that will enable more client satisfaction to be generated."[62]

Thesis

There are many strategies by which a society can improve the conditions of children; schooling is only one way. Additionally, there are many strategies for improving schools; improving teaching is only one way. Eventually, however, almost no matter how tortured the logic, one is led to the need to upgrade teachers and teaching. Thus, to this point our argument is threefold: *First,* the United States faces a forthcoming period of increased teacher demand. The demand is both quantitative and qualitative in nature. *Second,* conventional policy responses such as diluting entry-level standards and increasing remuneration will probably do little to reduce the need for skilled teachers, but may provide an expanded pool of candidates. *Third,* in expanding the labor pool by these means, there is little prospect of upgrading the professional attractiveness of teaching, but the risk is substantial that the already low ability level of teacher candidates may be further reduced, and excessive hierarchical and bureaucratic controls left unremediated.

Productive professional training, while unlikely to reduce labor demand, might hold the promise of maintaining and perhaps enhancing the effectiveness of the teacher workforce. Better teacher preparation, by itself, certainly offers no panacea for the nation's education ills. Nevertheless, if appropriately restructured, it could contribute to maintaining and promoting the quality of the nation's educators. For this to occur, many of the structural features of schools of education will have to be altered. *However, as they exist today and as we will argue in subsequent chapters, schools of education are in a weak position to contribute forcefully to the forthcoming challenge of improving quality.*

Schools of education are perpetual targets for criticism. Indeed, there are periodic proposals to abandon them altogether.[63] Meanwhile, states have enacted policies that enable prospective teachers

62. Ibid.

63. See, for example, Gene Lyons, "Why Teachers Can't Teach," *Texas Monthly* (Sept. 1979): 123–29, 208–22.

and local school districts to circumvent them.[64] Any forthright appraisal must acknowledge and dissect their several weaknesses. Before beginning our discussion on this dimension, however, we would like to present a statistical and comparative portrait of the nation's schools, colleges, and departments of education. The data refer to 1983, the last year for which comprehensive statistics were available.

Schools of Education

The historical distinction between the normal school or teachers' college and the liberal arts college did not entirely fade when they came to share the same campus; the tensions, sometimes conflict, continue within many institutions. Despite the proliferation of professional schools and colleges on general university campuses, the situation remains as T. R. McConnell described it in 1962: "Many of these professional schools still do not feel at home in the university, and the university does not feel comfortable with them."[65] This unease has been exacerbated by the emphasis on research which has characterized all major universities since World War II.[66]

About 400 American institutions offer doctorates in one or more fields; 160 of these offer doctorates in education.[67] The appearance, in all kinds of collegiate institutions, of faculties trained at the major research universities, has placed values and norms in conflict. Schools of education, business, social work, nursing, law, journalism, optometry, architecture, or whatever have been relentlessly exposed to university culture that stresses graduate schools, research institutes, grantsmanship, the quest for regionally or nationally recruited students, and the prescription to "publish or perish." Of those professional schools, however, education programs are the most numerous, existing in some 80 percent of all four-year institutions of higher education.

There were 1,287 teacher education programs operated in Uni-

64. See Doyle Watts, "Can Campus-Based Preservice Teacher Education Survive?" *Journal of Teacher Education* 31, no. 1 (Jan.–Feb. 1982): 50–53.

65. T. R. McConnell et al., "The University and Public Education," in *Education for the Professions,* 61st Yearbook of the National Society for the Study of Education, part 2, ed. N. B. Hunter (Chicago: University of Chicago Press, 1962), 257.

66. Harold L. Hodgkinson, *Institutions in Transition: A Study of Change in Higher Education,* (Berkeley: Carnegie Commission on Higher Education, 1970), 102–5.

67. Data regarding education programs presented in the following section are derived from Emily Feistritzer, *The Making of a Teacher.*

ted States colleges and universities in 1983. The slight majority of these, 645, were in private institutions. Public institutions, however, prepared the majority of future teachers, as they educate the majority of all college and university students. By way of contrast, there were baccalaureate (or first professional degree) programs in business in 202 accredited institutions, engineering programs in 243, law schools in 172, and journalism and mass communications in just 74 institutions. There are roughly fourteen times as many education schools as medical schools in American higher education.[68]

Undergraduate enrollments in education totaled almost 444,000, concentrated in the 1,190 institutions which awarded undergraduate degrees in education. While this represents a 35 percent decline from the more than 687,000 undergraduates enrolled a decade previously, it dwarfs other professions that require college graduation, such as public affairs, theology, medicine, law, and engineering; only business enrollments surpass education and that change occurred during the later 1970s when the market for teachers shrank precipitously; the decrease in public school enrollment resulted in fewer jobs, and prospective teachers reacted accordingly.[69] Data regarding graduate enrollments in education, which are certainly large, are not available centrally. But in 1980, 7,900 doctorates were awarded in education—more than the combined total of those awarded in English, mathematics, the physical sciences, and the social sciences.[70]

There were, in 1983, slightly more than 38,000 faculty members instructing in education programs. This was some 8 percent of all college and university faculty in the United States in institutions offering four or more years of instruction. By an almost three to one margin these were full-time as compared to part-time employees. Interestingly, despite a dramatic drop in college enrollment, the total number of full-time and part-time faculty members at these institutions declined a scant 800, only 2 percent, over the decade from 1973 to 1983. Apparently education school faculty members were as protected

68. American Council on Education, "Professional Education," in *American Universities and Colleges*, 12th ed. (New York: Walter de Gruyter, 1983), 37–116. The figure for law schools (172) is for programs accredited by the American Bar Association.

69. In 1972 bachelor's degrees in education were 21.4 percent of all degrees awarded, compared to 13.8 percent for business degrees. By 1982 the percentages were virtually reversed: education 10.6 percent and business 22.6 percent of the nation's total of 952,998 degrees in all fields. See *The Conditions of Education*, 130, 132.

70. W. Vance Grant and Thomas D. Synder, *Digest of Educational Statistics, 1983–84* (Washington, D.C.: National Center for Education Statistics, 1984).

from declining enrollments as were the workforces of local school districts.

For all their numbers, education faculty are an intellectually-fragmented group, more divided into "sects" than their nineteenth-century medical counterparts.[71] Their mutual differences in training, values, expectations, and backgrounds may be as large as those which separate them from professors in arts, letters, and science departments on their own campuses. Some are former elementary or secondary school teachers or administrators, who have carried a particular orientation into the college and university world. Still others have had no such experience and are proud of that fact. "Educationists" embody training in every conceivable discipline and some "have no discipline at all—*only Education!*" according to their detractors. While some capitalize upon their "roots," others have rejected their past associations. While the majority nationally are engaged in some facet of teacher education, the self-proclaimed leadership of the education professoriate is dominated by those who "do no such thing, thank heavens!"

Teacher training is not a large part of the nation's total higher education budget, consuming only 2 or 3 percent. As an absolute amount of money, however, a substantial investment is being made. Assuming conservatively that each faculty member's support costs $50,000 annually in terms of salary, fringe benefits, secretarial assistance, libraries, and supplies, the United States spent approximately $2 billion in 1983 on teacher training. Additionally, large graduate programs in education already exist, and serious proposals to move all the professional components of teacher education to the graduate level, if implemented, will increase costs significantly.

More Effective Schools of Education

Some might contend that the numbers of students and faculty involved and the magnitude of resources committed to education programs argue for their strength and power. The evidence suggests otherwise, although much of it is anecdotal. Generally, schools, colleges, and departments of education are politically impotent. Most of their faculty are marginal figures in institutional politics and naïve about state political processes. While their millions of alumni are a potential source of political protection and financial support, teachers are not

71. William R. Johnson observes that "in medicine, sects were destroyed by science; in education, science has bred sects" ("Empowering Practitioners," 233).

generally loyal to their training alma mater, and would be unable to contribute much financially if they were. In the euphemism employed by one school of education dean familiar with the politics of building endowments in private universities, programs in education are considered by campus administrators and trustees "not to yield many alumni, and, hence, have marginal political leverage."

The only substantial hope for an effective political shield for schools of education might come from alliances with statewide teacher unions. Approximately 16 percent of faculty union membership is composed of school of education faculty members. Even here, however, there seldom exist tight institutional linkages. The overwhelming proportion of practicing teachers is too estranged from schools of education to care much about protecting them. Rather, any protection schools of education experience is more likely to come from their small stature in the overall scheme of educational things. Resources to be gained in any one state from eliminating them probably do not justify the political effort. Moreover, schools of education are money makers on many campuses; they bring in more tuition or state funding than they generate in costs. Hence, inertia is likely to prevail.

On prestigious research campuses, where schools of education are conventionally quite small, intense competition for fixed numbers of faculty positions may motivate internecine faculty squabbles, and in subsequent chapters we describe the course and results of such friction. The positive financial advantages of education enrollments on smaller private school campuses and at publicly supported teacher training colleges, however, generally dampen such overt institutional cannibalism. All of this is what Gary Sykes has referred to as "Higher education's dirty little secret."[72] Nonetheless,

> Despite all the crises and closures and the cutbacks, the fact remains that teacher education *will* go on in universities and colleges, *will* continue to be one of the most important areas of professional preparation undertaken by our educational system, *will* continue to employ large numbers of professors and administrators and support staff, and *is*, fortunately, susceptible to improvement through the application of rational knowledge and conscientious effort.[73]

These are the words not of an American educationist, but of the former head of the Institute of Education of London University, com-

72. Gary Sykes, in *Against Mediocrity,* Chester E. Finn, Jr., Diane Ravitch, and Robert T. Francher, eds. (New York: Holmes & Meier, 1984).

73. William Taylor, "The Crisis of Confidence in Teacher Education," 44.

menting on the international crisis of confidence in teacher education and the challenges it poses.

Thus, our contention that schools of education are potentially a useful resource in meeting the mounting problems of teacher quality and educational performance is based neither upon their current technical effectiveness nor upon their political strength.[74] Rather, we believe that with appropriate strategies they can be transformed into effective instruments, and that such a transformation can be accomplished more quickly than attempting to build parallel institutions to take their place. Moreover, there is ample historical evidence that *alternatives* to schools, colleges, or departments of education are *not* institutionally viable. Academic departments, cross-campus teacher education committees, school districts, teacher corps, or whatever—none is sufficiently motivated, interested, capable, long lived, or trusted to conduct teacher preparation—as we will shortly see.

We wish to be careful not to promise more than professional school programs can deliver. By themselves, and particularly under current arrangements, they are rather fragile institutions. They certainly cannot, even with allies, overcome the ambivalence in American culture regarding education, the historically low estate of teachers, the consequences of lay control, the bureaucratic mentality of many school district managers, and the relative economic and political weakness of schoolchildren and of the women who are the majority of education school graduates. Nor can they remove schools from the political process and the struggles among competing values and interest groups in which public schools are entangled.[75]

However, the reform of schools of education does not require vast new resources. It could, perhaps, be done within a decade as happened with business schools in the 1950s. And, in the process, their transformation could assist in enhancing the quality of America's public schools. To do so will involve abandoning many ideas about teacher competence and enlisting teachers in partnerships in both research and professional training. Schools of education, strengthened in these ways, are, we believe, essential to any significant hope of realizing the professionalization of teaching.

74. Johnson argues, however, that they are more successful at clinical training than they realize, blinded by an inappropriate conception of the difference between clinical and experimental outcomes ("Empowering Practitioners," 238–40).

75. For provocative analyses of some dimensions of the politics of public education, see Paul E. Peterson, *The Politics of School Reform, 1870–1940* (Chicago: University of Chicago Press, 1985) and Diane Ravitch, *The Troubled Crusade: American Education, 1945–1980* (New York: Basic Books, 1983).

This book will confront many questions as courageously and candidly as we know how. Our accounts of past and present may both overgeneralize and omit important exceptions. Our case studies will be uneven in the amount of detail and the depth of analysis they offer. We think that is inevitable given the task of posing answers to the questions we set before ourselves. What is it about teaching and the training of teachers that is so vulnerable to attack and criticism? How did these weaknesses evolve? How does the situation of schools of education parallel that of the schools they exist to serve? How can schools of education be strengthened? Can they learn from other professional schools or are their problems unique? These are the central issues to be addressed in this book.

We attempt to delineate appropriate reform strategies for America's schools, colleges, and departments of education in the final chapter of this book. Before doing so, we believe it essential to understand more fully the evolution of these institutions and to analyze their traditional vulnerability, since our reform agenda rests on this understanding. The story we tell is of an existence periodically beset by ambiguity, confusion, irresolution, self-doubt, and stalemate. We are convinced that this is a tale in the historical sociology of American higher education that needs reciting, three decades after Paul Woodring wrote that "the most persistent and troublesome of all the problems is the deep chasm that separates the academic community from the professional educators in many of our universities. The problem is accentuated by the reluctance on both sides to admit that it exists and that it will not be solved until it is faced squarely and traced to its origins."[76]

We pursue that task in the next several chapters.

76. Paul Woodring, *New Directions in Teacher Education* (New York: Fund for the Advancement of Education, 1957), 78.

2 The Formative Years of Schools of Education, 1900–1940

Two The School of Education in the University

The graduate school of education in the American university in the last years of the twentieth century owes much of its character to developments that occurred between 1900 and 1940. In that period a handful of institutions rose to become models for other schools, colleges, and departments of education. Their collective character derived, in part, from the responses that they were required to make to their academic environments: to the college or university campus ethos, to the traditions and values of assertive and sometimes jealous arts and sciences departments, and to the insistent spread of graduate school norms through significant parts of American higher education. As professional schools, however, they were also pressured to supply the needs and wants of schools: for teachers and other educational personnel, for consultative services, for leadership in the development of a body of professional knowledge, and for a degree of protection from the whims of public opinion and political expediency to which all professions, but especially that serving public education, were constantly exposed.

The accommodations that schools of education made to the academic and professional pressures between which they were squeezed—between what has been called the "cool" culture of the university and the "hot" culture of the public schools—were remarkably alike at the leading private and public universities. They established, it is argued here, a particular kind of professional school "culture." This culture was spread to similar universities, and even to essentially dissimilar institutions, by the mechanisms of influence which prestigious and well-placed schools of education came to have on education faculty nationally. To the extent that other schools of education imitated the better-known of their breed, they acquired something of their problems as well as their achievements. As in the larger world of American higher education, strong alternative forms of professional education were stunted when quite diverse institutions came to be dominated by "a monolithic status system" based on the model of the prestigious research university.[1]

The faculties of a few institutions achieved early success in seizing leadership of the professional school of education model. This power enabled them to exercise much influence on certain aspects of the public school world and extended even to those church-run school systems that were seeking to establish their legitimacy as "American" rather than alien institutions.[2] Roman Catholic–sponsored colleges and universities established programs in both legal and teacher education similar to those in the secular sector.[3] The Catholic University of America established its doctoral program in education in 1906 and teachers and administrators of parochial school systems began to appear for advanced degrees in education, sometimes in secular universities.

Influence over American schooling came through the design of curriculum, the authorship of school textbook series, the articulation of the tenets of orthodoxy in school administration, and the development of standardized testing programs. Education faculty wielded authority in national and state organizations for research, curriculum, instruction, and administration. State and national elites of professional educators were disproportionately trained in a small group of interconnected public and private universities of national stature. These institutions came to represent a model for aspiring professors and administrators in newer or less-favored but ambitious institutions.

These model schools of education also experienced major disappointments. They were frustrated by a lack of prestige and power on their own campuses. Unlike the medical schools across the quad-

1. Ernest A. Lynton. "The Once and Future University: Reviving an American Tradition" (1984–85 Distinguished Lecture Series, University of Massachusetts at Boston, 29 April 1985), 3.

2. In a similar legitimizing movement, most of the religious sects formed theology schools to help advance their status from "cult" to "church." See H. Richard Niebuhr, *The Social Sources of Denominationalism* (New York: World Publishers, 1929).

3. The experience of a Catholic law school, Marquette University Law School, is instructive of this broad tendency in professional education. See William R. Johnson, *Schooled Lawyers: A Study in the Clash of Professional Cultures* (New York: New York University Press, 1978), 160–63.

rangle, they were unable to secure the presidential support or philanthropic patronage that made "learning by doing" so spectacularly successful in the reform of medical education.[4] In addition to suffering a lack of status on campus, they found their legitimacy denied by many practitioners, especially by ordinary classroom teachers—although many physicians similarly remained skeptical of academic medicine as well. There were also disaffections among those school administrators who labored outside of the charmed circles that united certain education professors with state and federal officials, education publishers, and big-city school superintendents in what was later called the "interlocking directorate in education."

Like leading professional schools in other fields, the vanguard schools of education became enmeshed in unresolved conflicts between the demands of theory and those of practice. Competing pressures on teacher education were never ending. Academic departments wanted improved subject-matter training. Local schools in a more pluralistic America wanted better management, disciplinary and teaching skills, and ample opportunity for supervised practice of the craft. To escape these conflicts, some schools of education reduced or eliminated their work in teacher training if they could get away with this. Other institutions relegated teacher education to a marginal position. Thus, unlike other professional schools, some education schools were able to avoid the preparation of novices.

Teaching had long been considered a temporary career for "males of ambition." Poorly paid relative to other respectable occupations, under the control of lay boards, and suffering by reflection from the immaturity of its clients, teaching was dogged by negative images. Nor were matters appreciably better in the upper levels of the profession. School administrators were frequently chosen for political reasons or by incompetent school boards. Yet status from one's work was an important ideal in a fluid society that valued ability over birth. In the struggle for status, the concept of professionalism became infectious.[5]

In the nineteenth century, the parlous situation of teaching was compounded by letting women into the occupation, for teaching was considered merely a way-station for women before they married. In

4. Kenneth Ludmerer, *Learning to Heal: The Development of American Medical Education* (New York: Basic Books, 1985).

5. Terry Johnson, "Professionalism: Occupation or Ideology?" In *Education for the Professions: Quis custodiet . . . ?* ed. Sinclair Goodlad (Guilford, England: Society for Research into Higher Education/NFER–Nelson, 1984), 19.

the latter part of the century it was common to appoint untrained but college-educated men as principals to preside over normal school–trained women teachers. In the words of a long-time normal school professor, however, since the colleges would not recognize the science of pedagogy, the men were "definitely biased and pompous" in their management of teachers.[6] These conditions deprived teaching of a strong, autonomous professional culture of its own. It was unable to exert the kind of countervailing pressures on schools of education that could have retained for practitioner training the primacy it had in medical and legal education, for example, where strong professional cultures did exist.

The low social status and lack of economic power of teaching in the general society and the preponderance of women in the field also deprived education schools of the resources of money and power which certain other professional schools received as compensation for maintaining the training of new practitioners as their primary mission. The rapid development of doctoral programs in education devalued the work in baccalaureate and master's degree programs, the staples of most other professional schools' programs. Ironically, as the numbers of graduate matriculants grew and the doctorate in education assumed an ever larger place in American higher education, even the dominant and more self-confident schools of education failed to quiet their critics, on and off the campus.

Nonetheless, in common with other professions, the leaders of the movement to professionalize teaching through extending educational requirements believed that more desirable candidates would be recruited by a more demanding program of training. Collegiate and university education would be a finer screen and, thus, an essential mechanism in raising the prestige of the entire education profession. The broad culture of the university would defeat the parochialism of public education. Being a significantly larger occupation and one controlled by laymen and not by a professional body like the bar, education could not, however, hope to do what the legal profession sought to accomplish in the 1920s through *its* educational reforms: to control the entry of immigrants, including Jews, to the bar.[7] It resembled

6. Charles Waddell (1875–1958) of the Colorado State Normal School at Greeley and the Los Angeles State Normal School, quoted in Robert E. Treacy, "Progressivism and Corinne Seeds: UCLA and the University Elementary School" (Doctoral diss., University of Wisconsin, 1972), 78.

7. Johnson, "Professionalism," 155; Jerrold S. Auerbach, "Enmity and Amity: Law Teachers and Practitioners 1900–1922," *Perspectives in American History* 5 (1971): 551–601.

business in being unable to control entry and licensure.[8] Teaching recruited heavily among the children of immigrants, of blacks, of the upper reaches of the working class. Nonetheless, the spokesmen for professional education for teachers pushed ahead as best they could.

This chapter develops these issues by an integrated, thematic review of the histories of ten education schools in elite, graduate-oriented universities. In chapters 3 and 4 two major sets of outcomes (here called *tensions*) will be analyzed. These are tensions that helped to estrange education schools from their natural constituencies, especially from teachers in elementary and secondary schools, without resolving their chronically troubled relations with their academic fellows on campus.

Exemplars: A Ten-Institution Survey

Inspired by academic and popular interest in ranking institutions for their graduate work in the arts and sciences, various attempts have been made to determine the relative standing of the nation's major schools of education.[9] The consensus list developed from surveys in the 1970s and '80s is surprisingly similar to that derived half a century before in the first national study that included schools of education: the Report of the Committee on Graduate Instruction of the American Council on Education in 1934. Then, the "most distinguished" schools of education, listed only in alphabetical order, were those at Columbia (Teachers College), Harvard, Ohio State, Stanford, the University of

8. Sinclair Goodlad, "Introduction," in *Education for the Professions: Quis custodiet . . . ?* 4.

9. Peter M. Blau and Rebecca Z. Margulies, "The Reputation of American Professional Schools," *Change,* 6 (1974–75): 42–47; Alan Cartter, "The Cartter Report on the Leading Schools of Education, Law, and Business," *Change* 9, no. 2 (1977): 44–48; Maurice Eash, "Educational Research Productivity of Institutions of Higher Education," *American Educational Research Journal* 20, no. 1 (Spring 1983): 5–12; Egon G. Guba and David L. Clark, "Levels of R & D Productivity in Schools of Education," *Educational Researcher* 7, no. 5 (1978): 3–9; H. Stephen Higgins, "The Ratings of Selected Fields of Doctoral Study in the Graduate Schools of Education" (Doctoral diss., Columbia University, 1968); M. G. Scully, "The Well-Known Universities Lead in Rating of Faculties' Reputations" [The Ladd-Lipset Survey], *Chronicle of Higher Education* 17, no. 18 (1979): 6–7; Herbert J. Walberg, "University Distinction in Educational Research: An Exploratory Survey," *Educational Researcher* 1, no. 1 (1972): 15–16. For a criticism of the enterprise of this "high-class form of gossip," see W. Patrick Dolan, *The Ranking Game: The Power of the Academic Elite,* Evaluation of Higher Education Committee of the Study Commission on Undergraduate Education and the Education of Teachers (Lincoln, Neb.: University of Nebraska, 1976).

California (Berkeley), Chicago, Iowa, Michigan, Minnesota, and Yale.[10] Yale subsequently closed its school and Iowa has dropped from the select group. In the last quarter-century, these two have been replaced among the most frequently mentioned top-ranked schools of education by the University of California at Los Angeles (UCLA) and the Universities of Illinois and Wisconsin.

A shared characteristic of the ten institutions of the 1934 list, like that of the consensus list of eleven drawn from the most recent studies, is that leading schools of education have been located in those American universities whose baccalaureate graduates are themselves among the most likely of American college graduates to go on to earn doctoral degrees *and* whose graduate schools are the numerically leading producers of the nation's doctorates. The first criterion suggests an academic environment that encourages its students to want further study, even if at some deferred time in life. The second criterion suggests a graduate school culture that induces an academic department or professional school to conform to an institutional ethos to extend its influence nationwide. This influence operates through the doctoral experience that produces scholars, researchers, academic authors, and college and university faculty and administrators. An institution-by-institution analysis of doctorates earned in the United States between 1920 and 1961, for example, reveals that the host institution of each of these schools of education was among the leading twenty producers of doctoral degrees during the entire period. Matching their institutions' overall record, these schools of education produced a disproportionate number of all doctorates awarded in education.[11]

The "premier" schools of education of 1934 did have their quite important differences, of course. Some were housed in well-established institutions (Harvard, Yale, and Columbia) or in younger, prestigious private universities (Stanford and Chicago). Others repre-

10. Raymond M. Hughes, "Report of the Committee on Graduate Instruction," *Educational Record* 15, no. 2 (April 1934): 205.

11. Six of the 1934 list of leading schools of education were in the top ten institutions for numbers of education doctorates produced, and all ten were found in the leading twenty institutions in this regard. The schools of education (and their institution's numerical doctoral production ranking in education) were as follows: Columbia (1), Stanford (3), Ohio State (5), Iowa (8), Harvard (9), Berkleley (10), Michigan (11), Chicago (15), Minnesota (18), and Yale (19). In Lindsey R. Harmon and Herbert Soldz, *Doctorate Production in United States Universities, 1920–1962,* Publication no. 1142 (Washington, D.C.: National Academy of Sciences–National Research Council, 1963), 19–26.

sented major state universities (Michigan, Iowa, California, and Minnesota) or the land-grant university tradition (Ohio State). None on the 1934 list of ten—and only one on the longer recent consensus list, UCLA—began its institutional existence as a normal school. Five of the institutional homes of the 1934 exemplars of "ed schools" were large, multipurpose private universities and five were large, multipurpose public universities. In the recent period the balance shifted somewhat, to include four private and seven public institutions. This change exemplifies the general trend in American higher education, especially in graduate education, whereby public universities have achieved parity with or have overtaken those private universities that once defined and largely monopolized "the best" in graduate training.

Institutional reasons for establishing schools of education were not precisely the same from place to place and, in making their decisions, universities varied significantly in their degrees of freedom from public, professional, trustee, or alumni pressures. For example, as the only general public university in Southern California after World War II, UCLA's School of Education could no more say "No!" to addressing the alarming shortages of trained public school teachers than its College of Business Administration could single-mindedly pursue its own wish to build a graduate school by disregarding the wishes of undergraduates to major in business.[12] The pressures and constraints at private Chicago or Stanford were different in magnitude and kind. Yet the locus of sponsorship in private versus public hands does not clearly differentiate these institutions; other factors are implicated. Thus, in the percentage that education doctorates represented of the institution's total production of doctoral degrees, Columbia and Stanford were far more "populist" than were Harvard and Yale, where education doctorates were a much smaller proportion of the whole; the public universities occupied the middle range on this continuum.[13]

When Ohio State's College of Education opened in 1907 it proposed to meet many of Ohio's needs for qualified specialists in educa-

12. Steven Schlossman and Michael Sedlak, *The Age of Autonomy in American Management Education,* draft report published by the Graduate Management Admission Council at Santa Monica, California, in 1985. A briefer version was published in the magazine of the Graduate Management Admission Council, *Selections* 1, no. 3 (Winter 1985): 16–26.

13. During the period 1920–61, Teachers College awarded 41.2 percent of all Columbia's doctorates and Stanford's School of Education, 28.2 percent of Stanford University's output. At Harvard and Yale the comparable figures are 7.5 percent and 6.8 percent respectively. Calculated from data in Harmon and Soldz, *Doctorate Production,* 20–22.

tion: to train high school teachers of academic and special subjects (including art, manual training, and domestic science), as well as normal school teachers, school supervisors, and district superintendents. In 1923 a faculty committee recommended a still-broader mission and constituency: to "meet all the varying needs of the public schools of the state," by training all public school workers including school librarians and psychologists, as well as educating researchers and professors for other institutions.[14] Nearly a half-century later, in 1965, given the breadth of such responsibilities, it is not surprising that a faculty committee of the Harvard Graduate School of Education characterized the genre of schools of education as "overwhelmed" with their obligations for training school personnel and "confused over how . . . to organize themselves to study the enterprise which they service."[15] And, as we will shortly see, presumably elitist Harvard University was every bit as confused as presumably populist Ohio State University.

We think their confusions are systemic: rooted in the evolution of university-based professional education, whereby old prejudices and disagreements were institutionalized and nourished even as new stresses were engrafted. In this chapter, therefore, we will examine in some detail the early histories of the ten 1934 top-ranked institutions. Our aim is to identify and explicate a small number of important tensions in the discipline of education—education conceived as both an applied social science and as the focus of professional training—as it was pursued and transmitted in these major American universities. From time to time we will relate these experiences to pertinent developments in professional education in other fields, viewing our subject in both historical and comparative perspective.[16]

These issues are, we think, both general to schools, colleges, and departments of education and particularly germane to the class of university represented by these ten institutions. Their graduates became the principals of normal schools, the presidents of teachers colleges,

14. H. G. Good, *The Rise of the College of Education of the Ohio State University* (Columbus: Ohio State University Press, 1960), 153–56.

15. Harvard Committee, *The Graduate Study of Education* (Cambridge: Harvard University Press, 1966), v.

16. For the interesting contrasts between the problems of professional practice and diverse mechanisms of professional socialization in law and medicine in nineteenth-century Wisconsin, see William R. Johnson, "Education and Professional Life Styles: Law and Medicine in the Nineteenth Century," *History of Education Quarterly* 14, no. 2 (Summer 1974): 185–207.

and the deans of other universities' schools and colleges of education, while heavily infiltrating their faculties. Today these institutions are also among the thirty-five schools of education that can be classed as "R & D" (research and development) institutions. Their faculties make from 60 to 65 percent of the contributions to the most influential and respected research and professional journals.[17] By these and other means they have had noticeable influence on most other schools, colleges, and departments of education, as their own universities have exerted corresponding weight on the character, or at least the aspirations, of American higher education generally.[18]

The Convergence of Institutional Types

The movement to professionalize one occupation after another had among its casualties two established alternative routes for the educating of practitioners. One, much the longest tradition of the two, was the apprentice system, the other the independent professional school. Apprenticeship placed a recruit under a seasoned performer. This ancient method had prepared the majority of lawyers, physicians, and architects, among others. While industrialization and schooling helped to doom the traditional apprenticeship system in the artisan crafts, the culprits in the learned professions were a loss of social-class homogeneity among practitioners and a growing specialization of practice (in some cases linked to industrial capitalism). Progressively fewer practitioners could convincingly claim to have mastered all the emerging subfields that were attracting aspiring and upwardly mobile lawyers, physicians, or engineers.

Yet, so familiar was the apprenticeship model that the earliest

17. David L. Clark and Egon G. Guba, *A Study of Teacher Education Institutions as Innovators, Knowledge Producers, and Change Agents,* National Institute of Education Project No. 4-0752. The reputations of individual scholars and academic departments is heavily weighted by publication in established journals. It is estimated that the majority of members of boards of editors of academic journals represent less than 2 percent of all degree-granting departments and schools in American colleges and universities. See Dolan, *The Ranking Game,* 43.

18. Individuals can "expropriate" institutional prestige. "Thus a professor may appear to carry with him some of the aura of Harvard as he moves to a state university, just as a physician 'keeps' some of the prestige of Stanford Medical Center and transfers it to a lesser teaching hospital or to private practice. It is harder to think of a General Motors executive appropriating in this manner some of G.M.'s power and prestige"; quoted in Margali Sarfatti Larson, *The Rise of Professionalism: A Sociological Analysis* (Berkeley: University of California Press, 1977), 205.

dozen American law schools—proprietary institutions like Tapping Reeve's school in Litchfield, Connecticut, that operated from 1784 to 1833—were essentially expanded law offices. Unlike the tiny college law schools of the period, unconcerned with general legal principles and awarding degrees, Reeve and his counterparts organized practical lectures and readings of the kind found in the offices of practicing attorneys. Student demand eventually spread this vocationalism to the college-sponsored law schools. As the law professor at the University of Virginia complained in 1830, "The necessity of some, and the impatience of others, urge most students into their profession after a year's study, or at most two years."[19] The nineteenth-century normal schools for teachers, with their model lessons and practice schools, were themselves as closely connected to the master-apprentice system and to learning-by-imitation as was practicable in an institution that taught students in sometimes sizable groups.

The second casualty of professionalism was the proprietary (for-profit) professional school: the independent, single-purpose schools of law, theology, engineering, medicine, dentistry, pharmacy, architecture, or teaching. Their faculties, they claimed, were the more prominent and orthodox portion of experienced practitioners. They gave systematic instruction and were more likely to remain somewhat closer to scholarly or scientific advances in the field.[20] In 1890 the Census reported that such independent professional schools, including teachers colleges and normal schools, together employed 34.1 percent of all college and university faculty.

Like apprenticeship programs, most independent professional schools have disappeared. This happened because, under the leadership of academics, successive groups of aspiring professionals and their new or reinvigorated professional organizations, like the American Medical Association, sought to lodge training in the reformed, multipurpose universities. By so doing they could borrow two kinds of prestige and at the same time make secure academic careers for themselves. The first source of prestige was from the traditional liberal arts, which became a prerequisite to the acquisition of the practitioner's skills. The second was from scientific research, which was enhancing the reputations of ambitious universities by the beginning of the twentieth century.

Professional education in many fields was affected by this broad

19. Johnson, *Schooled Lawyers,* 11.

20. Johnson, "Education and Professional Life Styles."

movement, although not uniformly nor for precisely the same reasons. Conditions of practice and the state of professional knowledge affected the development of each field in more or less unique patterns. Moreover, the annexed proprietary law and medical schools, through which several colleges and universities acquired their first professional schools, tended to maintain their autonomy, something which eluded almost all schools of education. Two reasons for the establishment of professional schools in the United States in the nineteenth century were to "guarantee orthodoxy" of practice and to proselytize. Both medicine and the ministry were so motivated, being divided into numerous and competing "sects" and susceptible to further fragmentation.[21] In comparison to this sectarianism, educational practice was not splintered by different schools of thought.

The Independent Professional School for Teachers

Yet, disagreements did exist about the essentials of professional training for teaching. An early justification for distinct institutions for the training of teachers was that academies and colleges did not care to do what was required to staff the proliferating common schools with well-prepared teachers. To the leaders of the common school movement, a single course in "the principles of teaching," offered in some academies and colleges, oftentimes erratically and always didactically taught, was not sufficient. Horace Mann complained in 1839 that existing work in pedagogy, did not command the undivided attention of the instructors. The reasons that it did not included a belief on the part of academy and college teachers that teachers' competence is based on, and largely limited to, mastery of one's subject matter. The normal school offered an alternative version: "one that combined raw experience and methodical training," to be gained through one or more terms at a normal school and its attached practice school.[22] The ideal of "superb craftsmanship in classroom management" distinguished the normal school from the liberal arts college and the university school of education.[23]

Between 1839 and the Civil War, in addition to the several private

21. Paul Mattingly, "Academia and Professional School Careers, 1840–1900," *Teachers College Record* 83, no. 2 (Winter 1981): 220–21.

22. Ibid., 224–25.

23. Merle L. Borrowman, "Liberal Education and the Professional Preparation of Teachers," in *Teacher Education in America: A Documentary History,* ed. Merle L. Borrowman (New York: Teachers College Press, 1965), 19.

normal schools founded for the training of teachers, ten eastern and northern states established one or more such public institutions. Mann wrote, thus, of his state's efforts to achieve such single-purpose institutions: "In Massachusetts the business of the normal school is to possess the entire and exclusive occupancy of the whole ground; to engross the whole attention of all the instructors and all the pupils; to have no rival of any kind, no incidental or collateral purposes, and the very existence of the school will be staked upon its success."[24] In the words of President Richard Edwards of the Illinois Normal University, the idea of future teaching "is the Alpha and Omega of schemes of study and modes of thought."[25]

In the case of westerly states, like Michigan, Minnesota, and Arizona, there was the additional wish to train teachers locally, rather than to depend upon teachers imported from New England, where they were thought to be better prepared than the usual native applicants: graduates of local common schools.[26] After the Civil War, normal schools became a serious force in the preparation of elementary school teachers. By 1898, the National Education Association (NEA) reported 166 state and 165 private normal schools in operation; they enrolled about 70,000 students. Most of the private normal schools disappeared by the 1920s. Not so with the public institutions; once established, strong local demand ensured the viability and expansion of state normal schools. The first national survey of the education of teachers, conducted by the United States Office of Education in the early 1930s, confirmed their importance in extending pedagogical training through America's corps of teachers, even influencing the training programs of other kinds of institutions in which teachers were prepared. For example, the investigators found that the existence of well-established normal schools and state teachers colleges in a state increased slightly the median numbers of semester hours in education and in practice teaching taken everywhere, even by senior high school

24. Quoted in Jurgen Herbst, "Nineteenth-Century Normal Schools in the United States: A Fresh Look," *History of Education* 9, no. 3 (1980): 221.

25. Richard Edwards, in National Teachers' Association, *Lectures and Proceedings, 1865,* 179. Quoted in Borrowman, *Teacher Education in America,* 24. Borrowman labels this one of the two "purist" positions. Its opposite was that of liberal arts theorists: that specialized professional concerns not distort liberal studies and general culture as the college's objectives. See pp. 25–26 especially.

26. Donald Warren, "Learning from Experience: History and Teacher Education," *Educational Researcher* 14, no. 10 (Dec. 1985): 9; Pamela C. Hronek, "Women and Normal Schools: Tempe Normal, A Case Study, 1885–1925," (Doctoral diss., Arizona State University, 1985).

teachers. In states where teachers were predominantly educated in liberal arts colleges, the opposite effect was noted.[27]

Although many academics had no interest in vocational instruction, the practical recipes for managing classrooms propounded in the normal schools made sense to youngsters from farm and laboring families. Most teachers came, after all, from families that lacked experience with vocational education based on academic abstractions. The normal courses in the proliferating public high schools had the same appeal; their location in urban areas complemented the county and state normal schools, most of which were found in rural communities. Although many teachers had no preservice training whatsoever, by 1900 or so, public and private normal schools dominated the scene, capturing 75 percent of the enrollment of prospective teachers; high schools prepared another 16 percent. In contrast, the colleges and universities enrolled a mere 8 percent of identified teachers in training.[28] Minnesota's development was probably representative in this regard. The University of Minnesota lacked a pedagogy department in 1869, but the lightly-settled state already had three normal schools and a normal course in twenty-two high schools.[29] Regardless, like ambitious physicians and engineers, the universities' new professors of pedagogy wished to make contact with a different tradition of professional education: that of higher education—the very arena that Mann had earlier found largely inappropriate, inadequate, and uninterested.

In 1890 Rutgers College President Merrill Gates told the National Education Association that "the great business of . . . education is to supply the world with teachers."[30] Despite the spread of university departments of pedagogy, not all university educators would have agreed with Gates that universities should give much weight to this activity. In 1929, desirous that his own University of Chicago Department of Education and other major education schools not have to bother much with that function, Charles Judd praised the Westfield (Massachusetts) Normal School and the Kalamazoo State Teachers College. Speaking before the NEA he predicted that additional normal schools and teachers colleges would continue to broaden their roles

27. *National Survey of the Education of Teachers,* Bulletin 1933, no. 10. (Washington, D.C.: U.S. Office of Education, 1935), 2:61; 5:51.

28. Burke A. Hinsdale, "The Training of Teachers," *Monographs on Education in the United States,* no. 8 (Albany, N.Y.: J. B. Lyon Co., 1899), 21.

29. Robert H. Beck, *Beyond Pedagogy: A History of the University of Minnesota College of Education.* (St. Paul, Minn.: North Central Publishing Co., 1980), 3.

30. Ibid., 1.

beyond "training immature young people" to enter teaching. Their expanded functions could include the further training of teachers-in-service and the preparation of school principals and supervisors.[31] Judd was half right in his prophecy: correct in that most teacher-training schools *did* expand their activities in the predicted direction. In 1938 under 20 percent of the member institutions of the American Association of Teachers Colleges offered any graduate work; by 1956 over 20 percent had a doctoral program, which is *not* what Judd had in mind.[32]

The American high school figured in this transformation of the normal schools. High schools achieved remarkable importance steadily after 1880, doubling their enrollments every decade until prevented by the low birth rates of the 1930s. This growth made it feasible for normal schools to begin requiring a high school diploma of their entrants, which in turn, hastened their own institutional evolution into teachers' colleges. By adding an optional four-year course, normal schools could train high school teachers along with their traditional elementary school–bound clientele. Despite objections to this trend, based partly on the inadequate training of many of their faculties, eighty-eight state normal schools become teachers colleges between 1910 and 1930. By 1940 the century-old term "normal school" disappeared into educational history.[33] High schools' growth and their need for teachers functioned to sustain enrollments in teachers colleges and university schools of education even in the depression years. If they were obligated to acquire pedagogical training, status-anxious prospective high school teachers were comforted by this association with higher, rather than lower, education.[34]

31. Charles H. Judd, "Teachers College as Centers of Progressive Education," *Proceedings of the National Education Association* (Washington, D.C.: National Education Association, 1929).

32. Karl W. Bigelow, "Moving Ahead in Teacher Education," American Association of Colleges for Teacher Education, *Tenth Yearbook* (Oneonta, N.Y.: AACTE, 1957), 18. The curricular problem of two-year normal schools, suddenly elevated to four-year institutions when two years of post-secondary schooling qualified teachers for certification in most states, are outlined in C. L. Phelps, "What Is a Teachers College?" *School and Society* 31, no. 739 (8 Feb. 1930): 183–85.

33. Paul Woodring, "The Development of Teacher Education," in *Teacher Education,* 74th Yearbook of the National Society for the Study of Education, part 2, ed. Kevin Ryan (Chicago: University of Chicago Press, 1975), 4. More than half of the faculty in normal schools and teachers colleges, of all types, did not have degrees of any kind in 1905. In *National Survey,* 5:63.

34. Arthur G. Powell, *The Uncertain Profession: Harvard and the Search for Educational Authority* (Cambridge, Mass.: Harvard University Press, 1980), 31.

With each passing year it was less common to find what Flexner observed in Maryland in 1914: "inconceivable confusion and lack of sequence and order" in the preparation of teachers, a body of practitioners "heterogeneous to the last degree."[35] Not only did normal schools and high school normal courses disappear almost everywhere in the United States, but the separate teachers colleges changed into general purpose universities; the same phenomenon occurred in the once separate theological seminaries and engineering schools.[36] Westfield Normal, founded in 1844, developed into Westfield State College and Kalamazoo became Western Michigan University. Although each continued to prepare teachers, each also joined the enlarging ranks of multipurpose institutions of higher education. Hence, Judd was mistaken in assuming that the particular institutional alternatives he spoke about in 1929 would long survive, to keep the major university schools of education freed from all pressures to prepare teachers.

Although, in fact, the nineteenth-century normal schools were never the single-minded and essential teacher-education centers that their supporters had wished, their disappearance took with it two professional assets: first, the ideal of the autonomous professional school devoted solely to the exalted preparation of teachers and, second, a dominating concern with "practical pedagogy."[37] As for the municipal and state teachers colleges, they proliferated and came to provide the bulk of the nation's teachers. There were two in 1900, ten in 1910, 125 in 1930, and 146 in 1933. By 1926 Detroit Teachers College was expected to provide one-third to one-half of the city's new

35. "For example, some teachers had entered the normal schools after high school graduation, as they should; but some had entered from the first, second, or third high school year, and not a few went straight from the elementary schools. Some went from the elementary schools to college in order to study 'education'; others spent a year or two in a normal school and then entered college; still others reversed this last mentioned process!" Abraham Flexner and Frank B. Bachman, *Public Education in Maryland* (New York: General Education Board, 1916), 58–60.

36. Jencks and Riesman, *Academic Revolution,* 216.

37. Many citizens sent their sons and daughters to normal schools and gave political support to their proliferation in order to use them as high schools, academies, or colleges. In the Midwest, at least, they represented "the people's yearning for access to liberal learning as a pathway to personal growth and social and vocational goals of their own choosing." Herbst, "Nineteenth-Century Normal Schools," 225. Paul Hanus, Harvard's first professor of pedagogy, secured his own secondary schooling at a Wisconsin normal school. Several of the first generation of American physicists attended normal schools in lieu of high schools or colleges, suggesting a far broader role for normal schools than is usually recognized. See Geraldine Jonçich, "Scientists and the Schools of the 19th Century: The Case of American Physicists," *American Quarterly* 18 (Winter 1966): 667–85.

teachers, in-service training for experienced teachers, and advanced preparation for identified "key teachers."[38] As public institutions they were natural candidates for subsequent expansion and transformation by state legislatures. This happened widely after World War II, when higher education enrollments ballooned under the impetus of federal and state programs to benefit military veterans.

As a consequence of internal and external forces, professional education, in almost all institutions, would have to coexist with academic interests in a competitive environment. What was being lost were the single-minded pursuit of professional training and the possibilities of a significant division of responsibility among distinctive institutional types. Also lost was the opportunity for competing schools of thought about how best to professionalize education, especially that part represented by teachers.

Into the Universities

The first university chair in pedagogy was established at Halle in 1779 by Frederick the Great's minister of public instruction. This was a century after August Hermann Francke pioneered the founding of normal schools with his Seminarium Praeceptorum (1696). In the United States the State University of Iowa is usually credited with founding, in 1873, the nation's first "permanent" professorship in education ("Didactics") although New York University, Brown, Indiana, and others had short-lived pedagogy programs or chairs before then. The University of Iowa's enabling act (1847) had specified that it include a professorship for the training of public school teachers; a subcollegiate "Normal Department" opened in 1855 as a start.[39] Minnesota had a similar provision in its 1860 university statute but was slower to act; its first professor of pedagogy was not hired until 1893—although speech professor Maria Mitchell, a normal school graduate and celebrated schoolteacher, inaugurated a series of lectures in education in 1887.[40] Michigan (1879) had the first of a few new schools founded in

38. *National Survey,* 3:52; Stuart A. Courtis, "Curriculum-Construction at Detroit," in *Curriculum-Making: Past and Present,* 26th Yearbook of the National Society for the Study of Education, part 1, ed. Guy M. Whipple (Bloomington, Ill.: Public School Publishing Co., 1926), 196, 202.

39. Timothy F. O'Leary, *An Inquiry into the General Purposes, Functions, and Organization of Selected University Schools of Education.* (Washington, D.C.: Catholic University Press, 1941), 240.

40. Hugh Graham, "The Rise and Progress of the College of Education of the University of Minnesota," *School and Society* 31, no. 798 (12 April 1930): 510.

the latter part of the nineteenth century, including Teachers College (1887), the ones at Chicago, Stanford, and Harvard in 1891, and at Berkeley in 1892. Although those who conceived the idea of the Ohio State University proposed, in 1864, that teacher education be provided, the Pedagogy Department dates only from 1895. Various Yale professors gave intermittent courses in "pedagogics" as early as 1891; a Department of Philosophy, Psychology and Education appeared only in 1910.

Within a few years the university department, school, or college of education became the modal type toward which other institutions gravitated. It was the preferred means to dignify education as a career for the better-educated and ambitious, to develop competent practitioners, and to build and codify a base of technical knowledge to guide practice and free professionals from outside interference.[41] The college or university professor of pedagogy combined two traditions of professional preparation: one an emphasis on academic preparation, the other elements of apprenticeship exemplified in the normal school's explicit pedagogical training and supervised practice. By 1902 there were sufficient numbers of pedagogy professors to form a new organization: the National Society of College Teachers of Education (later the Society of Professors of Education).

When Carter Alexander of George Peabody College for Teachers surveyed college and university departments of education in 1915, he found them in forty state universities, twenty-two nonstate universities, in women's colleges, agricultural, and technical schools. At a time when America possessed slightly over 600 colleges and universities, over 300 baccalaureate-granting institutions already offered courses in education. Alexander concluded that they offered work in education "as a part of a liberal education, with an idea of making it at the same time valuable for prospective teachers."[42] Like the normal schools, they all claimed to prepare teachers, but already an academic or liberal arts orientation was evident. The private institutions, especially, concentrated their training efforts on the high school teacher whose work was thought to be more like that of the college teacher; their stronger public counterparts did the same. In order to distinguish themselves from the normal schools, university departments of peda-

41. Arthur G. Powell, "University Schools of Education in the Twentieth Century," *Peabody Journal of Education* 54, no. 1 (October 1976): 3.

42. Carter Alexander, "Aims of Departments of Education in Colleges and Universities," *School Review Monographs,* no. 6 (Chicago: University of Chicago Press, 1915), 2–6.

gogy purported to emphasize the theoretical or philosophical aspects of teaching. The larger, moreover, already included courses for school principals and superintendents. A few (perhaps seventeen) of the universities also aimed to prepare normal school and college instructors and to give training for conducting research on education.

The objectives for the University of Michigan in the 1880s illustrate the many-sided ambitions of the pioneer university chairs in the "science and art of teaching." They included articulating secondary with higher education, training graduates for "higher positions" in the public-school system, teaching the history of education, promoting the study of "educational science," and securing "the rights, prerogatives and advantages of a profession."[43] The idea that they would be preparing leaders was present from the start. Because university graduates were a tiny minority of teachers, President Angell argued to the regents that Michigan graduates would be "called directly from the university to the management of large schools, some of them to the superintendency of the schools of a town."[44] His professor of pedagogy, Burke A. Hinsdale, even succeeded, in 1891, in persuading the Michigan legislature to authorize the University itself to award state teacher's certificates. This move enhanced the appeal of university training among aspiring teachers and their families, just as their own "diploma privilege" aided some contemporary university law schools in attracting students because their graduates were permitted to practice without further tests.[45]

The ambitious and fortunate among the early university schools of education quickly moved, as did Berkeley, from a regental authorization in 1889 for instruction in the Art of Teaching, to a two-man Department of Pedagogy in 1892, to a School of Education in 1913. When the nearby and potentially competitive Leland Stanford Junior University opened in 1891, History and Art of Education was one of its twenty-five initial departments; a School of Education was authorized a quarter-century later, in 1917. Ohio State's and Iowa's pedagogy departments became colleges of education in 1907. Despite the initial coupling of education with philosophy at Chicago, Minnesota, Yale, and Harvard, education soon won its organizational separation and attained departmental or school status in each. It was nearly a half-century before Michigan's education department became a school, in 1921; the University's president, M. L. Burton, who had

43. O'Leary, *An Inquiry,* 9.
44. Quoted in Hinsdale, "The Training of Teachers," 34.
45. Johnson, *Schooled Lawyers,* 55–57.

founded the College of Education at Minnesota, was instrumental in that upgrading.[46] Yale's Education Department (1920) was unusual in being a unit in the Graduate School. Of our ten institutions only Teachers College was truly unique. It was an independent professional school in 1892 when it became part of Columbia University, and it was able to maintain a greater degree of independence and professional character in its subsequent history than the others could ever assert.[47]

The Channeling of Diversity

By hiring one another's graduates and raiding one another's faculties, these ten institutions helped to create a shared culture that transcended many differences in their own universities' historical character or regional identity. The majority of the Teachers College senior faculty by the late twenties had earned doctorates at Teachers College or Chicago.[48] In addition, Teachers College helped prepare Ellwood P. Cubberley and Jesse Sears for Stanford; Edwin A. Lee, John Hockett, and George Kyte for Berkeley; Lotus Coffman, Marvin Van Wagenen, and Fletcher Swift for Minnesota; Ernest Horn and F. B. Knight for Iowa; F. D. Curtis for Michigan; B. R. Buckingham for Ohio State; Truman Lee Kelley and Alexander Inglis for Harvard; William Clark Trow for Yale; and Walter Dearborn for Yale, Chicago, and Harvard. By 1930, one-fifth of the faculty and administrators in education departments nationally were Teachers College graduates.[49] Teachers College had a still larger influence on the faculties of many normal schools and state teachers colleges; during the 1920s some boasted that half their faculty had degrees from "TC."[50]

Not all flowed *from* Teachers College, however. Will Russell was dean at Iowa before succeeding his father at Teachers College. (Obviously Teachers College remained first among equals.) Stanford gave

46. O'Leary, *An Inquiry,* 196.

47. Teachers College acquired unprecedented influence among educators around the world, a subject just beginning to receive systematic study. See Ronald K. Goodenow and Robert Cowen," The American School of Education and the Third World in the Twentieth Century: Teachers College and Africa, 1920–1950," *History of Education* 15, no. 4 (1968): 271–89.

48. Lawrence A. Cremin, David A. Shannon, and Mary Evelyn Townsend, *A History of Teachers College, Columbia University.* (New York: Columbia University Press, 1954), 245.

49. Ibid., 221.

50. Woodring, "The Development of Teacher Education," 8.

David Snedden and Henry Suzzallo to Teachers College and took Grayson Kefauver, who succeeded Cubberley as Stanford's dean in 1933. William Webb Kemp, Berkeley's dean from 1923 to 1939, studied at Stanford, but Chicago had the dominant influence on Berkeley's faculty; Kemp's successors as deans—Frank Freeman, Luther Gilbert, and William Brownell—were but a few of Berkeley's Chicago contingent. Luella Cole and Edgar Dale took their Chicago degrees to Ohio State. Harold Rugg taught at Chicago before he made himself famous, even notorious, at Teachers College. Although a somewhat late entrant into the network, by 1940 Yale doctorates had spread its influence—Lawrence Thomas going to Stanford, Theodore Reller to Berkeley, and Robert Beck to Minnesota. George Kneller, Ross Mooney, and Paul Sheats crossed the continent from Yale to UCLA, already an up and coming school, and showing it by recruiting faculty from among the institutions it sought to emulate.

The early demand for professors of education caused institutions to bid against one another. Ohio State, for example, lost its first professor of education, John Gordy, to New York University in 1901—only the beginning of a long series of defections caused by the small budgets from the Ohio legislature combined with the large demand in the expanding world of education schools. When Stanford University dawdled with his promotion in 1907, Henry Suzzalo courted offers from Ohio State, Missouri, Chicago (a professorship and principalship of John Dewey's former elementary school), and Teachers College. "Surely something ought to bob up out of that batch," Suzzalo confidently predicted to Charles Judd, then still at Yale.[51]

The Siren Call of Graduate Education

The "logic" of the academic profession is predicated upon a successive movement from teaching undergraduates in the upper division, to teaching graduate students, to working with post-doctoral students; this applies to both individual faculty and institutional rankings. The combined presence of normal schools, as well as state teachers' colleges and liberal arts colleges which offered some work in pedagogy, permitted early university professors of education to set their sights also far beyond undergraduates and responsibility for the initial preparation of teachers. The existence of alternatives relieved them of much of the pressures that came from students from modest social

51. Donald T. Williams, "Henry Suzzallo and the University of a Thousand Years," *History of Higher Education Annual* 5 (1985): 63.

backgrounds who were attending many of the nation's young schools of education, business, and engineering. Prospective teachers, like most business or engineering students, saw little reason to delay entry to their occupation by lengthy, expensive preprofessional requirements and a postgraduate course.[52] Only a few schools in the professional school sector could ignore such demands and confine themselves to graduates. Chicago was one of these. By the early 1930s it had closed its College of Education (that prepared teachers) and abolished the bachelor's degree in education. Berkeley was another example. Of over one thousand Berkeley graduating seniors in 1924, only sixty-five were education majors; most of these already held teacher certificates earned elsewhere, and wanted a baccalaureate degree. By 1939 the education school was responsible for only fifteen of fifteen hundred graduating.[53] Thus the Berkeley School of Education was freed to concentrate on advanced studies and training.

The Differentiating Functions of Graduate Education

The importance of being admitted into the elite of graduate institutions cannot be overstated. The signs of it were everywhere in the academic community of opinion. The first attempt to classify American institutions of higher education was an effort of the United States Bureau of Education in 1911. Conducted with the encouragement of the Association of American Universities, it grouped 344 institutions on the basis of how well their graduates were likely to perform as students in the nation's best regarded graduate schools.[54] The report was suppressed before it could be generally circulated, but not because of the criterion being used; there was little disputing the right of graduate

52. Jencks and Riesman, *Academic Revolution,* esp. p. 229. The existence of alternatives also shaped institutional preferences in other spheres. Thus, Barbara Solomon points out that elite Catholic colleges benefitted from the existence of the vocational programs in Catholic-sponsored secretarial junior colleges and nursing colleges, "freeing flagship colleges like Emmanuel to serve those desiring a liberal arts education," *In the Company of Educated Women* (New Haven, Conn.: Yale University Press, 1985), 156.

53. George C. Kyte, "Education in the University of California at Berkeley, 1892–1965" (ms., Education-Psychology Library, University of California at Berkeley, 1965).

54. David S. Webster, "The Bureau of Education's Suppressed Rating of Colleges, 1911–1912," *History of Education Quarterly* 24, no. 4 (Winter 1984): 499–511. The report itself is published in Richard Wayne Lykes, *Higher Education and the United States Office of Education (1867–1953),* (Washington, D.C.: United States Office of Education, 1975).

education to be the measure by which academic quality was judged. Rather, institutions not included among the fifty-nine "Class I" entries objected vehemently to being passed over. In America no institution will admit to being anything but first class, if only "of its type."

The ten schools of education that we are observing were early to recognize the importance of graduate education to the prestige of institutions in the twentieth century. Where formerly most college faculty and presidents were A.B.'s or doctors of divinity, by the first quarter of the twentieth century, master's or doctor's degrees were becoming expected in the more aggressive institutions. Moreover, graduate programs added lustre to the parvenue schools that were trying to move from apprenticeship training to learned profession. Education schools anticipated business, engineering, library, social work, nursing, and journalism schools in this development. They did so by first recruiting, as their preferred students, the graduates of normal schools who wanted university degrees as a means of advancement in the profession. They later sought a more prestigious student: the college or university graduate.

University education schools went further by limiting their teacher training, as much as was politically or financially possible, to preparing college graduates for teaching in high schools or, perhaps, in the new junior high schools. They designed advanced degree and certificate programs in emerging specializations for experienced professionals. The fact that, in the early years, salaries of elementary school teachers were so low that few could attend even an inexpensive public university like Ohio State, encouraged the faculty of ambitious education schools to look elsewhere for their clientele.[55] By not emphasizing elementary school teacher preparation and by plowing other fields, university education schools could also maintain good relations with potentially competing institutions—as Iowa did with the State Teachers College at Cedar Falls. This worked until the state teachers colleges themselves became more ambitious, to prepare, first, secondary school teachers and, then, other nonteaching education specialists. When many eventually aspired to offer doctorates, they entered into the most telling competition with university schools of education.

In some sense this early accommodation paralleled the recommendation of a 1920 report on legal education, funded by the Carnegie Foundation. The night law schools, attended largely by urban dwellers of working-class origin, would, as under the previous system of ap-

55. Good, *Rise of the College of Education*, 148.

prenticeship, prepare lawyers for the "minutiae of private practice"—especially for local probate, criminal, and trial work.[56] Graduates of university law schools would enter the corporate and governmental law fields. University law schools would also serve as the "nursery for judges" and "produce a minority of our actual legal practitioners, but textbooks for all."[57]

This report on legal education assumed a differentiated profession not unlike that which characterized public education. For example, in 1930, about one thousand institutions of higher education in the United States offered programs or courses which enabled their graduates to earn a teacher's certificate; in nearly half the institutions, more graduates entered teaching than entered all other fields of work combined. One's position in teaching or other educational work, however, still differed rather systematically according to the type of institution attended. Approximately 95 percent of the students in normal schools and teachers colleges planned to teach.[58] Ninety normal schools and 154 teachers colleges (private, municipal, county, or state sponsored) supplied two-thirds of the nation's elementary school teachers. In contrast, 85 percent of secondary school teachers possessed a bachelor's degree and, of these, only 13 percent were earned in public or private teachers colleges.[59] The preparation of high school teachers, education faculty, researchers, and school specialists of various kinds remained largely the province of the 105 schools or colleges of education in multipurpose colleges and universities. For example, in 1930 a study of 3,866 faculty in 28 normal schools and teachers colleges revealed that 74.6 percent received their last preparation in a college or university; 64 percent had a master's or doctor's degree.[60]

The Demands for Graduate Professional Education

Market and social conditions supported the ambitions of schools of education. In this period, the number of administrators and managers was growing even faster than that of teachers as school systems tried to cope with a bewildering profusion of political, cultural, and tech-

56. Auerbach, "Enmity and Amity," 557.

57. Johnson, *Schooled Lawyers,* 157.

58. *National Survey,* 5:160. These figures exclude racially segregated institutions that prepared black teachers only.

59. Ibid., 2:45.

60. Ibid., 3:121.

nological changes.[61] City school systems were swollen by annexations of their suburbs and, before 1923, by the yet-uncontrolled immigration from Europe. Pupils were being "classed" and graded, as the newly efficient hospitals were sorting their patients by medical condition, as well as social class. Urban teachers confronted the doubtful benefits of increasingly bureaucratic supervision under selectively-applied principles of scientific management. The head teacher had evolved into the school principal, and this role was increasingly said to require special training. It had always seemed difficult to make teachers into independent professionals because of the large numbers involved and the high rates of turnover. It appeared far easier to accomplish professionalization with the new educational bureaucrats; with proper study *they* could tell teachers how to perform, apply the rules, and then supervise their work.

Middle management in education grew as it was doing in business corporations. Urban schools, especially, were adding services like academic counseling, vocational guidance, school libraries, transportation, nutrition, recreation, and health programs. In California a new institution, the junior college, began to appear when a 1911 law authorized high schools to establish the thirteenth and fourteenth grades as lower-division college studies. The dean of Berkeley's School of Education was one of several university leaders in the state who assumed that such institutions would soon provide all the teaching of college freshmen and sophomores. They argued that the schools of education should be creating programs to train junior college faculties, and Berkeley and Stanford both did so. By 1920 California had twenty-one such junior colleges and, by the early years of the depression, about half the students enrolled in the state's public schools of higher education were in the state's thirty-five junior colleges.

Each specialization acquired its own national organization and professional journals. Schools of education, especially the leading institutions, legitimated these specializations by adding courses and professors to represent these interests and to protect them from the preferences of the uninitiated laymen on school boards. Specialization systematized what was increasingly a bureaucratic experience, one buttressed by concepts borrowed from business management. Thus,

61. Merle L. Borrowman, "About Professors of Education," in *The Professor of Education: An Assessment of Conditions,* ed. Ayres Bagley (Papers of the meeting of the Society of Professors of Education, College of Education, University of Minnesota, October 1975), 57–58.

one did not have to be a "free" (i.e., fee-charging) professional in order to have one's expertise sanctioned by university study; it worked for bureaucrats as well, whether in education, engineering, accountancy, or social work.[62] There were certain preferred strategies for doing so. Thus, the women who created the School of Social Service Administration at the University of Chicago in 1920 took care that the core of the curriculum was composed of the "hardest" of the soft social sciences: government, economics, law, history, public administration.[63]

At the same time, state government was extending its control over local school districts, as Horace Mann had wanted to see happen. In 1914 the General Assembly of Maryland authorized a comprehensive survey by an educational commission, to examine the state's entire educational system "with a view to correlating and coördinating the different institutions wholly or partially supported by state appropriations." At the time state law required only that teachers have six weeks of professional training, a provision that was "violated with impunity."[64] The Commission sought expert help from Abraham Flexner of Rockefeller's General Education Board; Flexner was credited with conceiving, in 1910, a widely-cited plan to reform medical education.[65] Not surprisingly, Flexner's Maryland study concluded that admission to teaching should be much more strictly regulated by a central agency, and that "effective schools require skilled and specialized leadership," decently paid, tenured, and supported by professional staff.

Also in 1914 the Ohio legislature showed *its* progressivism by requiring that the College of Education at Ohio State University establish the Bureau of Educational Research. No funding was provided, but the salary of the first director, B. R. Buckingham, was 25 percent greater than the dean's. Buckingham had previously headed the too-successful Bureau of Educational Service at the University of Illinois. The Bureau developed and sold thousands of standardized tests in

62. Larson, *Rise of Professionalism,* 182–187, 193.

63. Clark A. Chambers, "Women in the Creation of the Profession of Social Work," *Social Service Review* 60, no. 1 (March 1986): 21.

64. Flexner and Bachman, *Public Education,* vii, 159.

65. In fact, the conception and institutional framework of Flexner's reforms were set in the nineteenth century; his report represented a consolidation. See Ludmerer, *Learning to Heal.* For the role of the American Medical Association in the shaping of Flexner's report, see Ronald Movrich, "Before the Gates of Excellence: Abraham Flexner and Education, 1866–1918" (Doctoral diss., University of California at Berkeley, 1981).

various school subjects, arousing the envy of commercial publishers and the ire of President David Kinley.[66] Although not usually so profitable, such research units spread, allowing faculty and students to work with school districts in conducting surveys and studies of their enterprises. Berkeley opened its first school study unit in 1919, and most of its peer institutions followed suit. Further inspiration came from Washington. By 1919, the United States Bureau of Education had grown from an original staff of four—the Commissioner and three clerks—to a cadre of 91 professionals and 133 office workers.[67] It also had 380 "dollar-a-year men," collaborators in its various specialized surveys and projects; many of these were professors in schools of education. Before World War II the larger state departments of education had 100 or more professional employees. Before this formative period ended, three-fourths of the states required that their chief state school officer have professional qualifications.

City, state, and federal officials in education looked increasingly to the universities for manpower. By the 1930s, when a number of states had established credentials for such specialties as school administration and supervision, the universities had anticipated them: the courses were already in place.[68] By expanding their faculties into various specializations, education schools could offer attractive training to potential new clients. A broadened enrollment justified, in turn, employing still more faculty. The list of instructors in the catalogues of Teachers College grew from eighteen in 1897–98 to ninety-two a decade later. There, as elsewhere, many of the faculty came to be largely or exclusively identified with graduate education.

The advancement of Dr. William John Cooper illustrates the career ladders that were being constructed in education for ambitious men. Cooper graduated from Berkeley in 1906 and taught history and Latin in the high school of Stockton, California, before moving to the more attractive position of chairman of the history department in high schools in Berkeley and Oakland. Armed with a master's degree from Berkeley in 1917, he sought the post of district superintendent of schools in nearby Piedmont. He became successively, superintendent

66. Henry C. Johnson, Jr., and Irwin V. Johanningmeier, *Teachers for the Prairie: The University of Illinois and the Schools, 1868–1945* (Urbana: University of Illinois Press, 1972), 248–52.

67. Richard Wayne Lykes, *Higher Education and the United States Office of Education (1867–1953)* (Washington, D.C.: U.S. Office of Education, 1975), 79.

68. David Tyack and Elisabeth Hansot, *Managers of Virtue: Public School Leadership in America, 1820–1980* (New York: Basic Books, 1982), 98.

in Fresno and San Diego. In 1927 he became State Superintendent of Public Instruction in California and left that position when President Coolidge named him United States Commissioner of Education in 1929. Cooper served until 1933 when he resigned and became professor of education at George Washington University.[69] Unlike a generation later, however, Cooper's doctorate was an honorary degree from the University of Southern California. Earned doctorates characterized most of Cooper's successors, as they marked Americans of ambition in other university-influenced fields.

This was a variant of the process that was reshaping professional competence in the older, high-prestige professions. In the law it meant a reduction in the weight given to advocacy in the courtroom, when the bar examination and the law school assumed larger responsibility for certifying to the public and profession alike the competencies of a new breed of lawyer. In medicine the need to practice "heroic therapy" to establish one's reputation was curbed by the creation of medical societies, restrictive legislation on entry to practice, and medical schools to enforce a new orthodoxy.[70] In education ambitious younger men substituted university credentials and the contacts made thereby for some of the traditional experience and professional contacts; at the least it provided a shortcut.

The appearance of graduate work in education is striking, for it came earlier than in other professions. Stanford's first "majors" in education were three graduate students, one undergraduate, and four special students.[71] Minnesota listed pedagogy as a subject for graduate study in 1893. The first Ph.D. in education at Berkeley was earned in 1897, for a thesis on child study, awarded to the first woman to get a Berkeley doctorate; this was just six years after the initial faculty appointment was made in pedagogy. It also appears to have been the first doctorate in education awarded in the United States.[72] Before 1906, education came to enroll the largest number of graduate students of any Berkeley department. The same thing happened at Chicago by the

69. Lykes, *Higher Education*, 99–100, 107.

70. Johnson, "Educational and Professional Life Styles," esp. p. 203.

71. O'Leary, *An Inquiry*, 289.

72. The date of Millicent Shinn's Ph.D. is variously given as 1897 or 1898. Hers is described as the nation's first Ph.D. in education by Erwin V. Johanningmeier and Henry C. Johnson, Jr., "The Education Professoriate: A Historical Consideration of Its Work and Growth," in *The Professor of Education: An Assessment of Conditions*, ed. Ayers Bagley (papers of the meeting of the Society of Professors of Education, College of Education, University of Minnesota, October 1975), 2.

1920s. At Michigan in 1900–1901 graduate students in pedagogy were already 14.4 percent of the graduate total.[73]

Courses open only to graduate students appeared at Iowa by 1897; one featured statistical and descriptive studies of public school conditions, the other Herbartian methods in German elementary schools—both "trendy" subjects at the time. Teachers College had sixty-two doctoral students in 1910, a year in which only thirteen Ph.D. degrees in education were awarded nationally. The journal *Science* reported in 1911 that education already trailed only English, history, and philosophy as fields for the earned doctorate in the United States. When Frederick Bolton published his survey in 1915, only Chicago and Columbia were characterized as having large numbers of graduate students, but graduate programs were proliferating. By the 1930s, only chemistry produced more doctorates in the United States than did education schools.[74] Teachers College alone awarded 1,600 doctorates in education between 1898 and 1941. Not too surprising, then, that the designation "Graduate" was part of Harvard's title from its transformation from a Division of Education to a School in 1920. In that year education's share of all doctorates awarded nationally was already 8.6 percent; by 1940 it would be 14.3 percent and still rising.

The Slim Storehouse of Knowledge

One of the most influential figures in professional education at the turn of the century, Dean Christopher Columbus Langdell of the Harvard Law School, cautioned, "If law be not a science, a university will best consult its own dignity in deciding to teach it. If it be not a science, it is a species of handicraft, and may best be learned by serving an apprenticeship to one who practices."[75] Was education, however, a science? Did it possess, much less control access to, information of high value? Not in 1891, wrote Harvard's philosopher, Josiah Royce, in "Is There a Science of Education?" He did, however, assume that

73. Alan Creutz, "From College Teacher to University Scholar: The Evolution and Professionalization of Academics at the University of Michigan, 1841–1900," (Doctoral diss., University of Michigan, 1981), 222.

74. Hughes, "Report"; Frederick E. Bolton, "Curricula in University Departments of Education," *School and Society* 2, no. 50 (11 Dec. 1915): 841.

75. Quoted in Robert B. Stevens, "The American Law School," *Perspectives in American History* 5 (1971): 435. See also his *Law School: Legal Education in America from the 1850s to the 1980s* (Chapel Hill: University of North Carolina Press, 1983).

inductive science would eventually offer help to the *art* of the teacher.[76]

The eagerly made decision to offer graduate education put pressure on the small store of scholarly or technical literature on the ancient practice of education. A corpus of knowledge had to be attained quickly—to have something to teach and to justify the new place of education in universities. The reformed American universities that emerged in the 1890s were open to offering professional training "in fields that had a genuine but still only potential and undeveloped scientific or scholarly content."[77] Elmer Ellsworth Brown, who went from the position as Berkeley's first appointment in pedagogy, to United States Commissioner of Education, to chancellor of New York University, would have characterized his field as "only potential." In 1923 he looked back to the difficulty he had experienced at Berkeley in spending even the "modest sum available to start a pedagogical section in the university library."

> Many of the volumes ordered, although standard hand-books of the teaching profession, made a trivial showing as compared with the collections in agriculture, engineering, jurisprudence, and other professional subjects. For use in the classroom there was nothing available that could be compared with the texts of the older professions.[78]

Thus, Harvard's President Lowell was not altogether wrong when, in 1912, he reminded his chairman of education, Professor Holmes, that "one reason why the history of education has been considered so important in the training of teachers is that we have had so little so far to teach them about the way that things should actually be done."[79] Education was perceived to be in about the situation of the medical profession in 1793, when the College of Physicians proposed that a

76. Royce's essay is reprinted in Borrowman, *Teacher Education in America: A Documentary History* (New York: Teachers College Press, 1965), 100–127.

77. Robert Wiebe, *The Search for Order, 1877–1920* (New York: Hill & Wang, 1967), 121.

78. Elmer Ellsworth Brown, "The Development of Education as a University Subject," *Teachers College Record* 24, no. 3 (May 1923): 193. Of the wisdom of those older professions, recall, however, the criticism of Dr. Oliver Wendell Holmes, Sr., in the mid-nineteenth century. He wrote, "if the whole materia medica, *as now used*, could be sunk to the bottom of the sea, it would be all the better for mankind—and all the worse for the fishes." Quoted in Burton J. Bledstein, *The Culture of Professionalism: The Middle Class and the Development of Higher Education in the United States* (New York: W. W. Norton, 1976), 33.

79. Powell, *Uncertain Profession*, 99.

cholera epidemic be halted in Philadelphia by firing a cannon from the steps of City Hall. A dedicated empiricist, Charles Judd brooked no philosophy of education courses during his long tenure as head of Chicago's Department of Education. By 1910, statistical studies of the organization and problems of schooling were joining the historical and philosophical theses on the shelves of education school libraries. It was his psychological experimentation that prompted Lowell to try to lure E. L. Thorndike from Teachers College to Harvard in 1910. But such work was appearing elsewhere; scientific topics characterized many of the dissertations. "Here was no dabbling with the tricks of the trade that had been the earmarks of the normal school; here was *Wissenschaft* with a vengeance."[80]

The opinion that there remained very little of substance to teach had not been confined to Harvardian aristocrats nor soon quenched. The president of the University of Illinois commented on his reaction to the science of education in 1924, thus: "When one reads the literature of this field he is tempted, as he is when he reads some of the literature of sociology and psychology, to wonder whether after all the so-called field of study did not emerge into public attention largely because its devotees invented a terminology and then thought they had a science."[81]

The rudimentary state of the field was both a challenge and an opportunity for enterprising researchers. Investigations were proceeding on several fronts. Indeed, Teachers College's Paul Monroe observed little agreement among students of education "regarding the types of problems worthy of investigation, the methods to be used, the purposes involved, the organization of work of research, and the encouragement to be given to it."[82]

Stanford's Ellwood P. Cubberley was typical of the first generation of university educationists in developing and teaching courses that he could not have himself taken as they had not existed two decades before. As early as 1900, Ohio State's Department of Education offered two courses which none of the pioneers had available to them: "A Study of Scientific Method" and "Pedagogical Research." Faculty

80. Lowell to Thorndike, May 9, 1910, quoted in Geraldine Jonçich, *The Sane Positivist: A Biography of Edward L. Thorndike* (Middletown, Conn.: Wesleyan University Press, 1968), 296; Lawrence A. Cremin, *The Transformation of the School: Progressivism in American Education, 1876–1957* (New York: Knopf, 1961), 200.

81. Johnson and Johanningmeier, *Teachers for the Prairie*, 230.

82. Paul Monroe, "Co-operative Research in Education, Its Organization and Encouragement," *School Review Monographs*, no. 1 (Papers presented at the Society of College Teachers of Education, Mobile, Ala. 23–25 Feb. 1911), 14.

had to teach about a subject, that "hardly existed at all in the sense of other academic subjects."[83] Minnesota's College of Education had a mere six-man faculty in 1905–6, while the College of Agriculture had ten specialists in "sweet curd cheese work" and "cultures and starters" alone.[84] In their tiny departments early education faculty resembled the stereotype of the professor in the smaller American colleges, described in 1871: "a jack of all trades, equally ready to teach surveying and Latin eloquence, and thankful if his quarter's salary is not docked to whitewash the college fence."[85]

The paucity of modern, scientific knowledge about teaching and learning was especially unsettling given the consequences of the contemporary child study movement and progressive theories of instruction. Current theory rejected the idea of the student as passive receiver of whatever the school offered. This placed greater responsibility on the school to structure effective classroom experiences rather than rely on the child to grasp whatever the school offered."[86] Everything needed to be determined, from the stages of children's intellectual and psychomotor development and their variations from the norm to the effects of correlation of school subjects and the best pace for teaching, and the knowledge disseminated to teachers and specialists.

Graduate education, as well as the state of the field, argued for taking research promise and scholarly activity into account in making faculty appointments. Chicago and Berkeley were doing this in pedagogy before World War I. Harvard was being pressured by President Lowell to do the same. When Minnesota recruited Lotus Coffman from Illinois in 1915, it did so in the pursuit of a dean "well-trained in modern scientific methods." Cubberley took a leave from Stanford to earn a doctorate at Teachers College in 1905 and made sure that younger men aiming for a career at Stanford did the same.[87] For this reason the faculties of university schools of education were progressively less likely to hire school superintendents for professorships than were

83. Theodore Sizer and Arthur G. Powell, "Changing Concepts of the Professor of Education," in *To Be a Phoenix: The Education Professoriate,* ed. James Steve Counelis (Bloomington, Ind.: Phi Delta Kappa, 1969), 62.

84. Beck, *Beyond Pedagogy,* 48.

85. Quoted in Bledstein, *Culture of Professionalism,* 28.

86. Don C. Charles, "Expectation vs. Reality: Behavioral Science Response to Teacher Education Demand." In *Responding to the Power Crisis in Teacher Education,* ed. Ayres Bagley (Major papers and abstracts of the 1971 Conference, Chicago; Washington, D.C.: Society of Professors of Education) 31.

87. Jesse Brundage Sears, *An Autobiography.* (Palo Alto: 1959), 45.

normal schools or state teachers colleges, where a sixth of the faculties in 1933 possessed such experience.[88]

By founding journals and monographs series, education schools could do what other ambitious departments were doing to build their reputations: stimulate research and ensure a place for the publications of faculty and graduate students. The scope of Teachers College's publications was widest of all: from *Studies of the International Institute of Teachers College* to the *Teacher's Lesson Unit Series.* The *Educational Research Bulletin* of Ohio State University, begun in 1921, was intended both for other researchers and school professionals. Teachers College, Chicago, and Harvard each launched a journal labelled *Record.* The *School Review,* published at Chicago since 1896 as a journal of secondary education, was meant, by Judd especially, to demonstrate that the scientific study of the phenomena of education was both estimable and useful. "It is a curious fact that in academic circles and high school circles it is eminently respectable to be a student of the lowest forms of animal life and a very doubtful distinction to be a student of education," he mused. By the 1920s the journal was disseminating the results of research.[89]

In 1911 Houghton Mifflin Company and Stanford's Cubberley saw a large market for textbooks among advanced students of education; so began the Riverside Textbooks in Education.[90] The series linked professors from the leading education schools in an informal network, solidifying their institutions' influence on the development of the entire, many-sided field. In 1915 Chicago's Judd announced that his colleagues were beginning to prepare textbooks "which will give expression to the special methods of treating education which are characteristic of this department." He confidently predicted that as soon as Chicago could standardize its scientifically-oriented courses to textbook form, "there will be a great many other institutions which will adopt our formula."[91] The venture of publishing school textbooks would, however, also bring education faculty into competition with academics. At Michigan, for example, the academic faculty had pub-

88. *National Survey,* 2:172. Proportionally speaking, however, in both sets of institutions a superintendent had a far greater probability of becoming a member of an education faculty than did a teacher.

89. Harold S. Wechsler, "The Primary Journal for Secondary Education, 1893–1938: Part 1 of a History of *School Review,*" *American Journal of Education* 88, no. 1 (Nov. 1979): 98.

90. Jesse Brundage Sears and Adin D. Henderson, *Cubberley of Stanford* (Stanford, Calif.: Stanford University Press, 1957), 201.

91. Quoted in Bolton, *Curricula,* 840.

lished over 600 textbooks in the nineteenth century.[92] Much of the market in the next century would be captured by professors of education and their students. Some of the resentment, by academics, of educationists' growing claims to exclusive expertise in matters of education may be traced to this shift.

Creating the Common Denominator

Imitation has been a powerful force in the history of American higher education, and no less so than among the professional schools.[93] When Cubberley left the superintendency of the San Diego public schools for Stanford in 1898, he prepared for his new post by reading about what "twenty of our best universities" were doing in education.[94] In his struggles with Presidents Eliot and Lowell, Harvard's Paul Hanus repeatedly contrasted his 1905 total of 31 graduate students and 85 undergraduates with Teachers College's 250 and 800 respectively. Eliot's acid response to one such comparison was that Teachers College was an "exaggerated and undesirable standard."[95] Minnesota's David Kiehle reminded President Northrup that his own was twenty years behind other institutions in organizing itself to offer work in pedagogy.[96] When the president of the University of California argued fruitlessly in 1884 for the "importance of Pedagogics as a department of university work," he did so on the basis that it was "tardily receiving proper recognition in some of the best universities in the east."[97] On the same line, the regents of the University endorsed a resolution in 1919 calling for resources for Berkeley adequate to "train men and women for the teaching profession on lines comparable to opportunities offered in the Teachers College of Columbia University and University of Chicago."[98] In the School's own self-study (1933–35), Berkeley's courses were compared with those of forty other universities.

92. Creutz, "From College Teacher to University Scholar," 452.

93. Deans of business schools and their key faculty were also agents of institutional imitation. Vanderblue brought Harvard ideas and faculty to Northwestern's School of Commerce in 1937 and UCLA acquired Chicago's values with Dean Jacoby in 1948. See Schlossman and Sedlak, *Age of Autonomy,* 14–20.

94. Sears and Henderson, *Cubberley of Stanford,* 59.

95. Powell, *Uncertain Profession,* 80.

96. Beck, *Beyond Pedagogy,* 29.

97. O'Leary, *An Inquiry,* 363.

98. Kyte, "Education," 36.

Although competition thrived among the leaders, the faculties and deans of education schools also collaborated in the crucial early years. In a subtle fashion, one undoubtedly familiar to their counterparts in other fields, the collective task was to create and maintain a favorable image and set of arrangements that would secure a privileged status for all of the members of the elite group. In other words, the pie had to be secured before it could be divided. An example of collaboration that would protect the energies of the whole was the private agreement made in the 1920s between Teacher College and Harvard: that the latter would stay out of offering work in vocational education.[99]

In their building strategies, education deans sought outside assistance. Abraham Flexner once commented that "education is by all odds the field to which foundations have up to the present time given most of their energy, thought, and money, and in which, whatever may have been their errors, they have been most effective."[100] There was, however, no counterpart in the universe of education schools to the influence that the Carnegie Foundation for the Advancement of Teaching exercised on medical education after 1910, or the Ford Foundation on graduate business education after 1955.[101] For one thing, the number of education programs was so much greater. For another, education lacked a powerful professional organization, like the American Medical Association, to stimulate and control the reform thrust. Education's largest, the National Education Association, was not strictly a professional organization, being a general advocacy organization for public education and, like engineering associations, a voice for its members' grievances and aspirations.[102] Moreover, it was riddled, before 1920, with rival factions including women classroom teachers who were trying to gain some influence at the expense of university leaders like Nicholas Murray Butler of Columbia University and Charles William Eliot of Harvard University. As in the case of business

99. Powell, *Uncertain Profession,* 8.

100. Abraham Flexner, *Funds and Foundations* (New York: Harper & Row, 1952), 125.

101. The sponsorship of the study of medical education, led by Abraham Flexner, is told in many places, including Movrich, "Before the Gates of Excellence." On the role of the Ford Foundation–commissioned study of business education, by Robert Gordon and James Howell, see Schlossman and Sedlak, *The Age of Autonomy.*

102. Michael Burrage, "Practitioners, Professors, and the State in France, the USA, and England," in *Education for the Professions: Quis custodiet . . . ?,* ed. Sinclair Goodlad (Guilford, England: Society for Research into Higher Education/NFER–Nelson, 1984), 34.

schools, education seemingly lacked those nascent tendencies which could be legitimated and channeled by a single report.

Nonetheless, organized philanthropy did enhance opportunities for graduate programs, the establishment of professorships, and support for research. Rockefeller money opened the University of Chicago, sustained the School of Education until Judd put it on its feet, and, through the General Education Board (G.E.B.), made a major gift in 1929 that strengthened Chicago's graduate programs.[103] G.E.B. money launched the Harvard Graduate School of Education in a tardy effort to catch up with the competition.[104] Under Abraham Flexner, the G.E.B. was also a major benefactor of Teachers College, permitting the founding of its Lincoln School in 1917. In 1920 it announced a million dollar gift to Teachers College to endow and construct a new library and classrom buildings, recognizing its having "done more for the elevation of professional training of teachers and educational administrators than any other institution of its kind in the country."[105]

Public universities also received support for research and graduate education. The G.E.B. helped finance the staffing of Michigan's University Elementary School from 1930, and the Kellogg Foundation supported Michigan's research in the 1930s, on child development. Later, the G.E.B. funded community studies by Harvard, Ohio State, and other schools on issues of school administration. W. W. Charters secured large grants for Ohio State's Bureau of Educational Research from the Commonwealth Fund and the G.E.B. Banker Felix Warburg was a trustee of Teachers College; appointed to the Visiting Committee of Harvard's School in 1913, his contributions and energies pushed that School in new directions. But philanthropy tended to promote a certain sameness rather than clearly defined alternatives—as we will see again in the post–World War II period in the Master of Arts in Teaching programs.

103. Woodie T. White, "The Decline of the Classroom and the Chicago Study of Education, 1909–1929," *American Journal of Education* 90, no. 2 (Feb. 1982): 145–74.

104. Powell, *Uncertain Profession,* 3; Hugh Hawkins, *Between Harvard and America: The Educational Leadership of Charles W. Eliot* (New York: Oxford University Press, 1972), 256.

105. This was the largest appropriation to an education school in G.E.B.'s history. "Gift of the General Education Board to Teachers College, Columbia University," *School and Society* 11, no. 271 (6 March 1920): 286.

Conclusions

From the perspective of a sociologist of professions, the turn-of-the-century movement removed professionals from their "dependence upon the power and prestige of elite patrons or upon the judgment of a tightly knit community"; in their place, the modern professions depended upon specific formal training and "anonymous certificates."[106] Law, medicine, and theology had been the three professions of the medieval university, and were among the first to attach themselves to the modern American university. The first two gained prestige by their association with the changing universities. Despite their best efforts, university schools of divinity were unable to rise above the declining status of religion in modern society; thus, they reached the approximate position of schools of education: wedged in among the class of "minor professions," with fields like social work and town planning.[107]

Historians of education have frequently noted the other links between religion and education. For example, leaders of the early American colleges and public schools typically perceived their professional responsibilities in moral and oftentimes doctrinal terms, and a number of them actually had ministerial training. Normal school educators still thought of their profession as a quasi-religious calling, as older nursing educators used religious and maternal self-sacrifice to describe their mission.[108] But "profession" was coming to mean something different to the advocates of professions as secular undertakings. The referent was no longer the minister who professed his faith in a religious vocation—the ideal professional man of earlier generations in America. The new exemplar of the professional man was the reformed physician. Drawing on an expanding body of scientific knowledge and deepening specialization, the new-style medical doctor was confident, prosperous, and powerful. Well-organized, nationally through the American Medical Association, and in local medical societies, physicians had succeeded in eliminating other sects ("quacks") as serious competitors, closed large numbers of medical schools, and

106. Larson, *Rise of Professionalism,* 4.

107. Nathan Glazer, "The Schools of the Minor Professions," *Minerva* 12, no. 3 (July 1974): 352; William Alonso, "The Unplanned Paths of Planning Schools," *Public Interest,* no. 82 (Winter 1986): 58–71.

108. There are revealing comparisons to be drawn between teaching and nursing in their twentieth-century efforts to professionalize through esoteric knowledge and advanced credentials. See Barbara Melosh, *"The Physician's Hand": Work, Culture, and Conflict in American Nursing* (Philadelphia: Temple University Press, 1982), 15–35.

erected effective barriers to the widespread practice of what was becoming a lucrative and prestigious craft. They now aroused only envy and emulation among other professionals. How much their situations had altered since the nineteenth century can be estimated by reference to the complaint of a physician writing in the *Pittsburgh Medical Review* in 1896. He had deplored the humiliation he felt in making "a comparison of the economic and social positions of our leading physicians and surgeons with leading lawyers and other professional men."[109]

Meanwhile the legal profession was itself being upgraded. Although not ready to turn its back entirely on the "unschooled Abe Lincoln" image of the charismatic country lawyer, and unable to repudiate the public and even democratic character of the law, the future of the legal profession was increasingly being shaped by a private nexus of legal scholars, corporate lawyers, and judges. In contrast to those lawyers and physicians whom they aspired to imitate, educators, especially teachers, remained closer to ministers in the sources of *their* expertness, their calling, and their rewards.

Education's self-defined leaders—nationally visible school administrators and prominent professors of education—were impatient with that reality and struggled to change it. Abraham Flexner, a southern schoolmaster before he became an instrument of organized, reformist philanthropy, was appalled that, of twenty-three county superintendents of schools in Maryland in 1915, only fifteen had college degrees and not more than six of the fifteen "made special and professional preparation for their work."[110] He also disapproved of the fact that the faculty of the Baltimore Normal School, whose graduates were found in important school positions in the state, were themselves only graduates of the Normal. Flexner in 1915 and other prominent educational figures for a longer period, saw in educational science and advanced training the way into a better future—at least for persons like themselves. Professors in elite education schools would perform the same service as professors in elite law schools: provide the reform movement of professionalization with its necessary educational foundation.[111]

The single-minded pursuit of the prestige and legitimacy which academic and especially graduate education could confer was, however, threatening to the *professional* mission of all professional

109. Quoted in Larson, *Rise of Professionalism,* 159.

110. Flexner and Bachman, *Public Education,* 44.

111. Larson, *Rise of Professionalism,* 167.

schools, including education schools. As their deans and professors come under the influence of the graduate school and its ethos, they become more concerned with academic skills than with the professional values that distinguished them. As its historian has said of Harvard's Graduate School of Education and its repeated attempts to get on course, it "had not sought to re-examine the ends for which the School existed, but instead had sought to upgrade its product to conform to Harvard tradition."[112] Something similar could be said of the others. The "solutions," approaches, and prejudices of one dean became that of the others. Despite their important differences and the specialness of each one's host university, these ten schools of education became much alike in their responses to the developing profession and to their academic environments. Alternative conceptions, especially of the teacher and teacher education, once embodied in the stronger normal schools and state teachers colleges, were stillborn as these institutions withered in the face of the greater prestige of the college and university. As such they presented distressingly few real options to up-and-coming emulators.

It is a truism, that "as is the teacher, so is the school." When John Brinsley argued in England in 1622 for trained teachers it was because "so few of those who undertake this function are acquainted with anie good method, or right order of instruction, fit for a Grammer schoole."[113] The results were "the endlesse vexation of the painfull Maisters, the extreme labour and terrour of the poore scholars." In the succeeding two chapters we will look more closely, first, at how schools of education faced their responsibilities to the "Painful Maisters" and the "poore scholars." Then, second, we try to answer this question: How well did the nation's premier schools of education secure their own positions as academic enterprises on the campuses of America's leading universities?

112. Arthur G. Powell in Harvard Committee, *Graduate Study* 88.

113. John Brinsley is quoted in Robert H. Quick, *Essays on Educational Reformers* (New York: Appleton, 1890).

Three Tensions: The Academic and the Vocational

There is a powerful myth abroad in American universities: that colleges, and even universities, were once—in some golden age—purely academic places. This fiction ignores the historic function of formal education in maintaining or enhancing the social status of individuals or groups. "It is not only (or perhaps primarily) *what* you know but *who* you know that counts" is a truism that applies as well to collegiate experience as elsewhere. In every era and every society we know of, successful graduates have benefitted from the contacts made and the cachet of a diploma at least as much as from formal instruction. Most students have attended institutions of higher education for implicitly practical reasons—whatever the catalogue suggests. Those who would be ministers in the eighteenth century were largely replaced by those who would be businessmen or engineers in the twentieth; while these shifts were important indicators of social and economic developments in American society, they did not as radically alter the character or meaning of higher education as the academic tories would have us believe.

The vocational principle operated even in the expansion of women's education, the other great revolution of the latter nineteenth century.[1] Scholars usually consider women's education beyond basic

1. For a discussion of the neglect by historians of the revolution that women were introducting into education see Geralding Jonçich Clifford, "'A Hopeless Tangle of Tormenting Questions': History, Gender, and Education" (Paper presented at the annual meeting of the American Educational Research Association, San Francisco, April 1986).

literacy as nonvocational because, until well into this century, a minority of women entered and remained in the labor force. The prestigious women's colleges that opened after the Civil War—like the female seminaries that preceded them—appear different from the public state universities or colleges for black and Catholic students which "openly emphasized vocational education."[2] Yet, many who attended female seminaries and women's colleges did, in fact, intend to become school teachers or to prepare themselves to do so if personal circumstances required them to become self-supporting. The numbers of women making such contingent plans only increased with time. Arguably, the women who attended such schools to be "finished" as ladies and later, to increase their competence and value as prospective wives and mothers—women's "true profession"—also acted out of "vocational" motivations.

The important word is *openly:* public institutions, the teachers colleges, and those created for racial and cultural minorities, could not as well disguise their useful functions under the rubric of "liberal education for ladies and gentlemen." Conspicuous consumption in academia is a luxury that relatively few institutions of higher education in America could afford—then or now. In the middle and later years of the nineteenth century another class of universities, state institutions, some with land-grant status, spoke explicitly of the social benefits conferred by their vocational programs. At the University of Wisconsin, for example, its new normal department would be "the nursery of the educators of the popular mind . . . the *school of the schoolmaster.*"[3]

Although the modern university was created in a context of professionalization, its clearly vocational departments and professional schools have borne the burden of a conventional wisdom, however mistaken, that holds that their presence on college campuses debases higher education by encouraging unworthy motives and suspect curricula. This encourages professional school faculty and their apprentices to make their work appear progressively "more academic." What William R. Johnson writes of education for the bar—that institutions of higher education exercised "a more decisive impact than did the legal profession on the eventual configuration of the twentieth-century law school"—also describes schools of education in the leading American universities.[4]

2. Solomon, *In the Company of Educated Women,* 151.

3. Quoted in Johnson, *Schooled Lawyers,* 15–16.

4. Ibid., xii. In the academic professions the aim is to maintain and develop the cognitive resources of the culture, in the applied professions to attain practical goals.

In the case of education schools the academic ethos divides, *internally,* the faculty into two unequal groups: those who profess allegiance to scientific and disciplinary methods and those bound to the field by the mandates of professional training, especially for emerging and higher status occupational specializations. By the end of this formative period it was possible to find two faculties in the leading education schools: those men "who had the tools but no contexts other than the university laboratory or library in which to use them to illuminate education" and the men "who knew the schools but had few tools of inquiry to organize that experience, reflect on it, and generate new ideas."[5]

Among the professional schools of the prototypical American university there are, of course, gradations of acceptance or toleration. Knowing this, the early leaders of schools of education commonly tried to emulate law or medical schools, as they understood them. Employing this model, it may be said that the professional school has (1) as its sole purpose, training personnel for a profession; (2) a program that focuses on the development of practical knowledge and skills; (3) a program designed without interference by other departments and schools; and (4) a program influenced by professional organizations and public criticism. Employing these criteria, we can say that leading schools of education—whatever else they achieved—did not become or remain *professional* schools. Dominated by the ethos of graduate academic norms, lacking substantial independence, and weakly attached to the occupation of teaching, "their faculties are oriented to pedagogical studies that ultimately focus on research for the doctor's degree rather than on competence for either positions in the public school or in the training function of pedagogical schools."[6] Indeed, Robert Beck calls his history of Minnesota's College of Education *Beyond Pedagogy*—a state to be achieved through the pursuit of scientific research. But educational research often meant the construction of educational problems on the basis of academic or theoretical interest in phenomena of as little interest to the school-based practitioner

---

"In a word, the fiduciary responsibility of the academic professions is primarily cultural and in the applied professions it is primarily social"; Robert E. Roemer and Marian L. Martinello, "Divisions in the Education Professoriate and the Future of Professional Education," *Educational Studies,* 13, no. 2 (Summer 1982): 211.

5. Sizer and Powell, "Changing Conceptions," 67. See also Roemer and Martinello, "Divisions in the Education Professoriate," 203–23.

6. B. Othanel Smith, *A Design for a School of Pedagogy* (Washington, D.C.: U.S. Department of Education, 1980), 11.

as the work of the divinity school archaeologist was to the preacher laboring over his Sunday sermon.[7]

An academic problem is defined as "some lacuna or ambiguity in the data or interpretations of a world-wide discipline," a question asked by colleagues who are other academics in one's field.[8] They are "fellow professionals" in the sense of belonging to the *academic* profession. Even if motivated by problems of practical importance, academic researchers first translate them into theoretical questions to be answered theoretically.[9] Thus, their questions and concerns may appear unintelligible or irrelevant or unimportant or downright silly to the practitioners for whom professors in professional schools may claim to speak. Hence, what has been said of professors in engineering schools—that they usually become more interested in imparting the skills appropriate to teachers of engineering—also became true of many professors in leading schools of education: they were increasingly satisfied with reproducing *their* kind and with publishing for non-practitioner audiences. These tasks were easier to accomplish than was communication with the impatient, task-oriented practitioner.[10]

It is said of professors of education that their lives have a Janus-like nature, looking toward both the school and the university.[11] We think this is true of the largest number of schools, colleges, and departments of education. Their faculties are still composed primarily of those with professional experiences in elementary and secondary education. Drawn to higher education less to promote scholarship and doctoral education than to improve schooling by teaching future teachers, they are likely to spend longer hours on the campus in teaching and advising than on research projects—all characteristics found by questioning education faculty in nonelite universities.[12] In this chapter, however, we will describe the unraveling of this field-rooted professional purpose in the leading schools of education, institutions

7. Glazer, "Schools of the Minor Professions," 351. This recalls Steven White's observation about journalism schools: that their faculties and doctoral students conduct studies on such sociological aspects of the profession as the differences in alcohol consumption of reporters and editors. "But the working journalist's concern is whether his own editor is drunk, not how many editors are drunk"; Steven White, "Why Journalism Schools?" *Public Interest,* no. 82 (Winter 1986): 51.

8. Jencks and Riesman, *Academic Revolution,* 242.

9. Roemer and Martinello, "Divisions in the Education Professoriate," 211–12.

10. Ibid., 253.

11. Edward R. Ducharme and Russell M. Agne, "The Education Professoriate: A Research-Based Perspective," *Journal of Teacher Education* 33, no. 6 (Nov.–Dec. 1982): 36.

12. Ibid., 30–36.

that had a freedom not available to the fee-charging proprietary school or the free-standing public normal school or agricultural college scrutinized by a tight-fisted state legislature.[13] Once teacher education institutions, they came to identify ever more closely with the academic and graduate orientations of arts and sciences departments, and to recruit students who were redefining the education profession in ways that ignored, repudiated, or "transcended" pedagogy. In their efforts to justify the presence of their discipline in the university, the mission of professional education was being changed, albeit unevenly and unequally. Given all the social and political forces at work, it would have been courageous and farsighted for university presidents or education deans and their faculties to have acted otherwise. That such qualities were in short supply has haunted the teaching profession ever since.

A Vision of Wholeness in Professional Education

The pioneers of the university study of pedagogy oftentimes took their inspiration from medical education. If, in the early twentieth century, the vast majority of medical practitioners were skeptical about both medical science and the scientific elite in the reformed medical schools, they were certain that they wished to see their professional and economic status raised.[14] A key theme in the labors of the new and "scientific" medical educators was the union of research and practice. Early in this century, Franklin Mall wrote, for *The Michigan Alumnus,* of the value of research in the medical school:

> There has always been a great deal of discussion of the question whether a physician's training should be scientific or practical. It appears to me it should be both, for if he is educated only in the sciences underlying medicine, he is not a physician, while if he is educated in the practical

13. Proprietary schools had to advertise "an intensely practical curriculum designed to attract large numbers of students"; Johnson, "Education and Professional Life Styles," 201. How loath public officials were to spend taxpayers' monies was indicated by the Educational Survey Commission authorized by the Maryland Legislature in 1914. The Commission's appropriation from the state was $7,500 and so it sought its experts at the General Education Board. Rockefeller money paid Abraham Flexner and Frank Bachman. The Commission asked the G.E.B. "not to draw a plan for an ideal school system in Maryland that would be beyond the state's resources, but rather to indicate whether or not the State of Maryland was getting the best results from the money now expended, and if not, in what manner the same sum could be expended to better advantage," Flexner and Bachman, *Public Education in Maryland,* viii.

14. Larson, *Rise of Professionalism,* 164.

> branches alone, he is likely to become a shoemaker-physician who will drift into ruts and never get out of them.[15]

The earliest advocates of the systematic study of education possessed a similarly organic view of their task: the academic pursuit of science, and all that it promised, was believed consistent with, and indeed necessary to, strictly professional ends. "By basing our instruction and text-books upon a scientific ground-work, our department and our profession gain dignity and weight," a language professor at Hamilton College told his colleagues in 1886. "By introducing scientific methods, we shall show before very long that everybody cannot so teach, that the teacher must be as specially and as scientifically trained for his work in our department as well as in any other."[16] Similarly, in 1897 Cubberley described the work of the pedagogy faculty at Stanford University as a unified endeavor: "The scientific aim of this department is the study of the higher human life. . . . The practical aim is the training of teachers. . . . The two aims are organically united in the work of the department."[17]

In this view there was no necessary division perceived between the "academic" and the "professional," between the theoretical and the vocational needs of the field of education. Nor was the "science of education" in the tiny pedagogy faculties yet divided into departments or divisions along the lines of disciplinary or occupational specializations. Himself a former high school teacher, school principal, normal school instructor, and teachers' association official, Harvard's Paul Hanus had perceived a unity among those tasks.[18] Apparently, so did other pioneers of university schools of education.

Yet, this proved easier to assert than to demonstrate. Theory and practice did not so naturally blend as when the apprentice lawyer "read law" in a working law office, gradually assuming new responsibilities "in real cases, in concrete situations, and with specific person-

15. Quoted in Lawrence A. Cremin, "The Education of the Educating Professions" (Nineteenth Charles W. Hunt Lecture, American Association of Colleges for Teacher Education, Chicago, 21 Feb. 1978), 8.

16. H. C. B. Brandt, "How Far Should our Teaching and Text-books Have a Scientific Basis?" *Transactions of the Modern Language Association of America, 1884–85,* vol 1. (Baltimore, 1886), 59.

17. O'Leary, *An Inquiry,* 292.

18. Arthur G. Powell, "Speculations on the Early Impact of Schools of Education on Educational Psychology," *History of Education Quarterly* 11, no. 4 (Winter 1971): 407.

alities."[19] In comparison to the isolated student in the university law school, prospective teachers did receive some "hands on" experience in *their* training. Nevertheless, by 1923, if not sooner, some prominent participants saw problems, as well as progress, in the pursuit of a unified science of professional education.

Dean James Earl Russell of Teachers College was one. At the fiftieth anniversary of the 1873 founding of an education department at the State University of Iowa, Russell thought it necessary to remind his audience that "the duty of a professional school is to give the novice, so far as possible, what he will need in his practice."[20] Russell was also known for saying that, "if the surgeon needed to sew, the medical school taught sewing; and there was no question of graduate credit or whether sewing was truly a 'liberal' discipline."[21] Despite Russell's cautions about straying from one's training function in the pursuit of academic status, Stanford's Ellwood P. Cubberley issued a better prediction about the evolution of leading education schools, when he quoted an Englishman to the effect that "the distinctive function of a university is, not action, but thought."[22]

"'Winged Theory' and 'crippled Practice' do not easily work in the same yoke."[23] Put differently, Dean Russell warned that academic and professional workers are uneasy colleagues since "the academically-minded teacher is at his best when he is concerned with what the subject that he teaches will do for the student; the vocationally-minded teacher . . . does best when he thinks of what the student can do with the subject." Since "true professional training" rests on a prior "cultural education," Russell deplored the merging of the two in the same institution; he viewed this action as inimical to professional training—about which he saw "nothing esoteric" nor pretentious.[24] We would add, in hindsight, that the threat to professional education is arguably greatest when organizational merger is compounded by concentration upon offering academic degrees (especially the Ph.D.) about which arts and sciences faculties and the graduate school feel both responsible and thoroughly expert. An additional deterrent to

19. Dan C. Lortie, "Laymen to Lawmen: Law School, Careers, and Professional Socialization," *Harvard Educational Review* 29, no. 4 (Fall 1959): 363.

20. James Earl Russell, "Further Development of the School of Education," *School and Society* 17, no. 438 (19 May 1923): 535.

21. Cremin, Shannon, and Townsend, *History of Teachers College*.

22. Ellwood P. Cubberley, "The College of Education and the Superintendent of Schools," *School and Society* 17, no. 438 (19 May 1923): 542.

23. Good, *Rise of the College of Education*, 168.

24. Russell, "Further Development," 534.

maintaining concentration upon practitioner-centered instruction appears when the professional field has, like education, a parlous status—as low-paying, "suspiciously feminized," and respectable but not respected work, teaching being a widely offered service with many low-status clients. The education school could not expect to confer on its undergraduates the return some law schools promised theirs: "being, in all cases, personal wealth and distinction."[25]

A different kind of early warning came from Edward C. Elliott, at a conference on educational research held in 1911. Director of the Course for the Training of Teachers at the University of Wisconsin, Elliott had already seen the "easily detected tendency" in the scientific study of education to select "minute issues." Unless it was stopped, he argued, it "promises to produce a new form of scholasticism in education, a scholasticism as barren of service to human life, not to say real scholarship, as was the scholastic period of medieval thought."[26] What was said of the case method of legal study—that it replaced content with method—could be validly extended to the young scientific movement in education.[27]

This was, moreover, a period when many teachers, especially in rural schools, were unable to cope even with the simpler pedagogical ideas of the contemporary progressive education movement. Too

25. Chancellor of the University of Wisconsin to the legislature, on the advantages of a law school, in 1857. Quoted in Johnson, *Schooled Lawyers,* 2.

26. Edward C. Elliott, "Cooperative Research within the Field of Education," in "Research within the Field of Education, Its Organization and Encouragement," *School Review Monographs,* no. 1 (Papers presented at the Society of College Teachers of Education, Mobile, Ala., 23–24 Feb. 1911), 57–58. Elliott gave an example of a more promising line of research: "A scientific, comprehensive survey of the financial factors of education in two dozen typical American cities would, it may safely be affirmed, lead to an understanding of things not now understood, and to necessary reconstructions of the foundation support of public schools." It was more than a half-century later that such "necessary reconstructions" in the bases of school finance began, and it was led by law school professors concerned about equity issues, rather than by school finance specialists like George Strayer and Paul Mort of Teachers College. Their tradition was that of using well-financed "lighthouse districts" to generate pressure for additional state aid to *all* public schools. Our thanks to our colleague, Charles Benson, for pointing out this history to us.

27. Johnson, *Schooled Lawyers,* 104. One might speculate what could have happened if leading education schools had looked to the innovations in legal education coming from Yale, where a group of scholars deplored Langdell's emphasis upon legal principles. They stressed the factual content of cases and social policy concerns. See Laura Kalman, *Legal Realism at Yale, 1927–1960* (Chapel Hill: University of North Carolina Press, 1986).

untrained to introduce manual arts, domestic science, field trips, creative writing, or dramatic play into their classroom routines, some kept their classes occupied with time-killing "busy work."

> Hence little children are required to copy the alphabet over and over, or to write again and again the numerals from one to a hundred, or, on occasions, up to two or three thousand. Older children, having acquired some ability to write, are set to copying page after page of their readers, or to solving on paper long lists of problems placed on the blackboard.[28]

In their haste to develop an instant science of education to justify their presence in the modern research university, training such pitiable novices was downplayed while investigators seized upon the more manipulable, quantifiable, and often peripheral, aspects of pedagogical and management issues. In an ironic sense, the subject of education was greatly *under*estimated. A respectful appreciation of the complex, interconnected, and sometimes seemingly intractable variables involved in teaching and learning was slow to develop—perhaps slower than would have been the case had education become less fragmented within schools of education and had the barriers between many professors of education and those working in public and private schools not been accepted as either inevitable or desirable.

The Claims on Behalf of Theory

It was widely argued in the proliferating university professional schools that theory is the most practical of all knowledge. "What we demand then is, not rules, but principles; not mere tricks of art and slight of hand, but science; science which explains and authenticates art; which makes men masters in their work, and not mere imitators and operatives." So promised William Folwell in his 1869 inauguration as President of the University of Minnesota.[29] "Principles before practice is the true watchword," advised Folwell's contemporary, the dean of Columbia University's Law School.[30] As the new university was distinguished from the old college by a set of cultural values embodied in the word "science," the university pedagogy department would be

28. Flexner and Bachman, *Public Education,* 110.
29. Quoted in Bledstein, *Culture of Professionalism,* 285.
30. Quoted in Johnson, *Schooled Lawyers,* 102.

marked off from the normal school with its direct approach to practice. What the Johns Hopkins Medical School was doing for the medical arts, the education department at Chicago, especially, wanted (and long claimed) to be doing for the science of education.

A familiar theme was sounded early when William Payne, first incumbent of Michigan's Chair of the Science and Art of Teaching, made the appealingly simple case for university study of education as a liberal science. It is based, he wrote, on "fundamental principles" rather than "mere rule or method." Payne propounded an oft-repeated theorem: "The teacher who goes to his work provided with specific methods will start promptly but will not grow much; while the teacher who is grounded in principles will start slowly, will sometimes stumble, but will grow rapidly, and, better than all, will continue to grow."[31] Rejecting his own empirically derived pedagogical knowledge and normal school roots—Payne had been superintendent of the Adrian, Michigan public schools and lecturer at the Adrian Normal School—Payne preferred to teach only theory; it was up to his students to turn principles into practice, knowing into doing. This position was proudly contrasted with that of the faculty in teachers' colleges and normal schools, who professed to see little value in "theory courses."[32] In the minds of the pioneer generation of pedagogy professors, systematic theory was clearly preferable to random and uncontrolled experience as the basis for a science of education. In keeping with a more general movement, one also evident in the leading law schools as early as the 1890s, the curriculum in education schools was reducing practice and extolling theory.

Payne's successor, Burke A. Hinsdale, argued for chairs of pedagogy without necessary reference to the "practical phases of the subject." Before the Normal Department of the National Education Association convention in 1889, he made what would become the standard argument:

> Even if the work done by the pedagogical chair should pay no immediate attention to the preparation of teachers, it could not fail to be of much practical value. The scientific study and teaching of a science and an art in their purely theoretical aspects always promote the practice of the art; and the presence in every university in the land of a pedagogical

31. Quoted in O'Leary, *An Inquiry,* 177.

32. Obed Jalmar Williamson, *Provisions for General Theory Courses in the Professional Preparation of Teachers,* Teachers College Contributions to Education no. 684 (New York: Teachers College, 1936), 102–8, 163.

> professor, thoroughly devoted to his chair, could not fail to quicken interest in the subject, and to promote the teaching art.[33]

Such optimistic assessments of theory's inherent and inevitable contributions to practice cannot hide the fact that status considerations were also at work. This fact would assert progressively more influence than would "theory" on university programs in education as they became more ambitious. Vocational training for curriculum specialists or textbook writers or test makers came to carry greater weight than did practical training for teaching. "Practical courses," "concrete" and "scientific" work, and "specific methods" were tolerated much more for prospective school administrators than for teachers, given the compensating greater prestige and power of the administrative elite. Under Charles Judd's editorship, for example, the *School Review* emphasized "perennial and immediate practical questions" in both its editorials and articles, with administrative issues receiving a predictable emphasis.[34] What was in unrelieved disgrace were "philosophical musings" and normal school-style courses in the "principles of teaching" which, their critics charged, depended excessively on obsolete issues or personal experience and common sense. Such relics did persist, under less challenge, on the publishing margins and at the least prestigious institutions, removed as they were from the direct influences of the graduate school culture.

The Retreat from Experience

It has been noted of academic departments that they are loath to hire persons without academic credentials, even when their experience and talent might enliven the curriculum. Thus, political science departments seldom employ politicians nor physics departments engineers nor psychology departments psychiatrists; their "craft knowledge" represented a prescientific lore which arrogant academics scorned.[35] But what of professional schools? Do they carry their own quest for academic acceptance and theoretical science so far as actually to discount professional experience?

Harvard Law School excited contemporary comment when, in

33. Burke A. Hinsdale, "Pedagogical Chairs in Colleges and Universities," *Pamphlets on Higher Education,* no. 2 (Syracuse, N.Y.: C. W. Bardeen, 1889), 4.

34. Harold S. Wechsler, "From Practice to Theory: A History of *School Review,* Part 2." *American Journal of Education* 88, no. 2 (Feb. 1980): 221, 228.

35. Jencks and Riesman, *Academic Revolution,* 248.

1873, it hired James Barr Ames as assistant professor; a recent graduate of the school, Ames was without experience in legal practice. Although most new faculty appointed at major law schools continued to have some experience at the bar, a strong sense of separate cultures dividing law faculty and lawyers emerged in the twentieth century. The period of experience was being shortened and university-transmitted expectations of academic careers grew, promoting a cultural schism.[36] No longer were law teachers largely indistinguishable from practicing attorneys.

Medical education had an even greater appeal for professors of education. Subsequent research has uncovered pertinent differences in orientation and identification between those teaching the basic sciences and those in the clinical departments of medical schools, between those who have never practiced medicine and those who are qualified physicians. These differences encompass values, attitudes, and teaching practices. Medically qualified professors identify less with the academic profession (with university professors in the basic sciences, for example), looking instead "to other physicians in the community as a preferred local reference group."[37]

Most of the early professors of education, like those in contemporary medical and legal education, were themselves experienced and successful practitioners of their arts. Many education professors had been self-taught but effective administrators in an era when the rapid growth of public education meant that an able man could move quickly and directly from the classroom to the principal's or superintendent's office. In that early generation "the essential expertise that the professors offered was experience."[38] But the university environment and the emergence and proliferation of occupational specialization in education diminished the claims of experience. The full-time law or medical professor, committed more to the academic than to the legal or medical profession, had his counterpart in the coming type of education professor in the premier university schools of education. The library—not the courthouse, the examining room, or the schoolroom—was becoming the natural habitat of professors and students alike.[39]

36. Auerbach, "Enmity and Amity," esp. pp. 551, 563.

37. Henry Walton, "Overview of Themes in Medical Education," in *Education for the Professions: Quis custodiet . . . ?*, ed. Sinclair Goodlad, p. 51.

38. Sizer and Powell, "Changing Conceptions," 63.

39. Harvard's Dean of Law, Christopher Langdell, quoted in Johnson, *Schooled Lawyers*, p. 103. Johnson calls the emergence of career law teachers the most significant event in late nineteenth-century legal education (p. 105).

Criteria for Selecting Faculty

A nationwide study of the professional experience of faculty in schools, colleges, and departments of education in various kinds of institutions revealed that in 1931–32 faculty had less in common professionally with their students than had formerly been the case. Except in the teachers colleges and surviving normal schools, the significant majority of faculty had no professional experience in elementary schools—as either teacher, school principal, or supervisor, and a slight majority had no secondary school experience either. Education faculty in private, state, and land-grant universities lacked elementary school experience in over 73 percent of the cases and secondary school experience in over 50 percent.[40] These were the kinds of institutions in which our ten schools of education were located.

The lessening concern with teaching practice and the growing chasm of mutual indifference among the different workers in the education field was manifest in the selection of faculty and in the admission of students seeking advanced degrees and specialists' certificates. It was not that experience ceased to matter, except perhaps to those professors who identified closely with theoretical disciplines. Rather it was that the rapid change and increasing complexities of the profession made the "test of experience" an increasingly difficult one to administer. Experience in education was, ironically, less credible and more likely to seem "out of date" than academic credentials.[41] There was some justification to this in that the isolated world of the classroom teacher and the continuing transiency in the field did not provide the kinds of experience and contacts that the engineering, legal, and medical professions afforded their members, all of whom were expected to be careerists.

There were also other factors at work. "Young men must make their way 'up the academic ladder' . . . [and] this may leave some men

40. *National Survey of the Education of Teachers,* 2:120.

41. Developments in faculty selection in the once-elite Central High School of Philadelphia from 1880 to 1920 roughly parallel those in education schools. An open, proven record, as grammar school teachers and principals, of preparing boys for the competitive high school entrance examination was gradually replaced by appointing inexperienced university graduates. "The old performance standard . . . was abandoned in favor of a new credential standard," a hard measure (experience) for a soft measure (prospects). Bureaucratization under the stimulus of great expansion in high school enrollments drove the change. See David F. Labaree, "Proletarianizing the High School Teacher" (Paper presented at the annual meeting of the American Educational Research Association, San Francisco, April 1986).

in the 'practical fields,' whose work does not allow of production of detailed scholarly studies, at a disadvantage." These words were written about faculty in university schools of theology, but their applicability to education schools is clear.[42] To demand wide, varied, and fresh professional experience for a professorship in education in a graduate-oriented university school of education was to run counter to the standards of an increasingly rigid set of expectations for academic professionalization. These expectations included completion of the doctorate at a younger age, some demonstrated commitment to inquiry, an extension of personal influence through published writings, visible activity in university-based professional or scholarly organizations, and, perhaps most important of all, specialization. The commitment to specialization itself limited the acquisition of additional experience during one's graduate training to a restricted subfield of education and to its peculiar methods, problems, and developing traditions.

Although Chicago aspired to prepare administrative leaders and teachers of teachers, Charles Judd scorned the retired superintendents found in the faculties of teachers colleges; they contributed, he said, to a scant hospitality for research.[43] This was, however, the period in which law, medical, and divinity schools were still making professors out of leading practitioners. In this regard, then, some education schools were becoming more like the lower status agricultural and engineering departments of the land-grant universities, which were appointing faculty from traditional colleges. In doing so they generated disputes with some of their students and with public representatives. They persisted, nonetheless, for an institutional division of responsibilities between the academic and the applied failed to hold firm in the face of the near-universal effort to elevate status even at the risk of alienating farmers or industrial interests—or teachers.[44] Education school leaders, given their uncertain status among their academic counterparts, felt a special urgency to promote the norms of graduate universities.

No less a person than Dean Christopher Langdell of the Harvard Law School, himself a former practitioner, placed experience in researching the law far ahead of office or courtroom practice. But the untried younger education faculty did not always inspire confidence

42. H. Richard Niebuhr, Daniel D. Williams, and James M. Gustafson, *The Advancement of Theological Education* (New York: Harper & Brothers, 1957), 57–58.

43. Judd, "Teachers Colleges," 877–78.

44. Jencks and Riesman, "Academic Revolution," 225–26.

in the minds of the experienced professionals who came to study at Harvard's Graduate School of Education; the alumni complained about some faculty appointments on this score.[45] There were other, unrecognized costs in this approach to faculty selection. Subsequent investigations have shown that practitioners want to learn from the experiences of those who have been in their own roles. Teacher culture, like that of nurses, lawyers, and other workers, respects craft methods, on-line experience, and self-control, while it suspects "theory."[46] In minimizing significant teaching or administrative experiences, some education schools also relinquished the important influence over their students and former students that comes from such "within-guild" legitimation.[47]

The Quest for "Better Students"

A characteristic of education for the professions in these years, especially for the premier professional schools, was to place progressively more weight on prior scholastic achievement and academic credentials in the selection of both faculty and students. Judd considered the ten years of teaching and administrative experience of the average M.A. recipient as evidence of a retardation of career, a "handicap rather than an asset."[48] After all, one of the arguments on behalf of creating university departments of education had been that the field would thus be able to recruit among the nation's most desirable students. Would not that aspiration be effectively thwarted if it was primarily "normal-school types" who presented themselves for advanced degrees and credentials?

By the 1930s even at Teachers College, by all accounts the institution that most consistently accepted a professional school culture, its Division of Organization and Administration of Education thought that "for this highest type of professional training," it was a "distinct advantage" to recruit young people directly from college or after a limited experience. Internships should suffice to ready this inexperienced

45. Powell, *Uncertain Profession,* 139, 152. Dean Edwin Bryant of the University of Wisconsin Law School (1889–1903) anticipated such student reaction when he criticized the lecture method and the absence of recent legal experience on both pedagogical and professional grounds. See Johnson, *Schooled Lawyers,* 110–12.

46. See Melosh, *"The Physician's Hand."*

47. Michael Huberman, "Recipes for Busy Kitchens: A Situational Analysis of Routine Knowledge Use in Schools," *Knowledge: Creation, Diffusion, Utilization* 4, no. 4 (June 1983): 503.

48. White, "The Decline of the Classroom," 169.

group to use local schools "for observation, for the solution of professional problems, and for the conduct of significant research."[49] The Harvard education faculty yearned for more such students, at a time when only 6 percent of its students were inexperienced and full-time matriculants. They well knew that these were some of the characteristics of the student bodies at Harvard's other professional schools for they were often enough compared unfavorably with them.

When Alexander Inglis recruited a schoolteacher to take over his own role as Harvard's supervisor of practice teaching, he told him that "an able person would be sick of kids by the time he was thirty-five." Male teachers who stayed too long in the classroom—in the regular company of women and children—might even raise doubts about their manliness and, therefore, their suitability for dealing with the local power brokers on school boards and in chambers of commerce.[50] Were these the men to save school administration and educational research careers from the threats of feminization, the men able to deal with businessmen and civic leaders in the hurly-burly world of *realpolitik?* Clearly not. Instead, graduate students in education must be drawn early from their classrooms or recruited from among the graduating seniors of high-status colleges.

This campaign, probably fitful at best, failed abysmally. In 1920 the national lapse in years between earning the A.B. and the Ph.D. degrees averaged 6.6 years for doctorates in the physical sciences and 10 years for education doctorates. By 1940 the mean doctorate in education was awarded more than fourteen years after college graduation, and the difference between education students and other doctoral recipients had increased.[51] Moreover, to the extent that schools of education admitted the products of teachers college to their graduate programs, as they had to, they were more likely to educate many who had interrupted scholastic careers. The 1933 *National Survey of the Education of Teachers* reported that about one in five teachers college students had one or more such interruptions; in 40 percent of those cases, financial necessity caused temporary absences from college in order to teach school.[52] Thus, the social origins and economic status of teaching prevented the student's early move into graduate study in

49. O'Leary, *An Inquiry* 142–43.

50. Geraldine Jonçich Clifford, "'Shaking Dangerous Questions from the Crease': Gender and American Higher Education," *Feminist Issues* 3, no. 2 (Fall 1983): 48–54.

51. Harmon and Soldz, *Doctorate Production,* 41.

52. *National Survey,* 2:120.

education, and when the move was finally made it was commonly done through part-time study.

Again the example of Harvard is instructive. In the 1920s its education school tried mightily to conform more closely to Harvard's expectations on several related fronts. It sought to reform a curriculum of vocational subjects, like guidance, combined with such borrowings from academic disciplines as psychology and history.[53] The retirement of an older faculty, with its roots in the schools, left the field to younger professors who identified more readily with academic disciplines than public schools.[54] Like other education schools, however, Harvard found that its ability to imitate the Law School was frustrated by the absence of a student body of full-time students just graduated from college and expecting to enter a lucrative field. In their attractions for students, education schools were more like engineering and agriculture schools than like the schools of the elite professions. Education graduate students demonstrated their uncertain professional commitment, their lower economic status, and their lesser social sophistication all too clearly. Thus, the future generations of education faculty might well appear to include the "action-oriented" and "less reflective" parts of the American professoriate.[55]

Of our ten institutions, Harvard made the most conspicuous efforts to recruit a "higher class" of students, especially recent Harvard graduates. By this means Harvard sought—then and again in the 1950s and 1980s—a higher status and attractiveness for a career in education and it thought subsequent improvements in teaching were bound to follow. There was a model in the new science of medicine which was believed to be enlisting a better recruit in the twentieth century than it had in the nineteenth. Ambitious or altruistic young men, many from comfortable and even wealthy families, were ready and able to enroll in a long, rigorous, and expensive preprofessional and professional course of study in medicine. Education, however, could not compete. Ironically, to the extent that large numbers of well-off, as well as able and altruistic students could be recruited to education, they were more likely to be women than men.[56] This fact, unfortunately, could only work against education in the prestige game.

53. Powell, *Uncertain Profession,* 151.

54. Powell in Harvard Committee, *Graduate Study,* 90.

55. The terms are from Milton Schwebel, "The Clash of Cultures in Academe: The University and the Education Faculty," *Journal of Teacher Education* 36, no. 4 (July–Aug. 1985): 3.

56. Teaching recruited heavily among the graduates of socially elite and expensive women's colleges and among the daughters of the upper middle class who attended

The Retreat from Teachers

Open adventures in vocationalism had been part of Harvard University's history even before it launched its professorship in pedagogy. Charles W. Eliot's predecessor as Harvard's president was Thomas Hill, a Unitarian minister, mathematician, and president of Antioch College at the time of his election in 1862. Antioch College's first president (1852—59) was Horace Mann. Mann had agreed to lead Antioch so that it would make a higher education available to women who would become teachers.[57] Some Harvardians opposed Hill's selection for Harvard because of fears that he planned to use Harvard for "educational experiments." Their concerns were legitimate. In his aim to see Harvard made "a university of a high order," Hill unsuccessfully promoted professional schools of dentistry, mining, and agriculture. He envisioned a normal school within a university: a place which "teaches to teach."[58] The Harvard faculty majority set the institution's tone, however, as its newcomers quickly learned. Paul Hanus, Harvard's first appointment in pedagogy, resented his own title of Professor of the History and Art of Teaching. Later, his colleague Alexander Inglis shunted the supervision of student teachers to a junior member of the faculty and developed courses on broad policy issues in secondary education, for experienced students without intense concerns about classroom operations.[59]

Other education schools responded similarly to their environments. Ohio State dropped its course in "The Science and Art of Teaching" in favor of more specialized and academic-sounding offerings. Institutional publications came to reflect this movement. The University of Chicago journal, *The Elementary School Teacher,* was retitled *Elementary School Journal* in 1915. Although Judd stated that individual classroom problems would not be ignored, the journal was already stressing school organizational issues under his leadership: it seemed wiser to concentrate, for the time being at least, upon the effort to develop a "general science" of school administration.[60] Al-

---

the state universities. See Clifford, "Dangerous Questions," especially pp. 27–28. See also Solomon, *Educated Women,* 32–34, 127–28.

57. On Mann's Antioch years see Jonathan Messerli, *Horace Mann: A Biography* (New York: Knopf, 1972).

58. Hill, "Remarks," 177–79; Hawkins, *Between Harvard and America,* 38, 318.

59. Powell, *Uncertain Profession,* 6, 112–13.

60. Harold S. Wechsler, "Primary Journal," 101.

though Harvard, before 1940, was far more openly vocational than was Chicago, eventually its *Harvard Teachers Record* became the *Harvard Educational Review.*

The "democratic West" was no more immune to academic professionalism than was the "snobbish East." When Cubberley began his career at Stanford, four of his courses were the History of Education (in Europe and in America), Organization and Supervision, and a Seminar in Administrative Problems. The fifth, "Theory and Practice of Teaching," a year-long offering, was closest to a beginner's interest. It was next listed as "Introduction to Educational Theories and Practices" and later retitled "Public Education in America" and reduced to one semester. The course content became the basis of a textbook before the teaching was given over to a younger colleague.[61] Was it not symbolic that when John Dewey left Chicago's education department it was not for Teachers College but for Columbia's department of philosophy?

Alert men appreciated the differences between the connotations of art or science of *teaching* and science of *education;* it was the latter with which they wished to be associated. Cubberley maintained that even in a state university, where "the training of secondary teachers . . . must always be an important part of the work of a college of education . . . , the training of leaders for the executive direction of the schools of the state is a still more important service." He contrasted the highly centralized school systems of Europe, which advance school officers through a civil service system, with the American pattern of decentralized administration operating through lay boards of education. America, Cubberley argued, required "in the interests of efficiency and reasonable progress" that universities study the problems of the organization, administration, and supervision "of the schools which the people have demanded that the state create."[62] By means of academic credentials school administrators might attain the professional autonomy and freedom from lay interference that other nations afforded educators.

Faculty opinion outside of education schools typically agreed. The President's Committee on Programs in Education, of the University of California, endorsed the proposition that "fundamental research in the various areas of education" constitutes the function which, "more than any other, is the distinctive feature of a school of

61. Sears and Henderson, *Cubberley of Stanford,* 67.
62. Cubberley, "College of Education," 542, 544.

education in a first-rate institution emphasizing graduate work."[63] Chicago began, with Judd's coming from Yale, to "lay greater emphasis upon the empirical side of the work." This included developing a course on the principles of education for undergraduates and work in statistics and experimental methods for graduates.[64] In leaving his Cleveland Superintendency, Frank E. Spaulding explained, "I should be able to render at Yale University a larger and farther-reaching service to public education," than possible in a "strictly administrative" position. Yale offered unsurpassed opportunities for the preparation "not only of teachers, but especially of educational leaders—superintendents, principals, supervisors, and normal school and college teachers."[65]

Such scenarios could be recited for others of the faculties of our ten schools—and for those in other institutions which hoped to concentrate their efforts on the further education of already proficient teachers preparing themselves for management positions in the schools or research bureaus, or as faculty for other schools of education. Together these promised to advance, as teachers could not, the development of education as a liberal or, better yet, a scientific study. Those faculty with genuine research drives and sufficient institutional resources could, like E. L. Thorndike, hide in the new research institutes—remote, even, from advanced professional students. Thorndike's *Journal of Educational Psychology* with its appeal to "precision and professionalism," supplanted G. Stanley Hall's *Pedagogical Seminary,* which would "embrace all educators in the search for truth." The mania for educational measurement grew despite occasional protests.[66] Research on the teacher's "art" was overshadowed by that on the administrator's "science."

63. University of California at Berkeley, School of Education, Historical File, President's Committee on Programs in Education, "Report," n.d. (1950?), 30.

64. Bolton, "Curricula," 840.

65. Frank E. Spaulding, "Dr. Spaulding's Letter of Resignation from the Superintendency of the Cleveland Schools," *School and Society* 11, no. 266 (31 Jan. 1920): 133.

66. Powell, "Speculations," 408. After a talk by Leonard Ayres before the Harvard Teachers Association in 1912, Boston statistician Edward Hartwell pleaded that we "discriminate in our investigation and consideration of educational matters between methods and criteria that are applicable to living mechanisms and their activities and those which pertain to the realm of the inventor, the engineer, and the manufacturer," Edward H. Hartwell, "Discussion" [in response to Leonard P. Ayres, "Measuring Processes Through Educational Results"], *School Review* 20 (May 1912): 317.

Teacher Education—On the Margins

In 1925 J. O. Creager of New York University questioned the deans of education in thirty-two state universities. He found that only six states, including California and Minnesota, required that students preparing to teach be registered in the professional school. Even in some of those cases it was possible for liberal arts majors to take a few education courses, but not meet the school's full requirements; by applying directly to the state department of education they could still secure certification. Creager concluded that those sent out to teach "who have received the best professional training that the university can offer" were probably only as numerous as those "who have pursued the hit-or-miss path to a teacher's certificate." On behalf of schools of education, he deplored the lack of fit between their authority and their responsibility; "schools of education are, in the last analysis, made responsible for both types of product," he warned.[67]

Education faculty recognized the threat to their reputations coming from their failure to seize or maintain control over the education of future teachers. Like faculty in other professions, they worked to secure official recognition of their "right" to control the training of practitioners. But they also knew, instinctively perhaps, the threat to their prestige that came with too large an involvement with either prospective teachers, especially women elementary school teachers, or working teachers who needed assistance. In his very letter of acceptance to Stanford, the "practical school man," Cubberley, wrote, "I so long for the university atmosphere and for higher work." In the same quest for association with things of higher status, "A and M" colleges and teachers' colleges were diversifying their offerings, adding academic departments and programs that prepared for more prestigious callings than breeding cattle, building highways, and teaching children.[68] Not surprising, then, that the implications of Melvin Haggerty's research on reading and arithmetic were *not* applied to changing Minnesota's teacher-training programs; this issue fell beyond Haggerty's concerns and those of most of his colleagues.[69] Was it for such reasons that at Ohio State, which suffered large undergraduate pro-

67. J. O. Creager, "The Professional Guidance of Students in Schools of Education in State Universities," *Educational Administration and Supervision* 13, no. 3 (March 1927): 194.

68. Jencks and Riesman, *Academic Revolution,* 223–31.

69. Beck, *Beyond Pedagogy.*

grams of teacher education and added the preparation of elementary school teachers to its initial concentration upon the high schools, Dean George F. Arps reported in 1921 that the State's teachers had long regarded the University's work in education as inadequate, and subjected it to "caustic comment?"[70] Ohio's and Minnesota's teachers were as unimpressed by the professors of education as Wisconsin's lawyers were with the "narrow legal logic" that the University of Wisconsin Law School dispensed in imitation of Harvard's view of the lawyer as a scientific expert.[71]

The clarion call in education schools was, however, "to prepare leaders." At Stanford the euphemism was that the department of education should "aim more toward the attainment of ideals in the future than of small practical results in the immediate present;" that meant train principals and superintendents, future leaders, rather than teachers of high schools. Thus would Stanford have "an uplifting influence on the schools of California and an ennobling influence on the teachers of the state."[72] Cubberley was ready to give up the requirement that students planning to teach be counted as education majors; after 1902 he admitted only experienced teachers or normal school graduates to his department of education. This reduced one source of friction with other departments and, after a period of adjustment, was not costly in enrollment; there were sufficient experienced professionals who wanted preparation for upward career mobility. By the 1930s, the School of Education awarded 13.75 percent of all Stanford's doctorates; in the next decade the figure climbed to 17.7 percent, a proportion second only to Teachers College among our ten institutions.[73]

From the ambitious public universities one heard, "Let the state colleges train undergraduates to be teachers"—or, they might have added, businessmen, policemen, or dental assistants. At one time Minnesota's dean of education and the principal of University High School had identical offices in the same building, symbolizing both a linkage and a parity of theory and practice. In 1926 the College moved out and the relationship became hierarchical. That move was another step in an odyssey: it was reported within the University that the College of

70. Good, *College of Education,* 110.

71. Johnson, *Schooled Lawyers,* xvii. In 1930 a recent graduate told the Dean that he regretted spending so much of his time in the library rather than in the courtroom. "The law is easy to find once you get the hang of it, but God help you if you don't know how to address the Court" (p. 164).

72. Sears and Henderson, *Cubberley,* 57.

73. Harmon and Soldz, *Doctorate Production,* 22.

Education was "out of touch" and had "lost the confidence of the public schoolmen of the state. . . ."[74]

Other institutions demonstrated similar responses. By the 1920s the College of Education at the University of Illinois, which began life as the Illinois Industrial University, was distancing himself from the issues facing educational practitioners. Its historians determined:

> The problems of the small rural school, the crucial question of adequate distribution of financial aid, the relation of the schools to rapid social change, the need for the teacher to become an intelligent practitioner of the politics which decisively shaped the institution he served—these were their [the state's] major concerns. The College of Education did little or nothing about any of them.[75]

The teachers and administrators of Illinois concluded that there was more professional help to be found at Teachers College, Columbia, or even from the state's teachers colleges than was available in Champaign-Urbana.

Minnesota's College of Education under Deans Coffman and Haggerty pursued a general strategy of extending control over education, requiring that all future teachers enroll in the College. Academic politics dictated a different approach at private Chicago and Stanford. Allowing academic departments to retain responsibility for teaching subject matter to prospective teachers, with whatever provisions for "professional methods" they saw fit to develop, enabled Chicago's education program to concentrate its energies elsewhere. In 1901, at the request of Chicago's president, William Rainey Harper, Colonel Francis Parker's old normal school faculty was incorporated into the University, to form the nucleus of the College of Education, while the Graduate Department of Education pursued advanced work.[76] Such con-

74. Beck, *Beyond Pedagogy,* 53, 59.

75. Indicative was the dropping of its sole course on rural education when the state still had over ten thousand one-room schools, see Johnson and Johanningmeier, *Teachers for the Prairies,* 261–62.

76. The transformation of the Cook County Normal School into the Chicago Normal School in 1896, under control of an unsympathetic board, was what prompted Francis Parker to accept Harper's invitation. With Harper's assurances of the independence of the normal school faculty to continue their pedagogical innovations, the alliance was formed. Ida B. Depencier, "The History of the Laboratory Schools, The University of Chicago, 1896–1957" (ms., 1957), 18–20.

tainment of "vocational" programs in separate units was a common strategy in the wider fraternity of professional schools.[77]

Containment was sometimes succeeded by elimination of teacher education. When Harvard's new president, James B. Conant, visited Chicago in 1933, he mentioned his School of Education. As he recalled in his autobiography, "Bob Hutchins told me that they had abolished theirs and that Professor Charles H. Judd was the man to tell me what to do."[78] Judd had already conceded his own lack of interest in teacher education—putting "pedagogical patches" on the underlings of a system that would be shaped by the administrative leaders on whom Chicago and the others were concentrating. Although he disparaged the normal schools and state teachers colleges as places that educated teachers without a regard for research, Judd was willing to abandon teacher education to such institutions and to the academic departments of universities that, like his, denied pedagogy much legitimacy. Through the 1920s Judd advised Dean Henry Holmes to reduce Harvard's preoccupation with practitioner training via the master of arts degree; instead Harvard should help to develop education as a science through training for research, especially in educational psychology, Judd's field, where Harvard was notoriously lackadaisical.[79] President Conant did, indeed, take secondary school teacher preparation away from his education school, as President Lowell had, in 1923, eliminated undergraduate teacher training. Despite scant evidence of demand for graduate teacher education, Conant created the Master of Arts in Teaching program—giving direct responsibility for it to the Graduate School of Arts and Sciences, "with the cooperation of the Graduate School of Education."[80] Thus, Harvard's education school was effectively put out of the business of initial teacher preparation.

With their limited and left-handed approach to teacher education, the leading centers of educational research and theory-building unwittingly sustained the views of those academics who, in the words of Henry H. Hill of George Peabody College for Teachers, "seem

77. Dean Neil Jacoby of UCLA's business school also wished to rid his curriculum "of course content inappropriate to a prestigious university program." He did so by eliminating office management from the M.B.A. program and confining its courses and professors to a separate undergraduate Department of Business Communication and Office Management. Schlossman and Sedlak, *Age of Autonomy,* 20.

78. James B. Conant, *My Several Lives: Memoirs of a Social Inventor* (New York: Harper & Row, 1970), 183.

79. Powell, *Uncertain Profession,* 145, 160, 191.

80. Ibid., 128; Conant, *My Several Lives,* 184.

happiest flying backwards."[81] Withdrawing from teacher preparation, or secluding it in isolated and low-status units, had crucial effects on the young field of educational psychology. The learning theory of this new profession was developed from laboratory experiments and animal research. By 1910 it was abandoning the briefly practiced "natural history" approach of the child study movement. It "effectively excluded not only practitioners, but more decisively the world of practice itself." Without the pressure of a practice-oriented education school, and "needing neither first-hand experience nor access to practice, and with no clear responsibility for the larger normative and social problems embraced in the earlier science of education," educational psychology could pursue an independent and isolated academic course.[82]

The Fate of the Practice Schools

The wedding of theory to practice is an issue general to professional schools. The teaching hospital attached to the university medical school was a model for those deans and professors of education concerned about "sterile theorizing," on the one hand, and "unreflective, habitual practice" on the other. It also became the source of advances in the application of discoveries that gave medical science an aura no other aspiring profession could emulate. Law schools established legal aid clinics in the attempt to imitate the emphasis on clinical training in the best medical schools. These failed to assume a major role in providing the practical education the professional wanted, however, perhaps, in part, because their clients were the indigent.[83] For prospective teachers and for educational researchers alike the laboratory, demonstration, or practice school represented a potential bridge, a meeting ground, a synthesis. Laboratory schools would be the sites for testing the values of theorizing, places where the development of a corpus of applied research might be hastened even while novice teachers learned to view their craft in more experimental terms. Let the elementary and high schools serving as observation and practice centers "represent an advanced type of education properly corresponding

81. Henry H. Hill, "Preparing Teachers for the High Schools of the Future," in *The High School in a New Era,* ed. Francis S. Chase and Harold A. Anderson. (Chicago: University of Chicago Press, 1958), 252.

82. Powell, "Speculations," 408–9; Sizer and Powell, "Changing Conceptions," 64–65.

83. Johnson, *Schooled Lawyers,* 140.

to the instruction in academic subject matter and in educational theory given in the training classes," John Dewey advised in 1904.[84]

A common feature in the stronger normal schools, a few practice schools survived the transformation of normal schools to state teachers colleges and then to university schools of education. The University Elementary School of UCLA was one such, and it became the fountainhead of progressive elementary school education in California for decades.[85] Disdain for the normal schools and academicians' prejudices against "methods," practice teaching, and what Payne called the "illiberal effects of fixed habits," delayed, however, arrangements for practice teaching and practice schools in most university education departments.

When Michigan's Professor of the Science and Art of Teaching addressed the Normal Department of the National Education Association in 1889, on the new pedagogical chairs in colleges and universities, his audience gave him pointed comments about the need to provide practice facilities; they sounded like medical educators advocating the replacement of didactic instruction with clinical experience in the laboratory and at the bedside. Payne was on record as opposing practice schools in universities, however—believing they tended toward excessive concern with methods, rather than "that quickening into the intellectual life which is, of all gifts, the most precious endowment of the teacher."[86] The NEA discussants, however, pushed the distinction between professors of didactics, who give general lectures, and professional schools, which provide specific help; what was needed, they argued, were schools of practice, where students could acquire the opportunity to "feel the pulse, as it were, of real, living pupils—and not empty theorizing."[87]

Perceiving the merit of such instruction, Frederick Bolton predicted, in 1915, that "the time is not far distant when every university will have a practise school as a part of the necessary equipment of its

84. John Dewey, "The Relation of Theory to Practice in Education," 1904. Reprinted in *Teacher Education in America: A Documentary History,* ed. Merle L. Borrowman (New York: Teachers College Press, 1965), 171.

85. Treacy, "Progressivism and Corinne Seeds," 110.

86. O'Leary, *An Inquiry,* 11.

87. Hinsdale, "Training of Teachers," 11. About this time J. J. Findlay remarked on the English system which reduced the contents of two or three textbooks to a paper examination, issued a certificate to the successful testee, and "is content to have fulfilled its duty to pedagogics in this fashion." See J. J. Findlay, "The Problem of Professional Training: Recent Developments in Germany and England," *School Review* 1, no. 5 (May 1893): 286.

work in the training of teachers." At the time, only Chicago and Columbia, of the fifty-eight universities polled, had practice schools. In 1908, only sixteen of fifty universities even required practice teaching.[88] When Minnesota's Board of Regents created a College of Education in 1905, it was reported that the majority of the regents "seriously questioned the wisdom of conducting a model school in connection with the work done in the University, believing that provision . . . might better be made in the normal schools."[89] But the legislature mandated practice teaching in 1914 and that settled the matter for Minnesota.

Politicians sometimes intervened elsewhere. In 1910 President Thompson of Ohio State endorsed practice teaching despite opposition among some arts and letters faculty. His point was clinched in 1914, when the state legislature substituted "actual teaching under supervision" for an examination for candidates for teaching certificates. Fifty-six women, all prospective teachers, forthwith transferred from the College of Arts to the College of Education.[90] While the legislature promoted the concept, however, it resisted spending state funds for practice schools. Funding problems frustrated many other campus school efforts. When the endowment for the new Harvard Graduate School of Education was announced the plans included a laboratory and model school and a clinic "for the study of children, their growth and work." Their scheduled fall 1920 opening was postponed without explanation; neither the funds nor the institutional will materialized.[91] In 1957, Henry Hill recalled that the Peabody Demonstration School teachers were once the best in Tennessee, each one paid a thousand dollars more than any other teacher in the state. He lamented "that is no longer true at Peabody or any other laboratory school that I know."[92] Over the years, inadequate financing caused some practice schools to close and forced others to depend on affluent parents with decidedly independent opinions of their own about what constituted "good education."

Ultimately competition, legislative pressures for practice facilities, and the costs of campus practice schools motivated Harvard,

88. Bolton, "Curricula," 839–840; Bird T. Baldwin, "Practice Schools in University Departments of Education," *Journal of Educational Psychology* 2 (1911): 459, 461; O'Leary, *An Inquiry*, pass., esp. p. 29.

89. Beck, *Beyond Pedagogy*, 27, 252.

90. Good, *College of Education*, 68–69.

91. "The Harvard Graduate School of Education," *School and Society* 11, no. 267 (7 Feb. 1920): 166–167); *School and Society* 11, no. 277 (17 April 1920): 467.

92. Hill, "Preparing Teachers," 254.

Berkeley, and Stanford, among others, to make alliances with local school districts for practice teaching placements and demonstration sites. Trying hard to avoid competition with the normal schools and their successor institutions, the state teachers colleges, and sensitive to the higher prestige of secondary than of elementary schools, Berkeley labored to confine its own direct work in teacher education to high school teachers. The public University High School in Oakland was finally given official sanction by the regents in 1919, the faculty of the school assuming the principal burden of offering student teachers the "practical work."[93] For years the college-oriented high school recruited an academic elite from Oakland, San Francisco, and neighboring communities. The numbers of commuting students were seriously depleted by gasoline rationing during World War II, however, and enrollments in English VIII declined to a point that the course could not be sustained.[94] In 1946 the school, now surrounded by a black ghetto as the result of wartime changes in the city's population, was closed and its faculty removed to the School of Education—as Supervisors of Teacher Education. There they continued to have almost sole responsibility for teaching methods as well as the supervision of practice teaching in other local schools.

In 1926 Teachers College's Harold Rugg explained the limited influence on school practice of the F. W. Parker School in Chicago: its lack of affiliation with a teacher training institution.[95] The obvious remedy also failed to yield desired results, either for invigorating practice or stimulating research on teaching. The administrative strategy of forming lab schools to get scholars involved with schools failed most of the time—at Chicago, Berkeley, Michigan, and elsewhere. Chicago's Laboratory School has a complex history, including at one time or another Parker's well-endowed Chicago Institute (an elementary private school), John Dewey's Laboratory or University Elementary School (whose parents did not wish their children to be practiced upon), the Chicago Manual Training School, and the South Side Academy. All became part of the School of Education by 1902.[96] For a period, around 1908, there was a short-lived effort to exercise more

93. Kyte, "Education," 32.

94. Lonnice Brittenum, "Alumni of University High Reunited," *Oakland Tribune,* 4 May 1986.

95. Harold Rugg, "Curriculum-Making in Laboratory Schools," in *Curriculum-Making: Past and Present,* 26th Yearbook of the National Society for the Study of Education, part 1, ed. Guy M. Whipple (Bloomington, Ill.: Public School Publishing Co., 1926), 99–100.

96. Depencier, "History," 25.

faculty control and participation in the elementary school, but it was shortlived. A flurry of testing appeared around the time of World War I, but by the late 1920s few University of Chicago faculty were using the Laboratory Schools for their investigations.

For their part, practice school faculties remained remote from the major activities of professors of education—unless they, too, were also being prepared to escape the classroom through doctoral study. Although they might conduct experiments there in connection with theses and dissertations, the norms of graduate study precluded the expectation that advanced students would take internships in practice schools as a part of their preparation either for research careers or other high-status professional careers in education. Their employment in practice-demonstration schools was often merely expedient: a way to finance graduate studies, not part of a systematic university effort to wed theory and practice. Symptomatic of the schools' uncertain status was the turnover in their leadership. Between 1918 and 1944, eight principals of the University of Chicago High School came and went.[97]

During their entire history many campus schools fell victim to confusion in functions, expecting themselves, "all at once and in a single setting, to design new instructional approaches, to evaluate their effectiveness, and to demonstrate them in such a manner as to impress visitors from the public schools—while at the same time showing preservice teachers the best known ways to teach."[98] Small wonder, then, that most university officials, including deans of schools of education, decided to close their campus schools if a good excuse could be found.

"TC's" four practice, demonstration, and experimental schools—one of which antedated Dewey's Laboratory School at Chicago—were doomed to extinction, made irrelevant as teacher preparation withered and research moved into institutes and doctoral theses. A visitor from England, Sara Burstall, had been impressed in 1908, most of all, by the focus upon the Horace Mann School of "all the ability of the professors of Teachers College."[99] The "Golden Age" of Teachers

97. Ibid., 148–49; Margaret Willis, *The Guinea Pigs after Twenty Years: A Follow-up Study of the Class of 1938 of the University School, Ohio State* (Columbus: Ohio State University Press, 1961), 8; Good, *College of Education* 164, 171.

98. Henry M. Brickell, "State Organization for Educational Change: A Case Study and a Proposal," in *Innovation in Education,* ed. Matthew B. Miles (New York: Teachers College, Columbia University, 1964), 508.

99. Sara A. Burstall, *Impressions of American Education in 1908* (London: Longmans Green, 1909), 93.

College, reminisced Corinne Seeds, principal of the University Elementary School at UCLA, were the happy years at the Lincoln School "when the professors were helping teachers."[100] But high tuition, concern about the "city streets" expressed as early as 1913, and the steadily changing social and racial composition of their neighborhoods sealed the fate of the College's schools. Between 1919 and 1948 all were closed.[101]

What these data illustrate is the pressure, in place after place, of the social factors moving university schools from being "practice" or "lab" schools to "model" schools to *avante garde* or orthodox "safe" schools—havens for the children of faculty and upper-middle-class professionals in a changing America. Such progressions persuaded many educators to argue for more realistic instructional settings for training prospective teachers, i.e., local public schools. While the education school thereby gained a further reason to "let the other fellow do it," control over its product and over the persons most responsible for teacher training was again being sacrificed—this time to often scattered public school personnel, many of whom probably shared the low regard in which schools of education and "their theories" were held. This reinforced the particularistic and parochial character of American schooling as school professionals continued to "identify more with the local school than with the profession."[102] It also meant that teacher training lost coherence and whatever theoretical integrity comes with concentration and control.[103]

The fact that professors publish more than do practitioners means that their reformist or other views distort the image of the profession, failing to reveal the basic conservatism of the professions.[104] Too often, whether in their lecture classes or in their model schools, educationists talked about kinds of schooling that existed in few places in the United States or elsewhere. In adapting to the

100. Corinne Seeds, 9 February 1955. Quoted in Treacy, "Progressivism," 281.

101. Cremin, Shannon, and Townsend, "History," 99–113, 229–237. See also Jonçich, *Sane Positivist,* 552–74; Depencier, "History," on Chicago; Willis, *Guinea Pigs,* on Ohio State's University School.

102. Smith, *Design for a School,* 22; Roemer and Martinello, "Divisions in the Education Professoriate," 217.

103. It might be profitable to explore the contrast with hospital nursing schools which, although dispersed among one-fourth of the nation's hospitals by 1910, had a critical mass of students each and a resident faculty and administration to supervise classroom and bedside practice. Could biweekly visits of practice teachers by university supervisors hope to achieve the same results?

104. Larson, *Professionalism,* 154.

realities of public education, many graduates of schools of education understandably faulted their professional training as "idealistic" or "too theoretical."[105] This gave universities further incentive to use public schools for training sites, placing much of an otherwise unwanted burden of professional education on representative but sometimes poorly prepared local teachers.

The supervision of practice was the lowest-status element in teacher education. The salaries of "critic" or "master" teachers were typically set at only the level of elementary school teachers in large city school systems.[106] Although it divorced theory from practice, a compromise, of sorts, could be reached by subcontracting this component to public schools, and reserving theory to the education school. Since practice teaching often gave student teachers their only sense of identity with the profession during training, it was not surprising that young teachers acquired a much stronger loyalty to and identification with the public schools than with the university's education school.[107] If the sorting, certifying, and socializing functions of professional schools are, indeed, more important than those of transmitting knowledge or imparting skills, leading education schools were also delegating these prerogatives. This contrast with certain other professions has been noted. "The consultative professions like the clergy, medicine, law, engineering, and academic research seem to depend on formal schooling to socialize their novices more than do the managerial-bureaucratic professions like business and schoolteaching."[108]

Early on, and in their own ways, then, the prestige schools of education either eliminated teacher education or confined it to a limited and peripheral role in their increasingly graduate-oriented organizations. Education schools focused professionalism on those who were *leaving* teaching, rather than those entering the classroom.[109] A path was being cleared that led as far as possible from the teacher, the classroom, the pupil. This may help to explain the widening chasm

105. Woodring, "Development of Teacher Education," 12.

106. *National Survey,* 5:64.

107. David L. Clark and Gerald Marker, "The Institutionalization of Teacher Education." In *Teacher Education,* 74th yearbook of the National Society for the Study of Education, part 2, ed. Kevin Ryan (Chicago: University of Chicago Press, 1975), 53–86.

108. Jencks and Riesman, *Academic Revolution* 251–52.

109. Arthur G. Powell, comments at the session "Learning from the Past: Research and Experience in the Reform of Teacher Education," American Educational Research Association, Chicago, 3 April 1985.

existing between the "best thought" about practice that appeared in the professional journals and the realities of classroom practice.[110] These things were happening even as public schools were being rhetorically touted as a pillar of the American republic and a key factor in shaping the nation's future.

Conclusion

In 1929 George Counts faulted schools of education for claiming to speak for a broad, society-wide function—*education*—when they were, in fact, "nothing more than a teachers' college."[111] This student of Charles Judd's, himself a professor at Teachers College, had to know that he was not correctly characterizing *those* two institutions. If they were indeed ignoring *non-school* education in conceiving and conducting their numerous professional and research programs, it was *not* because they were preoccupied with teachers.

Jeanne Chall of the Harvard Graduate School of Education asked, in 1975, why many teachers seem unsure of themselves, hanging back at conferences, listening to educational researchers and administrators often less expert on the subject than themselves.[112] Paradoxically, the formative years of university schools of education—institutions avowedly created to professionalize teaching—reinforced this insecurity, supporting the perception of teaching "as an activity of low prestige, suitable chiefly for women."[113] In the minds of influential schoolmen the understandable repudiation of normal schools and their preoccupation with direct practice was extended to teachers in general, to pedagogy, and to the women with whom normal schools were associated. It was, as Chall states, a period that conferred its honors on its "spokesmen," writers and scholars, not teachers.

110. For an example of the discrepancy between expert thought and actual practice in the English curriculum, see Dora V. Smith, *Instruction in English,* Bureau of Education Bulletin, no. 17. (Washington, D.C.: U.S. Government Printing Office, 1933).

111. George S. Counts, "What Is a School of Education?" *Teachers College Record* 30, no. 7 (April 1929): 647.

112. Jeanne S. Chall, "Restoring Dignity and Self-Worth to the Teacher." *Phi Delta Kappan* 57, no. 3 (Nov. 1975): 170.

113. Samuel R. Ellis, "The Social Status of the American Teacher," *School and Society* 31, no. 785 (11 Jan. 1930): 47–50; Jurgen Herbst, "Professionalization in Public Education, 1890–1920: The American High School Teacher," in *Bildungsbürgertum in 19. Jahrhundert,* vol. 1: *Bildungssystem und Professionalisierung in internationalen Vergleichen,* ed. Werner Conze and Jürgen Kocka (Stuttgart: Klett-Cotta, 1985), 496.

Accordingly the growth of specialized organizations, journals, and university courses met the aspirations of *former* teachers for alternative career identities.[114]

Those other careers in education point to the importance of relative autonomy in defining "real" professional status, as contrasted with that of the "semi-professions." Except in remote rural schoolhouses, twentieth-century American teachers were progressively surrendering much of their occupational status and *de facto* power to supervisors and regulators; lay boards still possessed the *de jure* authority. Schools' new managers claimed specialized, technical, and theoretical knowledge, and their salaries overtook those of even the best paid teachers. While teachers were themselves better educated (or, at least, longer schooled) than before, their numbers and their sex (most were women) left them poorly positioned in society to attain professional parity with the less numerous would-be managers, most of whom were men. Teachers anticipated the position of nurses and social workers: each group struggling after the same university-dispensed knowledge that was in the more-secure possession of the physician, hospital administrator, or welfare agency bureaucrat. As Barbara Melosh has pointed out in her detailed analysis of the nursing profession, as apprenticeship programs in hospitals gave way to collegiate programs of certification, competence was ever more strongly identified with formal education. This reinforced nurses' subordination to doctors, while depriving them of the vestiges of an alternative claim to professional authority, such as special aptitude, service, altruism.[115] The "apprenticeship culture" of the hospital persisted largely as a kind of underground, disputational and scornful of the technical culture of "medical science." The parallels with the apprenticeship culture of the school and with teachers' attitudes toward "educational science" are striking indeed!

The professionalization of education through the route of academic specialization in university-oriented schools of education was, however, both fragmenting the field and loosening the bonds between professional practice and professional education. In the process, school administration and educational research were being made self-

114. Powell, "Speculations." By 1960 the path for many doctoral recipients in education was well established; more than half had left classrooms for nonteaching appointments prior to earning their doctorates. See Laurence D. Brown and J. Marlowe Slater, *The Doctorate In Education,* vol. 1, *The Graduates* (Washington, D.C.: American Association of Colleges for Teacher Education, 1960) 81–83.

115. Melosh, *"The Physician's Hand."*

conscious professions; teaching was not. The dreams of teacher activists, like Margaret Haley of the Chicago Teachers Federation, went largely unrealized. Their campaigns to wrest control of the National Education Association from university presidents like Harvard's Eliot and Columbia's Butler were successful. But the power passed not to teachers but to school administrators and professors of education.[116]

The subordination of teachers to administrators was intensified by the growing bureaucratization of schooling and by the mantle of expertise and legitimation thrown about administrators and other specialists by schools of education.[117] The efforts of grass-roots organizations like the Cincinnati Association of Public School Teachers, organized in 1920 to win salaries sufficient to stem the erosion of teachers from the field, may have raised sympathy in education schools. Its second aim, "to promote such other policies as shall tend to the elevation of teaching as a profession," promoted no discernible rethinking of their two-track strategy: to upgrade teachers' general and technical education (especially through the state teachers colleges) and to professionalize school management through university study and educational research.[118] The mounting assertiveness of teachers in Illinois, for example, beginning in the late 1920s, on behalf of improving their own economic status and expressing concern about systematic inequalities affecting students, progressed without assistance or recognition from the education faculty at the University of Chicago or the University of Illinois.[119] Schools of education, especially those in the class of the ten institutions on which we are concentrating our analysis, "were strangely mute about the problem of the teaching career."[120] Despite a flurry of renewed interest in teacher education during the 1920s, most notably at Teachers College and Harvard, the effort had disintegrated by 1940.[121] The countervailing forces, herein detailed, were evidently too strong.

116. Marvin Lazerson, "If All the World Were Chicago: American Education in the Twentieth Century," *History of Education Quarterly* 24, no. 2 (Summer 1984): 173.

117. See Larson, *Professionalism,* et passim, for a general discussion of this phenomenon in professions operating within bureaucracies.

118. "The Organization of the Cincinnati Association of Public School Teachers," *School and Society* 11, no. 272 (13 March 1920): 326–27.

119. Johnson and Johanningmeier, "Teachers," 233 (note 20), 237.

120. Powell, "Schools of Education," 6.

121. Ibid., 15. Nor were school administrators exempt from this historical process. J. W. Getzels contrasts the 1946 and 1964 *Yearbooks* on school administration of

The so-called theory courses of the advanced degree curricula actually represented occupational or research specialization far more than they did theory. They were unarguably credentialing devices that promoted onetime teachers into school or district administration or into instructorships in normal schools, teachers colleges, or university schools of education. Even the elite among school teachers—the small percentage of the total who were working in high schools—failed to gain stature from the steady shift of teacher education into colleges and universities. Indeed, they lost status as the elementary and secondary schools became linked, philosophically and organizationally, sharing the same mission: the transmission of popular culture. No longer were male high school teachers called "professor" as some had been in the nineteenth century.[122] The clear gain in prestige coming to those who left teaching diminished the standing of those who remained in the classroom. School superintendents earned from two and one-half to four times the salaries of high school teachers in 1913.[123] The "leading practitioners" whom schools of education hired, although in descending proportions, to mix with their scholars, were persons who had built their reputations as educational administrators rather than as teachers.

The appellation "laboratory school" attached to some campus or affiliated schools was an empty promise, although some of the child-centered variety were indeed showpieces attracting hundreds of visitors annually. The medical model of the teaching hospital as the locus of both experimental treatment and medical research failed to transfer to pedagogy. "Radical" departures were usually eschewed. For the Iowa University Elementary School, for example, it was decided in 1915 to avoid innovations that could not be adopted by existing public schools because they lacked suitable textbooks, trained teachers, or "intelli-

---

the National Society for the Study of Education. The nine authors of the former volume included five practitioners. No school superintendent or state school official was present among the fifteen who authored the successor volume; social and behavioral scientists had come to speak even for educational administration.

122. This is called "downward coupling" in Burton R. Clark, "The High School and the University: What Went Wrong in America, Part 1," *Phi Delta Kappan* 66, no. 6 (Feb. 1985): 393.

123. Herbst, "Professionalization," 527. In 1880 teachers at Philadelphia's Central High School earned from three to four times that paid grammar school teachers. The gap closed thereafter but equally telling was the proliferation and advancement of administrators. Male grammar school principals' salaries moved past that of Central High teachers in 1913. See Labaree, "Proletarianizing," 8.

gent support on the part of school patrons."[124] Reflecting the status preferences of universities, secondary schools were preferred to elementary schools although the opportunities to innovate in the latter were arguably greater, being farther from the pressures of preparation for college. Experiments were pallid and uncontrolled, if not actually proscribed by parental resistance. When Professor Frederick G. Bonser of Teachers College listed the common purposes of laboratory or experimental schools, he did not include research, even loosely defined. "Bases of appraisal . . . are subjective and philosophical, rather than scientific," he readily admitted.[125] Educational research largely ignored classrooms, in either model or regular schools, for several reasons: their overwhelming complexity for research that was conceived in narrowly positivistic terms; the lack of academic distinction attached to labors in schools; the marginal status given by the culture to work with children and women; the testiness of many teachers, principals, and parents to perceived university hauteur. Questionnaires, surveys, studies in campus educational clinics, psychology classrooms, and libraries made the education school itself the locus of most educational research—in marked contrast to the relationship of medical school to hospitals.

When Teachers College's Jesse Newlon reviewed studies of the training offered to school superintendents, he criticized it as preoccupied with mechanics of administration, as overly technical treatment "of such important and social questions as the function and control of education."[126] His was essentially the voice of a maverick. There were probably as few critics of public education on the faculties of either major or minor schools of education as there were social reformers among law school faculties.[127] Thus, when John Dewey lectured to a crowd at the University of Illinois in 1927–28, it was under the sponsorship of the College of Liberal Arts and not the College of Education. Except for a cluster of radicals at Teachers College, Ohio State, or Minnesota where Theodore Brameld was "odd man out" in

124. Ernest Horn and Maude McBroom, "Curriculum-Making in the University Elementary School of the State University of Iowa," in *Curriculum-Making: Past and Present,* 26th Yearbook of the National Society for the Study of Education, part 1, ed. Guy M. Whipple (Bloomington, Ill.: Public School Publishing Co., 1926), 271–72.

125. Frederick G. Bonser, "Curriculum-Making in Laboratory or Experimental Schools," in *Curriculum-Making: Past and Present,* pp. 353, 360.

126. Jesse H. Newlon, *Educational Administration as Social Policy,* (New York: Scribner's, 1934), esp. 93–102.

127. "What linked all career law teachers together . . . was a commitment to science, not a commitment to reform," quoted in Johnson, *Schooled Lawyers,* 166.

the late 1930s, faculty at the leading schools of education offered, at best, a tame version of progressive educational theory. As Burton Bledstein had noted, it was characteristic of academic professionals that they distanced themselves from social reformers: "The containment of ideas in the university placed them in a context where they could be managed in functional terms rather than radicalized in a socially demanding ideology."[128] In their general acceptance of the status quo in education, professors of education probably expressed the conservative opinions of the American public and of the majority of the teachers in the nation's schools.[129]

Still, reformist possibilities occasionally sprang up like mushrooms in a shaded lawn. By the end of this period Ralph Tyler had succeeded his mentor, Charles Judd, as chairman of Chicago's Department of Education, and a new interest in normative questions and curriculum appeared in course offerings, faculty appointments, and publications like the *School Review,* which moved curricular and instructional issues ahead of school administration practices. In addition to considering "how to carry on the required educational program most effectively and efficiently," Tyler argued that "some of the most critical problems facing our generation are questions about what the educational program should be." He wrote Chicago's president that he hoped for "a reduction in the tendency to glorify research which had no significance to mankind."[130]

Yet, even in a year like 1937, the more serious researchers among professors of education undoubtedly shared the desire of their counterparts in other departments. That was to be given peace and a place for pursuit of their entrepreneurial careers as "scientists" within the protective embrace of the increasingly bureaucratic organization of the modern American university.[131] On this issue academics and educationists could agree. As we will see in the following chapter, there was often too little else on which they could achieve harmony. Accommodation was the best to be hoped for.

128. Bledstein, *Professionalism,* 329. Michael Katz argues that the specialization of the curriculum along vocational lines promoted conservatism in school of education faculty. This was unlike the orientation of John Dewey and other early educationists whose approach was normative: "they thought in terms of education as it should be rather than as it was." Michael B. Katz, "From Theory to Survey in Graduate Schools of Education," *Journal of Higher Education* 37, no. 6 (June 1966): 327.

129. Cuban, *How Teachers Taught,* esp. chap. 6.

130. Tyler to Robert M. Hutchins, 4 December 1937. Quoted in Wechsler, "*School Review,* Part 2," 225.

131. Larson, *Professionalism,* 200, 290 (note 67).

Four Tensions: Relations on the Campus

Just as education professionals, especially teachers, often found too little in common with the professors in leading schools of education, the latter found their campus colleagues not very accepting of them. Nor were education schools able to ally themselves with the more prestigious professionals schools on their campuses, each working to establish its own protective domain of "expertise." Was there no systematic body of knowledge about education that could be disseminated through the elaborate degree structures of the modern university?

Academic opinion had not altered all that much since 1581 when Richard Mulcaster proposed a reorganization for Oxford and Cambridge that would have included a "colledge for training Maisters." He rightly foresaw that "some difficultie there will be to winne a colledge for such as shall afterward passe to teache schooles." The persisting lack of confidence in pedagogical instruction can be seen in many ways. Typical is the Master of Arts in Teaching degree, promoted by Harvard's President Conant and Yale's President Griswold, a degree that consisted of a small amount of pedagogy added to some advanced work in the student's subject-matter specialty. It was a reaffirmation of the traditional view that a liberal education and strong knowledge of one's field plus intelligence, plus, perhaps, some ineffable personal quality, all certified by diploma, was adequate as the elite universities' response to the state's interest in educating teachers.[1] Experience would provide the rest.

1. John Brubacher et al., *The Department of Education at Yale University, 1891–1958* (New Haven, Conn., 1960), 51.

Given the adverse posture toward departments of pedagogy, what then *was* the American university's reason for launching and maintaining a school of education? From the sociologists we can learn why education and other professions sought the sponsorship of the university: "For the younger and less-established professions, reaching the university means that they can develop their own distinctiveness: they are, indeed, under tacit command to develop their specific body of 'theoretical knowledge' from a firm institutional base, which has given them academic control of a captive audience."[2] What did universities gain in return?

The Universities' Interests in Education

American universities established chairs of pedagogy not in deference to the idea of a science of education nor in imitation of a few German universities which had pioneered chairs in education. It was not to create a discipline of education nor because such noted German intellectuals as Immanuel Kant and Wilhelm Dilthey taught courses on *Pädagogik* in international centers of learning. Rather they launched their intially modest ventures in professional education because it directly served their *own* interests. What were these self-interests?

Public relations was an important motive. As some elite colleges and universities found it convenient to have a theological seminary as a token to quiet critics of their "godless modernism," they similarly found that educating a few teachers could project an image of contributing to the public weal. Enrolling prospective teachers in the expanding state universities was a concession to populists protesting tax support of higher education at a time when public schools might be open only a few weeks a year or were not yet universally free. In Michigan, where the citizens of Berrien County had petitioned the legislature to disband the University of Michigan, sell its properties, and give the proceeds to the Common School Fund, President Frieze in 1870 supported giving assistance to the public schools "to obtain for the University a livelier interest on the part of the citizens."[3]

In response to the "apathy on all sides" toward the University of Iowa, one of its friends acquired for it a private law school thus giving it powerful allies. While the creation of a normal department would not "allign the interests of powerful groups" on the side of the university, as it might in the case of medical and law schools, there were

2. Larson, 201.
3. O'Leary, *An Inquiry,* 185.

important benefits in public good will.[4] In California, the University's professional departments and schools were developed on the initiative of members of the public, not professors or regents. The location of the law and medical affiliates in San Francisco, not Berkeley, symbolized the attitude of the letters and science faculty toward these vocational programs, regardless of their political or economic status in society. It was petitions from California's teachers to the Superintendent of Public Instruction and subsequent pressures from the legislature that finally forced the regents to take action to create a chair in pedagogics. Similar pressures and responses occurred throughout America, moving a variety of business and professional training programs into the university. To gain admittance, however, was not to be vouchsafed a welcome.

There was also the strong motive of attracting more students to an American system of higher education which had been overbuilt in the nineteenth century as a result of sectarian competitiveness, local boosterism, and states' willingness to charter institutions if not to fund them adequately. Even before the post–Civil War movement to modernize higher education, it was common to see colleges imitating one another in shifting their orientations in the hopes of surviving and, perhaps, prospering. Institutions went from denominational identification to nondenominational "Christian" status; from religious to secular orientation; from local to regional and, perhaps, national student markets; from liberal arts to professional curricula, and back to the first if that was warranted. The founder of the new and quickly popular Cornell University described it, in 1869, as "an institution where any person can find instruction in any study."[5] It was with some justification that Daniel Coit Gilman, first president of Johns Hopkins University, reportedly observed that, "It is neither for the genius nor for the dunce, but for the great middle class possessing ordinary talents that we build colleges."[6]

Even as the more ambitious colleges were striving to become universities by adding professional and graduate work, there were numerous patches on the system. Many colleges still retained their preparatory or subfreshman departments, left-over programs from the nineteenth century when the absence of sufficient high schools and

4. Johnson, *Schooled Lawyers,* 3, 17–18.

5. Ezra Cornell; quoted in Harold Perkin, "The Historical Perspective," in *Perspectives on Higher Education: Eight Disciplinary and Comparative Views,* ed. Burton R. Clark (Berkeley: University of California Press, 1984), 37.

6. Gilman is quoted in Bledstein, *Professionalism,* 293, 296–97.

the low demand for "real" college work had made these useful and sometimes economically essential parts of the institution. In 1912, United States Commissioner of Education Philander P. Claxton saw this as one of the unmet challenges facing American higher education:

> Of the four or five millions of young men and women of college age in the country, only about 200,000, or about 5 per cent, are doing college work in standard institutions. Less than 2 per cent do the full four years' work and take a degree. The best interests of the civic and industrial life of the country demand that a larger per cent of its citizens should have the preparation for leadership and direction of affairs which the colleges are supposed to give.[7]

Already engaged in an aggressive competition for enrollments on as broad a base as possible, institutions were increasingly forced to be consumer oriented. Adding new programs and adopting the elective system helped to fill classrooms and dormitories, and made local merchants and landladies smile. With more diverse students responding to this new curricular flexibility, college and university enrollments came out of their nineteenth-century doldrums. In terms of sheer enrollment, teacher education may have accounted for more than half of higher education growth between 1870 and 1930.[8] But, again, such growth did not necessarily win over the faculty. Liberal arts professors, while seeing more students than they ever had before, nonetheless resented the claims of professional departments on students' time.[9] They might believe that departments of pedagogy, like law schools, were less *alien* institutions than were medical or engineering schools because of teachers' and lawyers' historic association with the liberal arts.[10] But their self-interests alone were bound to cause conflict with those in pedagogy and other professional school faculties.

The Needs and Demands of Women Students

In a period of curricular flux, academics also fretted that enrollments in classics, philosophy, and other traditional liberal arts fields were becoming increasingly female. The women's presence, they maintained, pushed male students to elect courses in the social and physi-

7. Quoted in Lykes, *Higher Education,* 39–40.
8. Borrowman, "Professors of Education," 58.
9. Jencks and Riesman, *Academic Revolution,* 199–200.
10. Johnson, *Schooled Lawyers,* 3.

cal sciences, business, and engineering. Female students became scapegoats "for faculty frustration in a time of transition when the release of students from a required, set curriculum gave professors and administrators less control over students' academic direction."[11]

Gender was both a problem and another reason to admit pedagogy into the university curriculum. As colleges had hesitatingly discovered in the later nineteenth century, women wanted higher education—not only to prove they could study without expiring under the strain but also to prepare for the rapidly growing profession of high school teaching. In her study of midwestern colleges from 1890 to 1930, Joan Zimmerman found that a major reason among women for going to college, even among the middle class, was the practical concern of preparing for a better teaching career than could be obtained in the country school.[12] By admitting women, and by assisting their plans to teach, a college might double its potential pool of applicants—more than double it, in fact, because girls were two-thirds of high school gradutes at the turn of this century.

It is no coincidence that virtually all of the fourteen institutions identified by Edwin Slosson in 1910 as "the great American universities"—California, Chicago, Columbia, Cornell, Harvard, Johns Hopkins, Illinois, Michigan, Minnesota, Pennsylvanis, Princeton, Stanford, Wisconsin, and Yale—were the largest and were coeducational or had affiliated women's colleges.[13] At a time when young men were enrolling in commerce and other vocational courses, the presence of women helped to sustain the arts and letters departments. These subjects would dominate women's academic programs: first, because they represented the ideal of a higher education, which had so long been denied to women and, second, because they were the subjects that women could teach in the schools.

In its first decade a third of Stanford's graduates became teachers. At Berkeley in 1900, in a graduating class of 221, 77 women and 37 men applied for a teacher's license.[14] By 1915, over half the grad-

11. Solomon, *Educated Women,* 60.

12. Joan Grace Zimmerman, "College Culture in the Midwest, 1890–1930," (Doctoral diss., University of Virginia, 1978), 176.

13. Edwin E. Slosson, *Great American Universities* (New York: Macmillan, 1910). By the 1970s and 1980s, Princeton, Columbia, and Yale had finally concluded that coeducation permitted an institution both to be more selective in admitting male students and to generate revenue to strengthen liberal arts departments. Accordingly, each became fully coeducational.

14. University of California, "President's Biennial Report, 1898–1900," 14.

uates of Michigan's liberal arts college planned to teach.[15] In neighboring Wisconsin it was reported in 1909 that two-thirds of the women graduating from the University entered teaching and their rates of persistence in the teacher work force equalled that of the larger numbers of normal school graduates.[16] A study of 16,000 women college graduates, as of 1915, found that 58 percent were teachers; among those who were employed, nearly 85 percent were teachers.[17] By the early 1930s, over 40 percent of the graduates of public and private liberal arts colleges and universities nationally were becoming teachers.[18] The administrative rule of thumb for those institutions that followed was, "If you have a college, you'd better have teacher education."[19] This attraction of large numbers of students exacted a high price in prestige, however. In many instances prospective teachers were intellectually and socially unprepared, for attendance at a would-be elite institution, and the gender of the larger portion of them was only tolerated, at best.

When, around 1910, various universities contemplated steps to limit and confine women's presence, Helen Olin raised the spectre of a public-relations nightmare for public institutions if they failed to fulfill their obligations—both to the state for professional training and to parents whose daughters sought such training. This alumna of the university issued a thinly-veiled threat when she reminded officials of the University of Wisconsin that "any marked decrease or check in the tendency of women to increase their attendance would be in itself a warning to the people that the university was not, in a very important respect, justifying the claims which it is constantly making upon the state."[20] Like most other universities, Wisconsin learned to live with its women students, tempering its prejudices with prudence.

The University of Michigan became a coeducational institution in 1870 and, by the end of the decade, established its professorship in education. Nor was it coincidental that Stanford opened as a coeducational institution with an education department. A pedagogy

15. O'Leary, *An Inquiry,* 195, 297.

16. Helen R. Olin, *The Women of a State University* (New York: G. P. Putnam's Sons, 1909), 197. Only 5 percent of Wisconsin's women teachers were university graduates.

17. The study by Mary Van Kleek is reported in Solomon, *Educated Women,* 127.

18. *National Survey,* 5:53.

19. Clark and Marker, "Teacher Education," 77.

20. Olin, *Women,* 201.

department was, like the department of home economics, a structure to contain women students—lest they should wander about the institution unrestrained and bother the faculty and threaten male students. Ohio State opened its departments of pedagogy and of domestic science in the same year, 1895–96.

At a time when the most elite of the men's colleges would not admit women, Yale imitated Harvard and Columbia by inaugurating, in 1905, a short-lived summer school program for teachers; women were the majority of students. In 1920 Yale created the opportunity for matriculated graduate study in education when it opened a department of education in the graduate school. Yale granted its first Ph.D.'s to women in 1923 and even hired a woman, Bessie Lee Gambril, for the faculty; she and a woman professor in the Harvard Medical School were the first women to teach in Ivy League universities. Harvard was, however, still more daring—by admitting women as undergraduates into its new women's college, Radcliffe, and into the Graduate School of Education.

Relations of the High School to the College

Another interest of universities would be served by having an education department to assist college graduates to become teachers. The argument sometimes went that "it would be a disservice to our students and to society, if the nations' brightest youth were hampered in their ability to become teachers." This was also a way to protect the quality of the freshman class from the uncontrolled growth of yet-unregulated high schools. Colleges and universities were disturbed at the refusal of most American states to distinguish the training of high school teachers from that of their elementary school counterparts. California was unusual when, in 1905, the State Board of Education adopted a resolution requiring a full year of graduate work in order to receive a general secondary school teacher's credential; a decade later no other state had followed suit.[21] Nonetheless, establishing chairs and departments of education furthered the trend toward college-educated high school teachers, and high school teachers became more likely to have both academic and professional training.[22]

21. O'Leary, *An Inquiry,* 384.

22. Herbst, "Professionalization in Public Education," 507, 509.

In 1935, 10 percent of elementary school teachers, 56 percent of junior high school teachers, and 85 percent of senior high school teachers were college graduates. By 1955 the figure for elementary school teachers reached 70 percent and virtually all

Between 1890 and World War I, higher education gained an unprecedented influence on American schooling through the schools' employment of college-educated teachers. The many issues attending an expanding secondary education were largely ignored by university leaders, however. Their overriding concern was with the better articulation of high school to college. As a critic of this stance, Edgar Wesley, put the issue, "Thus the welfare of nine-tenths of the students was ignored in order to concentrate upon the college prospects of the one-tenth."[23] Some spokesmen of the education profession also claimed that college faculties' preoccupation with college preparation infected many of the teachers whom they educated.

Yet it must be remembered that some academics demonstrated a vital interest in the fuller range of services performed by public schools. One of the most famous of all American academic men, the historian Frederick Jackson Turner, offered a special course at the University of Wisconsin on the teaching of history in the public schools, traveled about the state visiting high schools as one of the University's official inspectors of their curricula and teaching, served (during the 1890s) on a statewide committee to standardize history instruction in the public schools, addressed audiences of teachers and clubwomen on education issues, and favored bringing normal schools under university influence. In describing these activities, his biographer, historian Ray Allen Billington, reveals how he himself viewed such activities: Turner was forced by his interest in teachers "to spend too much time at their meetings;" his speaking at high school commencements "meant more squandered time" and were "faint honors" and "burdensome activities"; these were "chores" demanded by his educational interest; the women's and social clubs he spoke before were "the supreme enemies of all academicians." In a non sequitur, Billington wonders of Turner that "an undue proportion of his time should be squandered on largely indifferent high school teachers. A constant stream of letters from teachers seeking advice flowed across his desk, and all were answered, often at great length."[24] While we think the Billingtons

high school teachers were college graduates. See Sedlak and Schlossman, *Who Will Teach?* 36.

23. Edgar B. Wesley, *NEA, The First Hundred Years: The Building of a Teaching Profession* (New York: Harper & Bros., 1957), 67–68.

24. Ray Allen Billington, *Frederick Jackson Turner: Historian, Scholar, Teacher* (New York: Oxford University Press, 1973), 135, 145–47, 151, 249–50. We are grateful to Dr. Paula Gillett for this reference.

outnumbered the Turners among academic men after 1900, Turner did have company.

At the University of Michigan in the 1880s and 1890s, for example, there were several professors whose visits to accredit high schools caused them to take a lively interest in the range of problems that teachers daily encountered. Even so, they tended to express the academic view: that subject matter was at war with teaching methods. They complained, for example, that discussions at teachers' meetings subordinated subject matter to methodology.[25] It was difficult for professors in leading universities and colleges to come to terms with the consequences of the fact that, after 1880 or so, the public high school had usurped the position of private academies in dispensing education to American youth. Each year the probability increased that their own undergraduates would be the products of public secondary schooling. By 1930 the ratio of public to private high school teachers in the United States was 8.5 to one.[26]

William Bagley of Teachers College was essentially correct when he analyzed the increasingly discrepant perspectives of college faculty and public school educators, including professors of education—it was rooted in the unprecedented popularity of secondary education in the United States:

> As long as an educational institution is highly selective, the problems of the curriculum, and the problems of administration are relatively easy to solve. Both materials and methods tend to become highly standardized, and pupils and students who are not adapted or cannot adapt themselves to these materials and methods are quickly eliminated. The responsibility of adaptation rests distinctly and heavily upon the learner rather than upon the institution or upon the teacher. When the school or the college opens its doors to the masses, however, the situation is exactly reversed. The responsibility for adaptation rests now upon the institution and the teacher; and with an increasing demand for ever higher and higher levels of mass education the intricacies and difficulties of the problem are very rapidly compounded.[27]

University spokesmen tried to contain the threat they saw coming from the popularization of high schools. An important medium for

25. Creutz, "From College Teacher to University Scholar," 455–57.

26. *National Survey,* 5:49.

27. William C. Bagley, "The University School of Education, a Source of Educational Leadership," in *The Changing Educational World, 1905–1930,* ed. Alvin C. Eurich (Minneapolis: University of Minnesota Press, 1931), 82.

exercising their influence was the regional high school accrediting associations that college and university representatives helped to form. Another was the work of university-dominated committees and commissions on secondary education. The most notable example was that of the Committee of Ten, chaired by Harvard University's president, Charles W. Eliot. Its report, issued in 1893, although arousing active opposition, solidified university influence on the American high school curriculum for nearly a quarter of a century and was consequential even longer.[28] Prominent university professors and presidents were also important in the leadership of the National Education Association. By World War I, however, the general influence of higher education on secondary schooling was waning. And university figures resented it, as they scorned educational "experts"—those former schoolmasters who would view the university, too, "as a sublimated high school," in the words of the dean of the graduate school of the University of Minesota.[29] Regardless, the young schools of education remained on the university campuses, testimonials to academe's self-interest in monitoring if not controlling secondary education.

Harvard offers a particularly instructive example of university self-interest at work. President Eliot, who consistently underestimated the nation's demand for secondary eduction, established a chair in pedagogy to preclude the appearance of a coeducational "high normal school" in Massachusetts to train college graduates as high school teachers.[30] When Eliot hinted that Harvard would prepare Harvardians to teach, the legislature abandoned the normal school plan; it was cheaper to have private Harvard do it than to create another state-funded institution for teacher education. With the support of prominent faculty like William James, Josiah Royce, and George Herbert Palmer, the Harvard faculty received Eliot's plan, dropped the word "normal" from the proposed one-year course, precluded women from enrolling, and grudingly acquiesced to the rest. Eliot hired Paul Hanus in order to advance Harvard's interests and to embellish his personal reputation as America's educational statesman. But as Hanus became more interested in the high school as a terminal institution and in

28. Herbst, "Professionalization," 508.

29. Guy Stanton Ford to President David Kinley of the University of Illinois, 5 December 1923; quoted in Johnson and Johanningmeier, *Teachers for the Prairies,* 231 (note 16).

30. Hawkins, *Between Harvard and America,* esp. 252–53; O'Leary, *An Inquiry,* 35; Powell, *Uncertain Profession,* 37–38.

such matters as vocational education, he lost the attention and support of Eliot and his successor.

The relations of education schools to their universities remain influenced by the differential function performed by academics and educationists in what is now called "social reproduction." A former dean of Rutgers University Graduate School of Education, expresses it thus:

> The mission of the dominant arts and science faculty is to reproduce the elite leadership of the nation and to produce new knowledge in the interests of government and the economy. By contrast, the mission of the education faculty is to reproduce the mass of workers and the unemployed. Differences in mission dictate differences in faculty roles and differences in knowledge production.[31]

One need not accept the full implications of Milton Schwebel's analysis to agree that in the period 1900 to 1940, American universities were more socially elitist institutions than many were later to become, and that high schools had become mass institutions only toward the end of this period. Recall, also, that the institutions upon which we have concentrated preferred to devote their professional activities to educating high school teachers, managers, and researchers. To do so was to lessen the ravages of clashing cultures on campus.

Delegating Functions to the Pedagogy Faculty

The faculty of schools of education provided other services to colleges and universities. Before state departments of education and accrediting associations assumed the responsibility, it was common for university professors to be asked to visit and approve high schools. The objective was to simplify college admissions by allowing graduates to enter the university without examination. To perform this administrative service was also to assert educational leadership in the state. Michigan's faculty had been doing this since 1871, and had grown weary of the duty.[32] Education faculty could assist with and perhaps take over that onerous task.

This delegation of university responsibilities was clearly on the minds of some university presidents when they contemplated making an appointment in pedagogy. In 1884, President Bascom of the

31. Schwebel, "Clash of Cultures," 2.
32. Creutz, "College Teacher," 97.

University of Wisconsin noted the high school accreditation movement and declared that more must be done to improve the state's high schools: "We trust that the professorship of pedagogy just established will be very helpful in this direction."[33] In its early years Michigan's Department of the Science and Art of Teaching housed the Inspector of High Schools; the same situation obtained at the State University of Iowa in the early years. An experienced superintendent, William Boyd, was named High School Visitor at Ohio State and later became that university's first dean of education. The appointment of Albert W. Rankin, state school inspector, as one of the two original education professors at the University of Minnesota smoothed the way to two novelties: the provision of student- ("cadet"-) teaching experiences for prospective high school teachers and the establishment of the University High School.[34]

Early incumbents of pedagogical chairs also began to give lectures to the teachers' institutes and state education conventions which were formerly the nearly exclusive province of normal school instructors, county superintendents, local ministers, and college professors promoting their own books or disciplines. Leading American scientists, who had formerly published school textbooks, did so progressively less often as professors of education and their emerging specializations became organized.[35]

The very existence of the pedagogues made it more difficult for other university professors, even those most like education professors in their experiences and sympathies, to feel other than superceded. While many nineteenth-century college professors and presidents identified themselves as participants and leaders in the various school movements of their age, increasingly after 1900, they were being told, in effect, to stand aside.[36] Consider the case of Henry Judson, professor of history at the University of Minnesota from 1885 to 1891 and later president of the University of Chicago. Before Minnesota acquired its first professor of pedagogy, Judson lectured to seniors on "the science and art of teaching." His fifteen-year stint as a public school teacher in Troy, New York, was the basis for his lectures. Judson's approach, like that of others of his generation, came to seem superficial and unscientific to those trying to professionalize

33. Quoted in Olin, *Women*, 175.

34. Graham, "College of Education," 511.

35. William E. Brownson and Joseph J. Schwab, "American Science Textbooks and Their Authors, 1915 and 1955," *School Review* 71, no. 2 (Summer 1963): 170–80.

36. Mattingly, "Academia and Professional School Careers," 221–22.

education through the new departments of pedagogy in major American universities.[37] An older kind of expertise was having to share the stage with another. Jealousy and conflict simmered, and sometimes erupted.

The introduction of chairs and departments of pedagogy provided another service to universities from the income derived by summer instruction. Largely attended by normal school graduates and teachers, summer schools also broadened a university's appeal. Beginning in 1893, Michigan's summer school made higher education available to more teachers than could matriculate in the regular program. Minnesota had a "Summer School for Teachers" fourteen years before it had a professor of pedagogy. Summer courses helped to counter the charge of elitism at private institutions like Yale and Harvard. At Berkeley, Ohio State, and undoubtedly elsewhere, summer schools for teachers introduced courses which might later become regular offerings, generated surplus revenues to cover less popular courses, and gave professors in a variety of departments an opportunity for additional income. In many universities they were also the opening wedge of coeducation, and were therefore something to be concerned about.[38]

Ed School, the Poor Relation

Cross-cultural studies of higher education demonstrate the near-universal, simultaneous presence of three kinds of systems of stratification. One form is the status differentials that exist on the basis of sectors of higher education. The sectors may be defined as private versus public, two-year versus four-year institutions, colleges versus universities. However defined, there are systematic and persistent prestige barriers between them. A second system of stratification ranks institutions within a given sector. Thus, our sample of ten institutions represents a major portion of the elite universities within the university sector. The third basis for allocating prestige is the intra-institution ranking: that which awards unequal status to the several schools and departments within a university.[39]

In accord with the prevailing intra-institution status system, the

37. Beck, *Beyond Pedagogy,* 11.

38. Clifford, "Dangerous Questions," 3–62.

39. Martin A. Trow, "The Analysis of Status," in *Perspectives on Higher Education: Eight Disciplinary and Comparative Views,* ed. Burton R. Clark (Berkeley: University of California Press, 1984), 137.

various efforts of their education faculties were met with little sustained respect or appreciation on university campuses. Dean James Earl Russell of Teachers College described the problem of schools of education as general to professional schools: "The lack of interest, not to say persistent hostility, on the part of college professors" was, generally directed, he thought, "toward each new move in professional training."[40] Education faculty could be forgiven for thinking that among professional schools they got more than their share of criticism. Each of these ten schools of education—and many of lesser reputation and influence—faced enmity. Some experienced recurrent threats of reorganization or dismantlement.

Opposition to creating the College of Education at Ohio State was described as based on both budgetary competition and "the doubt that anything could be taught about teaching." The naming of an opponent of the College of Education, history professor G. W. Knight, as its dean in 1914 may have been a strategy "to mollify the faction of the University faculty which opposed the College by appointing one of their number."[41] *School and Society* published in 1928 a graduate student's report of an unidentified professor of English "who suggested . . . that we begin a reform by killing off the professors of education"—a desperate remedy for ending a chronic complaint by academics.[42]

But this could hardly have been news to Stanford's Ellwood Patterson Cubberley. While Stanford's newness and freedom from tradition might have created a more favorable environment for its department of education, insiders knew better.[43] President David Starr Jordan warned Cubberley, on his arrival at Palo Alto in 1898, that the young department was already "in serious disrepute" and that faculty sentiment would strongly support closing it. Despite the school's eventual successes, its work faced persistent misunderstanding, misinterpretation, and condemnation. University-wide representation on the school faculty, designed to aid collaboration in the preparation of high

40. Russell, "Further Development," 533.

41. Good, *College of Education,* 47, 75.

42. G. R. Pease, "A Graduate Student Criticism of the College of Education," *School and Society* 28, no. 724 (10 November 1928): 576.

43. O'Leary, *An Inquiry,* 289. When Alvin Eurich, later of the Ford Foundation's Fund for the Advancement of Education, was acting president of Stanford (1948), he recommended closing its school of education. He took a similar position later, as first chancellor of the State University of New York. It did not help matters that Eurich had received his own doctorate from Minnesota's College of Education and been Melvin Haggerty's assistant dean in the 1903s before going to Stanford as professor of education in 1938.

school teachers, seemed frustrating and obstructionist to Cubberley. Nor could he, one of the University's internationally known professors, himself gain election to any of Stanford's major committees.[44] Small wonder that he would speak, with intimate knowledge, of the plight of university education schools, "met for long with bitter opposition from professors in other lines of work afflicted with a form of myopia which prevented their seeing beyond the limits of the subject matter which they taught."[45]

In 1929 Charles Judd of the Department of Education of the University of Chicago told the annual convention of the National Education Association that "teachers colleges have suffered perhaps more than any other group of American education institutions from isolation."[46] That distinction appears to have been passed on to the major education schools. In 1923 Elmer Ellsworth Brown, who went from Michigan to organize the work in education at Berkeley and then to become United States Commissioner of Education, said of such schools and departments that they "have been built up in the face of simply unbelievable distrust and opposition in the academic world." He praised Dean Russell's role as a "cheerful crusader" at Teachers College in the face of well-known opposition by the Columbia University faculty to the perceived "coddling of this parvenu institution" of Teachers College.[47] The corporate arrangments between the two were frequently readjusted in the effort to improve their troubled relations—or, perhaps, only to give Teachers College greater freedom from its imperious host. After nearly a quarter century of University attacks for its suspicious professionalism, Charles Judd proposed in 1932 that both teacher education and the publication of *Elementary School Journal* and *School Review* be taken over by the undergraduate college.[48] Relations may have gotten better at Minnesota. By 1938, according to its historian, Robert Beck, "it was no longer necessary for the College to fight for survival; deans and faculty members alike no longer had to expend precious energy on simply justifying their existence."[49]

44. Sears and Henderson, *Cubberley of Stanford*, 63–64, 70, 99; Tyack and Hansot, *Managers of Virtue*, 121–28.

45. Cubberley, "College of Education," 541.

46. Judd, "Teachers Colleges," 879.

47. Brown, "Development of Education," 194. See also Cremin, Shannon, and Townsend, *Teachers College*, 70.

48. The former function was divested but not the latter. See Wechsler, "Primary Journal," 102–3.

49. Beck, *Beyond Pedagogy*, 119.

Education at Harvard was launched despite the attitude of the faculty majority, which felt what Eliot described as "but slight interest or confidence in what is ordinarily called pedagogy."[50] As Harvard College and its other professional schools thrived, Eliot's interests in education waned, and Abbott Lawrence Lowell succeeded to the presidency, Hanus and his successors found little support and few students, and faced many rebuffs. Harvard's famed professor of French literature, Irving Babbitt, wrote in 1929 that "our professors of pedagogy and sociology are held in almost universal suspicion in academic circles, and are not infrequently looked upon by their colleagues as downright charlatans."[51] Professor of English Barrett Wendell was willing to have "educationists" at Harvard if housed in a separate school and not in the faculty of Arts and Sciences.[52] Even as the School's founding was being celebrated in February 1920, Dean Holmes learned that all of his recommendations for new faculty had been disapproved. No wonder that, at the dinner honoring the new School, Paul Hanus could, at embarrassing length, air a flood of embittered memories. After years of obstructing its efforts to secure endowment and occupy its own building, Lowell retired in 1933, telling the overseers that the Graduate School of Education was a "kitten that ought to be drowned."[53]

President Conant succeeded Lowell and found the school in serious financial trouble. He described himself as forced to spend more time than he wanted on an arrangement "which I had inherited but for which I had no special enthusiasm."[54] Years later, in his book *The Education of American Teachers,* Conant recalled:

> Early in my career as a professor of chemistry, . . . I shared the views of the majority of my colleagues on the faculty of arts and sciences that there was no excuse for the existence of people who sought to teach others how to teach. . . . When an issue involving benefits to the graduate school of education came before the faculty of arts and sciences, I

50. O'Leary, *An Inquiry,* 12.

51. Quoted in Brubacher et al., *Yale University,* 44.

52. Suggestions of this kind were not limited to schools of education, however. Liberal arts faculties, in fact, usually preferred to have *all* their "vocational" programs located in separate schools and colleges—if not entirely off the campus. See Hawkins, *Between Harvard and America*, 370.

53. Another problem was that, unlike the law and business schools, which drew their students from throughout the nation, Harvard's Graduate School of Education was "provincial": three–fourths of its students came from Massachusetts. See Powell, *Uncertain Profession*, 176.

54. Conant, *My Several Lives,* 180.

automatically voted with those who looked with contempt on the school of education.[55]

Between 1925 and 1934 Harvard's School slipped from third to tenth place in national surveys. It seemed an institution adrift, buffeted by nagging, draining, intractable status problems, small in the terms of human history but too large in Harvard's institutional life to be resolved to anyone's satisfaction. Two decades of efforts to produce large numbers of practitioners went unappreciated by Harvard's faculties and administrators. Struggling against its chronic inferiority complex, Harvard's education faculty aped Harvard University and endlessly debated standards. "I have seen us twice put on a high hat, and later take it off again," one member recalled in 1944.[56] At the end of this formative period in the history of schools of education, a dispirited Dean Holmes wrote privately, "The one instructional distinction we can point to is that we are operating on the graduate level and admitting only qualified students—and that might almost be taken for granted.[57]

The Absence of Intellectual and Social Distinction

Even away from Cambridge, Massachusetts, education schools were faulted for the qualities of what they taught, for their student bodies, and for their faculties. The influential Abraham Flexner, author of the previously mentioned report in 1910 on medical schools, widely credited with boosting those institutions into the universities' orbit of acceptance, was also asked to conduct studies on the education of teachers. After examining teacher training in the public normal schools of Maryland in 1916, at the behest of the legislature, he dismissed the possibility of effecting a similar upgrading in education schools. Unlike in the training of physicians, there were already too many and too varied institutions preparing teachers for the state to be

55. James B. Conant, *The Education of American TTeachers,* (New York: McGraw-Hill, 1963), 1–2. As Harvard's president, Conant thought that the Graduate School of Education might better justify its existence by studying social issues and education, becoming, in effect, a school of applied social science; his support of the School rested on this and not a professional hopefulness. See Powell, "University Schools of Education," 17.

56. Powell, *Uncertain Profession,* 226.

57. Harvard Committee, *Graduate Study*, 89. Holmes retired in 1940, a lame-duck dean, his successor chosen by President Conant the year previous, in impatience with the school's leadership and faltering vision.

able to wrest control of the situation.[58] Flexner praised major schools of education, early in their histories, with having made "an unquestionable contribution of genuine value" to American education through their efforts on behalf of an enlivened school curriculum. However, he scored both schools of education (along with departments of sociology, with which he frequently lumps them) and their host universities for having "lost their heads"—for having thrown out the best of the past along with the barren parts of the curriculum, for having an unwarranted devotion to technique, administration, and socialization.

In a period in which Robert Maynard Hutchins and other influential educators ridiculed most expressions of vocationalism in American higher education, Flexner found little to commend in university professional education. He placed journalism schools "on a par with university faculties of cookery and clothing," deplored business schools (especially the "more pretentious and for that reason more dangerous" ones like Harvard's Graduate School of Business Administration), and dismissed "schools of pharmacy, library science, town-planning, social service, etc." as not belonging in a university. As for the leading schools of education, he castigated Chicago and Teachers College for the "absurdities and trivialities" of their curriculum and dissertation topics. He thought that these derived, in part at least, from an excessive devotion to tests, measurements, organization, and administration. He also scorned most of Harvard's faculty in education: dealing, as they were, with "simple practical problems, which would quickly yield to experience, reading, common sense, and a good general education."

From a status perspective, the schooling enterprise seemed beset by the "3 Ps": powerlessness, prosaicness, and penury. Its immediate clients were children, a dependent population. Everyone having been through school, it lacked "mystery"; to walk down the halls of schools of education and observe the displays of flash cards and finger paintings conveyed none of the esotericism of the college of engineering's aerodynamic models. In 1930 the president of George Peabody College for Teachers noted that "any one of a half dozen medical schools has a larger endowment than all the teachers colleges on this continent."[59]

As a publicly funded service, both schooling and its caretakers often appeared threadbare. A teacher who had attended a normal

58. Flexner and Bachman, *Public Education*.

59. Bruce R. Payne, "Difficulties in the Integration of Subject Matter and Method in Teachers Colleges," *School and Society* 31, no. 808 (21 June 1930): 826.

school in 1858 recalled the struggles that upwardly striving youth had even in entering such modest classrooms:

> We were very poor, but very plucky. We boarded ourselves, mainly on corn mush, washed the floors and built the fires in the Normal Hall, and were poorly provided with all things; our parents were sad-faced, struggling pioneers of the prairies; but we were cheery, resolute, and happy in our life and our work. To the toiling youth of frontier homes, thirsting for knowledge, the Illinois Normal University opened the gateways of a new life.[60]

In that same era, colleges like Yale and Harvard had reluctantly accepted schools of science, believing that they, too, attracted déclassé students, persons of practical interests and too-modest social origins. Their solution was to restrict these programs to the fringes, but eventually they won their way to respectability.

What about the prospects of departments of pedagogy? Howard Bowen, a specialist in the economics of education, maintains that the prestige and "objective" quality of institutions of higher education are judged more by their "inputs" (what the students bring to the institution in the way of social and other resources) than by their "outputs" (what they contribute to the learning and personal development of their students).[61] Clearly education students produced fewer inputs as the field continued to recruit many students of modest social background: from rural areas, immigrant families, and upwardly mobile black families. Teaching was replacing the ministry as a path for improving one's social status.[62] Students educated in exclusively teacher-training institutions, the normal schools and state teachers' colleges, were like the students from municipal and Catholic colleges who attended independent and night law schools—coming disproportionately from the lower-middle and working classes.[63]

60. Quoted in *National Survey,* 5: 18.

61. Howard R. Bowen, *The Cost of Higher Education: How Much Do Colleges and Universities Spend per Student and How Much Should They Spend?* (San Francisco: Jossey-Bass, 1980).

62. In examining faculty characteristics in four midwestern colleges, Zimmerman ("College Culture," 220) found the ministry and school administration in the backgrounds of most of those who preceded academic life with other careers in 1890; by 1930 schoolteaching was clearly the most likely path to academe. Also important was the fact that senior faculty in 1930 were *less* likely to have had any other career than were the 1890 group; the relative percentages were 53 and 27.

63. Such law students are contrasted with the university graduates who attended the University of Chicago Law School in Lortie, "Laymen to Lawmen," 361–62.

Lower social status was joined with lesser academic standing. A study that tested high school and college youth in Pennsylvania between 1928 and 1934, initiated by the Carnegie Foundation, suggested academic marginality among prospective teachers. The data showed potential teachers falling below the averages of all college seniors except those majoring in business, art, agriculture, and secretarial fields, and the research eventuated in the experimental testing of teachers and the development of the National Teacher Examination Program.[64]

Some of those students would eventually make their way into the graduate programs of education schools. Conversely, except for the elite women's colleges, relatively few graduates of prestigious undergraduate institutions went on to earn doctorates in education. The chances of an A.B. graduate of Harvard or Yale going on to get an education doctorate were not appreciably greater than that obtaining at Princeton, which did not even have an education program on its campus.[65] Thus, in their social origins, most education students could not confer prestige upon their departments, although such "borrowed status" has been an important factor in the sociology of institutions. Nor was it unprecedented for interior or exterior critics of schools of

---

See also O. Edgar Reynolds, *The Social and Economic Status of College Students,* Teachers College Contributions to Education no. 272 (New York: Teachers College, Columbia University, 1927), 24–25. The 1933 study of the teaching population found that, compared to teachers educated in liberal arts colleges, teachers-college students came from larger families and had less well-educated parents. While 10 percent of liberal arts students came from farm or ranch homes, a quarter of teachers-college students had these origins. They were less than half as likely to have received a scholarship or fellowship, and their scholastic careers were more frequently interrupted by financial hardships. *National Survey,* vol. 2, *Teacher Personnel in the United States.*

64. Ann Jarvella Wilson, "Knowledge for Teachers: The Origins of the National Teacher Examination Program" (Paper presented at the annual meeting of the American Educational Research Association, Chicago, April 1985), 8.

65. Between 1920 and 1961, 42 graduates of Princeton, 95 graduates of Yale College, and 137 graduates of Harvard College took education doctorates. As a percentage of all the doctorates earned by graduates of these institutions education doctorates were as follows: Yale, 5.4 percent; Harvard, 4.8 percent; and Princeton, 3.6 percent. The baccalaureate origins of education doctorates favor the state univerities in our sample. For example, 13.5 percent of all doctorates earned by baccalaureate graduates of the University of Iowa were in education; the comparable figures for Berkeley and Ohio State are 9 percent and 14.6 percent. The significant exception to this private-public dichotomy was Columbia University: nearly a quarter of all those who graduated from Columbia and went on to earn doctorates took them in education. New York University (private) and City College of New York (public) followed closely as the leading baccalaureate institutions for education doctorates in the United States. Harmon and Soldz, *Doctorate Production,* 86–119.

education to equate social status with intellectual or professional "quality." The world of higher education has never been itself a democracy, even when it has contributed to democratic ends.

Flexner thought that education schools and sociology departments were the more likely parts of higher education to promote "authors of nonsense" to professorships in leading universities.[66] Others had formed that opinion earlier. In 1921, University of Illinois President David Kinley wrote to the dean of his College of Education that he found himself "unable to escape the feeling that many of our appointments in education are weaker than appointments in corresponding places in other departments."[67] Such a view of the inadequate supply of talent in even the higher reaches of the education professoriate eventually gained some acceptance in the leading schools of education themselves, as it was heard that the presence and influence of "absolutely first-rate people" in education could not keep up with the growing numbers in what was becoming a mass profession.[68]

Our institutional accounts and general propositions do not deny that some individuals associated with schools of education enjoyed high regard among their academic contemporaries—both on their own campuses and afar. We think that their numbers were probably very small, however, at the most prestigious universities. In 1920 Minnesota's dean of Education, Lotus Coffman, became the University's president, and fifty-three years later Ruth Eckert became the first College of Education member named Regents' Professor. Berkeley's first professor of pedagogy, Elmer Ellsworth Brown, became the distinguished and successful chancellor of New York University after he left the United States Commissionership of Education in 1911. Edward C. Elliott, who once directed the Course for the Training of Teachers at the University of Wisconsin, went on to the presidency of Purdue University. Charles Judd was made, in 1929, distinguished service professor by the University of Chicago. Other examples could no doubt be brought forward. Edward L. Thorndike and John Dewey come readily to mind as recognized ornaments of Columbia University. But, was it not Thorndike, *as a psychologist* or Dewey, *as a philosopher* who was

66. Abraham Flexner, *Universities: American, English, German* (New York: Oxford University Press, 1930), 96–97, 102, 109n, 160, 162, 172.

67. David Kinley to Charles E. Chadsey, 11 July 1921. Quoted in Johnson and Johanningmeier, *Teachers,* 247.

68. The conclusion to be drawn was that there was insufficient talent on *either* side of the desk in the classrooms of schools of education. See Harvard Committee, *Graduate Study,* vi–vii.

esteemed? Trained in his respective discipline, each was well honored by its organizations and leading scholars—although, we suspect, that about each one could have heard it said, "Just think what he *could* have done had he not gotten "mixed up with" (i.e., diverted by) education." In addition they may have shared, as Schwebel maintains, similar backgrounds, training, and intellectual orientations with their academic counterparts.

Quarrels on Campus

Schools of education were becoming, every day, better situated to arouse the hostility which any discipline or department in the modern university feels when its own expertise is challenged. Even though teachers' "products," unlike that of engineers and some businessmen, are intangible and fraught with problems of definition and measurement, schools of education claimed, first, a superior interest and a superior and growing knowledge of pedagogy: of how to teach. They conveyed, as they had to, the false impression that academics had an overweening confidence in "mere knowledge of subject matter."[69] Indeed some "educationists" might go so far as to wonder aloud whether there was an inverse relationship between an individual's disciplinary mastery and depth of scholarship, on the one hand, and, on the other, his ability to teach his subject. They introduced ideas of complex variables concerning the "learner"—his various aptitudes, abilities, interests, motivations, needs, learning styles, attitudes, backgrounds, previous experiences—and developed scales and surveys to plot them. This challenged a long-held view: that knowledge and character alone determine a teacher's success. Implicitly or explicitly they undermined the academicians' ritual contention that all university professors were "in the business of teacher education." While their graduates often became teachers, they were seldom consciously prepared to do so unless the educationists had a hand in their educations.

They also attacked the school subjects as curriculum problems. To protect themselves from the ennui and suspicion of the disciplinary scholars, they prepared their own specialists in the psychology, sociology, history, and philosophy *of education*—recruiting, in most instances, their experts in these fields from among their own or other schools of education, not from academic departments. In the process

69. For a corrective view see Merle L. Borrowman, "Liberal Education and the Professional Preparation of Teachers," in Borrowman, ed., *Teacher Education,* esp. 1–6.

of building up their own supply of arcane knowledge of the sciences of curriculum-building and teaching, however, they intruded on the turf of all the other teachers in the university. At the same time that their very belonging in the university was in doubt, they implicitly questioned college professors' competence to give direction to teaching and learning in the elementary and secondary schools—and, perhaps, beyond them. They did so through their pedagogical, administrative, textbook-writing, and testing activities. Some professors of education courted danger still further—by becoming "experts on higher education," sometimes through taking as part of their jurisdiction the new junior college sector which was first developed as an extension of "lower education." Consider the daring of Charles Judd. Soon after his arrival at Chicago in 1909, he lectured the Association of Doctors of Philosophy on the problem of turning Ph.D's into efficient teachers. He maintained that it was a persisting problem because "form is neglected and often unrecognized in the eager pursuit of subject matter."[70]

Staking and Defending a Claim

It was not necessary that the faculty in each school of education be involved in the leadership of the movement to professionalize the academic study of education. The mere fact that it was going on, so visibly in such places as Teachers College, the University of Chicago, and Stanford made all schools, colleges, and departments something of Peck's Bad Boy. The organizational sources of certain academic quarrels are not difficult to discern. As early as the 1860s at the State University of Iowa, the Normal Department enrolled more students than did the Collegiate Department.[71] This alone could arouse the self-protective instincts of other professors. The creation of departments was part of the process by which a number of once-sectarian and small American colleges pursued the goal of becoming secular and large universities. Since, "by nature, the department in an American university was acquisitive," the traditional fields had to resent the effects of state licensing; it gave education courses some popularity with students since certificate holders were exempted from taking the teacher's examination or got other concessions that eased their journeys into careers.[72] Struggles over "student credit hours" in certain aca-

70. Charles Hubbard Judd, "The Department of Education in American Universities," *The School Review* 17, no. 9 (Nov. 1909): 608.

71. O'Leary, *An Inquiry,* 244.

72. Bledstein, *Professionalism,* 301.

demic departments led the Michigan faculty in 1908, for example, to reject various proposals of the Education Department. This was but one of many and recurring conflicts over resources.

Since all the departments in a graduate-oriented university are, moreover, in the business of preparing and trying to place future college and university faculty, the growth of professional schools could reduce the job prospects of new Ph.D.'s in traditional departments. In the "wide open elective system and the consequent scramble for students," the rivalry with the new chairs of pedagogy affected the competition for students and additional faculty positions.[73] Such contests became intense in the 1930s, when college positions were restricted by periodic budgetary crises.

In the competitions for student "headcount" and control over the preparation of secondary teachers, education professors criticized the "antiquated faculty psychology" and doctrine of formal discipline practiced in academic departments. "In the majority of institutions," Professor Frederick Bolton of the University of Washington charged in 1915, the method and techniques of teaching special subjects "is given by the academic departments and as a consequence in many cases the work is not of the best kind from the pedagogical point of view." He concluded that academics' offerings of "methods" courses were often given as an extra, did not count toward major requirements, and were only "welcomed as an opportunity to mortgage that much more of the student's time."[74] Many of his confreres in education would have strongly agreed.

This does not mean that education professors were necessarily satisfied with "normal school methods" or with the quality of the pedagogy curriculum that was intended to put their graduates in touch with their professional work. There was, for example, disagreement among them as to how teacher education should be structured, especially that part which constituted chiefly liberal and disciplinary education. The teachers college school of thought stressed the professionalization of subject matter: the presentation of *all* subject matter from the standpoint of effective teaching of children. It assumed faculty familiarity with procedures used in the professional curriculum and, perhaps, the demonstration with children in the training school. Other education faculty thought it essential that their students study side by side with those not preparing to teach, getting "contact and competi-

73. O'Leary, *An Inquiry,* 192.
74. Bolton, "Curricula," 839.

tion with students in other fields," as a "safeguard against inferiority complexes" among teaching candidates.[75]

But their own courses disappointed educationists as well. Bolton's survey concluded that confusion in the names of courses, course proliferation, and overspecialization were common. To illustrate this problem, he cited the example of a course called "The Question as a Measure of Efficiency of the Recitation." Bolton asked, "Is there sufficient material of an elementary character to justify a course open to all . . . on this topic?" He doubted that the subject qualified as more than a seminar topic.[76] There is merit, it would seem, in critic James Koerner's later assessment: that education was a victim of its own prosperity, growing faster as a profession than its knowledge could advance.[77] In this regard it responded as Flexner said the Harvard Graduate School of Business was forced to do: "Faced suddenly with the problem of training for business a thousand students—graduate students—the School had to manufacture a literature."[78]

Whatever disciplines the school of education might incorporate in educational studies were already the province of other academics. This left them only pedagogy as a unique possession. As was to be expected, academic faculty for their part repeatedly and insistently questioned the very existence, and sometimes even the possibility, of worthwhile, much less *essential,* knowledge in the art and science of teaching—aside from that which would be provided automatically by study of subject matter, which resided in common knowledge, and which came with experience. They repeatedly charged education professors with an excessive concern with "how" to teach, rather than "what" to teach. Had they known it, academics would have been pleased to quote the views on pedagogy of one of the most famous of history's pedagogues, Jan Amos Comenius: "puerilia illa mihi toties nauseata."[79]

Teachers College had been rejected as an aspirant member of the

75. Phelps, "What Is a Teachers College?," 184.

76. Bolton, "Curricula," 836.

77. James D. Koerner, *The Miseducation of American Teachers* (Boston: Houghton Mifflin, 1963), 28.

78. Flexner, *Universities,* 168. Flexner was referring specifically to the imitation of the law school in developing case books in business and to the rush to "do research" on business practices in order to have something to teach.

79. Roughly translated as "In my view those childish things are endlessly sickening"; quoted in William W. Brickman, "Power Conflicts and Crises in Teacher Education: Some Historical and International Perspectives," in *Responding to the Power*

Columbia University family, in 1892, because the subject of education did not exist. Academic critics continued to hold that view, despite the incorporation of work in pedagogy by many colleges and universities. In 1933, Committee Q of the American Association of University Professors reported on "Required Courses in Education." Its formation was, no doubt, occasioned in part by a perceived threat: "the movement that had been started in some quarters to extend such [professional training of high school teachers] to college and university teaching."[80]

The Committee's questionnaire had been sent to eighteen hundred teachers. The responses, received from 391 high school teachers who had graduated between 1924 and 1929, reiterated the widely heard charges of the superficiality, redundancy, and uselessness of most pedagogy courses. Responses from eighty-three headmasters or principals of private secondary schools showed that in only 20 percent of the cases was even lukewarm support given to courses in general or educational psychology, methods, and practice teaching—the best regarded parts of the education curriculum. "A decided majority of these men and women rate professional training as almost, if not entirely, negligible in importance, when compared with character, personality, general intelligence, and the mastery of subject matter."[81] The Committee acknowledged that subject matter departments sometimes failed "to fulfill their full duties in equipping teachers." The members attributed this failure to "local conditions that could, and should, be corrected"—rather than to "inherent weaknesses in the subject matter." (Such a particularistic explanation was not applied in the case of the failures of education programs.) Its survey satisfied the Committee, therefore, that the answer was "No!" to the more covert but alarming question: "Should the requirements of professional training be extended to college and university teaching?"

The more "academic" subjects of the education curriculum, such as the history and philosophy of education, continued to be offered in the first half of this period although they were widely reported by teachers to be of little direct utility.[82] They were credited, however,

---

Crises in Teacher Education, ed. Ayres Bagley (Washington, D.C.: Society of Professors of Education, 1971), 19.

80. Committee Q., "Required Courses in Education," *Bulletin of the American Association of University Professors* 9, no. 3 (March 1933): 173.

81. Ibid., 191.

82. Roscoe G. Linder, *An Evaluation of the Courses in Education of a State*

with enjoying "the benign favor of the scrupulous academic gods."[83] Committee Q recognized their low popularity with practitioners, however, and concluded that such courses would be better appreciated and of greater significance "if moved into the graduate schools, where they could be given a more substantial character." In general the Committee was more tolerant of education courses in the graduate program. This relative toleration constituted another incentive to schools of education to concentrate their activities at that level.

The Special Dilemma of the Doctoral Degrees

At Stanford, Harvard, Chicago, and probably the others, educationists perceived less distrust on campus toward training administrators.[84] To the extent that schools of education prepared professionals, here was a *safe* place. It turned out, however, that the attachment of advanced degrees to programs for ambitious professionals brought new scrutiny—especially intense if the end degree was the Ph.D. In 1930, 95 percent of the advanced degrees in education awarded were the master's degree; 4.4 percent were Ph.D. degrees; and a mere .06 percent the doctor of education (Ed.D.).[85] The early twentieth century appearance of the Ed.D. at Harvard, Berkeley, Stanford, and Teachers College promised, however, a greater degree of autonomy in setting and administering requirements, bringing, in theory, a reinvigorated professional emphasis. In 1935 the authors of the *National Survey of the Education of Teachers* hoped that the presence of the Ed.D. in twenty-two institutions represented professional preparation without the stress on traditional research.[86]

But the academic profession resisted the campaigns of professional schools to offer doctoral degrees independent of the administrative control of graduate schools, if the statement of the Committee on Graduate Instruction of the American Council on Education is representative. In 1934 the Committee's report recognized that "a fundamental distinction exists and should obtain between advanced

---

Teachers College by Teachers in Service Contributions to Education no. 664 (New York: Teachers College, 1935), 103.

83. Bolton, "Curricula," 838; Williamson, *Provisions for General Theory Courses,* 43n.

84. Sears and Henderson, *Cubberley of Stanford,* 71; Powell, *Uncertain Profession,* 53; Woodie T. White, "Decline of the Classroom," 145–74.

85. *National Survey,* 3: 450.

86. Ibid., 7: 139.

professional instruction and genuine graduate work in professional schools. The issue is raised as to whether professional degrees rather than graduate degrees should not be awarded for advanced professional work. Attention in this connection is drawn to the apparent trend in professional schools to abandon professional degrees."[87] The Committee questioned whether that trend was sound. It also concluded that "the close association of the professional schools and the university under a common administration of all graduate work would be reciprocally advantageous to all institutional units occupied with advanced work." Advanced studies in education had to respond more to academic folkways than to professional requirements.[88]

In its efforts to distinguish the degree program of school administrators from that of future researchers, the University of Minnesota tried to gain curricular independence before the doctorate. As part of a curriculum reorganization effort aimed at structuring professional education closer to the law school model, Dean Melvin Haggerty launched a battle in 1926 to acquire for education control over the master of education degree. "Such reorganization should give complete freedom to the faculty of the College of Education . . . for the mapping out of curricula for the training of public school workers of all sorts." He reminded President Lotus Coffman, formerly dean of the College of Education, that the education faculty did not have the autonomy that the Law School took for granted. Instead it was forced to submit "its curriculum for the professional training of public school administrators and teachers to a group of men [faculty of other colleges] who have no experience in this field and have no real interest in it."[89] The views of the dean of the graduate school prevailed over those of Dean Haggarty, and that battle was lost.

Many schools of education fought essentially the same battle at the level of the doctorate. Stanford instituted its Ed.D. degree in 1927, primarily with school administrators and master teachers in mind. It was initially successful in developing the degree program under the control of the education school, not the graduate school. Columbia and Harvard differentiated their Ph.D. and Ed.D. degrees chiefly by administrative separation: the Ph.D. was controlled by the arts and sciences faculty, the Ed.D. by the education school.

At Berkeley, however, where the Ed.D. was in place by 1921, the "shared authority" in awarding the doctor of education degree was

87. Hughes, "Report," 232.

88. B. Othanel Smith, *Design for a School of Pedagogy,* 15.

89. Beck, *Beyond Pedagogy,* 82–83.

technical at best; the education school had little more control over the Ed.D. than over the Ph.D. Nor did the professional degree break much new ground. Three decades after Berkeley established the nation's second Ed.D. program, a University committee reported to the president that the establishment of a Field Service Center finally "would make it possible to differentiate more sharply the programs leading to the Ed.D. and to the Ph.D. degree, candidates for the former degree obviously participating in considerably more of this field service."[90] The Center *did* appear but not the hoped-for differentiation of the degrees.

A decade later the American Association of Colleges for Teacher Education was still being exhorted about "the critical importance of differentiating sharply between the two degrees . . . so that the requirements and curricular designs of each would reflect the intended difference."[91] The foreign language requirement was eliminated from the Ed.D. before 1930 at California, Harvard, and Johns Hopkins, and professional experience was required at various places, including Stanford. It was proving impossible, however, for either party on elite campuses to acknowledge candidly that curricular issues and definitions of "standards" were inextricably entangled in prestige issues: the high prestige of research when compared to professional practice, and the low relative status of education and whatever degrees were attached to *its* name.

While others of the leading schools of education multiplied their degree options and tried to create rational distinctions between vocational and academic needs, Chicago stood firm. The faculty reiterated its unwillingness even to suggest that Chicago might qualify the requirement that candidates must produce "a piece of research comparable to the research required in any other department of the University for the Ph.D. degree."[92]

Harvard also affirmed that all doctoral dissertations produce "research results of general and lasting value." A representative Harvard statement about the relation of the doctoral program to its students' career objectives was that "the attempt to meet their needs as

90. University of California, "Report of the President's Committee on Programs in Education," 29. Field Service Centers were created to contract with school districts or other agencies to provide paid, expert services, performed by graduate students or faculty members.

91. American Association of Colleges for Teacher Education, *The Doctorate in Education,* vol. 1, *The Graduates* (Washington, D.C.: AACTE, 1960), 14–15.

92. Frank N. Freeman, *Practices of American Universities in Granting Higher Degrees in Education,* 19th Yearbook of the National Society of College Teachers of Education (Chicago: University of Chicago Press, 1931), 53.

prospective professional workers is strictly incidental, their programs being designed in every case to follow the lead of the lines of thought and investigation they have chosen."[93] Yet Harvard also elected to develop the Ed.D. and declared it "centered wholly in the solution of educational problems."

This approach satisfied almost no one. A comparative examination of the topics of Harvard's Ed.D. and Teachers College's Ph.D. dissertations in the 1920s concluded that any differences "derived much more from the differing size and character of the two institutions than from any fundamental difference in the problematics they embodied."[94] Meanwhile, the slippery differences between the two Harvard doctorates confused all concerned and, by the 1930s, Harvard saw the popularity of its own Ed.D. degree decline as that degree appeared in other institutions as an alternative doctoral degree.[95] The gap between Teachers College and Harvard widened and Iowa and Ohio State pushed ahead of Harvard by 1932. Doctorates in education declined steadily as a percentage of all Harvard doctorates awarded: from 11 percent in the period 1925–29 to 2.7 percent a decade later.[96] Teachers College added the Ed.D. in 1934, and the products covered a similarly wide range of topics, from the theoretical to the applied—wider, indeed, than elsewhere because of the exceptionally large size of that institution.

In his 1934 survey, Theodore Reller found little evidence of lowered standards in doctoral programs by the substitution of experience for some portion of university study or by other actions recognizing education's fundamental status as a professional field of study. Instead, his results suggested that the problem lay in the difficulty of differentiating the Ed.D. from the Ph.D.—in the programs of study or in the career destinations of recipients. Differentiation already presented a dogged challenge, a "target of opportunity" for the critics on campus. Stanford reported that nearly a third of its Ed.D. students later petitioned to switch to the Ph.D. option.[97] It is debatable whether this was due to the slightly greater difficulty in obtaining the Ed.D., as the

93. Ibid., 109–10.

94. Cremin, "The 'Education' of Educating Professions," 15.

95. Theodore L. Reller, "A Survey of the Requirements for the Degree of Doctor of Education," *School and Society* 39, no. 1008 (21 April 1934): 518; Powell, *Uncertain Profession,* 202.

96. Harmon and Soldz, *Doctorate Production,* 20.

97. Freeman, *Practices of American Universities,* 144. For a discussion of Stanford's experience see Lewis B. Mayhew et al., *Educational Leadership and Declining Enrollments* (Berkeley: McCutchan, 1974), 38–40.

school claimed, or to the greater prestige of the Ph.D. But it seemed obvious that the programs, qualifications, and requirements were sufficiently similar to permit ready transfer. Yale tried another tack. Its education department abandoned "atomistic" specialization and preoccupation with methodology in favor of breadth, "humanized knowledge," and the "social function which its graduates would perform."[98] Clearly it was becoming progressively more difficult to define what a doctorate in education actually represented. This, along with decreased emphasis upon pedagogy and growing specialization, fueled the exasperation that lay behind the question sometimes posed by faculty in other departments: "What *is* it that you folks *do* over there?"

Because major schools of education became places emphasizing advanced degrees for the credentialing of educational researchers or school executives, they predominantly enrolled experienced professionals—persons who had learned their technical skills (except for research methods) on the job. This cut away much of the ground for what Dean Russell had called the technique of the art of the practitioner, and which he considered an essential component in any professional school's curriculum. Lawrence Cremin calls the resulting process of fragmentation and incoherence at Teachers College one of "devolution," a process that was essentially completed by 1940. What he has written of Teachers College probably describes the situation in many other schools of education:

> The requirement of special scholarship . . . was not included in the requirement for the Ed.D., and . . . was abandoned as a requirement for the Ph.D. before too long. The requirement of professional knowledge was more resolutely honored than any other, but only a minimal core of common work in the history, philosophy, and psychology of education was insisted upon. And the requirement of technical skill was acknowledged rhetorically but neither honored nor enforced programmatically.[99]

The prevailing curricular approach at its sister institutions became some variant of that adopted at Teachers College: to make a virtue of near anarchy in the name of individualization. This meant designing a program of studies that accepted each student's *prior* preparation (itself highly varied, unlike that of medical or engineering school graduates, for example), professional experience, and personal

98. Brubacher et al., *Department of Education,* 24, 28.
99. Cremin, "The 'Education' of Educating Professions," 16.

ambition. This reduced the strain on the institution's diminished capacity to agree upon the desiderata of competence and knowledge in professional education and on how to achieve them. However, this also made it every year more difficult to obtain some national consensus on what an advanced degree in education stood for in the programmatic sense.[100] In this regard, too, schools of education bore scant resemblance to the law or medical school *ideal* that the pioneer generation of university professors had in mind.

The Additional Stigma of Sex

Gender has been recognized only sotto voce as a factor in the low relative status of schools of education in academe. Yet, it was a chronic threat to their prestige on university campuses, especially at those private and public universities which thought exceptionally well of themselves. Women were the majority of practitioners in this period—reaching a high point in 1920 when they were 85 percent of all elementary and secondary school teachers. "Didactics," the early label for the art and science of teaching, had long since been considered a "womanly" subject. In 1864, when only a few of America's colleges were coeducational, the President of Harvard College told the National Teachers' Association (forerunner of the National Education Association) that didactics should be taught in those colleges which admit young women to their courses and in those schools which are designed only for young women.[101] The homilies of his successor, President Charles W. Eliot, that were addressed to the Radcliffe women emphasized teaching.[102] At Berkeley, however, President Benjamin Ide Wheeler responded to the threat of "race suicide" that spinster teachers reportedly posed when they chose careers over domestic life. Accordingly he warned the women of his university, "You are not here with the ambition to be school teachers or old maids; but you are here for the preparation of marriage and motherhood."[103]

Many Americans were persuaded to accept women as teachers of young schoolchildren by the argument that it was a modest extension

100. Ibid., 17.

101. Thomas Hill, "Remarks on the Study of Didactics in Colleges," *American Journal of Education* 15, no. 38 (March 1865): 179.

102. Hawkins, *Between Harvard and America,* 256.

103. Quoted in Clifford, "Dangerous Questions," 44. Despite a faculty committee recommendation to the contrary, Wheeler established a home economics department in evident sympathy with the "back to the home" movement that motivated conservative supporters of home economics as a field of study.

of women's natural domestic role as the first teacher of the child in the home. Yet, as schoolmistresses' ambitions and careerism mounted, some found the effects "unlovely." As sympathetic an observer as William James, persuaded to lecture to teachers as a source of extra income, wrote privately to his wife about the lack of stimulation or pleasure this offered. "I have never seen more women and less beauty, heard more voices and less sweetness, perceived more earnestness and less triumph that I ever supposed possible."[104]

Men responded variously as women assumed more influence over American cultural life, challenged men in the political sphere, and pressed their quest for fuller access to all employment. Male strategies included efforts to perfect a rougher masculine culture and to protect masculine institutions. This was no less true in education than in other realms. The *Educational Review,* edited by a founder of Teachers College, Columbia University's President Nicholas Murray Butler, published several articles on "the woman peril" in American education. Records of the Appointments Committee (teachers' employment bureau) at Ohio State showed a repeated and "pronounced prejudice" against hiring women teachers for the high schools in the period around 1910.[105] Between 1895 and 1920 there was a general reaction against women's dominance of teaching, even stronger efforts to resist their push to enter higher-status professions including school administration, and opposition to women's growing share of college and university enrollments.

The Menace of the Female Student

In 1920 *The Harvard Alumni Bulletin* consoled its readers that the creation of the Graduate School of Education "was no occasion to consider these students the vanguard of a feminine army determined to invade every department of the university."[106] For over two hundred years American higher education had been an all-male preserve, but, by 1900, women were 40 percent of all undergraduates. To blunt the demand of women for Harvard degrees, University trustees and officials created Radcliffe College in 1894, as a "coordinate college" for women. Next, in 1902, they authorized Radcliffe to grant the Ph.D.,

104. Quoted in Charles, "Expectation vs. Reality," 30.

105. Good, *College of Education,* 82.

106. "Quotations: Women in the Harvard Graduate School of Education," *School and Society* (16 October 1920): 348–49.

deflecting the pressures from women graduate students to enter Harvard University.[107]

Helen Olin, in her book *The Women of a State University* (1909) noted the "new generation of beards wagging ominously over the seriousness of the situation."[108] They wagged far and wide, in as diverse places as medical and journalism schools. The former set strict quotas on women students after about 1910, a limitation effectively reinforced by the growing practice adopted by hospitals of accepting no female interns.[109] More recent arrivals on campus, journalism schools discovered their "woman peril" only later, of course. To keep his institution "from going feminine," the dean of the Journalism School of Syracuse University set a quota in 1937. "Wisconsin almost destroyed itself a few years ago when it allowed itself to be overrun with women," he warned. "Other schools have had a like experience."[110]

Economic change heightened the sense of eroding manliness as farm and other heavy work declined and office jobs, in increasingly bureaucratic organizations, made it seem harder "to be a man."[111] One advantage of the newer behavioral and social sciences over the humanities was that they were considered more "manly." Early in the twentieth century this gave "brass instruments" psycho-physics, which Chicago's Charles Judd especially admired, a distinct advantage over "arm chair" philosophy, the field from which psychology was fleeing. There was a lesson here for the new, status-anxious schools of education and their male clientele. When women reached, by 1928–29, "an alarming and unacceptable" 54 percent of the Harvard Graduate School of Education, the faculty discussed eliminating course credits and building a business school–like "esprit de corps." These were part of an aborted effort to prevent women entirely from getting Harvard degrees.[112] Heavy requirements of statistics courses not only reflected the prevailing view of what "science" meant, it also could be

107. Solomon, *Educated Women,* 134.

108. Olin, *Women,* 177.

109. Mary Roth Walsh, *Doctors Wanted, No Women Need Apply: Sexual Barriers in the Medical Profession, 1835–1975* (New Haven: Yale University Press, 1977).

110. Harvey Strum, "Discrimination at Syracuse University," *History of Higher Education Annual* 4 (1984): 111.

111. Peter Filene, *Him, Her, Self: Sex Roles in Modern America* (New York: Harcourt, Brace, Jovanovich, 1974), 77. See also Joe L. Dubbert, "Progressivism and the Masculinity Crisis," in *The American Man,* ed. Elizabeth H. Pleck and Joseph H. Pleck, (Englewood Cliffs, N.J.: Prentice-Hall, 1980), 303–19.

112. Harvard Committee, *Graduate Study,* 86; Powell, 1980, *Uncertain Profession,* 169.

used to discourage women—and the "feminized males" associated with prolonged careers in teaching—from cluttering up the graduate programs and further debasing the School's campus image.

Not surprising then that, despite the large base of women prepared nationally at the baccalaureate level for teaching, their graduate enrollments conformed to the steep-sided pyramid characteristic of the gender picture in higher education generally: women were a minority at the master's degree level and a still-smaller proportion at the doctoral level. In a field where financial assistance was very hard to come by, women found it almost impossible to receive fellowships for graduate study. Also, marriage virtually barred women from such consideration; not until 1929 did the American Association of University Women award one of its fellowships to a married woman student.[113]

Compared to other fields, however, the presence of women in many graduate programs in education—where single women predominated until after World War II—was sufficiently large to arouse sexist concerns. The profiles of female participation in graduate education had resembled that of the social sciences generally until the years of the Great Depression, when women's share of doctorates in education climbed sharply. Nationally, in 1920, forty men and eight women received doctorates in education; the figures climbed to 368 and 96 respectively by the end of this formative period. As a result, the percentage of doctorates in education awarded to women went from 15 percent in 1920 to nearly 22 percent in 1940.[114] In comparison, the percentage of women receiving doctorates in all fields remained close to fifteen percent during this twenty-year period. Many contemporary observers must have thought that women's participation in education would continue this upward trend, and both individuals and groups were undoubtedly alarmed at the prospect—especially in economic hard times when so many male doctorates felt underemployed and threatened, and their professors, almost all males, would undoubtedly at least be sympathetic.

It was not, however, a simple matter of direct competition be-

113. Solomon, *Educated Women,* 138.

114. Harmon and Soldz, *Doctorate Production,* 49–53. The increasing share that was going to women reached its peak during the years of World War II and then fell sharply, as it did in other fields, losing almost all of the gain made. The general upturn in women's share of American doctorates began again after 1955. It would be useful to learn if the increase in doctorates to women during the 1930s was related to the activities of the National Youth Administration, which gave grants and work-study funds to women college students on almost equal terms with men. Solomon, *Educated Women,* 148.

tween the sexes for the same positions, as women's graduate degrees in education were disproportionately concentrated in such "female-intensive" fields as elementary education and home economics. There existed in education the counterpart of the movement to direct women scientists into home economics and women doctorates into such roles as dean of girls in high schools and dean of women in colleges and universities.

"Teaching usually belittles a man; his daily dealing is with petty things, of interest only to his children and a few women assistants," wrote C. W. Bardeen, the author of "Why Teaching Repels Men," but executive officers, superintendents, and principals of large schools are "brought into business contact with the world and show it."[115] As school administration positions went increasingly to graduates of university programs, the percentages of women administrators dropped steadily. Even in the elementary school principalship, women's share went from 61.7 percent in 1905 to 19.6 percent in 1972.[116] In the Catholic parochial schools, too, where members of women's religious orders made up almost all of the elementary school teachers, men exercised administrative direction of local schools through their total control of the ecclesiastical hierarchy; male clergy ruled the National Catholic Educational Association as well.[117]

Gender was sometimes acknowledged as a factor in the status of education schools on campus. At Columbia and Harvard opposition surfaced when it was understood that women would be brought into the university through education. After the affiliation of Columbia and Teachers College, the boundary, 120th Street was called by the Columbia men "hairpin alley"—as well as "the widest street in the world."[118] At Stanford quotas had been established on women applicants for undergraduate places; various other devices were employed at the graduate level. Frank Freeman's 1931 study, *Practices of American Universities in Granting Higher Degrees in Education,* said of Stanford: "On account of the restrictions on number, the selection of

115. C. W. Bardeen, "Why Teaching Repels Men," *Educational Review* 35 (April 1908): 355.

116. Tyack and Hansot, *Managers of Virtue,* 183.

117. An early indicator of feminist restiveness at this situation of male domination was the remark of Dr. Mary Molloy (later Sister Mary Aloysius), dean of the College of St. Teresa in Minnesota, to the NCEA convention in Buffalo in 1917. See Karen Kennelly, C.S.J., "Mary Molloy, Women's College Founder," in *Women of Minnesota: Selected Biographical Essays,* ed. Barbara Stuhler and Gretchen Kreuter (St. Paul: Minnesota Historical Society Press, 1977), 129.

118. Cremin, Shannon, and Townsend, *History,* 21, 70.

women is really very rigid. Data on scholarship, aptitude, character, and experience are collected and carefully evaluated. About one-fourth of the applicants are finally admitted. Similar data are collected and evaluated for men, but entrance is denied to a much smaller proportion."[119]

Harvard combatted "creeping feminization" by limiting work available in elementary education and by longer courses of study, until some means could be found to make women ineligible altogether for degrees. It was understood that women's numbers should not exceed some "intuitive critical mass."[120] At Chicago that meant avoiding the graduates of teachers colleges; Judd called them the "immature girls who have had no contact with the great industrial machinery of modern life."[121] To teach future administrators and school leaders was to contain "the woman problem" because the school administration fraternity had learned the strategies by which to close that field to aspiring women.[122] Other "female-intensive" fields also recruited and promoted men into administration, to protect their incomes and prestige from the full effects of "feminization." Library and social welfare schools, and the subordination of university nursing schools to medical schools, furnish clear parallels.

Women on the Faculty in Schools of Education

Because the professoriate was one of the fastest growing professions, even before 1900, might not women graduate students in schools of education aspire to join their faculties on completion of their training? Apparently not. Writing in 1910, Helen Olin commented on what she found were prevailing attitudes toward women in graduate education in the progressive state of Wisconsin. As preparation for academic positions, she observed that teaching as a field for women "would be recommended as generally useful in high schools, normal schools, and even women's colleges. It would be acceptable in infinitesimal

119. Freeman, *Practices of American Universities,* 138. Interestingly, the author concluded that discrimination did not result.

120. Powell, *Uncertain Profession,* 154–55, 169, 284.

121. Judd, "Teachers Colleges," 880. A half-century later, after the Soviet Sputnik was launched, university-based, self-styled reformers tried to push through school innovations premised on a similar belief: that the problem could be traced "to inadequate personnel who were insulated from the larger society, the world of ideas, and the educational implications of the scientific revolution." Seymour B. Sarason, *Schooling in America: Scapegoat and Salvation* (New York: Free Press, 1983), 18.

122. Tyack and Hansot, *Managers of Virtue.*

quantities in higher coeducational institutions providing a woman would do a man's work for one-half his salary, in a position given no authority or influence in the control of the department."[123]

Statistical distributions of women teachers appear to bear out Olin's cynicism. United States Bureau of Education questionnaires reported women's share of positions reaching highs of 67.3 percent in public normal schools in 1920 and 65.9 percent in state teachers' colleges in 1910.[124] The figures were still higher for women faculty in women's colleges, being between 71 percent and 80 percent in the years from 1900 to 1940. Therefore, the prospects for women's academic employment darkened with the steady reductions in numbers of women's colleges and the upgrading of normal schools to state teachers colleges and then to multipurpose colleges and universities. One statistical analysis calculates that the changing institutional mix within American higher education—notably the demise of normal schools and most women's colleges—accounts for some two-thirds of the changes between 1900 and 1940 in the proportion that women represented in the professoriate.[125]

An alternative door by which women might gain entry into the faculties of coeducational colleges and universities opened, however, when a college or university created a program, department, or professional school in which women would be the majority of students. These were places where the subject matter or the career objectives were considered congenial to women's innate characteristics or probable destinies in life, fields in which women were "expected to assume responsibility for the 'primary care' of the most unrewarding and disorderly of clienteles: the young, the poor, the intemperate, the sick."[126] The formation of a normal or pedagogy course to train

123. Olin, *Women,* 292–93.

124. Susan B. Carter, "Academic Women Revisited: An Empirical Study of Changing Patterns of Women's Employment as College and University Faculty, 1890–1963," *Journal of Social History* 14, no. 4 (Summer 1981): 675–99; Lucille A. Pollard, *Women on College and University Faculties: A Historical Survey and a Study of Their Present Academic Status* (New York: Arno Press, 1977), 189–90.

125. The proportion of *total* U.S. faculty employed in women's colleges, normal schools, and teachers colleges declined from 21.4 percent in 1930 to 13.2 percent by 1940. Carter, "Academic Women Revisited," 681.

126. Joan Jacobs Brumberg and Nancy Tomes, "Women in the Professions: A Research Agenda for American Historians," *Reviews in American History* 10, no. 1 (June 1982): 288. For a brief period in the late nineteenth century, women gained a foothold in medicine, partly on the logic that it was more appropriate for them to care for certain female ills and partly because the unreformed medical professions was too weak to resist them. In the twentieth century this latter condition changed.

teachers was the earliest example of the acceptance of such a logic in a university setting. If the institution could find the means, the appearance of departments of domestic science, women's physical culture, librarianship, social work, and later public health and nursing were fairly certain to reflect the growth in numbers of women students and, hence, be the occasion to add women to the faculty.[127]

In higher-status universities, however, women's share of faculty positions never approached those of the women's colleges, the normal schools, or the teachers' colleges. The peak reached by Harvard University's faculty women in this period was 1.3 percent of the total faculty in 1940; theirs was consistently the lowest figure among our ten institutions. Minnesota's figure was the highest, women there becoming 24.2 percent of the university's faculty in 1930.[128] Compare this with the picture for all of American higher education: from 1900 to 1960, the proportion of women faculty has varied from 20 percent to 37 percent.

In *The Academic Marketplace,* Caplow and McGee characterize discrimination against women in the academic profession, while "not peculiar to the academic world," as operating such that "women scholars are not taken seriously and cannot look forward to a normal professional career."[129] In schools of education women also found themselves "outside the prestige system entirely." Committee W (on the Status of Women) of the American Association of University Professors reported in 1921 that there were 9 women and 190 men holding full professorships in education; among instructors, however, there were 43 women and 38 men.[130] The more prestigious the university, the more likely that rank and salary discrimination against women flourished.

Events had begun more auspiciously. In 1892 President Harper recruited Julia Buckley as Chicago's first professor of education, and sent her to Europe for graduate study.[131] Marion Talbot, dean of women at the University of Chicago, recalled that "in 1901 the organization of the School of Education brought a considerable addition of

127. Geraldine Jonçich Clifford, ed., *Lone Voyagers: Academic Women in American Coeducational Universities, 1869–1937* (New York: Feminist Press, 1988).

128. Carter, "Academic Women Revisited," 682.

129. Theodore Caplow and Reece J. McGee, *The Academic Marketplace* (New York: Science Editions, 1961), 111–12.

130. A. Caswell Ellis, "Preliminary Report of Committee W, on Status of Women in College and University Faculties," *Bulletin of the American Association of University Professors* 7, no. 62 (October 1921): 23.

131. Wechsler, "Primary Journal," 91.

women to the teaching staff" of the University.[132] As these normal school women inherited from Colonel's Parker's Cook County Normal School retired, however, their positions went to men or were closed.[133] Women's overall presence on the Chicago faculty declined, from a high of 22.5 percent in 1910 to 10.3 percent in 1940. This ran counter to a pattern of modest increases at some other leading private and public universities—especially at the land-grant institutions after the 1920s, with their growing programs in "women's fields."[134] Even in these fields, however, promotion rates of women faculty were consistently slower than for males, although they were better in departments where their numbers were greater. Corinne Seeds of the UCLA School of Education, who taught some 30,000 students who became teachers, elementary school supervisors, and curriculum experts in a career that stretched from 1928 to 1957, was made professor only on the eve of her retirement.[135]

At Minnesota, after ten years as a University High School English teacher and supervisor of student teachers, Dora V. Smith was appointed assistant professor in teacher education; a few other women dotted the large faculty. It occasioned much comment when Yale hired a woman to its new Education Department faculty in 1920, but Yale never repeated that experiment; the closing of the Department foreclosed that possibility entirely. Jesse Sears' account of Stanford under Cubberley speaks always of the men of the faculty. Harvard University had a similar taboo against women faculty, and the education school had enough problems without trying to nominate women to its faculty.

132. Marion Talbot, *More Than Lore: Reminiscences* (Chicago: University of Chicago Press, 1936), 133.

133. Woodie T. White, "Decline of the Classroom," 167.

134. An examination of the twenty universities with the largest proportion of women among their faculties in the mid-1970s found fifteen of them to be schools granting unusually large proportions of their bachelors degrees in the fields of education, home economics, letters, library science, and social work. Margaret Gordon and Clark Kerr, "University Behavior and Policies: Where Are the Women and Why?" in *The Higher Education of Women: Essays in Honor of Rosemary Park* ed. Helen S. Astin and Werner Z. Hirsch (New York: Praeger, 1978), 124.

Unlike the situation with academic women in general, those in education did not have appreciably higher social status backgrounds than their male counterparts if data on present education faculty are a reliable guide. See Carla Sue Weidman and John C. Weidman, "Professors of Education: Some Social and Occupational Characteristics," in *The Professor of Education: An Assessment of Conditions,* ed. Ayres Bagley (Papers of the meeting of the Society of Professors of Education, College of Education, University of Minnesota, October 1971), 88.

135. Treacy, "Progressivism and Corinne Seeds," 89.

At Berkeley women were occasionally appointed as lecturers to prepare future teachers of home economics and clerical subjects, and as supervisors of some facets of student teaching; most served briefly. Apparently only one, Dr. Edna Bailey of the University High School faculty, was put on the professorial ladder and then promoted to tenure in 1927; no other woman moved upward through the tenure ranks until 1967. Ohio State had some nationally prominent women on its increasingly large faculty, notably Luela Cole and Laura Zirbes, but typically women held nonprofessorial titles such as supervisor of practice teaching. They were also found disproportionately in the teaching of art, music, and domestic science departments of the College of Education.

Women had such a low presence, nationwide, in departments of education that a 1924 study of women's status on university faculties in academic departments only, decided to include education in order "to get at the workings of the masculine mind of those occupying our chairs of education."[136] Among our sample of institutions, Teachers College was the one best hope for the academic woman in leading schools of education; by 1950, 36 percent of the faculty were women.[137] When Lindley J. Stiles of the University of Wisconsin surveyed schools of education about their programs and resources in teacher education, for the Association of Land-Grant Colleges and Universities around 1961, his questionnaire asked only about the "present number of men on the faculty." If he assumed there would be no women to report he was not far wrong, even for teacher education. In their response to the "woman problem" at least, school of education faculty were in accord with the rest of the university. Yet this was a joining of prejudices more than a meeting of minds.

Conclusion

Professors of education, like professors in general, experienced success in becoming "professionalized," in the sense that Jencks and Riesman use the term: being more colleague-oriented than client-oriented, more concerned with the opinion of one's fellow practitioners than

136. Ella Lonn, "Academic Status of Women on University Faculties," *Journal of American Association of University Women* 17, no. 1 (Jan.–March 1924): 6.

137. Cremin, Shannon, and Townsend, *History,* 245. One of the most interesting of the Teachers College women was Mabel Carney, who took a special interest in the minority and women students and was active in the College's programs in Africa. See Goodenow and Cowen, American School of Education and the Third World in the Twentieth Century," 279–81.

with approval by laymen, more rewarded for talk than for action. Yet mutual understanding and parity of esteem did not result from their shared development of the professoriate in competition with the interests of parties outside the university. It appears difficult to refute Stephen Hazlett's notion that the survival of schools, colleges, and departments of education may depend more on their functions than on their purpose.[138] These functions included performing necessary but unwanted administrative tasks in connection with the state's interests in public education, attracting large numbers of upwardly mobile and sometimes marginal students into universities which needed their numbers to pay for more prestigious activities like faculty research and doctoral education, and preparing them for the socially vital but marginally respected services attendant on mass schooling.

At this point it may be instructive to employ some further comparisons with other professional schools, especially those that could not pretend to have their roots in the medieval universities, as did law, medicine, and theology—professions that did not automatically add to a university's prestige through their affiliation with it. For example, leading university engineering schools also became interested in developing the skills befitting future professors of engineering, assuming that these skills would also be useful to practicing engineers.[139] Representative American business schools enjoyed, until the 1970s, what Schlossman and Sedlak call an "age of criticism-free autonomy." Without achieving either autonomy or recognition, their counterparts in education pursued some of the same interconnected strategies employed by business schools. These included a broader curriculum that emphasized academic approaches or "applied social science" over functional specialization, the diversion of resources to graduate programs preparing for research careers at the expense of undergraduate "vocational" training, creating personal networks that enabled their advanced-degree holders to step into executive positions in the field, and curtailing the numbers of women in their programs.

Most nineteenth-century physicians and lawyers learned their trade through apprenticeships. Teachers, too, had not rushed to enroll in the normal schools; most were content to learn their poorly paid and often briefly practiced craft on the job. In the next century, however, state requirements filled the teachers colleges and universities

138. J. Stephen Hazlett, "Education Professors: The Centennial of an Identity Crisis" (Paper presented at the annual meeting of the American Educational Research Association, San Francisco, April 1986), 17.

139. Jencks and Riesman, *Academic Revolution,* 253.

with students, just as the growing prosperity of their patients enhanced the appeal of the medical schools for aspiring physicians, and the rise of modern corporations created lucrative new opportunities for ambitious lawyers. Emulating law and medicine, education schools made efforts to recruit more "raw A.B.'s" to graduate pedagogy programs but were frustrated by teaching's low salaries and the larger society's willingness to secure teachers cheaply.[140] Even when advanced education promised a better paying and more prestigious specialization, the insecurity bred in them by their class origins and the trauma of the Great Depression ensured that most education graduate students would be debtridden part-timers, loath to abandon the security of their jobs. The pattern of part-time study was to persist.

The doyens of professional pedagogy accepted the demise of independent normal schools and teachers colleges, just as the custodians of medical, theological, and engineering education were closing their separate institutions. They all did so in favor of linking their futures with the universities' ambitions, creating other reference groups than practitioners against which to measure how well they were doing. It was especially incumbent on schools that enrolled many poor students and which rarely produced wealthy alumni—like divinity schools and normal schools—to join forces with and partake of the resources of larger and stronger institutions. Even relatively secure Teachers College affiliated with Columbia and, much later, George Peabody College for Teachers joined with Vanderbilt University. It was too difficult to prosper alone, especially given the higher costs associated with graduate education and a research-oriented faculty. Moreover, affiliation with a university gives a professional school's faculty some protection from the "provincialism of the field"—whether it be doctoring, preaching, or teaching. Representatives of the public eagerly endorsed this co-mingling of institutional types, believing that the multipurpose university, like the comprehensive high school, was "more efficient, more productive, and more democratic than was separatism."[141]

If they looked about them at the other professional schools on their campuses, education faculty could well have taken comfort in

140. Nathan Glazer ("The Schools," 356–57) points out that, although medical research workers and perhaps legal scholars *might* have the edge on practitioners in terms of relative status, the much higher income potential of practitioners certainly evens the score. This situation did not, of course, apply in the relations between education professors and school teachers.

141. Jencks and Riesman, *Academic Revolution,* 215, 231.

their own course of action. What they would have seen were other professional programs that were often "not particularly useful and in fact, not even vocational." The divorce from professional issues was everywhere marked, especially in graduate professional programs.[142] Nor was it simply a matter of the slower growth of dependable knowledge in the highly complex, socially interactive, politically afflicted phenomena that constitute education. Examination of other fields suggests that the relationship of knowledge to professionalization is varying, inconsistent, also complex, and not yet fully studied.

But the similar evolution of more independent and prestigious professional schools, with their much smaller numbers of practitioners or their economically more powerful alumni to call upon, could not in itself secure the shaky status of education schools. There was little comfort in the knowledge that, for all their centuries of experience, academics were also baffled about teaching. Little comfort in the fact that other professional schools—of business, medicine, engineering, and even scientific research—also found little correlation between grades in professional schools and success on the job.[143] Little comfort in the sociologists' conclusion that the legal or medical practitioner's status is as closely related to his client's social position as to his own developed skills.[144] Nor would there have been much consolation in the news that, as professors of education, they combined the ambiguous, if not consistently unflattering, status of both the teacher *and* of the professor. As we discussed in chapter 1, American society has long manifested a strong streak of anti-intellectualism. In popular culture this was often expressed as ridicule of both teachers *and* professors.[145] Even the incumbents in the "learned professions" might agree with the Chicago attorney who acknowledged, in 1902, that "we all . . . feel a sort of contempt . . . for our academic brothers out at the university—we can't help it."[146]

Yet, for all they knew, they, in education, were alone culpable. All

142. Ernest A. Lynton, "Universities in Crisis," (Paper prepared for the Directorate of Social Affairs, Manpower and Education, Organization for Economic Cooperation and Development; Center for Studies in Policy and the Public Interest, University of Massachusetts at Boston, n.d.) 13.

143. Jencks and Riesman, *Academic Revolution,* 203–5, 241.

144. Larson, *Professionalism,* xi–xii.

145. In today's mass media, as in earlier popular culture, teachers and professors are typically portrayed as failures in love and defeated in life, good but ineffectual or evil eccentrics; in either case they are the butts of the society's jokes, humiliated and depressed in the telling. Gerbner, "Teacher Image," 66–92.

146. Quoted in Auerbach, "Enmity and Amity," 569.

that education faculty were told by teachers, academics, and newspaper editors was that their theory and even their methods courses did not much matter. As for their "science of education," it was likely to be linked with the pretensions of sociologists and the "mumbo-jumbo" of other fakirs. Estrangements from the field, the unreconciled differences and new tensions in the relationship of education schools to their universities, and the jaundiced view of the molders of public opinion would darken the prospects of schools of education in the future. In the next section we will bring our story and our analysis up to the late years of the twentieth century. In so doing we will encounter both continuity and change, prosperity and pain.

3 The Years of Maturity

Five Riding a Roller Coaster, 1955–85

The period of campus unrest was marked by struggles within schools of education between the partisans of collegiate interests and those of social interests. In the school world, teachers and school administrators were skirmishing with one another and the public. And, not least in importance, there was a growing contentiousness between majority and minority cultural interests. "Crises" in education, while numerous, often appear prosaic in comparison, for example, with those in the practice of medicine. "The state of ordinariness or normalcy which typically surrounds educational issues obscures the vital function that education is providing in the long term," notes Dean Patricia Graham of Harvard's Graduate School of Education. "Rarely is there a clear moment when education has failed; rather, there is a gradual accumulation of evidence providing concern about the quality of our youngsters' education."[1] Despite its lack of dramatic incidents, education is daily implicated in society's contentiousness, the public schools being microcosms of local communities in social and cultural transition. A reason for the vagueness of schooling's multiple goals is, after all, "in part to keep conflicting stakeholders at bay."[2]

The post–World War II years imposed numerous challenges on America's educational system and some on the universe of schools of education to which schooling was loosely connected. The number and variety of irritants almost defy belief. They include the strains placed

1. Patricia Albjerg Graham, "Memorandum to the Faculty," Harvard Graduate School of Education, 1985, p. 2.

2. Michael Huberman, "Recipes for Busy Kitchens," 490.

on the system by the baby boom and resulting shortages of classrooms, materials, and trained teachers; the scathing attacks on the "pedagogical mindlessness" of progressive education from scholastic fundamentalists; the tensions of the West's "cold war" with the communist bloc that linked the triumphant launching of the Soviet Sputnik in 1957 to alleged inadequacies in American public education; the sometimes violent struggles over school desegregation that followed the Supreme Court's decision in the Brown v. Topeka Board of Education case in 1954; the growth of teacher militancy and collective bargaining, taxpayer revolts in the context of inflation, the Vietnam war, and antiwar protest; and then a "baby bust" that forced first schools and then colleges into painful and divisive contractions.[3] The period was marked by particularly abrupt and often short-lived changes of course—for example, from a relaxation of requirements to the mandating of a core curriculum.

All schools, colleges, and departments of education were shaken to some degree by these events, with the leading schools presenting the largest targets. This chapter will trace the effects of some of the general, society-wide events on the relationships between education schools, their universities, and their constituencies in the professional practice of education. In chapters 6 and 7 additional case studies will demonstrate how external pressures affected the professional schools, in part through the operation of new university mechanisms: the standing campus-wide personnel and program review committee and the special audit committee.

Postwar Education: Growth amidst Discord

Increasing enrollments were the first external demand facing school boards, taxpayers, and planners. The number of school-age children, which had stayed at about 28 million from 1930 to 1950, leapt to 42 million in 1960 and to 51 million in 1970, before starting to drop. In the single decade of the 1950s, the numbers of kindergarten-through-twelfth-graders grew more than in the preceding half century. The rising birth rate, which reversed a longstanding decline in fertility, was accompanied by the increased "holding power" of schools. The gradual change of the high school from a selective to a common school quickened. The percent of the age group in high school grew from 51 percent before the war to over 80 percent by 1960.

3. For perhaps the best entrée into this period, see Ravitch, *Troubled Crusade.*

In 1940 only one in seven of eighteen to twenty-one-year-olds had been in college. In 1960 Robert J. Havighurst described two schools of thought about growth in college enrollments during the upcoming decade: the "realistic view" predicted a 50 percent increase or less; the "expansionist view" predicted a 100 percent increase.[4] The expansionists proved to be too conservative: the numbers in colleges and universities grew by 140 percent from 1960 to 1970, to enroll nearly half of the age group. Accordingly, while the numbers of elementary and secondary school teachers grew by 44 percent between 1960 and 1970, college and university faculty increased by 144 percent.[5]

For the first time in the history of American higher education, there was an excess of student demand over places. This allowed the better positioned colleges and universities to become academically selective and turn applicants away. It forced state officials to enlarge and build public institutions to accommodate them and the other children of voters. The "graduate virus" proved virulent; even many private liberal arts colleges began to offer graduate degrees. The fact that publically financed higher education grew disproportionately more than did that in the private sector probably intensified, however, the range of external demands on higher education.[6]

The Consequences of Growth for Education Schools

Enrollment growth in education programs exceeded the average for higher education generally. This fact was not as distasteful or threatening to the general academic community as it would have been had overall enrollments not risen so dramatically.[7] By 1977, there were over 45,000 professors of education in 1,367 institutions; 153 of those schools awarded doctorates in education, nearly double the number that did so in 1960.[8] Compensation for decades of insults directed

4. Robert J. Havighurst, "Who Goes to College and Why?" in *Recent Research and Development and Their Implications for Teacher Education,* Thirteenth Yearbook of the American Association of Colleges for Teacher Education (Washington, D.C.: AACTE, 1960), 103.

5. Larson, *Professionalism,* 251.

6. Lynton, "Once and Future University," 3.

7. Schlechty and Vance, "Recruitment, Selection, and Retention," 481.

8. Sam J. Yarger and Bruce R. Joyce, "Going Beyond the Data: Reconstructing Teacher Education," *Journal of Teacher Education* 28 (Nov.–Dec. 1977): 21; American Association of Colleges for Teacher Education, *The Doctorate in Education,* vol. 2, *The Institutions,* (Washington, D.C.: AACTE, 1960). As early as 1963, there were 35,888 in

against schools and departments of education came in the form of upward leaps in enrollments, the proliferation of postgraduate programs in education, new demands for services and research, and unprecedented state and federal funding to meet these demands. The "double happiness of demand" and the "bubble of cock-eyed optimism" persisted in most education schools into the early 1970s.[9]

The first priority of schools of education had to be addressing the teacher shortage, exacerbated by the low birthrates of the 1930s and the competition of teaching with other markets for college graduates in an expanding economy. Teacher numbers grew four times faster than the population from 1950 to 1970, going from one to nearly two million. The number of states requiring a bachelor's degree for certified elementary school teachers went from twenty in 1945 to fifty by 1975. While a quarter of the entire college graduating class in 1950 took baccalaureate and first professional degrees in education, they were 38 percent by 1972. In that peak year 317,254 college graduates completed their preparation for teaching positions.[10] The percentage of all teachers with bachelor's degrees climbed from 60 percent to 90 percent. Increases in student enrollment, however, combined with high teacher turnover and rising standards to cause the well-publicized problem of "underpreparation"—and nearly 100,000 taught with emergency credentials.[11]

The movement to upgrade teachers was not restricted to the public schools. The large and expanding system of Catholic parochial schools, which enrolled over 90 percent of youngsters in nonpublic schools, was also affected. The "sister formation" movement began in 1952 to ensure that nuns in teaching, nursing, and social work "had as much professional preparation as their secular counterparts." Only

---

the education professoriate; that was 10.2 percent of the total faculty in American higher education. Only 35 percent of the total had doctorates, compared to 59 percent of social science faculty—in part because only one-third were employed in universities. Study reported in James Steve Counelis, "The Professoriate in the Discipline of Education," in *To Be a Phoenix: The Education Professoriate,* ed. James Steve Counelis (Bloomington, Ind.: Phi Delta Kappa, 1969), 4, 7.

9. Jeffrey S. Kaiser, "Pessimistic Optimism in an Era of Slowed Growth: An Administrator's View," *Educational Perspectives* 14 (December 1975): 10.

10. William S. Graybeal, "Status and Trends in Public School Teacher Supply and Demand," *Journal of Teacher Education* 25 (Summer 1974): 207.

11. James C. Stone, *Breakthrough in Teacher Education,* (San Francisco: Jossey-Bass, 1970), 4–5. See also Woodring, "Development of Teacher Education," esp. 16–24.

13 of 377 teaching orders in 1956 were known to offer full bachelor's degrees. A commission was created by the National Catholic Education Association, analogous to the Teacher Education and Professional Standards Commission of the National Education Association. It looked successfully to the Ford Foundation's Fund for the Advancement of Education for help in designing a teacher education curriculum. As a result, according to the dean of the School of Education at Seton Hall University, the prewar educational isolation of Catholic practitioners disappeared.[12] Catholic teachers were attending new colleges sponsored by teaching orders, existing Catholic women's colleges, coeducational Catholic universities, and even public and private secular universities. Thus, the reform movement in teacher education encompassed public and nonpublic institutions at all levels.

In response to teacher shortages, private Stanford University began a program for elementary teachers in 1950; women had previously enrolled at nearby San Jose State College for professional courses while pursuing their Stanford baccalaureates. As in other states with accessible systems of state teachers colleges, the legislature also pressured the University of California to prepare more teachers. "Anytime you get twenty more student teachers, you'll get another supervisor," President Sproul told the deans at Berkeley and UCLA.[13] Their faculties, however, wanted more than teacher educators, he suggested, pointing to the accompanying need for professors in school administration, supervision, and curriculum fields—persons who could educate the specialists who were also needed in an era when a new school opened daily and entire school systems appeared to service the housing tracts that were displacing lettuce fields and almond orchards.

Although they did not openly say so, education professors knew that preparing more graduate students in education would restore some balance to the gender ratios in their student bodies. Male graduate students would compensate for the masses of young women preparing to teach since custom, veterans' preference policies, and hiring practices dictated that most of the new administrators would be men. Moreover, not to grow was to be left behind: graduate education in all fields was expanding, its status escalating. The unwillingness of grad-

12. Richard Ognibene, "Promoting Change in Catholic Education, 1940–1965" (Paper presented at the annual meeting of the American Educational Research Association, Chicago, April 1985), 17.

13. Quoted by Theodore L. Reller, former Berkeley dean of education, interview with authors, Geraldine Clifford, Berkeley, 11 September 1985.

uate education in general to justify itself in terms of social benefits would create, however, a special problem for graduate programs in professional schools—as we will subsequently see.[14]

The multiplication of degrees, faculties, service bureaus, and other units within schools of education was assisted by a flow of extramural and institutional funding. A study of 1956–58 doctoral recipients in education found that the "G.I. Bill of Rights" was important to 61 percent of the respondents. After 1945, the mean time lag from A.B. to doctorate in education declined from its high of over sixteen years. Education doctorates continued, however, to have more years of professional experience (a median of 7.2 years) than the average (4.6) of all fields, and more financial and family obligations (2.31 dependents compared to 2.00 for the total group).[15] Regardless, by the mid-1960s, 34 percent of all graduate degrees nationally were earned in education, and that figure went to nearly 39 percent a decade later.

Federal programs like the National Defense Education Act (1958) and the Education Professions Development Act (1967) contributed to graduate-level support, providing an unprecedented if shortlived opportunity to enroll recent graduates and permit full-time study for experienced professionals; the former program concentrated on subject matter specialists and the latter on education professionals.[16] Harvard's former dean of Education, Francis Keppel, was United States Commissioner of Education in the Lyndon Johnson administration; more money for "R & D" was one of his priorities.[17] Foundations also extended largesse, funding instructional innovations, student fellowships, and research and development activities.

With this outside assistance and the ambitions of their own upwardly mobile students, graduate schools of education increased their share of all doctorates awarded to 24 percent by 1980. Although a Harvard committee noted that the production of scholars was a rather new idea at the Graduate School of Education in the early fifties," by 1965 "'doctoral potential' became an important admission criterion

14. Jencks and Reisman, *Academic Revolution,* 250.

15. American Association of Colleges for Teacher Education, *The Doctorate in Education,* vol. 1, *The Graduates,* 82; Harmon and Soldz, *Doctorate Production,* 41, 46–47.

16. William A. Jenkins, "Changing Patterns in Teacher Education," in *The Teaching of English,* 74th Yearbook of the National Society for the Study of Education, part 1, ed. James R. Squire (Chicago: University of Chicago Press, 1977), 276–77.

17. Hugh Davis Graham, *The Uncertain Triumph: Federal Education Policy in the Kennedy and Johnson Years,* (Chapel Hill: University of North Carolina Press, 1984), 117.

for nearly every program in the School."[18] Excluding Yale, schools of education in our ten institutions contributed a significant and increasing share of their institution's total doctoral production. During the 1950s, for example, their contributions ranged from over 7 percent (at Chicago and Wisconsin) to 30 percent (at Stanford) to 45 percent (at Columbia).[19] This persistence is especially remarkable given a general downward trend in relative productivity of the leading doctoral institutions as more universities entered the competition.

Who Will Educate Teachers?

It had not been the intention of the founders of university schools of education to be the locus of all teacher training, as the pioneer university law schools did not intend to be the primary mode of legal training nor regulate entry into that profession.[20] Given the post–World War II national rush to college, however, it was inevitable that a higher education, some argued one built on a four-year liberal arts foundation, became the new standard of adequate professional preparation. About four-fifths of all higher education institutions prepare teachers.

The majority of America's new teachers were educated in ignored institutions, taught by those who lacked a national platform. While hundreds of liberal arts colleges each graduated two dozen teachers annually, and the elite universities ten times that number at their peak, the upgraded state teachers' colleges were the major producers. In 1973 Northern Illinois University, for example, granted 2,300 bachelor's and 1,500 master's degrees in education.[21] Their faculties themselves provided another reservoir of doctoral students for the graduate schools of education.

Two other groups of professionals—neither having deep personal interest or experience in teacher education nor much up-to-date working knowledge of the conditions of teaching—tussled for advantage in the public debate about teacher education content: professors in prestigious academic departments and professors in the graduate schools of education. The former group had acquired unprecedented

18. Harvard Committee, *Graduate Study,* 97–98.

19. Curtis O. Baker, *Earned Degrees Conferred: An Examination of Recent Trends* (Washington, D.C.: National Center for Education Statistics, 1981), 32; Harmon and Soldz. *Doctorate Production,* 20–22.

20. Johnson, *Schooled Lawyers,* 42. As late as 1951, 23 percent of lawyers had never attended law school. See Lortie, "Laymen to Lawmen," 351.

21. Clark and Marker, "Institutionalization of Teacher Education," 58.

power as a result of two phenomena: the intense demand for higher education and the association of academic scientists with the successful war effort, especially the development of atomic energy. Professors in a variety of fields, including the sciences, involved themselves in an unprecedented process of developing new curricula, especially for able high school students, and a program of teacher institutes designed to prepare teachers to use the new materials. In so doing they were coming back into the bailiwick of professors of education, even while stepping up their complaints about the educationists' guardianship of the public schools.

Among the academic critics of schools of education, the most informed and effective was probably Arthur Bestor, a graduate of Teachers College's Lincoln School, historian at Teachers College and the University of Illinois, leader of the Council for Basic Education, and author of *Educational Wastelands* (1953). He soon had company. Within a decade, Harvard's former president, James B. Conant, published *The Education of American Teachers* and James D. Koerner a less temperate book, *The Miseducation of American Teachers.* Bestor wrote critically of the "interlocking directorate" of influential figures in schools of education, state departments of education, public school administration, and the United States Office of Education, who together decided the quality and character of schooling. To break the stranglehold of "educationists" on schooling meant to intervene in the training, licensing, and employment of teachers. A place to begin was developing alternative emphases in teacher education. Students and graduates of the nation's leading colleges and universities were the preferred and most accessible focus for the attention of such academic critics.

Project English and the other curriculum projects of the period created teams of subject-matter specialists, education faculty, and teacher consultants, usually under the direction of academicians. Academicians participated in the teacher institutes funded by private foundations or the National Science Foundation for experienced mathematics, science, and foreign language teachers and by the College Board and the United States Office of Education for English teachers.[22] A spurt of Master of Arts in Teaching (MAT) programs also required cross-campus and university-school collaborations.

22. The typical institute format was that teachers enrolled in summer or yearlong graduate classes to extend or update their knowledge of subject matter. Workshops, sometimes without academic credit, were an optional feature, designed to help teachers apply this knowledge in their teaching situations; this component was gener-

Influential persons in Washington favored moving teacher education to stronger institutions. In 1966 President Lyndon Johnson created a task force on education, chaired by Sidney Marland, superintendent of Pittsburgh's schools. The task force agreed privately that it would like to see all remaining teachers colleges closed down. A politically untenable act when pursued directly, similar ends could be achieved by encouraging the process already underway: converting them to liberal arts colleges, with, it was hoped, higher academic standards. All teacher education, they thought, should be left to the stronger public and private universities, through fifth-year Master of Arts in Teaching programs.[23]

From More Teachers to Better Teachers: The MAT Solution. President Conant announced the first MAT program in 1936, primarily for graduates of Harvard and similar institutions. Low demand for teachers during the depression and poor salaries made the program unattractive to graduates of elite colleges, however, and the Harvard education faculty in 1946 disavowed teacher education. With the appointment, in 1948, of Francis Keppel as its dean and the better economic climate for teachers, Harvard's interest revived—although teaching was recruiting more heavily among blue-collar families than before.[24] With Harvard, the Ford Foundation supported a twenty-nine college arrangement, begun in 1952, to arouse undergraduate interest in secondary teaching, to develop introductory education courses, and to provide post-baccalaureate academic and professional courses and supervised student teaching; in its first five years approximately 550 secondary teachers were prepared through this collaboration.[25] Such Master of Arts in Teaching programs were the most numerous experiments in teacher education funded by the Foundation; eighteen of the twenty-five projects prepared secondary teachers exclusively. The fact that the teacher shortage was then most severe at the elementary school level, where women predominated, reinforces the observation that considerations other than teacher numbers operated in the design and funding decisions.

---

ally the least well planned and least satisfying to the participants. See Jenkins, "Changing Patterns," 275.

23. Graham, *Uncertain Triumph,* 169.

24. Harvard Committee, *Graduate Study,* 92–96; Sedlak and Schlossman, *Who Will Teach?* esp. 30–32.

25. Woodring, *New Directions,* 49.

From its outset in 1936, the Ford Foundation supported educational improvement in Michigan, but it began its national programs only in 1950. Through its Fund for the Advancement of Education, teacher education received the largest grants. From the initial support given a statewide experiment in Arkansas in 1951 (called "the Arkansas Purchase" by resentful local educators) through the 1960s, the Foundation invested $70 million in innovations in teacher education. With the breakdown of former prohibitions against married women in teaching, foundation officers thought that mature women might be drawn into the teaching workforce if they could find an alternative to the "conventional programs conceived for younger students."[26] "Breakthrough Programs," launched in 1958, also sought to involve academic faculty in teacher education. In all, forty-two institutions participated. Adopting a "trickle-down"or "rub-off" theory, the Foundation funded a group of mostly northern and eastern institutions, bypassing the colleges which prepared most of the nation's teachers, colleges which "lacked a dynamic, experimental climate or the high visibility and fame that would make them valuable as pace-setters."[27]

Personal networks played a part, as did institutional reputation and the merits of the proposed program. For example, the University of Chicago was a major beneficiary: its former chancellor, Robert Maynard Hutchins, a Foundation director, was a founder of the Fund for the Advancement of Education; Clarence Faust, one-time Chicago professor and dean, was president of the Fund; and a former chairman of the Department of Education, Ralph Tyler, was on the Advisory Committee. One-time Stanford professor and acting president, Alvin Eurich, was a senior officer of the Fund, and the architect of its new programs for teacher education; Stanford also proposed an MAT program and was funded.

Critics faulted the Fund's elitism, not its cronyism. In 1954, Professor Thomas Briggs of Teachers College resigned from the Fund's advisory board and published his charges in *School and Society.* He scored the Foundation for its hostile attitude toward professional educators, its arrogance, the absence on the staff of persons with intimate experience with the schools, its lack of "sympathy with the democratic idea of giving appropriate education to all the children

26. This was probably a euphemism for the poorly regarded teacher education programs believed to prevail. Paul Woodring, "The Ford Foundation and Teacher Education," *Teachers College Record,* 62, no. 3 (Dec. 1960): 227.

27. Stone, *Breakthrough,* 15.

of all the people."[28] If the charges were warranted, the Fund probably reflected the attitudes of most college professors. College teachers of literature, for example, "viewed the high school program in terms of its value for college preparation and its relations to the curricula of college English departments," according to a survey published in 1961. "They did not consider its value as general education for all kinds of high school students."[29] Even the smallest experimental programs in Fund-aided schools could not recruit many applicants unless they offered financial incentives. This was just one indication of the growing association of public education and public school teaching with social stratification as education expanded in the postwar United States.

Charting the Effects. What were the results of this campaign for collaborative experimentation through philanthropic generosity to teacher education in elite institutions? For one, the collaborations proved more administrative than intellectual. For another, they did not convert many academicians into pedagogues. The academic courses offered during the fifth year were rarely tailored or even adjusted with prospective teachers in mind; they remained designed for potential scholars and researchers. Yale officials acknowledged to the Foundation that "we no longer advise students to elect some of the graduate courses in academic fields which do not seem appropriate for prospective high school teachers."[30] Student opinion at Yale revealed even wider dissatisfaction among the mostly female MAT students: disappointment with the dull and irrelevant professional courses, the excessive academicism of their subject-matter courses, the belittling scorn shown them by graduate students and many professors. Of the twenty-two interviewed, fourteen described their experiences as "terrible," "bad and confusing," "a terrible disappointment." Nearly a third decided not to teach. As one woman expressed it, "The professors are so condescending to the MAT students. The students are worse. I am planning to enter the doctoral program next year in the ______ department, so I can tell the difference. As an MAT I

28. Paul Woodring, *Investment in Innovation: An Historical Appraisal of the Fund for the Advancement of Education* (Boston: Little, Brown, 1970), 238–42.

29. The 1961 study by Kitzhaber, Gorrell, and Roberts is reported in Henry C. Meckel, "Research on Teaching Composition and Literature," in *Handbook of Research on Teaching,* ed. Nat L. Gage (Chicago: Rand McNally, 1963), 994.

30. Stone, *Breakthrough,* 136.

was talked down to. As a doctoral candidate, my intelligence has improved."[31]

Chicago officials reported, however, that academic faculty found MAT students superior to their M.A. students and some actively participated in recruiting at other colleges, at least in the early years.[32] Chicago's original two-year postgraduate program was eventually "compressed" to a five-quarter plan when students reported the internship year longer than was needed, but it was also getting difficult to secure internships in the tightening economic situation facing schools by the 1970s.[33] At Berkeley the Graduate Internship Program (GIP), a School of Education program that operated through University Extension because of University policies on matriculation, was first funded by the Ford Foundation and then the State. Although not an MAT program, lacking both an academic degree and substantial contact with academic departments on the part of the interns, it had some vocal supporters in certain academic departments that benefited from the opportunity for their graduates to earn teaching credentials, if they wanted them, through an intensive shortcut approach. The staff was a group of dedicated and competent individuals who taught most of the courses and supervised the paid, full-time internships in which students were placed after a summer's study of education. The decision to close the GIP came when school districts, able to obtain regularly credentialed teachers, were no longer willing to employ untested talent as a condition of their being admitted to the program. Its closing provoked, however, charges that the School acted because of the program's success in comparison to the School's regular program.[34]

An extensive study of a sample of Breakthrough Program graduates revealed that the opportunity to study with well-known scholars in their teaching fields was the most attractive feature of the programs, and that the student teaching or internship component was the most

31. Levine, "Marital and Occupational Plans of Women." Nursing students report similar experiences in studies of medical schools. The Levine study is summarized in Seymour B. Sarason, *The Culture of the School and the Problem of Change,* 2d ed. (Boston: Allyn & Bacon, 1982), 64–67.

32. Stone, *Breakthrough,* 102.

33. Roger A. Pillet, "MAT–5 Quarter Program" (University of Chicago, Graduate School of Education, Fall 1969).

34. Theodore L. Reller, interview with Geraldine Clifford, Berkeley, 11 September 1985 and 28 August 1986. See also Theodore L. Reller, "Teacher Education in the School of Education: A Position Paper" (University of California at Berkeley, School of Education, November 1968).

highly rated; this latter is consistent with all the research on teacher education, regardless of kind of program. Graduates were most likely to fault their training for its limited help to them "in assessing and reporting student progress, interpreting test results, individualizing instruction, teaching students from different backgrounds or students with discipline problems, teaching slow learners, and dealing with parents—in short, with inadequate pedogogical training."[35]

MAT graduates were as likely to enter teaching as those with conventional training, mostly in above-average suburban public schools serving well-educated white parents who expected superior teachers and supported education—schools like the ones in which most took their internships. One-third of those entering teaching in the later 1960s were still teaching in the mid-1980s, but the average stay in teaching was only five years. Researchers concluded, however, that such wastage was only apparent: "Such a group of teachers provides 'fresh blood' to the profession, while holding down the costs of teacher salaries." Moreover, many of the dropouts from teaching, like the products of conventional programs, later pursued further degrees and other careers in education. Graduates of selective schools were less likely to teach and to continue in teaching, however, than those attending nonselective institutions. This was a sign of the continuing use of teaching for social mobility.[36]

A few four-year programs were funded in selective undergraduate colleges like Barnard, Swarthmore, and Carleton. Allowing a "bare minimum of classroom experience," such programs depended upon careful screening, close organization;, and assistance after graduation. As such, they were far more expensive than the average program in teacher education. In fact, while many academics spoke of overblown programs and the excess of professional courses in conventional teacher education, education faculty were complaining of inadequate institutional investment in teacher education and too little profes-

35. Richard J. Coley and Margaret E. Thorpe, *A Look at the MAT Model of Teacher Education and Its Graduates: Lessons for Today,* Final Report, sponsored by the Ford Foundation (Princeton, N.J.: Division of Education Policy Research and Services, Educational Testing Service, Dec. 1985), 28.

36. These social class linkages were confirmed in a comparative study of women in four professional programs at Yale in the 1960s. Compared to medical and legal students prospective nurses and teachers came from low-status families, had less-educated mothers, were more likely to express the conventional female willingness to defer career to domestic responsibilities, and felt treated as members of low-status groups within the university. Levine, "Marital and Occupational Plans of Women."

sional content. Their deans worried about a two-tier faculty. Academics had lost interest in pedagogy. And graduates were dismayed by the poor fit between their training and the workplace. Together these represent what we call structural barriers.

The Structural Barriers to Reform in Teacher Education

Education schools shared a problem with other professional schools and academic departments in major universities: the minimal resources and attention given to teaching and the diversion of resources to research. Thus, professors of medicine found it easier and quicker to be promoted and gain tenure for their research than for their teaching.[37] But, for a variety of reasons—philosophical and financial—educational research did not flourish in the same way that medical research did. Hence, schools of education acquired no halo to glorify their activities; instead they were faulted as inadequate in both teaching and research—and, as such, entitled to few resources.

A wider problem of chronic under-funding of teacher education relative to higher education in general was uncovered in the first federally sponsored National Survey of Education, published in 1935, showing the inadequacies of libraries in normal schools and teachers colleges.[38] The general problem persisted. In 1982–83, for example, the estimated average cost of undergraduate teacher education was $1,848 per university student; the comparable figure per pupil in kindergarten through twelfth grade was $2,566.[39] Some traced the causes of this low investment to the placement of the majority of teacher education programs in the undergraduate years; as a partial remedy they advocated certification following graduate professional study only.[40] In California, however, where the great majority of teacher credential students already had a bachelor's degree, the California State

37. Ludmerer, *Learning to Heal.*

38. *National Survey of the Education of Teachers*, vol. 5, *Special Survey Studies*, 243 ff.

39. Monica Murphy, "Teacher Preparation in California: A Status Report" (Prepared for the California Commission on the Teaching Profession, Sacramento, April 1985).

40. See, for example, Clark and Marker, "Institutionalization," 57, 76–78; Holmes Group, *Tomorrow's Teachers: A Report of the Holmes Group* (East Lansing, Mich.: Holmes Group, 1986); Carnegie Task Force on Teaching as a Profession, *A Nation Prepared: Teachers for the 21st Century* (New York: Carnegie Forum on Education and the Economy, May 1986). In 1986 the Holmes Group of deans of major graduate schools of education and the Carnegie Task Force report both endorsed placing all teacher education at the graduate level.

University system considered them upper-division undergraduates for funding purposes.[41] Funding teacher education as just another undergraduate program resulted in teachers being taught how to teach by being lectured to about teaching, often in large classes.[42]

Another solution to underfunding was the expedient placement of students for observation and practice teaching in local public schools whose practices often contradicted the pedagogical and curricular principles being enunciated in the university, and under the daily supervision of teachers often untrained and unrewarded for these duties. Small wonder, then, that education students complained that their university courses were "too theoretical." All in all, craft-based apprenticeship training might better describe much of teacher education than did the term professional education.

Unable to negotiate an appropriate share of institutional resources in a time of plenty, when education students were generating revenues for the colleges, there was little reason for optimism as higher education moved into its "era of limits" and schools of education were forced to shrink. University administrators, even education deans, were also faulted by teacher educators for applying accounting systems inappropriate to the multiple demands and "road running" attendant on field placement. University liaison with school sites devolved onto graduate students preparing for other careers, on low-status faculty hired on term contracts, and on inexperienced assistant professors not well positioned to defend themselves. As successful as John Goodlad was in steering UCLA between professional and academic waters, he failed to get those who spent significant time in teacher education promoted. The "remedy" at Harvard was to appoint respected educational practitioners to part-time or full-time positions in the nonladder ranks of the Graduate School of Education.[43] Thus, a troubling division of labor and status was created in many schools and departments of education, a two-class system unusual in American universities.[44]

41. Murphy, "Teacher Preparation in California."

42. Stone, *Breakthrough,* 9.

43. James K. Bonney, "A Profile of the Harvard Graduate School of Education: A Report Compiled for Professor Harry Judge's Study of American Graduate Schools of Education" (Feb. 1981), 17. By permission of Professor Judge, Oxford University.

44. Martin A. Trow, "The American Academic Department as a Context for Learning," *Studies in Higher Education,* 1, no. 1 (March 1976): 22. In 1966, a committee of the Berkeley School of Education was formed to try to resolve the issue of a large and growing bloc of low-status supervisors nominally attached to the school. While endorsing the importance of practice teaching and the supervision of that practice, it sug-

Depending as they did on extrinsic inducement, most of the MAT programs were discontinued with the end of their Ford grants and the collapse of the market for teachers after 1970. Some institutions did incorporate elements into their regular programs, but many MAT programs left few traces.[45] Additionally, and importantly, educational policy makers everywhere were switching their attention from the needs of rapidly growing suburbs and the interests of the middle class in better college preparation toward the problems of racism and educational deprivation in city schools. "The MAT concept, with its liberal arts, suburban orientation was no longer on the cutting edge of reform."[46] In 1964 the faculty of the Graduate School of Education at the University of Chicago intensely debated the revealing question of where MAT interns should be placed: in large urban centers (likely to involve them in minority neighborhoods or schools undergoing desegregation) or "in any system outside the Chicago area which would provide an appropriate situation for a profitable teaching experience."[47]

A professor of English and education, William Jenkins, wrote of professors of English that "for a brief period in the 1960s—less than a decade—their lack of concern for education programs was superseded by exemplary participation and cooperation."[48] Other contemporary observers agree that, by 1970, academics' interest and participation in teacher education had declined, especially on larger campuses where departmental and disciplinary organization was strong. At best, academic departments might wish for accessible programs for the prospective teachers among their graduates but, in the opinion of the President of George Peabody College for Teachers, too many had "learned to look down their Roman or Greek noses at the barbarians who teach professional education and at their students who are preparing to teach."[49]

Philanthropic funding for teacher education was an artificial sup-

---

gested that the burden of supervision be transferred to the public schools. The university "should not be as deeply involved in supervision as it is. On-the-job supervision is not practiced by the university in the case of training lawyers, engineers, or social workers, for example. . . ." Theodore L. Reller, "Report on Supervised Teaching Unit, Berkeley Campus," University of California at Berkeley, School of Education, 5 July 1966, 9.

45. For a description of the situation at Harvard, see Glazer, "Schools," 357.

46. Coley and Thorpe, *A Look at the MAT Model,* 29.

47. University of Chicago, Graduate School of Education, *Minutes of the Meeting of the Graduate School of Education Faculty,* 20 May, 1964, 2.

48. Jenkins, in Squire, p. 262.

49. Henry H. Hill, "Preparing Teachers," 253.

port; its withdrawal returned education, in most places, to the school, college, or department of education. The slogan that "teacher education is the business of the entire faculty" again proved more rhetoric than reality. It is hard to dispute the conclusion that the very concept of university-wide responsibility for teacher education "is belied by the basic organization of the institution itself."[50] A fundamentally different community of interests means that, "Given its structure and agenda, the high school must set its face against serving effectively as a feeder unit for the university" while the university "is biased against serving effectively in the selection and training of teachers for the high school."[51]

The Breakthrough Programs were predicated on another set of unwarranted expectations. One was that teachers were being prepared to work in ungraded classes, with teaching machines, educational television, team teaching, and flexible scheduling and classroom space. It was incorrectly predicted that university scholars, education professors, and teachers and school administrators would soon be engaged in continuous collaborative planning of classroom organization and activity. Another unmet expectation was that the public schools would take over more of the responsibility for recruiting, educating, and inducting new professionals. Initial teaching experience was to come through a prolonged internship as a junior member of a teaching team, under salary by the school rather than on grants from a foundation. The worsening fiscal situation of public education dashed that latter hope.

Interviews, by teachers, of those who entered the profession in the boom and bust years yield additional insights into the disparity between liberal arts–oriented teacher education and the realities of schooling. The Boston Women's Teachers' Group concluded:

> The ideology of a liberal arts background allowed teachers to resist seeing their education as a vocational training ground for a prescribed task. The prescriptive methods and specific classroom management techniques of the teacher colleges were not emphasized to liberal arts students. Instead, the education courses offered . . . underscored the importance of entering schools with a distinct philosophy of education that was not to be found in a static model of classroom life. The approach to understanding and handling the child was reformulated in terms of the new professional careers emerging from the rising sciences

50. Clark and Marker, "Institutionalization," 76; Woodring "Development of Teacher Education," 20.

51. Clark, "High School and the University," 392.

> of psychology and sociology. . . . When the liberal arts graduate began her career, she discovered that the position of teacher was not reformulated to accommodate her training.[52]

In their anxiety to shed the image of the normal school and teachers colleges, university schools of education adopted some or all of the features of the liberal arts approach described above. Here was another cause of the charge of "ivory tower elitism" hurled by practitioners.

Schools and Society in Turmoil

Rising but unrealistic expectations about the reform of teacher education and the meliorative effects of education on children created, first, an unprecedented worldwide expansion of schooling, followed by just as widespread a disenchantment. In the following section we discuss a quartet of social and political movements that affected all educational institutions, schools and departments of education included. These are the civil rights movement, teacher militancy, the consumer movement, and the constriction of resources resulting primarily from demographic change.

The Civil Rights Movement and Schools of Education

Decisions of the United States Supreme Court outlawing racially segregated schools unleashed, among liberals, high hopes for achieving educational equality and racial harmony. These hopes were punctured by accumulating evidence of persisting disparities in educational achievement and by rancorous and sometimes violent protests against busing students to achieve racial and economic desegregation in public schools. "White flight" deprived many schools of the middle-class support so long thought essential to the well-being of public education; some of that withdrawn support was represented on university faculties where professors abandoned neighborhoods and schools in social and educational flux. Despite the high idealism of many prospective teachers, the difficulties of urban schools, sensationally treated in the mass media, almost certainly discouraged many prospective teachers.

52. Sara Freedman, Jane Jackson, and Katherine Boles, "The Effects of the Institutional Structures of Schools on Teachers," Boston Women's Teachers' Group, final report, National Institute of Education G-81-0031, 1 September 1982, pp. 104–5.

Differences in fertility rates and immigration levels higher than at any time since 1923 together exposed schools in many regions to shifting ratios of majority to minority youngsters. The call heard in the 1950s, to prepare and recruit more men to teaching so that predelinquents might have favorable role models, was heard again in the 1980s as certain states faced the prospect of a majority of minorities among school children; this was already the situation in the nation's largest school districts. Primarily white education schools were thought insufficiently interested in the problems of teaching inner-city children. A liberal arts college graduate entering teaching through the federal Teacher Corps program recalled two requirements that appealed to her: working in a school in a low-income area and the exclusion of education majors. "They were supposed to find people who would be trained for teaching the culturally deprived," she recalled.[53]

Ironically, the civil rights movement, and its extension in the women's movement, presented women and talented minorities with unprecedented options—well-paid occupational alternatives to teaching, which was losing what little status it once had. In fact, the proportion of black students prepared to teach decreased by over one-third between 1975 and 1981. As standards of preparation were raised and competency tests for prospective teachers were imposed by state governments, minorities fell farther behind. Some southern schools of education with predominantly minority student bodies faced the prospect of losing their accreditation entirely.[54]

Given the redoubtable problems of learning and socialization faced by an increasingly diverse and differentiated educational system, there was an unparalleled need for educational research. Despite relatively generous expenditures for educational research, the expectations set were too high. Like the spending for public education as a share of gross national product, expenditures for educational research were declining by the late 1970s.[55] Academic departments whose disciplines were represented in the curricula of the elementary and secondary schools did not participate in research on how students learn their subject matter, typical sources of difficulty, and the poten-

53. Freedman, Jackson, and Boles, "Institutional Structures," 60.

54. William E. Trent, "Equity Considerations in Higher Education: Race and Sex Differences in Degree Attainment and Major Field from 1976 through 1981," *American Journal of Education* 92, no. 3 (May 1984): 280–305; and Gifford, "Teacher Competency Testing."

55. Torsten Húsen, "Research and Policymaking in Education: An International Perspective," *Educational Researcher* 13, no. 2 (Feb. 1984) 8–9.

tial of new technology in assisting teachers.[56] Instead, in the face of an unprecedented collection of challenges, they pursued a conservative, almost reactionary course: developing curriculum materials, based on existing disciplinary canons, primarily for the gifted segment of college-bound youngsters, while offering their regular courses to prospective teachers through MAT and similar programs.

The most famous piece of research of the era, a study designed to determine the degree of equality of educational opportunity in American public schools and supervised by sociologist James S. Coleman of Johns Hopkins University, illustrated that sometimes no research is better than the "wrong research." It was bad research in the technical sense of using data inappropriate to the questions being asked. Its policy implications were similarly wrong-headed. The "Coleman Report" (1966) was popularly interpreted to mean that the social class and family characteristics of a student's classmates matter more in determining academic achievement ("outputs") than do school resources, the students' background being the most crucial "input."

Minority schools were inevitably stigmatized by this research. If "schools don't matter," then neither do the schools of education whose faculties train the teachers and administrators, design the curriculum, write the textbooks, and study the learning and teaching processes—none of which counts for much. The policy inference was to concentrate upon racial desegregation of schools and intervention in the upbringing of young minority children in order to provide them with some middle-class cognitive advantages, rather than to improve the quality of the schools attended by minority and other underachieving youngsters. The pursuit of that policy alienated millions of Americans, however—with public schools, teachers, and teachers of teachers the losers. Nor did it achieve its objective: by the end of the period, except in the southern and border states, racial resegregation of schools was commonplace. In 1980, in a number of states including New York, Massachusetts, and Michigan, lower percentages of black students were attending predominantly white schools than in 1968. And educational equality of the races nowhere accompanied desegregation in a systematic way. The research community, too, found education a far more complex and confounding subject than it had once imagined.

56. In 1985 the American Association of Colleges sponsored a report recommending that departments in research universities devote one or two faculty positions to research on learning their disciplines, to their own benefit and that of the secondary schools. Quoted in Gifford, "Teacher Competency Testing," 64.

Militancy: America's Teachers Fight Back

In a period when the American labor movement began to lose momentum, along with its traditional members, the teaching profession became highly unionized; even lay teachers in Catholic schools organized and went on strikes. Between 1918 and 1962 there were 130 teacher strikes; in 1969–70 there were 114. Teachers felt subordinated in increasingly bureaucratized school systems, and collective action promised them more advancement than did the doubtful "science of pedagogy."[57] Changes in the nation's occupational profile showed that the place of teachers among professional workers had actually declined, while a three-fold increase in their numbers "blurred the distinctiveness of being a teacher."[58] Initial improvements in income as a result of the teacher shortages of the 1945–65 period did not survive the 1970s' inflation, taxpayer revolts against local school districts, or the greater income gains made by other college graduates. While many students in MBA programs also worked to finance their studies, they could anticipate future remuneration rates unthinkable to education students.

Teachers felt increasingly powerless in the face of the turmoil generated locally by state and federal government policies and court decisions. Teachers were minimally consulted in designing and implementing many of the curriculum projects emanating from university scholars; the arrogance of mathematicians, physicists, and biologists in the presentation of their "teacher-proof" materials did not escape teachers' attention. The strong endorsement which many education professors received from undergraduates for their personal devotion to teaching and advising did not hold when their students became teachers, and began criticizing their pre–student teaching experiences as not demanding or irrelevant.[59] As their professional organizations became ever more militant unions, teachers turned to them for relief. When a new school reform movement surfaced in the early 1980s, teachers were better positioned to demand representation in the political process than in any previous school reform movement.

As teachers' unions became less able to secure economic benefits

57. Larson, *Professionalism,* 184–85.

58. Ronald G. Corwin, "The New Teaching Profession," in *Teacher Education,* 74th Yearbook of the National Society for the Study of Education, part 2, ed. Kevin Ryan (Chicago: University of Chicago Press, 1975), 240.

59. Ducharme and Agne, "Education Professoriate," 33.

for their members, they turned to issues of professionalism: securing status benefits for teachers.[60] In the early 1950s the National Education Association refused to support federal funding for educational research; a quarter century later the American Federation of Teachers proposed that research funded by the National Institute of Education, much of it conducted by faculty members in schools of education, be analyzed with respect to the "teacher impact" of its projected outcomes.[61] Federally initiated Teacher Centers, seen by unions as a way to gain teacher control over continuing education, did not mandate participation by schools of education in their staffing; opposed by some education schools, this further embittered relations.

Contests for control over accreditation and teacher education also mounted. In 1970 teachers secured inclusion in the National Council for the Accreditation of Teacher Education (NCATE), the organization that accredits the majority of the nation's larger teacher education institutions. In Oregon and California teachers and public representatives secured the largest share of members on state licensing commissions. Organized teachers supported legislation, like that passed in Calilfornia and Texas, requiring that university-based teacher educators have recent and continuing experience in school classrooms.[62] Collective bargaining agreements with local school districts sometimes covered student teacher placements. One expert predicted, however, that teacher organizations would gain only nominal influence in preservice teacher education: "The primary orientation of teacher groups in terms of political and economic power means that they lack any comprehensive goals regarding changes in the content of teacher preparation; they have issues, not curricula."[63] "Warm body" programs in Los Angeles and New Jersey, permitting noncreden-

60. Lorraine M. McDonnell, "NEA Priorities and Their Impact on Teacher Education," in *1977 Yearbook of the American Association of Colleges for Teacher Education* (Washington, D.C.: AACTE, 1977), 62.

61. Administrators' groups also asked for an advisory role in setting research policy and in selecting NIE senior staff. David H. Florio, "Research and the Politics of Education," *Educational Forum* 42 (May 1978): 495.

62. The universality of complaints about excessive theory and the remoteness of professors from the realities of the schools is suggested by a study of teacher graduates in Australia. See John McArthur, *The First Five Years of Teaching*, Educational Research and Development Committee, report no. 30. (Canberra: Australian Government Publishing Service, 1981).

63. Martin Haberman, "Perspective on Tomorrow's Teacher Education," in *Teacher Education*, 74th Yearbook of the National Society for the Study of Education, part 2, ed. Kevin Ryan (Chicago: University of Chicago Press, 1975), 315.

tialled teachers to be hired, caused the unions to back off their attacks on education schools.

The breakdown of organizational unity in education was a prominent feature of this period. The American Educational Research Association (AERA), the major representative of researchers in schools of education, left the National Education Association and no longer held its annual meeting with the American Association of School Administrators. The NEA severed its ties with the American Association of Colleges for Teacher Education. It also threatened to leave NCATE because of persisting domination of the accrediting process by college and university interests, at the expense of representatives of teachers, state departments, school boards, and chief state school officers. By the mid-1970s the vaunted "educationist establishment" looked to be a shambles. Those who once complained that "all roads lead to the NEA" were advised that "the roads that now lead to NEA seem to consist chiefly of AFT cobblestones."[64]

Organized teachers were only one group engaged in a tumultuous political struggle for control of teacher education and accreditation. Also drawn into the arena as contestants were state legislators (oftentimes representing new constituents like ethnic minorities), educational commissions, federal agencies, school district lobbies, citizens groups, parent councils, and civil rights and public interest groups. A many-sided contest for influence came out of the political movements of the past three decades—movements which include judicial activism, consumerism, religious fundamentalism, anti-professionalism, the women's movement, community control.

The most likely casualties, according to some analysts, were some, even many, of the nation's schools, colleges, and departments of education. In the opinion of one spokesman, at the least their "teacher education role will probably be severely circumscribed within collaborative arrangements which favor organized teachers and administrators at the expense of university academicians."[65] Some proposed that all teacher education take place in the schools; the functions of colleges and universities would be limited to providing a general or liberal education. Nolan Estes, then superintendent of the Dallas public

64. Clark and Marker, "Institutionalization," 79. For more detail see Robert N. Bush and Peter Enemark, "Control and Responsibility in Teacher Education," *Teacher Education,* 74th Yearbook of the National Society for the Study of Education, part 2, ed. Kevin Ryan (Chicago: University of Chicago Press, 1975), 165–294.

65. Christopher J. Lucas, "Teacher Education and Its Governance," *Educational Forum* 42 (May 1978): 470.

schools, was one who advocated the apprenticeship model. Already some 10 percent of the nation's teachers were working as teacher educators, most supervising student teachers in their own classrooms with little training or guidance from schools of education. The dean of education at the University of Illinois worried aloud that strenuous efforts by the teaching profession to control teacher education form and content would jeopardize all teacher education in American research universities; these institutions would rather drop this low-status activity than have it be shaped by craft-based "wisdom."[66]

Unlike lawyers who perceived the economic and social advantages of viewing law as a teachable "science," the much larger, more varied, and newly unionized teaching profession remained alienated to the claims of theory and research as articulated by education professors. In 1985 the superintendent of the politically visible Fairfax (Virginia) Public Schools told the national Governor's Association Task Force on Teaching that he doubted that "foundation of esoteric knowledge exists for pedagogy."[67] For their part, educationists doubted the large claims on teacher preparation made by liberal arts faculty. Moreover, unlike all other professionals, teachers had some sixteen years of "anticipatory socialization" to teaching that they had received during their own schooling days—socialization which swamped what they learned in their education courses. And, by the 1980s, teachers had, on average, thirteen years of experience; its effects also dwarfed the influence of their year or two of education school.[68] Of what value to teachers was the "empty knowledge," of dubious utility, they were sometimes given—such as the number of words in an average four-year-old's vocabulary or the percentage growth of the brain during adolescence? In fact, the *increasing* emphasis in schools of education on "basic" research, on studies using technical methods out of proportion to the problem being investigated, often couched in unintelligible language, signified pretentious cant to the cynical and now more vocal teacher. And the numbers of cynics in teaching were reputedly growing daily.

66. J. Myron Atkin, "Institutional Self-Evaluation Versus National Professional Accreditation—or Back To The Normal School?" *Educational Researcher* 7 no. 10 (Nov. 1978): 3–7.

67. Robert A. Spillane, "Agenda for 1986: The Profession of Teaching" (Paper prepared for the National Governor's Association Task Force on Teaching, 12 Dec. 1985), 2.

68. Catherine Cornbleth, "Ritual and Rationality in Teacher Education Reform," *Educational Researcher* 15, no. 4 (April 1986): 5.

Consumerism and Accountability Exact Their Price

In their local schools, citizens and parents contested professionals for power. Formation of the National Citizens Council for Better Schools opened this period. Before it was over parents and their lawyers were bargaining with schools over the educational program and placement of children legally defined as "handicapped." Other manifestations in education of more inclusive citizen concern and consumer vigilance were decentralized school boards and ward selection rather than at-large elections. In part, the better organizing of teachers was a defensive reaction to the formation of these citizens groups and the proliferation of their attorneys and staffs in the contests over education policy.

Along with its indirect effects on schools of education and their universities, consumerism has had several direct effects. Members of the public came to outnumber representatives of higher education on state teacher licensing boards in some states. By the early 1970s state boards participated in the licensing of 300,000 teachers annually and the accrediting of some 1,400 teacher education institutions. As early as 1956 a meeting of the American Association of Colleges for Teacher Education discussed public participation in teacher education. A supporter contended that public examination of the situation would reveal that "most institutions of teacher education are dedicated primarily to serving the teaching profession, rather than the public, and that their concepts of the clientele they should serve are unbelievably narrow."[69] No longer. As part of its 1970 change of the teacher licensing system, California required that every teacher education program in the state have a citizens' advisory committee.

The most significant outcome of the consumer movement was application of the deceptively simple concept of "performance-based" or "competency-based" teacher education (PBTE).[70] The underlying assumption was that the teaching act can be dissected into discrete competencies or teachable skills—dozens or hundreds, according to the list makers; once learned, these skills would be usable on the job, making the teacher as methodical about her work as the engineer is

69. Probably Herbert McNee Hamlin, professor of agricultural education at the University of Illinois. Quoted in Ralph H. Woods, recorder, "Public Participation in Teacher Education," in American Association of Colleges for Teacher Education, *Ninth Yearbook* (Oneonta, N.Y.: AACTE, 1956), 47.

70. Gage and Winne, "Performance-Based Teacher Education," 146–72.

about his.[71] Although its parentage lies more in behaviorial psychology and military and industrial training models, the appeal of PBTE to representatives of the public lay in the unreflective but commonsensical slogan that "competencies" rather than courses or credits should determine the licensing of a teacher. The federal government appropriated over $12 million for PBTE between 1967 and 1973.[72] By 1975, nearly half the states had or contemplated a performance-based approach to teacher education. Its logic and practice badly divided teacher educators and probably discouraged some education faculty from participating in an enterprise with a dubious accounting system which was linked, conceptually, with Program Planning Budgeting in the discredited Defense Department.

Pupil competency tests were another innovation of the latter half of this period, intended to make teachers and schools *prove* that students were adequately educated. By the mid-1980s, such tests were being widely discussed and sometimes applied: to permit students to pass from one level of schooling to another, to determine high school graduation, and to define eligibility for athletic competition in schools. Using the same principle of holding institutions accountable, tests were being required of teachers: for entry into a teacher education program, for initial certification, or for recertification, only rarely (as in the case of Texas from 1985) for continuation in one's position. Increasingly, it seemed, the public was saying "Show me!"

The sponsorship that traditional professions acquired from upper-class patrons, the emerging professions now seek from government.[73] Licenses and credentials offer a legitimacy which may be denied by public opinion. Throughout the century professional educators had striven to centralize and elaborate a system of teacher licensing based on required programs at approved institutions. By the 1980s there were alternative systems of teacher licensing which bypassed education schools entirely. At the same time that Harvard was reviving its interest in preparing teachers and administrators and abandoning its heavy emphasis upon policy studies, twenty-two states allowed persons to be employed as teachers without having completed

71. Lee Harrisberger, "Curricula and Teaching Methods in Engineering Education," in *Education for the Professions: Quis Custodiet . . . ?* ed. Sinclair Goodlad (Guilford, England: Society for Research into Higher Education/NFER–Nelson, 1984), 133–40.

72. Bush and Enemark, "Control and Responsibility," 284.

73. Larson, *Professionalism,* 155, 199.

any teacher education, certification to come with satisfactory performance and various kinds of nominally supervised inservice training. Reformers billed such plans as incentives—like subsidized MAT programs, scholarships, and salary bonuses—to encourage bright, college-educated but impatient persons to enter teaching. The *Wall Street Journal* reported in 1984 that sixty Princeton graduates were placed in private schools the previous year sans credentials, while only nineteen Princetonians were enrolled in the University's teacher preparation program.[74] On this issue, however, organized teachers and schools of education were on the same side in arguing against such attractive but damaging shortcuts.[75]

Constriction: Declining Enrollments and Institutional Surgery

From 1960 to 1972, the share of the gross national product going to higher education doubled—from 1.1 percent to 2.2 percent—before it began to drop. Political economists began to say that education in general would never again have the favored place that it once enjoyed in the competition for public-sector dollars. The demands of other age groups, especially the elderly and younger workers paying high social security taxes, of environmental and energy activists, of defense and other government programs, would be powerful contestants for funding.

A special 1977 appeal to the alumni of the University of Chicago Department of Education acknowledged the "crisis" in higher education: "To meet the demands of this new era, many institutions will have to abandon programs, close departments, or shrink uniformly. The University of Chicago, wisely we believe, has chosen to do the last."[76]

Other institutions thought Chicago's an unwise response to the pessimistic outlook for higher education, a constriction expected to last through the balance of the century given the graduation of the "baby boom" generation, the much lower birthrates in effect, and cut-

74. Virginia Inman, "Certification of Teachers Lacking Courses in Education Stirs Battles in Several States," *Wall Street Journal,* 5 January 1984.

75. See, for example, the arguments in Bernard R. Gifford and Trish Stoddart, "Teacher Education: Rhetoric or Real Reform?" in *Education on Trial: Strategies for the Future,* ed. William J. Johnston (San Francisco: Institute for Contemporary Studies, 1985), 177–97.

76. University of Chicago, Department of Education, *Friends,* a newsletter, October 1977, 1.

backs in government and foundation support.[77] Berkeley's Chancellor Albert Bowker announced in October 1978 that his administration would pursue a different policy: the unimpaired retention of "academic excellence" rather than proportional cuts. "We simply cannot drive all our programs toward mediocrity," he asserted. "If it becomes necessary, we must prune units or programs, leaving the balance fiscally healthy."[78] To further that policy the administration would use existing faculty committees and their review mechanisms, as well as appoint special program review bodies as needed to implement "the new 3 R's: Reexamination, Retrenchment, and Retirement."[79] Whatever tolerance arts and sciences faculty had shown toward low-status fields during the flush times they would not willingly show in lean years. Indeed, one position taken about universitywide program reviews was that they should not be applied to arts and science departments: even if found weak, they had to remain on campus because of their reinforcement of other disciplines and professions. In this view, only professional degree programs should be subject to reviews and such discretionary acts as elimination.[80]

When the output of teachers peaked nationally in 1972, schools of education began to experience the consequences of an oversupply of teachers, something unknown since the Great Depression. Compared to 1971, there was a one-third decrease in the number of first degrees in education awarded in 1980, i.e., 58,445 fewer degrees. In contrast, some competing fields were growing. In 1962, there were 5,401 master's degrees awarded in Business Administration; women got 180 of them. Twenty years later, there were 61,428, and women, many of whom would once have been teachers, earned 28 percent of them.

The first employer of new doctorates in education was typically a college or university; in the period 1957 to 1961, for example, 60

77. During most of the 1950s the number of births per 1,000 population in the United States exceeded 25. A sharp decline brought that figure to 17.5 in 1968 and to under 15 through most of the 1970s. The small rise thereafter was considered a result of the larger number of women of childbearing age in the population, not a return to the pronatalist planning of the immediate postwar years.

78. University of California at Berkeley, "Chancellor Looks at Budget Cuts' Impact on Berkeley," *Monday Paper* 7, no. 7 (3 Nov. 1978), 1, 4.

79. The term is B. Claude Mathis's, in "The Teaching School—An Old Model in a New Context," *Journal of Teacher Education* 29 (May–June 1978).

80. Frederick E. Balderston, "Academic Program Review and the Determination of University Priorities," *International Journal of Institutional Management in Higher Education* 9, no. 3 (November 1985): 242–43.

percent became faculty.[81] Indeed, much of the postwar enrollment growth in American higher education was absorbed in supplying its own need for new professors. In all kinds of professional schools this resulted in cultivating academic rather than professional programs, no matter how dysfunctional in terms of professional needs.[82]

For a while schools of education lived on their graduate enrollments, but the disastrous market for teachers ultimately took effect since many with education doctorates were preparing to teach in the very schools, colleges, and departments of education that did little other than prepare teachers. In 1978, an unduly pessimistic projection was that many schools of education by 1980–81 would have 'melted' to a third or less of their 1970 faculty and a quarter or less of their students.[83] In a planning document for professional education in the University of California, its former dean asked of UCLA's graduate-student situation whether "the commitment of sixty faculty FTE to their production is desirable for cloning research-oriented professors," even if this cloning had been the best preparation for future teachers of teachers and administrators.[84] The University of Oregon began offering courses in "Interpersonal Relations" and "The Psychology of Adolescents" to police officers. Nonetheless, it had to release five of its eighteen untenured professors in the late 1970s.[85] At the state universities of Maine and West Virginia and the private New York University, omnibus schools of human services were created, swallowing up education schools, before this trend ended.

As with higher education generally, vulnerability to efficiency-minded administrators was greatest at those schools which had not diversified their activities. The decline in teacher demand was most telling at public universities with undergraduate education programs. In 1983, after ten years of retrenchment, the College of Education at the University of Minnesota was asked to prepare to reduce its budget by another 9 to 12 percent "to create a pool of flexible resources and

81. This was a higher proportion than in chemistry (25%) or the natural sciences average (41%). Calculated from data in Harmon and Soldz, *Doctorate Production,* 48.

82. Ernest A. Lynton, "Reexamining the Role of the University," *Change* 15, no. 7 (Oct. 1983): 20.

83. L. H. Browder, "Where are Schools of Education Going?" *Journal of Teacher Education* 29 (1978): 52–56.

84. John Goodlad, chair, *Report of the University-Wide Program Review Committee for Education* (University of California, Oct. 1984), 25.

85. Robert Vogel, "Teachers' Colleges Shift Their Focus to Related Fields," *New York Times,* 11 Nov. 1979.

cover possible reductions in state support." Only three other units in the university system were cut this deeply: Agriculture, Biological Sciences, and University College.[86] At the University of Hawaii, the chancellor appointed several task forces to study selected programs. Task Force C reviewed the College of Education to assess its needs and plans. Its conclusion was that the College's projection of a renewed demand for teachers in the state, and hence its efforts to recover some twenty lost positions, was wrong. Instead the College should raise its standards, thereby reducing enrollment by half over five years, losing more faculty positions in the process. The dean resigned, citing his refusal to comply with these recommendations.[87]

The School of Education of the private University of Pennsylvania came out of a threatening review in better shape than did Hawaii's demoralized and leaderless faculty. Martin Myerson, formerly chancellor at Berkeley, tried to close Penn's School of Education to conserve resources. The School was retained, reportedly because the response from "the field" was immediate and positive. A history of good relations with the profession and the strategic placement of many of its graduates in important positions in southeast Pennsylvania, New Jersey, and adjoining areas was credited by one alumnus with the result. The School eventually obtained a new dean and several faculty increases.[88]

The aging of the teaching force was another consequence for education schools of the teacher surplus. Fearful of being able to reenter a saturated market if they left teaching temporarily or sought other positions in education, America's teachers held on to their jobs to an extent matched only in the 1930s. Given the flat salary structure of the teaching profession, in some geographical areas a majority of teachers had reached the maximum of their districts' salary schedule and had no financial incentive to pursue further university course work. If they wished to improve their salaries, they could choose teacher-created staff development and teacher center programs at the expense of schools of education and university extension courses. For decades the master of education had been the most popular advanced degree for both men and women, being linked to many salary scales;

86. University of Minnesota, College of Education, *Points* 11, no. 7 (15 March 1983), a newsletter.

87. June Watanabe, "UH's Dean of Education Quits in Policy Dispute," *Honolulu Star-Bulletin,* 4 May 1984.

88. Theodore L. Reller, interview with Geraldine Clifford, Berkeley, 11 Sept. 1985.

before 1980, however, the master of education had declined as a share of all master's degrees.[89]

A further development of this period, one that we think confirmed schools of education as "suspect" and vulnerable institutions, was the growing percentage of women students, especially at the doctoral level. From having 21 percent of education doctorates awarded in 1971 and 34 percent in 1977, women went on to receive 44.4 percent in 1980 and 49 percent in 1982.[90] Between 1975 and 1980, women's share of the enrollments at Harvard's Graduate School of Education grew from 53 percent to 65 percent.[91] Responses to a survey conducted by Michigan's School of Education indicated that, in the period 1975–78, of thirty-one major public and private schools of education, only four graduated more doctoral women than men; the women's average for all the institutions was 48.1 percent. Among enrolled doctoral students in 1979–82, however, eight institutions enrolled more women than men and the all-institution average for women had risen to 50 percent.[92] Although distributed unevenly among programs, women students went from around 20 percent of those in school administration at Harvard and Berkeley in the early 1970s to a majority by the mid-1980s. By 1986 women were 43 per cent of the membership of the American Educational Research Association.

The modern-day counterparts of the late nineteenth-century colleges' "Ladies' Course" are today's schools of nursing, home economics, social welfare, librarianship, and education, as well as those academic departments with "dangerously high levels" of women students. Suzanne Hildenbrand, who has compared the development and status of differing professions, suggests that male sociologists invariably label "female-intensive" fields as the "semi-professions," a term seldom applied to such predominantly male occupations as optometry, city planning, and forestry.[93] Among professional schools, as among

89. Baker, *Earned Degrees,* 16.

90. Ibid., 34; Lois Weis, "Progress but No Parity: Women in Higher Education," *Academe* 71, no. 6 (Nov.–Dec. 1985): 31.

91. Bonney, "A Profile." Different figures are found in Paul N. Ylvisaker, "HSGE 1977: Another Stage of Growth," Harvard University, Graduate School of Education. He writes that women's share went from 45 percent in 1967 to 63 percent in 1976.

92. University of California at Berkeley, School of Education, Historical files. Eunice L. Burns to Robert B. Ruddell, 7 May 1979.

93. Suzanne Hildenbrand, "Ambiguous Authority and Aborted Ambition: Gender, Professionalism, and the Rise and Fall of the Welfare State," *Library Trends* 34, no. 2 (Fall 1985), note 1.

academic departments, the available research appears to confirm ordinary observation: Men's fields enjoy more prestige, self-confidence, power, and rewards. This affects their students, faculty, subject matter, and resources.[94] Even in an era when affirmative action was a publicly proclaimed goal of institutions of higher education, the prosperity and survivability of male fields was arguably much greater.

Conclusion

This period in the history of American education began with an external threat amidst internal disarray. The Soviet Sputnik and the ravages of progressive education were the respective markers. Thirty years later economic competition with Japan and a less-focused vision of the causes of school inadequacies gave a new impetus to the movement to save society through school reform. It was timely, therefore, that Derek Bok chose education as the subject for his 1985–86 president's report to the Harvard Overseers. He noted that education schools were missing in the intense contemporary debate about education, that their faculties were absent from the commissions and task forces framing the issues, and that the "surging interest in the schools" had failed to raise the campus status of schools of education in research universities.[95] The strong, if controversial position taken by the Holmes Group of deans of graduate schools of education, ended the near-invisibility of education schools in the 1980s reform movement, but the final issue remains in doubt.

Bok had in mind the 150 graduate schools of education, some 10 percent of the total that contribute to teacher education in the United States. Unlike the major teacher-producing universities, the big-name schools of education have been relatively more insulated from the demographic, market, and regulatory imperatives located beyond their campuses. Although not immune from these forces, the institutions featured in *Ed School* have been driven primarily by the institutional histories of the research universities in which they have been uneasily situated since 1900 or earlier. The universities remain their primary environment, other academics their chief critics. The shifting priori-

94. Saul D. Feldman, *Escape from the Doll's House: Women in Graduate and Professional School Education,* report for the Carnegie Commission on Higher Education (New York: McGraw-Hill, 1974), 46–57. See also Kenneth L. Wilson and Eui Hang Shin, "Reassessing the Discrimination Against Women in Higher Education," *American Educational Research Journal* 20, no. 4 (Winter 1983): 529–51.

95. Derek Bok, "The President's Report 1985–86, Harvard University" (Cambridge, Mass.: Harvard University, April 1987), 1.

ties of governments and foundations have been experienced by education schools chiefly in the scramble for research funding.[96]

Although universities have been far less affected by social vicissitudes than have been the elementary and secondary schools, their fivefold growth since World War II has left them more vulnerable to outside influence, and more ready to accept bureaucratic structures and rationalized planning models. In chapters 6 and 7 we turn, through case studies, to the interplay between old academic values, chronic tensions, and the new mechanisms for sorting among institutional preferences and prejudices.

96. For a critique of funds spent on problems as defined by federal functionaries see Theodore R. Sizer, "On Myopia: A Complaint from Down Below," *Daedalus* 103, no. 4 (Fall 1974): 337.

Six Case Studies in Academic Politics and Institutional Cultures

The experiences of Yale's Department of Education early in the post–World War II period, when college enrollments were booming and graduate education was prospering even more, furnish an instructive example of the potentially fatal consequences when chronic institutional tensions interact with external pressures. The intense postwar criticism of public schools and teacher education "was enough to reactivate and strengthen the group at Yale that have been lukewarm toward the professional study of education from the very outset sixty years before, and had never really slackened its opposition," in the understated words of Yale's John Brubacher, one of those left to "turn out the lights."[1]

In 1952 President Griswold announced a master of arts in teaching program "to revive the liberal arts as a force in American secondary education."[2] Some Yale College faculty were concerned about the teacher shortage and increased credential requirements set by Connecticut. The president was already a vocal critic of those "stifling, technique-oriented" courses of the usual teachers college program that reportedly repelled the better students.[3] Seymour Sarason, a Yale psychologist unusual for his persistent involvement in education,

1. Brubacher et al., *Department of Education,* 47. An internationally known historian of education and holder of an endowed chair, Brubacher found himself a teacher without students at Yale and finished his career at the University of Michigan. William Brickman chaired a committee to investigate the academic freedom issue and reported bitterly on the affair in "Power Conflicts and Crises," 25–26.

2. Woodring, *New Directions,* 50, 134–36.

3. Sarason, *Culture of the School,* 61.

recalled the principal reactions among the faculty: Some were indifferent provided that Yale "did not give education anything resembling an important status;" many preferred that nothing be done; others approved "if a token gesture would keep the president happy;" and still others saw the MAT as "fulfilling an obligation of a university to the larger society in a manner consistent with its traditions (*including that of noblesse oblige*); that is, the students would be of high quality, they would take the regular courses in the area of their special interests, and they would be treated and evaluated like any other student in the university."[4]

The director of the MAT program expressed his own hope that the study of education in terms of its philosophy, history, psychology, and sociology would replace the undue concern with methodology and technique in conventional teaching programs.[5] Innovation was primarily organizational, however, for the leading parties assumed, falsely, that the existing academic courses were perfectly functional for prospective secondary school teachers. One had to know, Sarason observes, that the new program was initiated in a setting hostile to teacher education.

Given a large Ford Foundation grant and placed under the direction of a professor of English, the program had no place for educationists. The junior year introductory course, "Basic Concepts of Education," was taught by a professor of philosophy and the senior year course, "Education in American Society," by a professor of psychology. The fifth-year program combined courses given by academicians with the desired "bare minimum" of professional courses offered by present or former secondary school teachers.

The "gradual dissolution" of the Department of Education, begun in 1951, was completed in 1958 when its last degree was awarded. There had been only six full-time faculty in 1952 and retirements without replacements and some joint appointments with other departments made the small faculty an easy target for elimination. Requests from the Department for meetings with President Griswold went unanswered. Despite the recommendation of a presidential committee that doctoral work be resumed, and without consultation with the education faculty, Griswold finally acted to put them out of the misery of prolonged uncertainty. At Yale, "the mother of universities," one of the nation's better-regarded departments of education disappeared.

4. Ibid., 62.

5. Stone, *Breakthrough,* 113. For a good summary of the relevant criticism and its consequences see Woodring, "Development of Teacher Education," esp. 16–24.

In the dramatic incidents of education school histories, individual actions often appear to dominate the script. President Griswold seemed stubbornly determined to close Yale's Department of Education. President James Perkins of Cornell, also a nationally known spokesman for postwar higher education, assumed that role—leaving behind, however, a department when he closed Cornell's school of education in 1963. Conversely, Presidents Kennedy of Stanford and Bok of Harvard emerge as their visionary opposites a quarter-century later when they urged elite universities to strengthen their schools of education, not to close them. Engineering professor Stanley Berger at Berkeley and mathematics professor Daniel Gorenstein at Rutgers live on in the annals while the faculty committees they chaired to review schools of education are forgotten; more about this later. It goes without saying that human agency, not "institutional will," causes actions. Nonetheless, individuals act in social contexts. Hence, our case studies were conceived and written to demonstrate how institutional cultures, historically evolved, guided the pen of even the strongest leaders.

We were not systematic in our selection of case studies for this chapter, and the amount of detail we could provide is quite varied—some examples are mere outlines. These institutions, however, represent a mix of leading and lesser places, each brought to our attention by fellow educationists who thought their stories both instructive and representative. The first account, of Yale, and the last, of Chicago, describe places that are, admittedly, uncommon on various dimensions. We feel sure, however, that readers will recognize in these diverse portraits features and phenomena that "ring true" in their own situations, that locate universals in particularities.

Institutions in Transition: Three Case Studies

In the examples in this section three types of institutional transformations are chronicled. The first, the disappearance of one of the nation's few surviving independent teachers colleges, represents the last act of a half-century-long process wherein autonomous professional schools closed or became mere units of multipurpose universities. The second case study illustrates a decision to sacrifice a program in professional education in order to secure an emerging institutional self-image. The third and most detailed example presents a less drastic but more commonly experienced event in the recent histories of schools of education: schools trimmed to meet severe economic realities and harsh academic criticism.

The End of Another Independent Teachers College: George Peabody

In 1960, 8 percent of America's institutions of higher education were teacher-preparatory schools; by 1980 none were so listed, as failures and mergers closed this chapter in the history of professional education. Southern traditions of regard for history and family had helped sustain George Peabody College for Teachers in Nashville, Tennessee. Long after other private teachers colleges had vanished, merged, or created an uneasy alliance with a nearby university—as in the case of New York City's Teachers College and Columbia University—Peabody had some 27,000 living and devoted alumni, an endowment of about fourteen million dollars, excellent facilities, and a beautiful campus in a region that valued longevity. In 1957 Peabody's President Henry H. Hill boasted of the harmony existing between its disciplinary and professional faculties, telling a national conference:

> At George Peabody College I preside over a unique situation: our liberal arts professors in history, mathematics, and other areas rub shoulders daily with our education professors. The result seems, in the climate of American academic opinion, unbelievable. They actually like each other and show as much respect for each other as can be expected of a group of professors. . . . The reason? Well, we live close together in an institution long dedicated to the teaching profession on a campus with a laboratory school and many interesting efforts to improve schools and school buildings and school teaching.[6]

Over the years Peabody had also diversifed, enabling itself to withstand fluctuations in the market for teachers. Its faculty offered liberal arts programs and a major in business, although the majority of its undergraduates prepared themselves to teach. The College also opened one of the best library schools in the South. An entrepreneurial faculty secured extramural grants as they became available; a third of its budget in recent years came through "soft money." The largest portion came from the National Institutes of Health for research in the area of mental retardation. While some faculty conducted basic neurological research on the brain, others pursued applied research on such matters as family intervention.

In the early 1970s, as the demand for teachers was about to plummet, the Board of Trustees decided to reassert the College's

6. Henry H. Hill, "Preparing Teachers," 259.

commitment to teacher education.[7] The faculty was reorganized into matrices as traditional departments were eliminated. Not only were faculty heads reeling, but many important items were left unattended in the reorganization. As the market for teachers worsened, the commitment to this new course was not reversed. Entrance requirements had to be dropped to fill the classes depleted by the potential teachers who were pursuing more promising careers. A higher-education program with an emphasis on the junior college was added. The school administration program was expanded as a money-maker; by the end there were well over one hundred Ph.D. students, most of them in school administration. Traditional distinctions between the Ph.D. and the Ed.D. were eroded. To increase their salaries some of the faculty took on as many as eight or nine classes. There was, by 1980, only one extramural grant outside the areas of psychology and special education. The board and president had guessed wrong, and with the signs of institutional decline everywhere, a merger was proposed with nearby Vanderbilt University.

Collaborations between Peabody and Vanderbilt extended back into "the good times." Before Vanderbilt had any programs in education, those of its students who wished to teach enrolled in Peabody courses. Peabody and Vanderbilt shared a large central library. Of a more questionable nature was an arrangement whereby Peabody students could play on Vanderbilt athletic teams; when Peabody's entrance requirements were lowered, this became a tempting way for Vanderbilt to recruit athletes of dubious academic status. More positively, there was an institutional commitment to professional education left over from Vanderbilt's experience with a Ford-funded MAT program. When funding ended, the chancellor made the firm decision that teacher education would be a permanent, institutionally supported component of the University and the faculty agreed after some initial resistance. Vanderbilt lacked, however, two things that Peabody possessed: a faculty who studied teaching and learning in schools and the cooperative relationships with schools needed to provide the supervision and cooperative planning needed for exemplary professional programs.[8]

Chancellor Alexander Heard was anxious to make Vanderbilt a

7. Most of the details of what follows come from a telephone interview by Geraldine Clifford with Dean Willis D. Hawley of Peabody College for Teachers in Vanderbilt University, 9 April 1986. We are also grateful to Dean Hawley for commenting on an earlier draft.

8. Coley and Thorpe, *A Look at the MAT Model,* 23, 27.

comprehensive university. It already had a highly rated theology school, was about to add a music school, and was making a substantial investment in its business school. It needed additional dormitory space, which Peabody had. Peabody's trustees were encouraged by Heard's agreement that additional resources would be invested in Peabody if it became Vanderbilt's school of education; Peabody would not live on as an embarrassment to the University. The Peabody faculty was divided on the merger, but in July 1979 it took place. Locally it was said that "Vandy took the place over." Promises, however, were kept. The University probably invested more money in Peabody than any other American university was then investing in its school of education. A new dean, Willis D. Hawley, was brought in from the Institute for Public Policy Studies at Duke University. Within three years after the merger enrollments had increased, the faculty's scholarly productivity almost doubled, and external funding was growing.

"Reaching for Excellence": Duke University

Not all decisions to close or curtail academic programs are taken in response to crisis or to reduce or reallocate an institution's financial obligations. Sometimes they are a response to rising institutional ambitions, as in the decision of Duke University to close its School of Nursing and Department of Education in 1982.[9] Duke University was a different institution in the late 1970s than it had been even a decade before. It had enormous ambitions to use its resources to become a front-rank university. Having the nation's fifteenth largest endowment—no longer dependent on the American Tobacco Company of the Duke family—Duke recruited talented faculty to improve its reputation. Virtually overnight it went from regional to national status, from a student body of 65 percent Southerners to one of 65 percent Northerners. Its most highly regarded professional schools and departments were medicine, a law school, and a new business school of which the University was very proud and which was attracting large gifts. There was, however, a sharp drop in the perceived status of its other professional programs: the engineering, divinity, forestry, and nursing schools, and the education department.

9. Details on the Duke case were supplied by Joseph Di Bona, professor of education, in a telephone interview by Geraldine Clifford, 5 September 1986 and by Willis D. Hawley, former professor of political science and member of the Assessment Committee that recommended the actions described. We are also indebted to Dean Hawley for his comments on an earlier version of our Duke case study.

Duke had been one of the original institutions to receive Ford money for an MAT Breakthrough Program in 1959, a program that was unconnected with Duke's standard undergraduate teacher education. Duke's president wrote the presidents of thirty colleges in the geographic area that did not have graduate programs in education, to entice their graduates to Duke to prepare for teaching and to identify faculty representatives who would advise them. A panel of superintendents of eight cooperating school districts was linked with the program's advisory committee.[10] By the time the MAT was discontinued in the late 1970s, however, whatever spillover prestige effects and important support it once possessed were gone. If there ever had been allusions to the "wonderful MAT students" they were no longer heard; anyway those had been "Duke students" and not "education students." The conventional wisdom had it that the small education department of about twenty mostly tenured faculty was a weak unit which, with a few exceptions, produced little research or scholarship—under ten publications in a good year.

The departments of Education, Sociology, Health and Physical Education, and the Schools of Nursing and of Forestry and Environmental Planning were selected for review by the chancellor and the provost. A fifteen-member Assessment Committee was carefully chosen by the Faculty Senate and the provost to confer legitimacy on whatever decisions were reached. No member of the scrutinized units was among the mostly senior and highly respected faculty impaneled. The two considerations placed on the table were cost savings and the possibilities of excellence; weaker units had to be sacrificed in order to strengthen those which could reasonably achieve excellence.

As it turned out, the review exonerated Sociology, although the experience caused a loss of students and serious erosion of faculty morale. Forestry and Environmental Planning was put on notice for future review, Health and Physical Education was demoted from an academic department to a service unit, and Nursing and Education were recommended to be closed, their faculties terminated or relocated. There was no protest within the state to "save Education." The review apparently captured widespread agreement that, despite its large numbers of students, the program was of little use. There was modest alumni concern, but the possibility of upgrading the school administration program appeared to appease that. There was little commentary about the fact that the two disappearing units represented "women's professions" and that Duke had no other professional

10. Coley and Thorpe, *A Look at the MAT Model,* 22.

schools in women's fields. News that the nursing students averaged three hundred points lower on the Scholastic Aptitude Test than the student body average and the fact that the nursing dorms kept these women students from being well integrated in the student body dampened this issue.[11] Had there been a more active local women's movement, the University could have disarmed it with the word that it was seeking actively to recruit women students to medicine, law, economics, and business—thus appealing to the elitism that was then so evident in the women's movement, especially on college campuses.

The Committee made no argument for retaining the Department of Education; it clearly appeared far from excellent. Its closing would cause little disruption: it had almost no undergraduates and the few small classes offered to provide students what they needed for certification could be taken at the University of North Carolina, eleven miles distant, or at the state's Greenville or Charlotte campuses. Its graduate programs, however, generated one fifth of the total income of the Duke Graduate School; most of these students were Ed.D. candidates, local school administrators. It was proposed that this lucrative professional program be continued through courses offered elsewhere on campus: school law in the Law School, developmental psychology in the Psychology Department, etc. A small core of faculty members with good connections with the schools would continue as coordinators or advisors. The plan seemed logical but doomed from the start, fatally flawed because very few academic faculty were willing to offer the courses desired by school professionals. No students were admitted for graduate degrees in education. No one cared much since the graduates of these programs were not expected to contribute much to the University's endowment. The position of Horace Mann over a century earlier seemed vindicated: that normal schools had to exist to do what college faculty did not want to do.

While eliminating the undergraduate major in education that led to state certification and ending all training in elementary education, Duke prudently followed the lead of other prestigious colleges in retaining an option whereby undergraduates could become secondary school teachers by combining an A.B. degree with certification in four years. It recognized that teaching paid poorly and students in high-tuition schools might resist more lengthy (and costly) programs. This abbreviated but state-approved arrangement was popular with

11. In fact, the decision to close the School of Nursing was later modified. In the context of a national shortage of nurses, the undergraduate program disappeared, but a dean and a small faculty remained to train a few graduate specialists.

humanities and social science majors; it recruited able students who scored well on the National Teachers' Examination and other measures; they were sought out by school districts in the state and region. Paradoxically, the five full-time, tenured faculty in the Education Program who survived the Department's elimination were all "foundation types"—social and behavioral scientists. Since they represented a poor fit with the practical needs of a teacher certification program, the University was forced to find part-time and nonprofessorial faculty to teach the methods classes and supervise student teaching.

While the education faculty offered nonprofessional courses that were attractive to Duke undergraduates, as program faculty they had less interaction in matters like service on dissertation committees than they had enjoyed as department members. Meanwhile Duke was pressured from the outside to do something affirmative in the area of teacher education. Duke was treading water and waiting to see what Ivy League and other private colleges would do with the issue of teacher education—an issue which, seemingly, would not go away.

Economic Adversity and the University of Michigan

The American economy posed another threat to schools and schools of education throughout the 1970s. High inflation, fueled by the Vietnam war and the Mideast oil crisis, reduced buying power and raised taxpayer resistance to government spending. The growing obsolescence of American manufacturing and transportation structures slowed economic growth. Reduced productivity and the high relative cost of labor made Americans increasingly conscious of the economic threat posed by other nations' more competitive industries. By the early 1980s a recession was evident on most fronts. Unemployment rates reached and exceeded any known since the Great Depression; in Michigan they were twice the national average.[12] State governments were forced to use more of their revenues to assist the unemployed and to stimulate economic development at the same time that their revenues were shrinking.

Particularly hard-pressed were the industrialized Northeast and North Central regions of the United States. These "snowbelt" and "smokestack" areas had been losing population and industry to the

12. Three consecutive quarters of downturn in key indicators made the recession official. Unemployment rates were rising in 1981 and broke postwar records in 1982; the previous postwar record had been set in 1975, in connection with the international oil crisis.

"sunbelt" states since the end of World War II. By the 1970s they were particularly disadvantaged by the aging of their manufacturing plants and high energy costs. As the center of the domestic production of automobiles, trucks, and tractors, Michigan—and its largest city, Detroit—were among the most affected. By 1980, state and local governments mandated budget cutting and hiring freezes as private employers laid off workers, reduced the state's income, and added to the welfare rolls. No publically funded institutions were exempted from the red pencil. In its application, however, lay the great threat of downward mobility in the prestige rankings that mean so much to American universities.[13] Meanwhile, another institution, Michigan State University, saw its chance and grew in estimation and usefulness, as we will later see.

One of the most prestigious of the nation's public and private universities, the University of Michigan pioneered in the articulation of a vision of the state university as capstone of an entire system of public education, assisted by a constitution that gave it unusual independence. In 1871 it began the nation's first high school accreditation process whereby university professors visited schools and approved those whose students could enter the University directly. The inheritor of this role, the Bureau of School Services in the School of Education, continued to perform the function which most other states ceded to their state departments of education. In 1923 the regents of the University formally expressed this tradition of involvement with schools by adopting a bylaw that recognized the function of "bringing all schools into closer relation with the University to give a more perfect unity to the state educational system."

Yet, on his retirement as dean of Education at Michigan, Wilbur Cohen noted, with restraint, that education schools, their faculties, and students "generally go unheralded among the medical, law, engineering, business, math, physics, and chemistry units."[14] Michigan's School of Education was one of the earliest founded in a state university and was rated "excellent" in the 1934 survey of graduate programs by the American Council on Education; it continued to appear well ranked nationally in subsequent reputational studies. By the 1970s,

13. Trow, "Analysis of Status," 136.

14. University of Michigan, School of Education, Wilbur E. Cohen, "Report to the President," *Innovator* 10 (30 Nov. 1978): 2. It is worth noting that Cohen was the bureaucratic father of social security in the 1930s, a highly respected undersecretary in the Department of Health, Education, and Welfare in the 1960s, an able academic. Nonetheless, he was unable to render Michigan's School of Education respectable in Ann Arbor. Cohen died in 1986.

however, it was mired in difficulties. These included traditional academic suspicion of schools of education and a swollen, underfunded structure that could not bear close scrutiny even before the budget cutters appeared on the scene. There were fifty-four identifiable doctoral and sixty-three masters' specializations. The School's faculty included former teachers of the University School, who concentrated upon teaching in undergraduate programs in education, faculty assigned to the School by campus administrators when other units were closed or cut back, as well as education professors of greatly varying degrees of scholarly productivity and widely divergent interests. The faculty numbered 125 at one point. Probably only the program in higher education was nationally regarded as excellent, however, while that in school administration ranked very well in the state.

As was also happening at other institutions since the mid 1970s, the School's balance between undergraduate and doctoral enrollments had shifted markedly. A study of the employment of doctoral students, based on 1964–70 and 1974–80 graduates, reported that 22 percent were employed in elementary and secondary education—as teachers, consultants, principals, and superintendents—while 55 percent had college and university positions. Overall enrollments in the School had declined, however, from a peak of nearly 2,400 in 1974 to 1,200 in 1980. The declines were, in part, a function of the market for teachers and, with respect to doctoral students, the associated reduction in opportunities for those who would be employed in primarily teacher education institutions.[15]

Since 1978, the School had attempted to reduce enrollments in a selective fashion—so as to bring faculty-student ratios into line with patterns existing in more highly regarded campus departments (and in comparison education schools) and to raise overall student quality. It tried to use enrollment decisions to strengthen programs thought to be stronger and to starve those of lesser quality. All of these goals responded to general criticisms of education schools made by their academic counterparts. Plans to maintain graduate enrollments while reducing undergraduates posed two threats: one was perpetuating the inadequacies of underfunded graduate instruction and the second was subjecting more of the School's students to the scrutiny of the Graduate School. The University's Rackham Graduate School had already conducted an examination of doctoral dissertations from the mid-1970s; Dean Stark characterized its report as having been written

15. From its peak production year (1969–70), when 1,480 teacher certificates were awarded, there was a consistent decline. By 1977–78 the figure had been halved.

"much more critically than [were] reports of similar studies for other U-M departments."

Given the state budget crisis, administrators in all of Michigan's higher education institutions were forced to economize, with budget reductions of up to 6 percent. In 1981 Dean Joan Stark and the School's Executive Committee began an internal review to reorganize the School. By January 1983, the remaining fourteen academic programs were consolidated into five divisions and a School-wide administrative structure was created to coordinate the whole, which included centralizing certain responsibilities for teacher education."[16] Despite internal differences of opinion about the need for and direction of the reorganization, the School's leadership believed that considerable internal housecleaning was inevitable, and essential to protect the School from the full consequences of external challenges. "We think we were following the president's mandate to get smaller and better on our own," Stark explained. "Smaller and better" was the central Administration's motto—meaning "reduce the University's activities, staff, and budget at the expense of weaker faculty and non-priority programs."[17]

The Budget Priorities Committee Takes a Look. Internal dissension paled in comparison with the threats from campus administrators and state budgetary officers. The administration seemed little interested in the plans developed by the School, as it had its own approach.[18] The University announced a five-year plan to reduce general fund programs by $20 million and to reallocate that money "into a selected set of high-priority programs." This was taken to mean new funds to support growth in business and such high-technology fields as engineering and robotics. In March 1982, Vice-President for Academic Affairs and Provost Billie Frye announced that, as part of the reduction-and-reallocation plan, three schools were being reviewed: Education, Natural Resources, and Art.[19]

16. John Beckett, "Dean Hopes to See Reorganization Incorporated in Education School's Review," *Ann Arbor News,* 6 January 1983. Copies of the *Ann Arbor News* are courtesy of Bobbi Figy.

17. Gerlinda S. Melchiori, "Smaller and Better: The University of Michigan," *Research in Higher Education* 16, no. 1 (1982): 58.

18. John Beckett, "Recommended Cuts in Education School Hard to Take, Dean Says," *Ann Arbor News,* 29 May 1983.

19. Also under review were the Center for Continuing Education of Women and institutes involved with labor studies and mental retardation. The University of Michigan Associates in the School Foundations of Education, "School of Education Threat-

At four large public meetings the Budget Priorities Committee took testimony from some one hundred students, alumni, educators, and friends of the School. No member of any of the interested schools and centers was a member of the Committee, and only one meeting was held with the School's executive committee. In the School's newsletter, *Innovator,* the Dean had already warned that proposals had been heard to reduce the School's budget far more than was proposed for other schools and colleges at Ann Arbor, and that the School might even be closed. Consistent with a campus goal of faculty shrinkage the School itself anticipated a 10 percent reduction over the period ending in 1986–87. The University-wide committee would, however, "review the school and portray scenarios that might result from budget reductions of 10 percent to 100 percent."[20] Those receiving *Innovator* were asked to examine the issues and to inform university administrators of their support for both the education profession and Michigan's School of Education."

The needs of the state and nation for leaders in all kinds of positions in education, as well as the challenges posed by new technologies for education, were stressed as the reasons to maintain and even to increase the School's current level of support. Since the School produced only 6 percent of the state's newly-certified teachers in 1980–81, it could not claim that it performed an essential service in this regard, or that a new teacher shortage must necessarily find it ready to meet that challenge.[21] Neither was there much evidence that Michigan academics, any more than faculty at other high-status universities, wanted to see the School concentrate its efforts on undergraduate teacher education. Nor was there notable support for the School's off-campus and "professional development" students. While Michigan State University proposed to meet its budget stringencies by giving greater emphasis to preparing teachers and other school personnel,

---

ened," *Notes and Abstracts in American and International Education,* no. 61 (Summer–Fall 1982) 1.

20. Joan S. Stark, University of Michigan, School of Education, "Annual Report to the President of the University," *Innovator* 14, no. 3 (December 1982): 1. Many of the data on the School of Education are drawn from this issue. We are grateful to Dean Carl Berger for information on events after 1983. He bears no responsibility for our interpretations, however.

21. Students receiving Michigan certificates in secondary school teaching areas might receive Letters, Science, and Arts degrees, rather than degrees from the School of Education. All told, and counting the campuses at Flint and Dearborn, the University of Michigan produced under 10 percent of all new teaching certificates in that year. *Ibid.,* 5.

the University of Michigan faculty in education and the academics who constituted the Budget Priorities Committee chose to reemphasize graduate education for the preparation of leaders and the development and dissemination of knowledge.

In its report the Budget Priorities Committee proposed large cuts in the three schools reviewed: a 25 percent cut in the budget of the School of Art, a 33 percent reduction in Natural Resources, and a recommendation that the School of Education's general fund budget be reduced by 40 percent. To bring faculty ratios closer to graduate school norms, it concluded that, by 1986–87, Education's then-current enrollments be reduced by over half, to 500 students. All undergraduate teacher education was to be eliminated. In recognition of the reduction in revenue and the negative political implications of this proposal, the Administration decided instead that enrollment be held to the 1983 level of 1,400 students while the ladder faculty, largely tenured, be cut from 75 to 45, and the School's annual general fund budget reduced from $4.8 million to $2.9 million. The Ed.D. was to become the School's primary degree; authority to grant the Ph.D. was limited to joint programs with other departments, at least for the time being. The Board of Regents subsequently endorsed this recommendation and a "Transition Team" was appointed to develop plans to realize the reductions by the target date of 1988–89. In what was becoming a widely repeated refrain, the regents also recommended that the central mission of the School be "the improvement of elementary and secondary education through significant, high-quality research, teaching, and service," by identifying "intellectual foci around which to establish 'centers of excellence'." A new "transition dean," formerly the associate dean, was appointed. Carl F. Berger pledged to try to meet the objectives and to begin to repair the damage: "For nearly twenty months the School of Education has been under review. During that time our reputation across the state, the nation and, most importantly, across the campus has eroded."[22]

The Aftermath. In the implementation phase the School's five major programs were reduced by the transfer of the program in physical

22. Dean Berger is quoted in Max Gates, "Education School Budget Axed—But Not Enrollment," *Ann Arbor News,* 16 September 1983. See also University of Michigan Associates in the Social Foundations of Education, "School of Education Reduced Dramatically," *Notes and Abstracts in American and International Education* 62 (1983): 1–4 and "School of Education Transition Team," *Notes and Abstracts in American and International Education,* no. 63 (1984): 4–6.

education out of the School and by the identification of four areas of intellectual and research emphasis. The enrollment goal was a student body of 60 percent graduates and 40 percent undergraduates. The target for teacher education certificates annually was about ninety each of elementary and secondary school teachers. Larger beginning courses would generate the "student head count" to justify small advanced and graduate courses. The projected reorientation from service to research was completed by a new Center for Research on Learning in Schools, the continuation of the Center for the Study of Higher and Postsecondary Education, and reorganization of the Bureau of School Services as a self-supporting Bureau of School Accreditation and Improvement Studies, with a policy focus. By early 1986 faculty reduction goals were on schedule; negotiations with twenty-six of the thirty faculty to be eliminated had produced agreements about their departures by 1988–89. While some of the faculty were angered, others were buoyed by the fact that new faculty searches had been authorized for four positions.

Between the faculty committee's report and the final decision by the administration and regents, University President Harold T. Shapiro was invited to attend a conference at Pajaro Dunes, California in the summer of 1983. The presidents of Stanford and Harvard Universities, Donald Kennedy and Derek Bok, on the advice of their deans of education, selected seven university presidents or chancellors and four deans of schools of education to consider how elite universities might collaborate with American public schools, in a new and mutually-respectful partnership. At the conclusion of the conference, the presidents pledged to "insure excellence" in education through joint ventures, involving education and academic faculty and school personnel. In the opinions of the organizers, three or four schools of education were "saved" as a result of this extraordinary event—which, behind the public rhetoric, was a message from two powerful university presidents to their counterparts "to lay off" bashing their schools of education.[23] The *Ann Arbor News* was not alone in wondering, however, whether the cuts proposed at Michigan—including the near-elimination of teacher preparation and the Bureau of School Services—were consistent with the Pajaro Dunes manifesto. Provost Frye disputed any inconsistency but acknowledged to reporters that

23. Correspondence of Dean Patricia Graham (Harvard) with Dean J. Myron Atkin (Stanford), January 1983, courtesy of Dean Graham; interviews by Geraldine Clifford with Dean Atkin, 15 April 1986, at Stanford University, and with Dean Graham, 21 February 1986, at Berkeley.

the school reform movement had "impressed upon him the importance of preparing teachers for those schools."[24]

Throughout its ordeal, Michigan's School of Education continued to claim the high regard in which it was held by the national community of schools, colleges, and departments of education. If it was merited, rather than merely a reflection of "herd instinct," this regard was rarely reflected on campus. The initiatives the pared-down School subsequently took were fated to receive little support by the campus administration. Thus, when the School proposed, in early 1986, a program to assist the Detroit public schools in retraining mathematics teachers, at small cost to the University, the initiative was quickly rejected by President Shapiro as being incompatible with the budget cuts assigned to the School of Education. Whatever momentum the School could generate would have to depend largely on its inner resources—that is, upon the 60 percent that remained.

Meanwhile, at East Lansing. At Michigan State University the College of Education emerged as both the most credible center for professional preparation in Michigan and a national resource on research and training for teacher education.[25] The new dean, Judith Lanier, attracted campus approbation from the start by viewing the budgetary crisis as an unparalleled opportunity to strengthen the College and its Institute for Research on Teaching. Forty faculty positions were eliminated by early retirements and buy-outs, and unproductive units were removed, including those that did not advance the clear image of a professional school that integrated training with applied disciplinary research in a creative amalgam. Within four years the lost tenure lines were regained and the College's faculty stood at two hundred. The conventional School of Elementary and Secondary Education had been transformed into the Department of Teacher Education. With eighty-five positions the College's largest unit, it merged all foundations faculty in the social sciences and humanities with curriculum and methods specialists and those responsible for supervising student teachers. This represented an unprecedented commitment to applied scholarship in preparing teachers and teacher educators.

24. "U-M Cuts, Shapiro Statement in Conflict?" *Ann Arbor News,* 17 August 1983; John Dunn," Bureau of School Services Cuts Bringing Howls From around State," *Ann Arbor News,* 22 April 1983.

25. Professor Lee Shulman of Stanford persuaded us to begin this case study contrast with the University of Michigan. We are also indebted to Michael Sedlak and Gary Sykes of Michigan State for some of the details.

Michigan State's old College of Education had little national or local status. The few highly regarded Education faculty tended not to be associated in people's minds with the College. The federally funded Institute for Research on Teaching had been secured in 1976 not because of the College's academic quality but because of its professional character and collaborations with teachers.[26] In 1984 another federal competition, for a research and development center on teacher education, was also won by Michigan State University in the recognition that it had become the national locus for research and training initiates in teaching. In 1980 the schools administration program was still being run by nonpublishing former school administrators who consulted actively with practicing administrators; it had skipped entirely the phase of hiring "context-free" administrative theorists. The Lanier-directed reforms included adding faculty with research and publishing capability to those existing in school administration. The College's broad strategies included gaining campus recognition for professional publications and activities, and designing mechanisms to protect applied researchers from conventional academic canons and traditional "accounting" systems. In what would be an interesting reversal, if true, persons with strong applied interests were believed to have higher salaries than the "theoretical types."

A conventional undergraduate teacher certification program was retained, including the income and political support it generated, but, as the nation entered a phase of the school reform movement that extolled more demanding teacher education and certification and that promised greater teacher professionalism as the reward, four innovative and highly selective alternatives were designed. Michigan State–trained teachers were a premium in the state. One of its organizers in 1983, Dean Lanier was made head of the aggressive new national organization of education deans in research universities: the Holmes Group. Even more remarkable than her national visibility was the perception on campus that the most highly regarded dean and the most credible, exciting activities in all of Michigan State's professional programs belonged to the Ed School.

As the story of the Univeristy of Michigan makes clear, external events like the worsening economic situation of its region were dealt

26. Such collaborations with practitioners include arrangements whereby teachers spend their mornings in their schools, teaching, and their afternoons at the Institute of Research on Teaching, conducting research. Michigan State University, Institute for Research on Teaching, *IRT Communication Quarterly* 9, no. 1 (Fall 1986): 1.

with by local actors who responded, as best they could, in ways they considered appropriate to the indigenous institutional culture and prevailing status system. While interest and perceptions of faculty committees were not identical with those of University administrators, there was sufficient agreement that the School of Education was an alien or wayward body. Even as parts of it were cut away, the rhetoric about "original research" and "centers of excellence" testify to the force of campus community values. At Michigan State University, however, the ethos of the land-grant university was dominant. And the College of Education's own actions were both aggressive and attuned to that campus's institutional character; the result was not constriction but enhancement.

The Expansion of Institutional Mechanisms of Control

While Yale's President acted in the fashion of the nineteenth-century college autocrat, most other presidents and provosts used or created faculty committees through which to operate. Schools of education and other low-status campus units were disproportionately their targets. With the transformation of normal schools and state teachers colleges into components of more general colleges or universities, a significant degree of discretion in teacher education was sacrificed. For one thing, education schools were assigned responsibility for a product over which they had only limited control. Prospective elementary teachers took approximately 60 percent of their preparation and secondary teachers 80 percent in academic departments; in elite colleges and fifth-year programs these proportions might be even greater.[27] This "shared ownership" confused issues of credit and blame. English or political science could claim the better students; the weaker belonged to education.

Neither could education schools exercise the "complete discretion" over student admissions which obtained in nearly all schools of law, medicine, dentistry, and theology.[28] One consequence was their student-faculty ratios: a mean in education of 37:1 in 1973, com-

27. Clark and Marker, "Institutionalization," 54, 75; Woodring, "Development of Teacher Education," 17. Whereas the nursing student spent 48 percent of her time in nursing courses and the social work student 36 percent studying the professional field, the future biology teacher's professional program consumed under 20 percent. Murphy, "Teacher Preparation," 3–5.

28. Rebecca Zames Margulies and Peter M. Blau, "The Pecking Order of the Elite: America's Leading Professional Schools," *Change* 5, no. 9 (Nov. 1973): 26, 27.

pared to the professional school average of 20:1. Education faculty at Michigan had protested that, like other schools of education, their's had less financial support and higher teaching loads than other colleges in their universities.[29] Rather than ease this problem, it was exacerbated by the administration's decision both to maintain student enrollments and reduce faculty size.

This suggests another critical consequence of restricted autonomy: that low-cost and income-producing departments such as education could be exempted from professional school or campus-wide campaigns to upgrade the institution's standing by more closely "sifting and screening" applicants. Presidents and trustees did not wish to see them raise their admission standards or upgrade their programs if it meant "pricing themselves out of the market," for high-number, low-status units brought the institution *only* enrollments and, perhaps, some public good will—*not* prestige or alumni gifts. If, as some sociologists claim, "sorting and certifying is considerably more important than what professional schools actually try to teach," then closely controlled schools and departments are disadvantaged in the prestige game.[30] With the aid of foundations and a more prosperous alumni, business schools "imposed a new, significantly different direction upon the field, one that academicized and broadened the curriculum, deemphasized functional specialization, legitimized research, and raised student qualifications and expectations."[31] Although they pursued some of the same strategies, education schools entered no "age of autonomy" of their own; quite the reverse happened.

Universities are frequently charged with caring relatively little about their undergraduate programs. Many have let their "majors" remain unexamined for years, to the detriment, among other things, of the future teachers being prepared in these fields. The expansion of their graduate programs, however, subjected schools of education to the invariably more critical eye of graduate deans, committees, and faculties. Increasingly the recommendations of education faculty about appointments, tenure, and promotions had to be scrutinized by the campus-wide academic personnel committees which advised chancellors and presidents. It is reasonable to conclude that even leading education faculty served on such committees less often than their counterparts from arts and science departments or the elite

29. Stark, *Innovator,* 2.
30. Jencks and Riesman, *Academic Revolution,* 254.
31. Schlossman and Sedlak, *Age of Autonomy,* 3.

professional schools and colleges, denied access to important "insider knowledge."

The universalistic criteria of publication in refereed journals, leadership in "recognized" scholarly and scientific societies, and service on powerful campus committees were being imposed on faculty in progressively more of the nation's schools, colleges, and departments of education. One outcome was to reduce further incentives to engage in teacher education and other time-consuming field-based activities. Instead of conceiving applied research and development activities for low-status professionals and school children, it was more prudent to pursue "basic" research in the disciplinary canons likely to be understood and valued on the high-status personnel committee. In some places, Chicago's Department of Education was one, it became the practice to give representatives of cognate departments a virtual veto on appointments and promotions, prior to submitting nominations to campus administrators and committees. Appointments of outside scholars to search committees for education faculty was another strategy of "building bridges," one that sometimes had deplorable consequences.[32]

Then there was the "injustice" in applying the criterion of research "productivity." Being part of a professional school, it was considered "natural" that law school faculty would primarily teach and not publish. A historian of legal education noted, "for a hundred years commentators have expressed surprise that despite the number of distinguished lawyers teaching in the law schools, the output of scholarly literature is small."[33] An empirical study published in 1985 confirmed the historical observation. Over a three-year period, and despite a plethora of law periodicals, 44 percent of the senior faculty in 138 schools accredited by the American Association of Law Schools

32. This happened at one well-known university, when a promising field-based researcher *in teaching* was not appointed as an assistant professor because a member of the appointed search committee from the cognate department wrote a letter stating that the candidate was not sufficiently well trained in the discipline to be able to establish linkages between the two departments or to induce members of the cognate discipline to develop their latent interests in education. It is impossible to conceive of a history department or a law school permitting such considerations to affect an appointment which it wanted, enabling another department or school to usurp its own estimates of what kinds of talent and training were required in its faculty.

33. He remarked, further, on the low social status that researchers had in law schools at such places as Columbia, Harvard, Yale, Michigan, Chicago, Berkeley. Stevens, "American Law School," 538.

had no publications whatsoever; the median number for the period was one publication.[34] Yet almost all law school professors were full professors. It was certainly true that many education faculty were similarly unproductive as scholars, especially those with heavy teaching schedules and employed in predominantly undergraduate institutions. Yet, the productive members of education faculties in schools where virtually all did publish captured fewer rewards and garnered less status and power than their counterparts in the law school across the quadrangle. The rules were clearly different according to who was playing the game.

Campus-Wide Review Committees and the University Ethos

We saw at work, at Michigan and Duke, a new mechanism to process hard decisions about resources and to bring lagging units into compliance with institutional ambitions and values. Unlike accreditation committees, which usually share the assumptions of the units under review, the special faculty committees appointed to conduct institutional self-evaluations typically were carefully salted with skeptics; they made a virtue of their "distance" from the problems at hand and their recommendations were often drastic. At Rutgers, the Graduate School of Education went from eighty to fifty-seven positions in five years following a critical campus review.

A "blue-ribbon" committee appointed at the University of Illinois in the early 1970s launched a similar series of cyclical reviews of every campus program, applying the general campus ethos. In an early cycle, three professional schools, each well rated in its respective field—the Library School, the Department of Architecture, and the College of Communications—came in for intense criticism on the grounds of inadequate systematic research programs or a lack of professional creativity. The former seemed more important, however; in light of the University's preferred self-image, "nothing substitutes for superiority of scholarship."[35] The recommendations about closing programs made by this elite faculty group were not accepted by the broadly based Campus Senate. But determined administrators and prestigious faculty leaders were always able to frighten the subjects of their scrutiny and sometimes to prevail. An interested observer was

34. Michael I. Swygert and Nathaniel E. Gozansky, "Senior Law Faculty Publication Study: Comparisons of Law School Productivity," *Journal of Legal Education* 35 (1985): 373–94.

35. Atkin, "Institutional Self-Evaluation," 5.

the dean of the University of Illinois School of Education. He concluded that "Whatever the reason—budget, publicity, or administrative pressure—campus expectations are being reasserted, slowly but successfully."[36] There was little question but that even respected professional programs could be forced to respond in order to reaffirm traditional or changing academic values.

Building Bridges across the Campus

Compared to those of the prewar period, schools of education were less insular as well as less independent places. Their undergraduates plied between them and academic departments. Their graduate students were encouraged and sometimes compelled to take work in other departments and professional schools, although the variation was great. More important for professional schools' internal operations was the growing disposition to employ doctorates from so-called cognate fields, especially the social and physical sciences. The hoped-for joint appointment was the ultimate token of acceptance by campus worthies, as was participation in prestigious university-wide research or policy centers.

Exporting Students

Always defensive about their academic standing, schools of education, like departments of home economics, overcompensated by encouraging their students to take courses in other departments to raise their academic respectability and counter the perennial charge of "isolation." Journalism schools went so far as to require more outside than inside course work.[37] Education schools were more vulnerable on this score than engineering schools, for example, the educationist lacking the "self-confident contempt for the humanities and social sciences that engineers displayed."[38] Michigan's School of Education required that ten credits for the master's degree and twenty credits for the Ph.D. be taken in cognate departments. Stanford required Ph.D. candidates, the majority of its doctoral students after the foreign language requirement was dropped, to have a master's degree in another field or take a minor outside the School.

36. Ibid.

37. White, *The Public Interest,* 40–41.

38. Jencks and Riesman, *Academic Revolution,* 235. On home economics see Margaret Rossiter, *Women Scientists in America: Struggles and Strategies to 1940* (Baltimore: Johns Hopkins University Press, 1982), 201.

Did the strategy benefit education students and their schools? Students, at Michigan and elsewhere, found few courses offered at times convenient to part-time students and their enrollment was sometimes challenged on the grounds of lack of preparation or space. In many cases they reported themselves treated as second-class citizens outside their own schools, and we have all seen the classic signs of their self-doubt and social marginality as a result. At the same time that Harvard's president was championing schools of education and having the University's governing body meet at the Graduate School of Education, a new Harvard doctoral recipient was telling us of the "incredible isolation" of HGSE.

Encouraging outside study also resulted in loss of student credit hours and a negative balance of payments, with doubtful gain to the sending department if not to the students involved. Education students at Harvard, for example, were taking twice the number of courses in the Business School as its students were getting in Education.[39] The situation appeared comparable at other institutions. Education schools' export policy was rather an affirmation of their collective weakness than a solution to their problems on campus, however much individual students may have profited from the experience.

Importing Faculty

Another outcome of the quest for respectability and acceptance was an increasing disposition to appoint to education, business, public administration, library science, public health, social work, nursing, and other professional schools, young professors whose training and experience were exclusively in some more respected discipline. In 1966, for example, there were already reportedly five thousand behavioral and social scientists holding appointments in professional schools in American universities. The increasing status of academics began to influence medical schools which formerly had employed, almost exclusively, only those trained in medical schools. Law schools hired a few social and behavioral scientists. The reverse did not apply: political science departments did not appoint politicians, physics departments engineers, nor economics departments businessmen.[40]

Academe prizes specialization and "rigor" as defined by the

39. Bonney, "Profile," 15.

40. Jencks and Riesman, *Academic Revolution,* 216–17, 248; Lewis B. Mayhew, *Changing Practices in Education for the Professions* (Atlanta: Southern Regional Education Board, 1971), 40–41.

canon of each discipline, despite occasional incantations about the value of interdisciplinary study. Professional schools were, however, more natural places for multidisciplinary if not interdisciplinary approaches. The difference in the postwar period was a growing propensity to appoint disciplinary-trained scholars and scientists fresh from their Ph.D. studies in their respective fields. Such men, and occasionally women, were free of any taint of experience in professional education and education schools. If nothing else their presence reinforced a "research environment" in schools of education, something which progressively more education schools were eager to cultivate if hard put to afford. While this hiring from outside was done with less and less apology, skeptics raised eyebrows at what were sometimes called "cowbird appointments," and alert doctoral students in education had to wonder about the market value of their *own* degrees. The awarding of fellowships for research in education, like those by the Spencer Foundation, given in apparent disproportion to social science degree holders, caused dismay among them on the same grounds.

As the academic job market tightened, younger economists, political scientists, anthropologists, psychologists, and historians were more willing to consider faculty appointments in professional schools. The considerable increase in federal grants and contracts for education-related research also "sweetened the pie." Well-funded subdisciplines in sociology, for example, caused scholars to migrate. By 1970, of fifteen major specializations, the sociology of education acquired the highest rate of external support.[41] Still, the low esteem attached both to schools of education and to applied, problem-oriented sociology caused some trepidation and a willingness to retreat if the opportunity was present or the extramural support withdrawn.

During the 1960s, however, funding prospects were bright in educational research. Research support went from an estimated $33 million in 1960 to $98 million in 1965 and $122 million in 1972.[42] While state dollars doubled, foundation monies grew by 250 percent, and federal support by nearly 400 percent. Institutional support for educational research and development went to schools of education in several forms: through research grants and contracts, in released time,

41. James L. McCartney. "The Financing of Sociological Research: Trends and Consequences," in *The Phenomenon of Sociology: A Reader in the Sociology of Sociology,* ed. Edward Tiryakian (New York: Appleton-Century-Crofts, 1971), 384–97.

42. In contrast, in defense-related fields research and development support was $8.3 billion. Lee Cronbach and Patrick Suppes, eds., *Research for Tomorrow's Schools* (New York: Macmillan, 1969), 240.

and by establishing or expanding doctoral degree programs. Augmented by extramural funds, one visible sign of a growing, multidisciplinary, and international community of educational researchers was the dramatic increase in the membership of the American Educational Research Association, which grew from 650 members in 1950 to 13,438 in 1977.[43] At the 1986 annual meeting there were 310 foreign scholars on the program and 900 in attendance, representing forty nations. The number of specialized journals in education increased by seventy-three between 1961 and 1975, enlarging the opportunities for dissemination of one's research and the building of academic careers.[44]

Greater diversity of education faculty undoubtedly enriched the curriculum in graduate professional education and the range of problems and methodologies admitted under the rubrics of professional preparation and educational research. The consequences were not, of course, entirely positive. Agreements on the core knowledge of professional education and on the qualities sought in faculty, applicants, and graduates became harder to reach. This encouraged individualistic course development at the expense of school-wide curricula and the curriculum integration effort of the prewar years. Research procedures sometimes drove the curriculum, with research apprenticeships and dissertations regarded as the best training, as in the sciences, although most graduates were practitioners, not scientists.[45]

Political stalemates or plain "horse-trading" operated in everything from faculty appointment priorities to academic and professional requirements; whether this was more prevalent in schools of education, we leave to others to say. There is certainly the general fact that major American universities tolerate, and perhaps encourage, an individualistic and even idiosyncratic behavior among professors. Nevertheless, as education faculty became more diverse, teachers, related professionals, and policy makers were more likely than ever to wonder about the purposes and utility of education schools.

A Case Study: The "Basic" and the "Applied" at Stanford

Stanford's appearance among the top five American universities is described as "meteoric."[46] Intensive self-study and planning in the

43. Harold E. Mitzel, "Increasing the Impact of Theory and Research on Programs of Instruction," *Journal of Teacher Education* 28 (Nov.–Dec. 1977): 15.

44. Corwin, "New Teaching Profession," 250.

45. Powell, "University Schools of Education," 17.

46. Mayhew, *Changing Practices,* 11.

1950s launched its advance. Although the strategy was predicated on strengthening key arts and sciences departments, graduate work, and research, the rise proceeded, in large part, through active engagement in the world of practical affairs—in business and industry, law, and medicine. Some thought that private Stanford expressed more of the land-grant ethos than the state-chartered University of California across the bay in Berkeley.

For decades, however, Stanford's clearly practical School of Education had produced scores of school administrators for northern California in the face of yawning indifference by the Stanford faculty.[47] In 1962, in what was, relatively, a very small school, there were eleven professors devoting much of their time to preparing administrators; ten of them were themselves experienced administrators, mostly in public school systems. Change was in the wind, however. By 1972, two of the three remaining from the 1962 group were about to retire. None of the replacements had previous experience either in a school of education or as a chief administrative officer, and only one had academic preparation in the field of education.[48]

A new pattern of appointments, beginning in the mid-1950s and lasting through much of the '70s, altered the character of the School; some two-thirds of the 1985 faculty were appointed in that period. Service commitments were deemphasized in the faculty reward system. Preparation of elementary school teachers disappeared. The policy of Deans I. James Quillan and Thomas James was to make Stanford's School of Education the equivalent of Chicago's Department of Education, featuring education as a social science. This approach collided in the 1960s with an active professional interest group in the state which pioneered and exported the junior or community college movement. Searching for a publishing scholar in junior college education provided fruitless, so a publishing scholar with minimal contact with a private junior college was appointed. "For this, key leaders among California junior college presidents attempted to boycott the Stanford program in junior college administration, and even tried to jeopardize funds for the program."[49] Lewis Mayhew may have exaggerated this account, but he correctly concluded that the trend was

47. Mayhew and Committee, *Educational Leadership,* 23, 54, 100.

48. Ibid., 23–24.

49. Mayhew, *Changing Practices,* 19. Between about 1960 and 1975, Stanford, UCLA, and Berkeley were linked in a ten- (later eleven-) center national project in community college leadership, funded by the Kellogg Foundation. The Stanford component was partially transferred to Berkeley before the program was ended entirely.

away from appointing practitioners to faculty posts in professional schools. For one thing, it was too difficult for most men and women with school careers to acquire the theoretical preparation and compete with a person holding a Ph.D. from the discipline.[50]

Stanford's development, especially in the 1960s and 1970s, exemplified the more general trend of seeking recognition on elite campuses, and the favor of foundation and federal patrons of research, by appointing behavioral and social scientists to the faculty. In the words of a Stanford faculty committee, the stated goal was "to improve the balance between research-oriented and practice-oriented professors."[51] Several joint appointments were secured, as at Chicago. If the strategy did not fully succeed at Palo Alto, where education students reported that they and their school were still viewed suspiciously by professors in academic departments and other professional schools, it looked good from afar. Stanford's School of Education moved to the top of the reputational rankings and secured numerous large grants for individual and group research projects, many housed in new federally financed institutes located at Stanford. The research and development center on teaching was the telling justification for retaining a small program to prepare secondary school teachers. The presence, just off campus, of the foundation-supported Center for Advanced Studies in the Behavioral Sciences, headed by Ralph Tyler, former chairman of Chicago's Department of Education, certainly assisted greatly. It brought leading scholars and scientists from the nation to Palo Alto for extended periods, where they might interact with Stanford's faculty and graduate students in a variety of specialties.

In the late seventies, however, yet another shift in emphasis was being expressed. In 1978 President Lawrence Cremin of Teachers College, a strong supporter of the movement, acknowledged that efforts during the previous two decades to bring education courses into closer relationship with the disciplinary canons of academic departments had led to "the disappearance of any relevance to the problems of education."[52] Two Harvard professors put it differently, alleging that academic disciplines, wherever taught, were "essentially elitist, while

50. Sizer and Powell, "Changing Conceptions," esp. 65.

51. Mayhew and Committee, *Educational Leadership,* 4, 20. The students responded appropriately, assisted by the decision in 1968 to drop the foreign language requirement for the Ph.D. In 1973, for example, 84 percent of those in school administration opted for the Ph.D. rather than the Ed.D. degree; a decade before, Ed.D. candidates were the majority at Stanford.

52. Cremin, "The Education of the Educating Professions," 20.

the most apparent problems of public schools were those of expansion to serve non-elite populations."[53] In the process of conducting a self-study to revamp its administration program, Stanford professors warned of a counterswing since many departments were so overloaded with discipline-oriented professors that viable contacts with the field were disappearing.[54]

By the early 1970s a certain irrelevance was indeed evident at Stanford. Students in the school administration program complained that they would likely graduate without either a cohesive grasp of the field of education administration or sufficient marketable skills in their intended administrative specialization, as their theoretically inclined professors lacked necessary experience in educational administration. The faculty Committee on Administration and Policy Analysis characterized an externally funded joint program with the Graduate School of Business as "fragile" and "ill-fated," a ready victim when the monies ran out and it openly acknowledged "our current contempt for practitioners, especially those in the local area."[55] Declining enrollments after 1965 or so, and faculty proposals to restrict admissions to a few applicants with high research potential who could be supported by external funds, threatened professorial positions.

At a time when Stanford's School of Education was the nation's top-rated, the *Chronicle of Higher Education* headlined, "Stanford U. Plans Revitalization of the Education School."[56] Given the relatively new academic orientation of its School of Education, the regard which it had captured among other graduate schools of education, and the value of high rankings on Stanford's campus, it seemed an unlikely choice, going into the 1980s, to lead the nation's major universities toward a renewed interest in collaborations with elementary and secondary schools and identification with their problems. Derek Bok at Harvard and A. Bartlett Giammati of Yale were major university presidents who lent their support to such a move but the key figure was Stanford's president, Donald Kennedy. Operating in a local political culture that grants unusual power to a university president, Kennedy gave a clear signal: "get closer to your field." He vocally supported the efforts of Stanford's new dean of education, J. Myron Atkin, to make

53. Sizer and Powell, "Changing Conceptions," 69.

54. Mayhew and Committee, *Educational Leadership,* 4, 20.

55. Ibid., 49, 53.

56. "Stanford U. Plans Revitalization of the Education School," *Chronicle of Higher Education* 23, no. 14 (2 Dec. 1981): 6.

Stanford a center of professional advancement in education. "I am an educationist," Atkin told the *Stanford Daily* without apology. A science educator and former dean of education at the University of Illinois, Atkin's coming to Stanford had excited the faculty who perceived that he had made Illinois a much stronger center for educational research; hence his interest in professional issues was not worrisome. Still, Atkin had criticized Illinois' educational research tradition as almost exclusively oriented towards behavioral science. "As a direct result of this research bias," he wrote in 1968, "we usually find that problems of education that are investigated turn out to be either trivial, or they bear little relevance to classroom practice."[57]

Stanford's relative standing was reinforced by Atkin's appointments of persons who combined solid research credentials with authentic interests in professional education and the realities of practice. Teacher education, which was preparing only thirty students in 1980, was revived; Dean Atkin and the senior faculty taught in the program.[58] But the faculty had long since concluded that teacher training, like pursuing practical research, was a tactical error for junior professors given the Stanford academic culture.

Various partnerships were begun with schools, reportedly less condescending than the typical university venture of this kind. Speaking of one, a three-year project called Study of Stanford and the Schools, a long-time local English teacher praised the effort as ending "long years of living in the shadow of Stanford." Early in 1985, however, the *New York Times* editor who reported on the project's progress, mentioned growing concerns, financial and otherwise. Fred Hechinger thought that "some of the more academic social science researchers in the school of education are jealous of the time and money spent on such hands-on research."[59] It might be more accurate to say that, while the Stanford and the Schools project was controversial within the faculty, it also secured enough funds from foundations

57. J. Myron Atkin, "Research Styles in Science Education," *Journal of Research in Science Teaching* 5 (1967–68): 339.

58. Stanford University, School of Education, J. Myron Atkin, "Report to the Stanford University Senate," 8 January 1981. Stanford was not prepared, however, to risk assigning a ladder-faculty member to the perilous task of directing teacher education. Late in 1986 Atkin's successor announced plans to recruit a "term" faculty member to that post. Marshall Smith, "Stanford School of Education Budget Presentation Outline," 19 December 1986.

59. Fred M. Hechinger, "Three Years of Lessons," *New York Times*, 29 January 1985. See also idem, "Colleges Reaching Out to Aid Public Schools," *New York Times*, 14 December 1982.

that other Stanford researchers found their traditional sources drying up.

Although somewhat misleading, Hechinger's words seemed prophetic, for later that spring a significant portion of the faculty signaled their lack of confidence in the dean and he resigned. For a few days in the late summer following a major review of the School instigated by the provost, it appeared that the University might close its School of Education in favor of an academic department or a research institute, on the models of Chicago or Johns Hopkins. Instead the School was advised to correct its fragmented character and acquire greater coherence. It proved impossible, however, to categorize the disruption of leadership as signaling another sea change at Stanford. As in other schools of education, ideological discussions seldom surfaced cleanly in the faculty and grievances were aired around other issues, including administrative style and the "soft monies" on which Stanford had thrived. The School lost several competitions for funds, culminating a several-years' decline. That retrogression appears to be the more decisive factor in the School's short-lived crisis.

In the opinion of former Dean Atkin, much as they might regret it, even the most discipline-bound professors of education accepted a reinvigorated professional thrust as a fact of life for schools of education—and even more so at Stanford under Kennedy.[60] Subsequent appointments and promotions appeared to confirm that judgment. The new dean, Marshall Smith, seemed determined to retain and expand the practitioner orientation even while supporting "strong and coherent research and research training programs."[61] As one Stanford professor said to us, Stanford could retain its number one ranking—an all-important factor on its own campus—with perhaps a third or less of the faculty holding the symbolic joint appointment or engaged in basic research, while the remaining two dozen behaved like responsible professional school teachers, applied researchers, and consultants. The admitted split between theory and practice was there but maintaining "balance" was the key operating principle; at Stanford having the best of both worlds was in sight.

60. J. Myron Atkin, interview with Geraldine Clifford, Stanford University, 15 April 1986. Kennedy's commitment was not short-lived. In September 1987 he spearheaded a conference of educators in Minneapolis and on September 17 issued an open letter to 3000 university and college presidents exhorting them to work to elevate the attractions of teaching as a career in their own institutions.

61. Marshall Smith, *Budget,* 1.

The Foundations Department at TC

Like psychologists and mathematicians, historians and philosophers of education frequently had more in common with discipline-oriented colleagues in other fields than with the specialists in curriculum, language arts, or counseling psychology on their own faculty. As disciplinary or interdisciplinary foundations courses were reduced as requirements for teacher candidates and doctoral students, this faculty found itself increasingly confined to preparing disciplinary specialists—presumably the beau ideal of any self-respecting modern academician—and to making new alliances. The job market precluded doing much of the former so coalitions with other social scientists became common. Programs in social and philosophical foundations of education were particularly susceptible to being merged with policy studies, a new, more theoretical speciality which was taking over doctoral programs in school administration, particularly in the smaller graduate schools of education.

The appearance of federal initiatives in education encouraged policy studies. So did the appointment of younger economists, sociologists, and political scientists who were displacing retiring former school administrators on many faculties. The 1960s and 1970s witnessed numerous absorptions of foundations faculty in policy-oriented units: at Berkeley, Wisconsin, and elsewhere. Chicago announced in 1979 the formation of a new "special field"—Administration, Institutional, and Policy Studies—in order to integrate comparative education, history, politics, sociology, and economics with organizational interests.[62] Harvard called its amalgam Administration, Planning, and Social Policy. The foundations at Teachers College ("TC" to educationists around the world) pursued a different route.

Among the schools of education we have examined in detail, Teachers College, Columbia University, was always something of an exception to many of our generalizations: a nearly autonomous corporate body, which gained in independence from its university over a time when the controls were tightening elsewhere; the first horse away from the gate in the education school derby, but increasingly hard-pressed to maintain its advantage in the postwar boom period for other schools of education; a large, multidepartment school when most private universities "sheltered" only small, single-department schools of education; and consistently the closest thing to a true, national professional school in our sample. But, Stanford's specialist in higher

62. University of Chicago, Department of Education, *Education News* (1980) 1.

education, Lewis Mayhew, saw Teachers College exemplifying important changes in emphasis in this period:

> Several of the best known professional schools—education at Columbia, engineering at Stanford, business at Harvard—gained their influence through direct and continuous concern with the practical problems of the field and through preparing the next generation of highly qualified practitioners. But as these schools turned their efforts toward more and more basic research, contacts with the field waned and the possibility emerged that their overall influence on the professions would ultimately decline.[63]

As one generation of leaders was succeeded by another, the Foundations Department at Teachers College became the Department of Philosophy and the Social Sciences. The change in name signified several dimensions of an interesting, nationwide shift in thinking about education. One was a fairly abrupt devaluation of what remained of interdisciplinary, school-oriented teaching and writing in the foundations of education. Another was a correlative rise in the value of disciplinary linkages between scholars in professional schools and their colleagues in the cognate academic departments and scholarly societies. A third, and more hopeful prospect, was the appearance in education schools of new approaches to educational research, like Teachers College's program in applied anthropology.

As historians, philosophers, and social scientists, the original foundations faculty had been professionally oriented in a special sense, inspiring graduate students at TC and elsewhere in the world—by their books, lectures, and example—with stirring challenges on behalf of a mélange of professional and social ideals: intellectual freedom, democratic education, social responsibility, secular humanism, and political liberalism.[64] The Foundations Division, encompassing psychology, philosophy, and the social sciences, had been founded in 1934–35 by William Heard Kilpatrick and his associates, as part of an overall reorganization of the College. It was also influenced by the movement toward interdisciplinary survey courses like Columbia College's Contemporary Civilization.

Along with provoking similar foundations of education groupings in colleges and universities nationwide, the Department of Social and

63. Mayhew, *Changing Practices,* 27.

64. Barbara Finkelstein, "Servants, Critics, Skeptics: The Place of Foundations Faculties in Professional Education," *Teacher Education Quarterly* (California Council on the Education of Teachers) 11, no. 2 (Spring 1984): 15.

Philosophical Foundations was home to a group of controversial activists or independent thinkers such as George Counts, John Childs, Harold Rugg, R. Freeman Butts, Ernest Johnson, Lyman Bryson, Bruce Raup, Goodwin Watson, Jesse Newlon, Edward Reisner, Isaac Kandel, and Harold Clark. As a member of the Graduate Faculty of Columbia University, historian Merle Curti belonged to the Foundations faculty. Author of *The Social Ideas of American Educators* (1935), Curti advanced a severe critique of the hold of conservative and even reactionary ideas on schooling a generation before the "radical revisionists" came on the scene in the late 1960s.

Its successor Department of Philosophy and the Social Sciences echoed the concerns of another one-time member of the Teachers College faculty in the Social Studies Department, Arthur Bestor, more than it recalled Curti's concerns; in the 1950s, Bestor's attacks on the intellectual flabbiness allegedly imposed on schools by educationists made him their *bête noire.* At TC, however, retirements and internal struggles set the Foundations Department on a new course, beginning around 1958 and culminating in the renaming of the Department in 1964.[65] In 1957 a former Department head reported on a shift away from "the crisis outlook and the social or reconstructive role of education" to greater emphasis on disciplinary scholarship, research methods, and empirical study.[66] The change was signified in recruitment of faculty from academic departments rather than from schools of education, their formal titles as professors of history (or sociology

65. The retirements are mentioned in R. Freeman Butts, "Reflections on Forty Years in the Foundations Department at Teachers College," paper prepared for the 1975 Alumni Day, 11 April 1975. The bitter disagreements can be "read between the lines." Professor Butts was also interviewed by Geraldine Clifford at Stanford University on 15 April 1986. For another perspective on the shift at Teachers College see the interpretation of Diane Ravitch (adjunct professor in the Department of Philosophy and the Social Sciences) on the work of her predecessors in the department, in *Troubled Crusade.*

66. R. Freeman Butts to W. H. Cowley, 2 October 1957. Printed in Charles J. Brauner, *American Educational Theory* (Englewood Cliffs, N.J.: Prentice-Hall, 1964), 204.

"As I viewed it the new department had come to believe that their predecessors had put too much stress on ideology rather than upon the social science disciplines, were more interested in social and educational actions than in solid, hard empirical research, too much enamored of the generalist rather than the specialist, too long on professional or social commitment but too short on scholarly depth and rigorous knowledge." (Butts, "Reflections," 34). He also pointed out (p. 37) that almost no members of the altered department belong to the new foundations organization, the American Educational Studies Association, established in 1968 by Teachers College graduates to promote a more integrated approach to the foundations of education.

or economics) *and education,* and their identification with the Graduate Faculties of Columbia University.[67]

The new breed of foundations scholar carried their orientations beyond their departments and into the learned societies in education. This thrust was especially notable in the history of education field. The History of Education Section of the National Society of College Teachers of Education had been organized in 1947, by Claude Eggertsen and Freeman Butts, and had founded a journal by 1950; parallel sections within the Society, on the philosophy of education and comparative education, spun off to form separate societies, in what was a wider movement toward specialization. The independent History of Education Society was organized in 1959 with Lawrence A. Cremin as its first president, and for a time his perspective shaped the organization. Cremin chaired the new Department of Philosophy and the Social Sciences and later became president of Teachers College.[68] Cremin's own books captured Bancroft and Pulitzer Prizes in American history—signal honors for any scholar and unprecedented for a professor in a school of education, especially in a field of scholarship which Harvard historian Bernard Bailyn had castigated in *Education in the Forming of American Society* (1960). The shapers of the field of the history of American education, Bailyn charged, were historiographically untrained schoolmen who used the field to advance professional, not scholarly, ends; their writings were but "the patristic literature of a powerful academic ecclesia."[69] Bailyn's book became something of a bible for younger historians of education in the 1960s.

In a related development, one also led by Cremin, one heard that the student of education should include study of the other places that

67. There were, however, earlier associations between the Foundations faculty and other departments of Columbia University: John Childs, Bruce Raup, and Ernest Johnson with the departments of Philosophy and Religion and the Union Theological Seminary; Sloan Wayland and Wilbur Hollenbeck with Sociology; R. Freeman Butts with the School of International Affairs; and others. In the opinion of Professor Butts it was a matter of a difference in identification, not orientation. R. Freeman Butts to Geraldine Clifford, 25 August 1986.

68. According to Sizer and Powell, the society debated, in 1968, whether a new "learned society" should be formed, one that considered the history of education in strictly academic terms. "Changing Conceptions," 83.

69. Bernard Bailyn, *Education in the Forming of American Society* (Chapel Hill: University of North Carolina Press, 1960), 8. Although Lawrence Cremin is closely, and correctly, associated with Bailyn's posture toward the field, see his caveats in Lawrence A. Cremin, *The Wonderful World of Ellwood Patterson Cubberley: An Essay on the Historiography of American Education* (New York: Teachers College Press, 1965).

educate, and concentrate less on schools: "Why cannot the professor of education concern himself with influences on children of all kinds, not just those that happen to occur in schools?" and "We are yet far too institution bound."[70] A desirable outgrowth of this attitude was a broadening scholarship in the history, sociology, or psychology of education. In political terms this diversion of emphasis relieved hard-pressed schools of some of the responsibility for the deficiencies of education in this society. But one can also interpret it as another repudiation of the education profession and *its* chief place of work.

What happened among historians had its counterpart in the other disciplines of the old foundations of education. Still more radical sentiments agitated the social sciences in graduate programs in education, from east coast to west. The intellectual and political exposés of schools and schoolmen, in a movement called "revisionism," linked the foundations disciplines more closely with university scholarship, especially New Left historiography and sociology—hardly a development calculated to appeal to most teachers and other school professionals. With the changing of the guard, the journals in the philosophy of education and the annual meetings of the Philosophy of Education Society "were replete with word-splitting, language analysis, argument assessment, and rational intellectualizing," in the dominant style of analytical philosophy—although there were those that resisted this tide.[71] Understandable in philosophy departments, this orientation ignored the untidy world of the classroom in which teachers and students accommodated ever more uneasily to one another in the United States and in most other industrialized societies. Schools of education appeared to be depriving themselves, at least temporarily, of yet other parts of their professional school character. As for Teachers College, the verdict on whether more was gained than lost awaits a longer historical perspective.

As a large public institution, Michigan possessed a less singular sense of itself than may flourish at prestigious private universities. Michigan's history was one of compromises and mixed functions, so that its institutional ethos had a latitude that gave even its low-status professional schools some room to exist and sometimes to prosper. Stanford, like Cornell, was a private university with a land-grant aura. Teachers College was, like Columbia, accommodating and entrepre-

70. Sizer and Powell, "Changing Conceptions," 75.

71. Paul Nash, "The Humanistic Foundations of Education," *Teacher Education Quarterly* (California Council on the Education of Teachers) 11, no. 2 (Spring 1984): 56.

neurial. The University of Chicago, however, believed itself to have had, from its origin, a single-minded devotion to the unfettered pursuit of new knowledge. This was, in theory, a clear standard against which the University was ever ready to measure curricular and organizational innovations. For this reason we devote the next section to an extended discussion of the situation at Chicago.

The Institutional Ethos at Work at Chicago

The annual issues of *Education News* distributed to alumni and friends by the Department of Education provide unfailing reiteration of its commitment to the unfettered pursuit of knowledge. Some representative statements from the 1980s give the flavor of the Chicago ethos. At the start of the decade, Charles Bidwell wrote:

> In each of its ventures, the Department is conscious of its paramount responsibility to provide leadership in education, first by scholarship of the highest order and originality and second by the preparation of intellectually perceptive and disciplined educational researchers and practitioners. [1980]

> The best of educational research arises from the application of disciplined intellectual curiosity to problems embedded in the conduct of education. The purpose of this inquiry, however, is general understanding rather than the solution of particular problems of practice. . . . [The practitioners we prepare] will apply disciplined intelligence and general understanding to develop solutions to particular problems of education, in schools and elsewhere. [1981]

As another school reform movement was heating up in the press, he wrote:

> At a time when the means of education—not only dollars, but disciplined and original minds, systematic knowledge, and informed practice—seem to lag farther and farther behind the need, the responsibility of this Department to increase the intellectual capital of education cannot be greater. [1982]

Remarking on celebrations of the careers of two emeritus members of the faculty, Benjamin Bloom and Allison Davis, he observed:

> Each [career] in its own distinctive way signified what has made the University of Chicago a great center of scholarship in education: intellectual power, discipline, and originality; the courage and stamina to pursue big questions; deep interest in fundamental educational and learning processes; and integration of these interests with theory and method in social science. [1984]

And, finally, in 1985 he stated, "The same commitment led Charles H. Judd and then Ralph Tyler to build at Chicago an intellectually diverse and powerful education faculty, and this commitment has been no less strong in the Department's ensuing years."[72]

The Department of Education

As director of the School of Education, and chairman of the Department for some three decades, Charles Hubbard Judd convinced himself, his colleagues, and many in the rest of the University of Chicago that the Department of Education was a trustworthy member of the family, driven by identical ideals and prejudices. With the closing of the School of Education in 1931, there was little to deflect the faculty of the Department of Education from the pursuit of wisdom and enlightenment without deliberate regard to its utility.[73] By all accounts most were pleased to be released from any commitment, implied or explicit, to train teachers. Professional training—with all its demanding distractions and illiberal realities—was confined to preparing educational researchers and administrative "leaders" and, hence, consistent with the University's conception of its elitist position and with the faculty's own strong preference for exclusively graduate education. The responsibility for preparing a few teachers was distributed across certain departments, more a "hobby" of scholars with pedagogical interests than an institutional function. A university-wide Board of Precollegiate Education exercised a degree of oversight over secondary teacher education lodged in the cognate departments, although in some cases, English and German specifically, interested

72. Charles E. Bidwell, Professor of Education and Sociology, was chairman of the department and author of these statements in *Education News* (University of Chicago, Department of Education).

73. The original School of Education contained the College of Education to train teachers in undergraduate programs, the Graduate Department of Education, the University High School, and the University Elementary School. The College was given a brief reprieve, closing in 1933.

faculty behaved like a school of education in assisting their majors to get state certification.[74]

During the 1931 reorganization, the former Graduate Department of Education became part of the new Division of the Social Sciences, one of the University's five divisions. Within the Department of Education a Center for Teacher Education evolved to provide counseling and administrative support for those undergraduate programs that permitted students to combine a modicum of professional course work (not including "methods of teaching" which was lodged in academic departments), observation in the University's Laboratory School, and ten weeks of practice teaching with the graduation requirements of academic departments, to secure certification in four years and one summer. On occasion, Department of Education professors were involved in such activities and in planning for more extensive professional programs; John Goodlad, who directed the Center in the late 1950s, was a case in point. Although perhaps the majority of University of Chicago faculty found the whole idea of teacher preparation suspect, pedagogical and training interests were tolerated as long as professors fulfilled their obligations as productive scholars.[75] As a Department of Education committee remarked in 1975, there existed a "well-established tradition of the University which accepts and recognizes the right of the faculty members to pursue their scholarly work in ways that they deem more suitable."[76] For some few of them teacher education furnished concepts, theories, methodological issues, and research subjects.

While a more theoretical- and discipline-oriented faculty was being recruited, the late 1950s was a time that demanded more of

74. Steven Gevinson, "What Happened to the Master of Arts in Teaching and the Graduate School of Education?" (unpublished seminar paper, University of Chicago Department of Education, 12 December 1984), 16; Professor William Pattison, University of Chicago, telephone interview with Geraldine Clifford, 23 April 1986. We are deeply indebted to Professor Pattison, secretary of the Department of Education, for his willingness to make available documents from the Department's files and for answering numerous questions on several occasions; to Mr. Gevinson, a graduate of the MAT program in English Education and a current doctoral student in the Department; and to other past and present Chicago faculty who were willing to be interviewed. None bears responsibility for our interpretations and conclusions, however.

75. Despite their hopes, the editors of the practitioner-oriented *School Review* rarely got articles from professors in the cognate disciplines at Chicago. Wechsler, "From Practice to Theory," 228.

76. University of Chicago, Department of Education, "Report of the Committee on the Merger of the Graduate School of Education and the Department of Education," (6 Nov. 1975), 3.

American higher education. In the case of public and less secure private institutions, the times demanded *more* teachers. In the case of prestigious colleges and universities, the demand was for *better* teachers—for arrangements to recruit and assist into teaching some of the brighter and more sophisticated undergraduates in elite colleges. This might mean "talking up" teaching careers to their students, or entering into compacts with an institution that maintained an education school, or employing a person to offer professional courses and supervise student teaching for liberal arts students, or inagurating a Master of Arts in Teaching program.

Chancellor Kimpton, Francis Chase, and the Scholar-Teacher

As a private university, exempt from some social and political pressures, the University of Chicago nonetheless emerged from World War II more deeply immersed in politics than some believed desirable, its administrators "irritably sensitive to public criticism and controversy."[77] It sheltered one of the nation's major nuclear development projects during the war. Some concluded that it should play a correspondingly great part in the preparation of the nation to win the "Cold War." With the launching of the Soviet Sputnik in 1957, the improvement of public education was again made a patriotic and strategic issue. How would the University of Chicago respond?

Postwar society breached the walls of academe in the proliferation of poverty-plagued black neighborhoods surrounding the University itself. In order to attract and retain faculty members in the 1950s and 1960s, the University had to be deeply concerned about the quality of local housing, services, amenities, and schooling—lest it share the declining reputation of other once top-ranked urban universities, notably Columbia and Johns Hopkins. In 1942 the Laboratory School Council had first discussed admitting black students and a few entered the primary grades in 1943.[78] By the mid-1950s the University was exerting leadership in a major urban renewal project. The Kenwood and Hyde Park neighborhoods were remade, in a sanguine view, into a "stable, integrated community of high standards," housing over 70 percent of the University of Chicago faculty.[79] Faculty children favored

77. Bledstein, *Professionalism,* 294.

78. Depencier, "Laboratory Schools," 142–43.

79. Professor William Pattison, interview, 23 April 1986. Other reports offered less rosy characterizations of the renaissance of the University environs. Urban re-

three neighborhood public schools—the Kenwood Academy for secondary schooling and Bret Harte and Ray Elementary Schools—along with the University Laboratory Schools. No longer experimental schools, the Lab Schools offered a preparatory education to a student body that eventually became a quarter nonwhite and 50 percent faculty offspring. As a community-stabilizing effort, the University built a new high school building, opening it conspicuously in November 1957 with ceremonies and a conference.

Lawrence A. Kimpton, chancellor of the University, was the "point man" in the era of expansion and social undertakings that he believed essential for the continued viability of the University of Chicago.[80] Kimpton's address to the conference, "The University and the High School—Past and Future," was published in the conference papers, *The High School in a New Era.* He blamed universities for having separated themselves from high schools and the education of their teachers. The problematic status of their schools of education was close to the heart of the problem:

> The professional educator was looked down upon by his colleagues within the university community until a professor hesitated to admit that he was a member of a school of education. It has been the habit of oppressed minorities through the centuries to band themselves closely together for common defense and, even though separated from the main part of the community, to play a powerful role in its life. And this is precisely what happened in the schools of education at the great American universities.[81]

Through their concerted influence on state licensing laws and their training of the faculties of normal schools and state teachers' colleges, Kimpton concluded that the "sneered at" and isolated professors of education effectively cut the American high school off from the influence of the American university. His solution offered both aca-

---

newal eliminated Chicago's jazz center and other colorful features of an earlier Hyde Park. Moreover, the riots after the murder of Martin Luther King in 1968 left blocks of devastation between the Midway and 63d Street. Some thought the University sat on a shrinking island.

80. Professor William Pattison, interview, 23 April 1986.

81. Lawrence A. Kimpton, "The University and the High School," in *The High School in a New Era,* ed. Francis S. Chase and Harold A. Anderson, (Chicago: University of Chicago Press, 1958), 35.

demics and professional educators a chance to reform the situation, through a new partnership:

> The universities must stop grousing about the education of our high school students and get back into the business of training teachers. The schools of education must become a real part of the universities, and the universities must begin to relate themselves properly and effectively to the work of the schools of education. The philosophy of education must be taught by a member of the department of philosophy. . . . The high school teacher of mathematics or the teacher of teachers of mathematics in the school of education must receive his training in subject matter at the hands of a competent mathematician.

Lest his examples slight educationists, Kimpton assured them that they would, in fact, "remain the real link between the university and the high school, translating out the theory and new discovery of the universities into the high school classrooms." In his faulting of university scholars for knowing and caring too little "about the real activities and problems of the classroom teacher," thus ensuring that university research seem "sterile and irrelevant" to that teacher, Kimpton could have been describing many faculty in departments of education. Chicago's was especially vulnerable on this score in 1957: it was a department of applied social science (some Chicago faculty would dispute the "applied"); except for a residue of persons with school connections, its members selected, first and sometimes only, with conventional disciplinary criteria in mind; there was almost no one on the regular faculty with nonuniversity teaching experience; its professors had little or no professional interaction with the Laboratory Schools, and were largely confined in their professional training to working with aspiring school administrators who came to partake of, but not to inform or refresh or test, the faculty's "general understanding" of educational phenomena and processes.

The following October, Francis S. Chase, chairman of the Department of Education, gave a speech in Oklahoma City that continued a theme in the emerging reform at Chicago. Despite the prevailing anti-intellectualism of American society, which was then an object of frequent reflection by intellectuals, Chase thought he observed some promising signs of greater value being accorded to intellect and knowledge. He spoke of the scholar-teacher as the type most likely to instill in all his pupils the attitude of "student," so much lacking in American high schools. "The good teacher is so full of his subject and so impelled by the desire to unfold its beauties and marvels to others that he seeks constantly for approaches which will get through to the inert, the inept, the inattentive and the unawakened."[82] In the months between its high school conference and Chase's Oklahoma speech, the University of Chicago created a Graduate School of Education as a structure to prepare such scholar-teachers.

The Graduate School of Education, 1958–75

When Kimpton and Chase supported the plan for a new *Graduate* School of Education to the governing body of the University of Chicago faculty senate, they did so in the context of this question: "Whether the University is properly organized to carry out its functions of teacher-training, operating the Laboratory Schools, and maintaining effective liaison with the elementary and secondary schools." The proposed new structure would be one of small size, authorized to grant only the Master of Arts in Teaching degree to prospective high school teachers who would study their subject specialization exclusively with graduate faculty in their respective disciplines. The *Minutes* record the chancellor as saying that "it would be 'an appalling thing' for the University to generate a typical 'normal school' with substandard training programs."[83] The Board of Precollegiate Education would continue and academic departments were not precluded from continuing or creating their own master's degree programs for teachers. As further safeguards, the majority of members of the School's faculty would hold joint appointments with the Department of Education and "all or nearly all members of the Department of Education would be members of the School." The Department chairman would be dean of the proposed School.

The Council was reminded of the University's historical objective of improving and advancing education at all levels.[84] The opportunity to attract and train larger numbers of well-prepared high school teachers and, through them, to improve the University's relationships with secondary education and elevate its standards was, Kimpton argued,

82. Francis S. Chase, "Can Teachers Be Scholars or Pupils Students?", speech given in Oklahoma City, 23 October 1958. Courtesy of Professor William Pattison, University of Chicago, Department of Education.

83. University of Chicago, Council of the University Senate, *Minutes*, 11 March 1958 and 15 April 1958.

84. University of Chicago, "Report and Recommendations Concerning a Graduate School of Education," 5 March 1958.

sufficiently important to justify the risks and administrative difficulties. The promise of external funds for scholarships was held out.[85]

At the Council meeting on 15 April 1958 where the faculty was to vote on the proposal, a professor in the Humanities Division reported sentiments ranging from "little enthusiasm" to "bitter opposition" among his colleagues; the University, "aware of what had happened in the name of graduate schools of education elsewhere, should resist such tendencies," he maintained, and exploit instead the possibilities already present at Chicago. On the other hand, a scientist supported the proposal, reporting that the Department of Education felt ill equipped to handle all its functions, that schools of education had become the traditional way to communicate with the schools, and "the Committee was assured the Department of Education had no intention of setting up a teachers' college; that it would provide the professional training necessary for certification of teachers; but that in all cases the substantive material would be taught by the appropriate departments." After further discussion which demonstrated their considerable confidence in the abilities of academic departments to prepare teachers adequately (if they would), their disdain for schools of education in general, and a willingness to capitulate to the wishes of the University administration, twenty-two Council members registered their approval and eight voted against the proposed Graduate School of Education.

By its action the University of Chicago clearly indicated that it intended *only* to create an arm of the Department of Education that would prepare secondary school teachers at the graduate level. It decidedly did not wish a full-fledged structure existing on equal terms with Chicago's family of other professional schools. "The limits on its independence, scope, and status were intentional and explicit at the outset."[86] Department of Education faculty bent over backwards to "avoid giving offense by any act that might be interpreted as implying that we thought of ourselves as the only University agency concerned with teacher education." A proposal for a convocation to announce the

85. Stone, *Breakthrough,* 196. In fact in the School's first year the Ford Foundation made its initial grant to support the MAT program; in all Chicago received $2.4 million, second only to Harvard's $2.8 million among the 42 colleges and universities which Ford supported for innovative teacher education. In 1958 the Ford Foundation already supported the School Improvement Program and the Comparative Education Center in the Department of Education, but it was argued that the proposed School of Education structure would facilitate the operations of these and the Midwest Administration Center. University of Chicago, "Report and Recommendations," 2.

86. Gevinson, "Master of Arts," 9.

Graduate School of Education was similarly rejected "as premature and likely to give offense by being thought too pretentious."[87] Some Department members abhored publicizing the fact of the School of Education, something which might confuse observers in arts and sciences departments into thinking that *they,* of the Department of Education, belonged to this controversial unit.

Identity problems notwithstanding, the Department gained some major advantages: freedom from the cross pressures that go with preparing novices for teaching, thus maintaining a desired parity with academic departments; as dean of a school, a direct route to the chancellor for its chairman; a structure which would bring the Laboratory Schools a reporting line to the dean; and, of much more interest to the faculty, an enhanced ability for Chicago education faculty to compete for the growing largesse of foundations and the federal government in the support of educational research and development.

The issue of faculty quality and qualifications was of vital interest to both the Council and the Department. It was promised that a "very limited number" of new appointments would be made to persons "without predominantly scholarly backgrounds." The School faculty did not grow much beyond the promised five "regular" (professorial) staff members and the ten field staff on term appointments. All had doctoral degrees if not scholarly records, except for some master teachers from the University High School who served as lecturers in the School and subject matter coordinators under the chairmanship of faculty members in the participating academic departments. Among the five criteria recommended in 1960 for promotion and tenure of School faculty were "continued inquiry in the teaching field" and "research and contributions to the literature." Joint appointments with the Department of Education were subject to the usual review process, necessitating approval of the dean and designated faculty in the Division of Social Sciences, as well as the Department of Education. Predictably, very few such joint appointments eventuated.[88] Nor, as was initially proposed, did many members of the Department be-

87. University of Chicago, Department of Education, *Minutes of the Meeting of the Faculty of the Department of Education,* 3 October 1958, pp. 5, 6.

88. The Department faculty eventually expressed (a) its wish to cooperate with the Graduate School of Education—as in offering social and behavioral science courses to prospective teachers; (b) its belief in some advisory role in GSE appointments; and (c) its disavowal of requirements for joint appointments unless proposed GSE faculty were "explicitly employed to perform substantial teaching, research, or other functions of the Department." University of Chicago, Department of Education, *Minutes of the Faculty,* 11 February 1964, p. 2.

come faculty of the Graduate School of Education; indeed some junior faculty in the Department were warned by those more experienced that they should have nothing to do with the School if they valued their careers. A recommendation from the Advisory Council of the Graduate School of Education that the Department and School faculties typically meet jointly was not followed.

Given their natural inclinations and primary interests, the academic departments did not challenge the Graduate School of Education for the doubtful privilege of mounting alternative graduate teacher education programs. In early 1959, for example, while nine departments claimed to prepare teachers, only five did so intentionally. As one department reported, "A very small number of our graduates have taught in high schools and some of our graduates are teaching in junior colleges. This is normally the result of accident, failure to complete the Ph.D., or failure to secure a college or university position, [rather] than of deliberate preparation."[89] Over the years the *Minutes* of the School report that cooperating departments were gradually "increasing their commitment to and acceptance of" the School's MAT programs.[90] Whether academics abandoned their conviction that future teachers are inevitably the inadequate and unfortunate among their students is debatable; the fact is that the few academic programs of teacher preparation that once existed did disappear.

The School expanded its offerings beyond those originally envisioned. It added a Master of Science in Teaching program for elementary school teachers; "refresher institutes" for experienced teachers in collaboration with academic departments; and a short-lived master's degree program in school counseling. More challenging yet was a large reading program that prepared specialists and, after 1970, a fast-growing doctoral program in teacher education through a joint committee with the Department, which alone was authorized to award doctorates in education. Along with normal institutional maturing,

89. University of Chicago, Department of Education, "Report on Master's Degree Programs for the Preparation of Secondary School and Junior College Teachers," 6 April 1959. The unknown authors went on to comment about the perpetuation of "mediocrity" in existing arrangements: "The present programs are preparations for the Ph.D. In some cases courses more appropriate for teachers than for research scholars have been included, but this is not the case in general. It seems incongruous to have such programs on the books, turning out few teachers, while students are going out as teachers from the same institution with the A.B. in some of the same fields."

90. University of Chicago, Graduate School of Education, *Minutes of the Council of the Graduate School of Education,* 12 May 1964, p. 1.

these additions represent the faculty's awareness of their limited effect given the small number of teachers being prepared and retained, and their limited impact upon the profession even if their graduates, scholar-teachers, became high school department chairpersons, as was envisioned.[91] A carefully selected and well-qualified faculty, as they saw themselves, they wished to be put to fuller use. Like their counterparts in the Department of Education, School faculty were expressing a natural interest in reaching and influencing the careerist and higher-status professional in teaching, a field still marked by debilitating turnover and low prestige. Thus, Chicago had acquired, albeit on a very small scale, what it did not want: a teachers college.

The Disappearance of the Graduate School of Education

In the first year of the School, Dean Chase wrote to officials of the Ford Foundation, describing the organization of its funded MAT program at Chicago: a School functioning as an administrative body, to coordinate teacher education and curriculum study in various departments and divisions of the University; a Department of Education dedicated to the study of education and the preparation of researchers and university faculty; and a small undergraduate teacher education program in the College. In an internal memorandum, a consultant raised the issue of how these several teacher education programs with their separate staffs and their separate relations with academic departments and with local schools live together, and more importantly, *why:*

> As near as I could tell from some pretty frank discussions about this matter, the answer is that no one wants to "rock the boat" at the moment. The general attitude of other-than-teacher education personnel, i.e., the group made up of the associate and full professors (and status members) of the Department of Education is that they could [not] care less about teacher education as such in any form. They are interested only in themselves, in their own research, and its theoretical contribution to the "theoretical" components of education. . . . Within this structure of disdain toward the training of teachers, the MAT program somehow flourishes and grows, thanks to [its director], an extremely

91. See, for example, the comments of Janet Emig and Richard Hodges in *Minutes of the Meeting of the Graduate School of Education Faculty,* 16 November 1966, pp. 2–3.

> able group of students, and several academic departments who find in the MATs the ablest graduate students at the University.[92]

Forty years after Chicago closed its first school of education, the still-young Graduate School of Education was in trouble. President Edward H. Levi—a "local" who attended the University of Chicago continuously from his matriculation in the Lab School kindergarten through the Law School, and a man with a deep understanding of the Chicago ethos—sent a memorandum to the GSE faculty. "We are delighted," he wrote, "that we did not let ourselves be persuaded by the largesse of foundations and government grants to change our traditional views." He endorsed "the wisdom of the University's long-term approach, which he downgraded to "having a small unit to help coordinate the teacher training aspects of work carried out throughout the entire University and within the Department of Education."[93] In 1969 Levi had put in an appearance at a School faculty meeting. Dropping the first shoe, he had commended the faculty for its decision to conduct a self-study since each unit should be obligated to scrutinize "what form and proportion of present structure would be determined to survive." Moreover, he reminded them, the mandate of the School should be shaped according to the University's mission to "search for important problems, place its bet on the generation of ideas and the teaching for those ideas and the testing of ideas."[94]

At its peak, the School enrolled a new cohort of ninety MAT students each year, compared to a Departmental enrollment of about four hundred. While large by University standards, the numbers were insignificant alongside those of neighboring institutions: Chicago State, Northeastern Illinois State, and the University of Illinois at Chicago. Moreover, it was increasingly difficult to place Chicago's interns in the changed market for teachers during the 1970s. The Ford Foundation and the federal government had moved on to funding other projects than teacher education. But neither the surplus of teachers nor the loss of external funding probably would have proved fatal to the School had the Department of Education and the University of Chicago had sufficient reserves of commitment to the reality, rather than the rhet-

92. James C. Stone to Alvin C. Eurich, 20 November 1963, Ford Foundation Archives; quoted in Coley and Thorpe, *MAT Model,* 25.

93. Edward H. Levi, memorandum to the faculty of the Graduate School of Education, 20 April 1973. Quoted in Gevinson, *Master of Arts,* 10.

94. University of Chicago, Graduate School of Education, *Minutes of the Meeting of the Graduate School of Education Faculty,* 15 January 1969, 2. The language is that of the author of the minutes.

oric, of the preparation and continuing education of teachers. These activities simply did not fit comfortably in the University's culture.

The request of the School faculty for an inquiry into the "appropriateness and adequacy of its resources" to carry out the University's commitment to teacher education instead brought a recommendation that the Graduate School of Education be merged with the Department of Education. At that point the Department was itself an old body. The professors brought in by Ralph Tyler to revive the faculty after he succeeded Judd as chairman in 1938—Benjamin Bloom, Lee J. Cronbach, Vergil Herrick, Chester W. Harris, Carl Rodgers, R. J. Havighurst, Joseph Schwab—were gone or retiring. The Chicago-based Spencer Foundation funded an infusion of young assistant professors—some dozen in the early 1970s. But almost none remained, either rejected by the Department for tenure or rejecting the institution and building careers elsewhere.

Early in 1975, the provost appointed a committee chaired by Chauncey D. Harris, former dean of the Division of Social Sciences. The Harris Committee was now ready to make public the difficulties of the Graduate School of Education. These included creation of a separate faculty of nationally visible subject-matter specialists with unmet expectations of becoming part of a full-fledged professional school, declining budgets and plummeting morale, inadequate consultation in the selection of the dean, and a heightened "sense of isolation and of nonrecognition." The Committee concluded, "The faculty of the School feel underappreciated, undersupported, and underrepresented and suspect a lack of sympathy for the professional orientation of the School."[95] Despite persisting difficulties in reconciling diverging views about scholarly study and professional training, the Committee nonetheless recommended a merger of the two incompatible units.

In October 1975 Professor Philip Jackson addressed the Society of Professors of Education at its Minneapolis meeting, on the topic of "Divided We Stand." His categories of educationists would have described his own institution, Chicago. To the "disciplinists" (psychologists, historians, philosophers, and sociologists of education) and the "generalists" (professors of educational administration, curriculum, higher education, counseling) of the old Department of Education was added with the closing of the Graduate School of Education, a component of "pedagogists." To the extent that their different orientations might cause friction, Jackson had no doubt that "the group we are

95. University of Chicago, "Report of the Committee to Examine the University's Resources and Future Commitments in Education," 16 May 1975, 3.

calling the disciplinists seem to have the upper hand." They were, he noted, in many institutions "a natural elite whose superior status is acknowledged and goes unchallenged within the education faculty."[96]

John Goodlad had been correct when, in 1957, he reported on a proposed Master of Arts in the Teaching of Science: "the scope of the administrative activities involved is such that the persons would be unlikely to do the scholarly work necessary for advancement" through the usual channels of research and publication.[97] Some School faculty left in apprehension of the results when their contributions were subjected to the test of congruence with the University's research mission; others failed the test and then left. The rare "accepted survivors" were those who, with the proper personal style, demonstrated unusual facility in combining professional leadership with serious research records.

The School's programs fared little better than its faculty. Its dream of exerting leadership in teacher education was viewed skeptically. Department faculty thought the quality of students in the collaborative School-Department teacher education doctoral program was low, the requirements too relaxed, the dissertations relatively inferior and perhaps damaging to the reputation of the Department. With the merger the program became one of the Department's "special fields" before vanishing from the books. The once-flourishing reading program virtually disappeared. Outreach programs shrank to weekend seminars with local school administrators when outside funding permitted. The concept of the scholar-teacher had never been taken seriously in the Department; the high intellectual calibre of the MAT students was not uniformly recognized by Department faculty at the time—although some thought them far superior intellectually to the Department's own students. The fact that Harvard and Yale dropped their own MAT programs encouraged the Harris Committee to think that ad hoc arrangements could suffice to meet the small demand. By 1985 there were under ten MAT candidates around, although prospects of supporting future mathematics teachers promised some renewal of numbers.

96. Philip W. Jackson, "Divided We Stand: The Internal Organization of the Education Professoriate," in *The Professor of Education: An Assessment of Conditions,* ed. Ayres Bagley (Papers of the meeting of the Society of Professors of Education, College of Education, University of Minnesota, October 1975), 67.

97. John I. Goodlad, "The Master of Arts in Teaching—Overview and Framework." Quoted in Gevinson, "Master of Arts," 11–12.

Whatever Happened to Reading at Chicago?

In recommending the disposition of the faculty and programs of the Graduate School of Education, the Harris Committee specifically mentioned the long history of the reading field at Chicago. In fact, Chicago's was once at or near the pinnacle of the nation's programs for the preparation of researchers, teacher educators, textbook writers, and curriculum specialists in the field of reading—this because of one man: William S. Gray. The first dissertations in reading were completed at the University of Chicago in 1917; Gray's was one of them.[98] He subsequently taught several generations of the field's leaders. He authored the most widely used basal reading series, the "Dick and Jane" books, incorporating the latest thinking in reading instruction, and, from 1925 until his death, the annual reading research summaries published in the *Journal of Educational Research;* no field exceeded reading in the amount of research undertaken in what public opinion and many educators considered to be the preeminent skill subject in the entire curriculum, from grade one to the university.

In the 1920s Gray shared with Arthur I. Gates of Teachers College credit for developing diagnostic techniques for assessing reading performance and for fathering the specialty of remedial reading. A president of both the International Council for the Improvement of Reading Instruction and the National Association of Remedial Teachers, which merged to form the International Reading Association (IRA) late in 1955, Gray was the first president of the new, thriving organization. Gray was instrumental in obtaining space for IRA's national headquarters in Judd Hall, and one of Judd's former students and an occasional lecturer in reading at Chicago, James McCallister, became its Executive Secretary-Treasurer.[99] Of all the well-known names on Chicago's education faculty over five decades—Judd, Bobbett, Buswell, Freeman, Tyler, Havighurst, Chase, Anderson, Campbell—Gray's was unquestionably the most familiar to teachers, principals, curriculum specialists, and publishers.

In 1960 William Gray was thrown from a horse and killed during a Wyoming vacation. Although emeritus for a decade, Gray's passing symbolized a closing chapter at Chicago. Direction of the reading pro-

98. Nila Banton Smith, *American Reading Instruction* (Newark, Del.: International Reading Association, 1934, 1965), 187.

99. Bob W. Jerrolds, *Reading Reflections: The History of the International Reading Association* (Newark, Del: International Reading Association, 1977), 40.

gram had already passed to Helen M. Robinson, Gray's student, herself a prominent figure in the reading field on its clinical side. One of the rare women on the tenured faculty, Robinson was promoted to professor and, in 1962, to the newly created William S. Gray Chair. A few subsequent appointments were made, designed to bring the program closer to the new work in linguistics, psycholinguistics, rhetoric, developmental psychology, and other fields where there were cognate disciplines to scrutinize faculty work—something which reading had not previously "enjoyed."[100]

In 1961 the International Reading Association moved from Judd Hall. In the measured words of IRA's historian, "The University of Chicago could not or would not provide adequate space on campus, and possibilities near the campus were extremely meagre."[101] During the 1960s the reading faculty retired or departed. With Helen Robinson's retirement the Gray Chair became vacant. H. Alan Robinson left Chicago for Hofstra University the same year in which he became president of the International Reading Association; Samuel Weintraub, later an editor of IRA's *Reading Research Quarterly,* left at the end of the decade. The Reading Center, a testing and clinical facility that was part of a national movement begun in the 1930s with strong support from Gray, was put on notice: unless it could come up with a research agenda, it would be closed. Chicago vanished from the ranks of the nation's leading centers of reading research and professional training. In contrast to the small, research-oriented Language and Reading in Instruction (LARI) program in the Department of Education, the Graduate School of Education had established a prospering professional program; some sixty graduate students were enrolled at one time. The disappearance of this program not long after the merger left some of the faculty and the students bitter. It was an example of the Department of Education "shooting itself in the foot," in the words of an unsocialized former faculty member, looking from the vantage point of another field.

In the opinion of the national "reading establishment," probably the ultimate betrayal of William Gray and his professional mission came when the Department, after prolonged discussions, reconcep-

100. Some of the disciplinary influences on language arts education are discussed in Geraldine Jonçich Clifford, "A Sisyphean Task! Historical Perspectives on the Relations of Reading and Writing Instruction," Technical Paper No. 7, Center for the Study of Writing, University of California, Berkeley, and Carnegie Mellon University, 1987.

101. Jerrolds, *Reading Reflections,* 65–66.

tualized one of its few precious endowed chairs and awarded it to a cognitive psychologist with no standing in the reading field. This decision was an instructive and dramatic one, a correct decision from the perspective of the prevailing ethos. Although the incumbent of the William S. Gary Chair of Education and Behavioral Science did not publish in *The Reading Teacher* or even the *Reading Research Quarterly,* she could converse on terms of mutual respect with Chicago professors involved in brain research, with cognitive psychologists, and with psychiatrists in the medical school about basic research on the acquisition of word meanings by very young children. Given these highly specialized interests, however, other leadership had to be found when, in 1981, the Department decided to "renew" and "revitalize" the reading program and recover some of Chicago's lost visibility in reading research and instruction.[102] Room 204 of Judd Hall was dedicated as the William S. Gray Room and made the headquarters of the programs in reading and elementary teacher preparation, and a national conference on reading was sponsored in 1982.

The decline of reading and its gradual transformation into cognitive psychology at Chicago after William Gray's death is symptomatic of other decisions made by the faculty of the Department of Education in the postwar years. It is the case, however, that reading's status had always been somewhat debatable, for it existed rather uncomfortably in Charles Judd's Department. Himself a product of a normal school, a classroom teacher, a student of Thorndike at Teachers College (M.A. 1914), Gray was a *rara avis* in Judd's faculty for both his background and his unremitting interaction with teachers and their classrooms. He did not eschew "service" to the profession; on the contrary, he ran workshops for teachers around the United States, in the style of a glorified "normal school instructor." He taught the much-maligned methods courses and administered student teaching at Chicago. When necessary, Gray quietly dissented from Judd's policies on a number of particulars, but prevailed only in his own reading program with its decidedly clinical cast. Almost alone among the senior faculty, he knew why those small children were to be found in the corridors of Judd Hall and utilized the Laboratory Schools for both instructional and research purposes.

102. "Designed for teachers updating their training or individuals seeking training as researchers in reading education, the program stresses the teaching of comprehension skills and strategies for integrating instructional innovations in reading, basic research, and practice." University of Chicago, Department of Education, *Education News,* 1984, p. 5. See also the 1980, 1981, and 1982 issues of *Education News.*

Future Prospects at Chicago

University of Chicago President Hannah Gray was another participant at the 1983 Pajaro Dunes conference. How was Chicago going to respond to its clarion call: that the nation's leading universities engage in an unprecedented active partnership with public schools? The Harris Committee had recommended "a united faculty to judge the promise and appropriateness for this University of current or proposed appointments, fields, or programs in education." A united faculty responded with characteristic revulsion at any talk of undergraduate teacher education, even in response to positive signals from academic departments and a looming teacher shortage.

When the Social Sciences Collegiate Division sent "an urgent request" that the Department of Education seriously consider the possibility of a "major" in Education, its faculty countered that, at most, "Education should be offered as a 'minor' associated with appropriate disciplinary concentrations, not as a concentration in its own right."[103] A six-year School Mathematics Project, chaired by a professor of mathematics and funded by a foundation grant, was allowable. So was using a gift to launch the Benton Center for Curriculum and Instruction. But to leap at opportunity, to snatch at bait even when offered by Chicago faculty or administrators who wished "to strengthen the ties of the College 'to the world of affairs,'" was not in the style of education at Chicago. Too many dangers followed from imitating ambitious schools of education. To Chicago's Education Department it meant more to house the editor of the *American Journal of Sociology* than of *The Reading Teacher* or even the *Reading Research Quarterly.* As it was worth more to their colleagues across the campus to be cited by scientists and scholars than by teachers or superintendents, it was with pride that the Department of Education reported its ranking for citations of its faculty's work by other social scientists. Unlike the reputational surveys, by this method Chicago came out better. "Department Rated Number One" claimed the headline in the 1985 issue of Chicago's *Education News.*[104]

103. University of Chicago, Department of Education, *Minutes of the Meetings of the Faculty of the Department of Education,* 8 October 1985 and 11 February 1986.

104. Richard J. Kroc, "Using Citation Analysis to Assess Scholarly Productivity," *Educational Researcher* 13, no. 6 (July 1984): 17–22.

Conclusion

In the foregoing exploration of some of the social, economic, and political developments of the years 1955 through 1985, we have witnessed both continuity and change in the situations of schools of education. Continuity lay in such facts as the lack of deep or sustainable regard for teacher preparation or interest in the issues of mass public education on the part of most academics in letters and science departments. Partly because of that, schools of education faced the persisting consequences of low status and academic marginality. These included the necessity to scramble after devices to answer their critics, tactics which reduced their independence, self-confidence, and discretion still further.

There were also new developments. The expansion and broadening of educational research was one, with positive potential for building the still-slender science of education. Some others, like the growing militancy among teachers and the new power of consumer groups, presented added difficulties. These problems, in turn, tempted many education professors to wish to see their schools quit being professional schools and become, instead, unabashed departments for the academic study of education. By making different kinds of faculty appointments, some, like the Foundations Division at Teachers College and the former school administration program at Stanford, approached that status; some in Chicago's Department of Education would claim that it never waivered from that stance.

University administrators were also thrown into doubt by the events of these three decades. Faculty review committees pressed for conformity to academic interests and styles. Yale and Duke let their departments of education disappear without discernible regret. But the crucial place of education in the larger society, and for their own futures, stopped most university presidents short of allowing their schools of education to disappear entirely. Most continued, if attenuated from their maximum size of 1970 or so—still caught, as they have been throughout, in the competing tensions generated by the university culture on the one side and the professional culture on the other.

Chicago's was a more typical case study than Yale's, which began this chapter. Chicago survived, as most schools of education did and will do. It demonstrates how external challenges can be reconciled to an institutional ethos. Embedded in this case study is a suggestion as to why almost all of the institutions which were preeminent in 1910 remained so in 1950 and 1985—despite a literal explosion in institutional formation. The situation in the United States was unlike that in Great Britain, for example, where teacher training colleges were separated from universities and other professional schools. Education schools in the United States *were* in the universities and in this fact lay their greatest challenge and their greatest opportunity.

After some seventy-five years, schools of education were still held up to unfavorable comparisons with the schools of the respected professions. The salaries of their professors were lower and their working conditions dysfunctional in important respects. While medical schools provide the extreme example of structuring different professional roles within the faculty, education schools were unable even to gain approval of a clinical track. Hence, these functions were delegated to subfaculty or performed, sometimes incompetently, by professors rewarded for other activities.

The fact that the curriculum of leading law schools was described as "unrelieved confusion" and "a mere aggregate or conglomerate of independently developed units," or that cyclical reform movements often "ended as intellectual disasters," gave cold comfort to the educationists. Law schools were fortresses of privilege and power, impervious to such attack.[105] It was galling to watch law and business schools creaming off many of the students, especially the women students, who once prepared to teach. Just a few years before, business had shared with education the status of academic marginality. Efforts of business schools, like that at Northwestern, to develop interdisciplinary programs with liberal arts departments had foundered on the rocks of academic indifference and negative attitudes toward business students, much like those that education still experienced.[106] By the 1980s it did not appear to damage the appeal of business schools when the popular press reported that the most successful MBA graduates of elite institutions were noted for their outgoing personalities and ambition rather than for their scores on scholastic aptitude tests.

Still, even the most prestigious professions and professional schools did not emerge from the tumultuous years of postwar America unscathed. In the spring of 1970, for example, the New York Court of Appeals reminded the New York University Law School of the limits of its independence, warning that its students could not take the bar exams if the spring term was curtailed to protest the shootings at Kent State University and the American invasion of Cambodia.[107] The

105. Stevens, "American Law School," 514–15.
106. Schlossman and Sedlak, *Age of Autonomy,* 45.
107. Stevens, "American Law School," 547.

president of Harvard University attracted wide attention in 1979 for his criticisms of the University's Graduate School of Business. His proposition that business schools should equip students to serve social purposes along with corporate interests got attention.[108] Derek Bok subsequently decried the rush of talented youth to law schools as a shameful waste of national resources. In contrast, his support of the proper mission of schools of education was hoped to signal a refreshing, if mild, change of atmosphere for schools of education on other campuses. Was anyone paying attention?

108. For an analysis of why a similar examination of an education school would be handled differently see Gifford, "Prestige and Education," 186–98.

Seven Sister Campuses in California: A Comparative Study of Institutional Cultures

For more than a century after its admission to statehood, California enjoyed a national reputation for leadership in public education from kindergarten through graduate schooling.[1] California's pioneering in education included strategies to professionalize teaching. It authorized a system in 1860 whereby teachers constituted the county and state boards of examiners that constructed and administered examinations to determine the awarding of teachers' licenses. Licenses based on examination quickly became obsolete, however, replaced by credentials gained through formal study. In 1893 California established a minimum requirement of a bachelor's degree for beginning high school teachers. It was also the first state to demand a bachelor's degree for elementary school teaching, this in 1930.

In 1913 normal schools were permitted to expand their curricula so as to offer prospective secondary school teachers an academic specialization in their teaching fields, and by 1923 normal schools were authorized to become state teachers colleges with a four-year baccalaureate program. Authority over these schools passed from local trustees to the State Department of Education. In 1935 they became general purpose state colleges when the legislature removed the declaration of intention to become a teacher as a prerequisite for admission. In 1948 there were seven such state colleges. The subsequent creation of a separate governing board permitted the formation of a

1. Charles J. Falk, *The Development and Organization of Education in California* (New York: Harcourt, Brace & World, 1968), 68–69.

system for the first time, parallel to the university system.[2] Their existence permitted the state colleges to concentrate more of their efforts on upper division and some master's degree work, bringing them into conflict with the University of California. We will later see the importance for schools of education of the existence of this parallel system.

When Robert Gordon Sproul was inaugurated President of the University in 1930, he told those assembled in Berkeley's Greek Theatre that his task was to maintain the University's acknowledged place as one of the world's great institutions. "It cannot be less and be worthy of the splendid public school system of which it is a part; worthy of this almost legendary land . . .; worthy of the pioneer people. . . ."[3] Sproul expressed for the University of California the mission which the University of Michigan had first claimed: the leadership of a state's entire system of public education. He exhorted the state's teachers colleges to give "honest devotion" to the education of elementary school teachers, the purpose for which they were founded as normal schools—regretting, in a telling phrase, that some "would hide in every way possible . . . the fact that they have anything to do with teachers."

President Sproul's own institution then contained two professional schools to prepare teachers—at Berkeley and UCLA. But he demanded more of them. "Why should we not look on education as [we would on] a problem in physics or astronomy?" he asked.

> The reason is that most of us either give no thought to the theory underlaying the system of education we support, or think of education

2. Ibid., 199. The seven state colleges were the California Polytechnic College and the Chico, Humboldt, San Francisco, San Jose, Fresno, and San Diego State Colleges. See University of California, Liaison Committee of the Regents of the University and the California State Board of Education, *A Report of a Survey of the Needs of California in Higher Education,* 1 March 1948, pp. 4, 18, 20–21. For a review of the earlier position of the University of California on the creation of this alternative system, see Verne A. Stadtman, *The University of California, 1868–1968* (New York: McGraw-Hill, 1970). The third sector in the state's organization of public higher education was the junior college; there were fifty-five in 1948. Junior colleges were first authorized in 1907, growing steadily until their post–World War II spurt.

3. University of California, "Inaugural Address of Robert Gordon Sproul as President of the University, 22 October 1930," Bancroft Library, University of California at Berkeley, pp. 1, 5. The contribution of the University to California's future elites is suggested by the twelve graduates of 1873, the first class to complete a four-year curriculum. They included a future California governor, a mayor of the city of Alameda, an engineer, a mathematics professor, two lawyers, and a bank president. See University of California at Berkeley, Capital Campaign, "Builders of Berkeley" (1986), 19.

> as an exception to the rule that every subject must rest on some cardinal theory. Such theories and investigations have been left in the universities almost entirely to departments of education, which for all the contumely that has been heaped upon their heads have been more progressive than other departments, for they have been making an honest, sincere study of a problem baffling in its complexity. Despite the exaggerated stressing of the theory of education, despite childish reliance on questionnaires, despite the weaknesses and foibles characteristic of any new effort, they have been hitting at least as close to the needs of the American university as those who will have none of educational theory.[4]

Sproul thus pointed to two problems of schools of education that have interested us throughout this study: the reluctance of many professors of education to be associated too closely with teacher education and the stubborn doubts within the larger academic community about the existence of a sufficient subject matter to justify education's existence as an academic unit. His call for assistance from the entire university in the scientific study of education was ignored. His promise that he would promote young professors on the basis of their devotion to advancing theory and conducting controlled experiments was not overlooked, however.

The two sister schools under Sproul's mantle were somewhat at loggerheads in 1930. And, given its different history, education at UCLA always retained more of its privileged and professional status. Thus, while Berkeley imposed higher grade-point averages for entering its teacher preparation programs than did UCLA, this did not raise education's status at Berkeley any more than it lowered education's status at Los Angeles. Ironically, north-south animosities meant that opposition to education at Berkeley generated some support for it in Los Angeles, even among academics who might otherwise share the persisting skepticism that afflicts the field at many other schools.[5]

California's public schools enjoyed wide support until beset by the financial and social pressures that accompanied rapid increases in the state's population, especially in its racial and ethnic diversity.

4. University of California, "Inaugural Address," 20–21.

5. Local protective sentiments did not always work, however. For example, in 1962 the Academic Senate of the University of California at Santa Barbara (until recently Santa Barbara State Teachers College) rejected the proposal of the new school of education to award a master's degree. It was widely believed locally that an important factor in that decision was the desire of a majority of the non-Education faculty to shed its "normal-school imagery" as quickly as possible.

When Maxwell Rafferty became State Superintendent of Public Instruction in 1963—in one of the state's periodic, populist indulgences—he rode and raised a tide of public concern. Some disarray in the profession and a defensive mentality left over from the salvos of Arthur Bestor and Admiral Rickover's post-Sputnik criticisms of schools strengthened Rafferty's hand. That history plus the education school's chronic lack of acceptance on the Berkeley campus made the School of Education vulnerable. Professional study of education now survives at Berkeley only by the decision of the chancellor to disregard apparently seriously-given advice from faculty committees and influential professors, advice that he disband the School.

What follows is a description and analysis of the more significant events that occurred over the decades, especially the years 1975 to 1983. Along with events, we probe the environmental and organizational conditions which contributed to the peril. We will visit, in turn, the two major schools of education during Sproul's presidency, tracing their separate histories to the present. UCLA's prospered in the City of the Angels, achieving the kind of balanced appearance that others also sought. Meanwhile Berkeley's fell on hard times, for reasons we dissect with excrutiating detail. Our story builds upon the clash of cultures and the new organizational arrangements introduced in earlier chapters; it also provides the grounds for the recommendations in the concluding chapter. Because of mounting interest in "research-sensitive practice" and "practice-sensitive research," the University Elementary School and its relations to the UCLA Graduate School of Education are highlighted. There may be lessons there also for contemporary advocates of the professional development centers urged by the Holmes Group.

A Sister Campus

That its particular history dogs an institution's steps is clear when Sproul's two schools of education are compared. Berkeley, opened in 1868, early favored liberal arts and science departments. For inspiration it looked to Yale and Johns Hopkins far more than to Cornell and Purdue. The faculty fought off the agriculturalists (in the body of the State Grange), the home economists, the physicians and nurses, even the lawyers for a time; satellite campuses at Davis and San Francisco were built as more congenial homes for these vocational fields. In marked contrast the Los Angeles campus originated as the Los Angeles State Normal School, situated in the protective embrace of Faith, Hope, and Charity streets. Founded in 1882 as a branch of the State

Normal School in San Jose, four hundred miles to the north, its sole mission was the preparation of elementary school teachers. It began that task with the heavy emphasis on practice that became characteristic of the institution.

In 1920 Los Angeles had more than one-half million residents, making it the fifth largest city in the United States. The growth of population and the new political and economic power in the southern region encouraged the Normal School's leaders in their dream of becoming a four-year, degree-granting teachers college comparable to Teachers College of Columbia University. It was already a large and thriving institution and, like other normal schools, anxious to appear more "academic." Notable members of the faculty included Lewis Terman (1906–1910), who went to Stanford and made his reputation there as a test developer and researcher, and Arnold Gesell (1908–1911), who inaugurated his famous studies in child development at Yale. It was difficult to keep such men in a normal school, and Angelenos chafed at the limits on their ambitions. By 1921, the Normal School's "largest laboratory," the Training School, enrolled 525 children. Yet, the fact that this, and other normal schools, could not grant the bachelor of arts, had begun to rankle. In response to *realpolitik* and to a regional vacuum in public higher education that the private University of Southern California threatened to fill, the regents of the University of California reluctantly accepted the normal school and added two years of general undergraduate education.[6]

These actions created the two-year Southern Branch of the University of California. It opened in 1919 with 2,300 students, one thousand of them in the teachers' course; this figure represented 40 percent of the state's teachers-in-training. The Normal School's principal, Ernest Carroll Moore, actively sought this union, arguing to Regent Edward F. Dickson, the sole Southern Californian on the Board, that "No really great teachers' college could be built successfully without contact with, and the prestige of a great university."[7] By 1925, with the persistent help of sympathetic legislators, a four-year course prevailed throughout, and the name of the institution was changed in 1927 to the University of California at Los Angeles. Its largest compo-

6. For the University's response to an earlier (1911) proposal to turn Throop Polytechnic Institute in Pasadena (later California Institute of Technology) into a second state university with its own board, see Stadtman, *University of California,* 214–17.

7. Treacy, "Progressivism and Corinne Seeds," 14. Most of the persons quoted and events at UCLA described in this section are drawn from Treacy. See also Stadtman *University of California,* 219 ff.

nent remained the Teachers College. A new and attractively located campus in the city's western hills was occupied two years later—a bond issue approved by local voters purchased the land. There were over 6,000 students ready for this promising new venture.

The conventional wisdom in the University of California community is that, somewhere along the line, UCLA administrators (but not necessarily the faculty) decided that their campus could not prosper by trying to compete with Berkeley's in the departments of the College of Letters and Science—at least not in the short run. Professional schools and colleges, rather than be merely tolerated as at Berkeley, were to be UCLA's path toward eminence. Enormous resources followed that strategy after 1945, especially to the Medical School which became a distinctive regional center earning UCLA considerable public good will and powerful friends among the Southland's business, entertainment, and political elites. It also worked exceptionally well bringing UCLA into the front ranks of American universities. Doctoral work was authorized in 1936, with support from Berkeley; the Academic Senate was more accepting of this than of teacher education.[8] UCLA initially appeared among the nation's leading graduate institutions in Keniston's 1959 study (placing fourteenth). By 1982, it had been rated eighth, "by far the best showing of universities founded in this century and perhaps the best showing ever of a predominantly commuter institution."[9]

The Opposition from the North

Ernest Carroll Moore, President of the antecedant Los Angeles State Normal School since 1917, functioned as both chairman of the Department of Education, Psychology, and Philosophy and provost (head) of UCLA until 1936. This was an incalculably great asset to education, especially given the "frustrating and distracting opposition" to its "little brother in Los Angeles" that came from unsympathetic regents, professors, and administrators at Berkeley.[10]

8. Stadtman, *University of California,* 267.

9. David S. Webster, "America's Highest Ranked Graduate Schools, 1925–1982," *Change,* 15, no. 4 (May–June 1983):23–24.

10. Treacy, "Progressivism," passim, esp. pp. v, 10, 108, 354. A Berkeley faculty committee had, in 1917, recommended against a proposal to offer requested summer session courses in Los Angeles. President Wheeler and allies among the regents nonetheless secured the summer session, opening the way toward UCLA. Stadtman, *University of California,* 218–19. Matters improved in 1933 when the UCLA faculty was formed into its own autonomous division of the Academic Senate, but Sproul exercised

Moore came to Los Angeles from the Harvard faculty with the warning of Harvard's President Lowell: "It will be a pretty fight; the interests of its people at the two ends of the state are diverse."[11] Feelings of sectional competition, even antipathy, were and remain strong in California. They explain some of the bitter opposition which the Southern Branch and UCLA received from Berkeley. The general disdain which the School of Education at Berkeley experienced on its own campus also redounded against the Los Angeles institution. Moore knew something of this at first hand, having been on the Berkeley faculty in both education and philosophy early in the century. Regent Chester Rowell reportedly had encouraged opposition to the plan for the Southern Branch among the presidents of California's seven other normal schools. He considered the training of elementary school teachers, including primary and kindergarten teacher, not the proper function of a university; it should restrict itself to preparing students to be high school teachers, principals, superintendents, and college and university professors.

Several "Stages of Purgatory," in Moore's words, were endured in the transition. At Berkeley in October 1923, the Educational Policy Committee of the Academic Senate concluded that elementary school teacher preparation did not belong in the University and asked the president to consider separating the Teachers College, the four-year course which granted the Bachelor of Education degree, from the University; the mixture of prospective teachers and liberal arts students was "unwholesome" and the operation of teacher preparation an illogical and distracting "sideline."[12] The next year President William Wallace Campbell proposed that the Teachers College not accompany the College of Letters and Science when the Los Angeles institution was moved to Westwood in 1929; he would have preferred that it be given back to the Normal School Trustees. Campbell specifically disliked having to sign credentials for prospective kindergarten teachers. Others reportedly objected to the presence on a University of California campus of the "little folks of the Training School" and to the "large group, predominantly made up of women whose objective was professional preparation for service at kindergarten and elementary school

---

close personal control in the highly centralized university during his presidency and he resided on the Berkeley campus.

11. Treacy, "Progressivism," 10–11.

12. Stadtman, *University of California,* 231–32.

levels."[13] Political support from the Los Angeles regent and local education and civic groups finally settled the matter in favor of retaining the Teachers College within UCLA. At the dedication of the new campus, Moore had the satisfaction of having his beloved mentor, John Dewey, give an address and receive an honorary degree. But, as Moore recalled, "I lived in that nightmare for four years and felt most of the time as though I had drunk kerosene."

The Intervention of the Women

The "constant criticism . . . that runs through the academic side, the so-called 'disciplined' fields"—in the words of a UCLA observer—surfaced again in the 1950s when friends of the campus University Elementary School (UES) sought the building funds to complete the school's relocation on the campus after it was forced out of its Los Angeles City School System building in 1945.[14] UES's historian, Robert Treacy, sees the campaign to retain the school, within the university and on the campus, as a feminist struggle.[15] Women, like Corinne Seeds, principal of UES from 1925 to 1957—an influential and idiosyncratic woman with a large and independent constituency—were a rarity in the University of California.[16] It must have annoyed some of her colleagues on the faculty that Seeds's supporters could "get to"

13. The words are Moore's, quoted in Treacy, "Progressivism," 41.

14. In 1955 a committee composed of regents and members of the State Board of Education, recommended that the University "defer completion of the University Elementary School at Los Angeles until a study had been made of the effectiveness of such schools." The committee also recommended that proposed laboratory schools at the Sacramento, San Jose, and Los Angeles State Colleges be deferred on the same grounds. University of California, Liaison Committee of the Regents of the University and the California State Department of Education, "A Restudy of the Needs of California in Higher Education: A Digest" (Berkeley, 1955), 80–81.

15. Ibid., 334. Treacy appears to accept the criticism that the hiring practices of UES "seemed to discriminate in favor of unmarried females" (p. 336). He suggests a "man-hating mentality" present in the school. But the career women in teaching whom Seeds needed and wanted for her school had, realistically, to be single women as the great majority of women teachers in the United States through the end of World War II were single, and married women were dismissed or demoted in many public and private schools until wartime shortages caused even "progressive" districts like Berkeley finally to change their policies and practices.

16. The chairmen of UCLA's departments of anthropology and political science, Harry Hoijer and Dean McHenry, parents of UES students, confirmed that 99 percent of public school supervisors in Southern California had signed statements supporting Seeds's school.

President Sproul when they could not. And Seeds did not even have a doctorate, at a time when this was becoming expected of faculty in up-and-coming institutions like UCLA. Dean Lee had urged her to "take a sabbatical, go to T. C. and knock out her Ph.D. or Ed.D.," but Seeds would not leave her school—an attitude about priorities that could have exasperated some of the younger, career- and research-minded members of the UCLA faculty.

The self-conscious support for Seeds by women in the state reflected the fact that professional women in education had been losing their places in school administration since the second or third decade of the century. The county superintendencies and positions as rural school supervisors which women once dominated in Western states were disappearing, or being downgraded in power, or given to the male products of education schools.[17] In the opinion of Corinne Seeds and her supporters, the mostly male faculty of the Department and School of Education also coveted the state funds going to UES; they would have them go to the Department instead, to hire more professors and to support research and experimentation rather than teacher training and demonstration work. Los Angeles City School Superintendent Susan Dorsey had been a vigorous supporter of teacher training at UCLA and of UES. Vierling Kersey, who assumed the superintendency in 1936, was another matter. He endorsed the campaign to evict UES, which had operated as a neighborhood public school.

The women teachers of UES and the mother-activists on the UES Family-School Alliance also believed that some members of the education faculty, particularly members recruited since the old normal school days, were uncomfortable in dealing with women—especially the single women, dedicated and independent careerists, who made up the faculty of UES and were badly out of style in the back-to-the-home and pronatalist climate of the two post-war decades. The organized, aggressive women of the UES campaign presented a challenge to conventional gender stereotypes. Of her good friend and major supporter of UES, Helen Heffernan, chief of the Elementary Bureau of the California State Department of Education from 1926 to 1965, Seeds said, "we had a powerful friend with a mind. I could safely say that she has the best mind of any women in education in the whole United

17. Reports of the State Superintendent indicate that, in 1920, there had been thirty women in country school superintendencies and twenty-eight men; by 1960 women held only nine such positions and, in 1970, one. Men also replaced women as principals of most elementary schools after 1920 or so.

States, and she has the ability to dominate that men hate."[18] Some men were known to refer to Heffernan as a "she-bull" and a proper model for matron in a Nazi prison camp. Even her strongest partisans among women recognized that when Seeds retired from the UCLA principalship, her successor, along with having to possess a doctorate, "had to be a man. . . . they were through dealing with women." This was reportedly "the conviction of only a few of them, who happened not to like to deal with women. But, they were a powerful little few."[19]

As devoted to the cause as were Corinne Seeds and her teachers, they might have failed to save UES without the assistance of the formidable women in the Family-School alliance. The school was exceedingly popular with a prosperous and sophisticated group of parents. The parents of present, former, or prospective UES students—the waiting list for four hundred student places ran into the thousands—were enlisted in the protracted struggle. Their members included the wives of powerful and well-connected men, and they used all the resources at their disposal. Personal friendships—with the Hearst publishing family, with prominent regents, and government officials—were exploited.

Appeals went to local, national, and international figures, including Aldous Huxley, Igor Stravinski, and Bertrand Russell.[20] Appeals were made to conscience and fair play. Mrs. Margaret Kiskadden, wife of a nationally known surgeon, challenged the chancellor by noting that "millions are being voted for a Medical School which had yet to prove itself, while a small but very bright jewel in his crown was being neglected completely." Another letter from a mother asked if the building project was delayed "because children do not vote, and because the staff is made up of women, women busy with their devoted attention to their jobs?"[21]

One objection heard to funding the UES building project was that the Berkeley School of Education had never had a campus school for teacher training, demonstration, or experimentation. But Berkeley's alternative model was not the major problem. More difficult to combat were subtle obstructions and the failures of University lobbyists to

18. Corinne A. Seeds, Oral History; quoted in Treacy, "Progressivism," 326.

19. Margaret Kiskadden, quoted in Treacy, "Progressivism," 300.

20. Russell, whose child had attended UES, concluded, however, that the mutual antipathy existing between himself and the Board of Regents would make him an ineffective supporter; his radicalism would, in fact, only alienate the Board.

21. Cited in Treacy, "Progressivism," 310, 312.

present and defend the UES budget item in legislative hearings in Sacramento. The personality of Corinne Seeds and the "eccentric feminism" or assertiveness of her female batallions was not the chief issue. Long-standing resistance to teacher education and direct University programs for children had become focused in the University of California community on the issue of the UCLA University Elementary School.

The struggle was also implicated in a now largely forgotten chapter of California history: the tensions associated with the Cold War, the Korean War, and the ravages of McCarthyism. Undoubtedly some among the UCLA faculty, in education and elsewhere, were frightened off by the fierce attack on progressive education as ultraliberalism. The wife of a member of the medical school faculty told Seeds that she was withholding public support of the school lest her husband's promotion be jeopardized. Such anxieties had to be heightened by the election, as State Superintendent of Public Education, of one of UCLA's own alumni, the demagogic Max Rafferty, and by an ever more politically and pedagogically conservative superintendent and school board in Los Angeles.

The Little "Red" Schoolhouse

The pedagogical theory that prevailed at UES was classic progressive education, featuring the project method and learning-by-doing or the "activity method." Seeds learned this at Teachers College, which, during the anticommunist campaigns of the 1920s and 1930s, was periodically branded as "Red." In the next two decades, UCLA students and faculty also periodically read in the local press about UCLA as the "Little Red Schoolhouse." Student-led protests on behalf of free speech on campus helped fuel the charges. So did Corinne Seeds. Her curriculum's principal goal was to bring the child "to become one with his world." This seemed to suggest to some observers a "one-world" internationalism, an undue regard for the United Nations, and pacifism—all considered unpatriotic in conservative circles. She had earlier fallen under suspicion for having organized a drive to collect toys for Japanese-American children placed in internment camps in 1942.

In 1945 Dean Lee wrote to UCLA's Provost Dykstra of the attitude of the local superintendent: "Mr. Kersey is at present riding the wave of 'return to the fundamentals' and following [William Randolph] Hearst's lead in 'emphasizing the three Rs.'"[22] A hostile former UES

22. Quoted in Treacy, "Progressivism," 304.

parent was elected to the Los Angeles Board of Education that year, precipitating the eviction crisis. Seeds believed she "was mad at us because we didn't joint the Moral Rearmament" movement; Seeds had, however, joined the Association for Promotion of Friendship with Russia.[23] Seeds had rebuked another parent when she objected to the temporary presence of a Negro teacher. Seeds was ordered to testify before the California Legislature's Fact-Finding Committee on Un-American Activities, called the "Tenny Committee" for its chairman, a former-radical-turned-anti-communist. In a room packed with teachers she was asked to verify the allegation that the UES curriculum of cultural units included study of Ukrainian collective farms. "Yes," Seeds replied. "That's the only kind they have."

Nonetheless, because of intense counterpressure by its friends, UES funding was finally scheduled to appear in the University's budget in the presentations made to the legislature in February 1956. When the item was removed, Mrs. Kiskadden went to the assemblyman representing the district in which UCLA was located, Harold Levering. He refused to help on the grounds that the school was "very, very pinko."[24] Levering was coauthor, with Jack Tenny, of Assembly Bill 61, the Levering Act, passed by the legislature and signed by Governor Earl Warren in 1950, during the Korean War. It required every civil defense worker and public employee in California to take an oath that the signer would not advocate or become a member of any party or organization advocating the overthrow of the United States government. This oath extended to others the controversial policy adopted in 1940 by the regents of the University of California not to employ communists as faculty or staff and implemented in the form of an oath in 1949. While the wounds within the University imposed by "three years of self-imposed conflict" were healing, officials remained skittish about public confidence and political charges of being "soft on communism," as events at Berkeley in the 1960s would subsequently demonstrate.[25]

It was quickly apparent that the University leadership and not

23. Ibid., 95, 303.

24. Ibid., 316. The identity of the unnamed assemblyman of the Sixtieth Assembly District was verified by means of *California Political Subdivision Maps. (Census of 1950: Reapportionment of 1951)*, Sheet 17, (Sacramento: California State Legislature, n.d.).

25. Among the 15 percent of University employees who refused to sign the regents' loyalty oath were Berkeley psychology professor Edward C. Tolman, for whom the building housing the departments of education and psychology was named in 1961, and UCLA professor of physics and future president of the University, David Saxon. See

the legislature was responsible for the obstacles thrown before UES. Failing to find help in Levering, Family-School Alliance leaders went to Assemblyman Joseph C. Shell, Republican minority leader, a graduate of the rival University of Southern California and frequent critic of UCLA. He lectured them on the politics of the budget process: horse-trading and the presence of UC alumni on strategic committees shape the process, he told them.[26] "Nothing is ever knocked out of the budget of the University of California except with the implicit consent of the University." Knowing this, pressure was next applied on James Corley, Vice-President of the University for Governmental Relations. The women confronted Corley in the legislature. "He was absolutely appalled," one recalled. "Nine women came down the corridor and just surrounded him." They threatened to put the affair on television. Corley was not through, however, in expressing the will of the University's administration in the matter of the University Elementary School of UCLA. After reinserting the UES budget item Corley failed to appear at the Capital Outlays Subcommittee meeting to defend it. Assemblyman Shell mischieviously intervened to hold the item over until Corley did appear. "Caught dead-to-rights," Corley capitulated and the item was approved; UES was saved. A few months later, perhaps ironically, the First Vice-President of the Family-School Alliance wrote that "we can never again lean comfortably back upon the idea that Mother (sometimes known as the University of California) will see to everything. We shall have to remember that the University Elementary School is our concern jointly with the University."[27]

When, in 1982, the University Elementary School was honored by a centennial celebration of the founding of the original practice school of the Los Angeles State Normal School, the featured speaker was Derek Bok, President of Harvard University. Bok was one of the former "little folks of the Training School." He was also a leader in the 1980s' effort to promote, through schools of education, new collaborations between leading universities and public schools. Significantly, few members of the faculty of the UCLA Graduate School of Education attended the event. Most failed to appreciate the fact that UES's large and loyal constituency secured not only the continuation of the University Elementary School—in whose activities education professors

David P. Gardner, *The California Oath Controversy* (Berkeley: University of California Press, 1967).

26. Treacy, "Progressivism," 316 ff.

27. Margaret Kidkadden, quoted in Treacy, "Progressivism," 319.

were little involved—but also buffered their own school of education from the consequences of estrangement from the field that so imperiled other education schools.

Becoming a Graduate School of Education

"We are now headed very definitely toward the abolishment of the Teachers College and the substitution for it of a School of Education about which there is nothing whatever that is unique or distinctive." This is what Director of Training of the Teachers College, Charles Waddell, wrote to Provost Moore in 1930.[28] While underestimating the continuing influence of its origins on UCLA's subsequent history, Waddell was essentially prophetic. We will end up with a few education courses, Waddell predicted, "superimposed upon an academic curriculum . . . with a little dabbling in practice teaching." By the late thirties he was saying that some local school administrators thought that teacher training at UCLA had upset the balance between professional and "purely liberal" education, in favor of the latter. Waddell hoped that the professional doctorate, the Ed.D., offered hope: "There is a better chance that those so trained can keep their heads out of the clouds and their feet on the ground."[29]

Waddell zealously promoted the specialist California teaching credential in kindergarten and primary education, which he pushed through the state bureaucracy in 1921. In 1942, however, Earl Warren, then attorney general of California, issued a ruling that teachers with general elementary credentials were suitably trained for kindergarten teaching. Waddell was agast at this intrusion of legal opinion into a matter of professional judgment. He, himself, retained an unchecked devotion to the turn-of-the-century belief in teacher professionalism through systematic child study learned from G. Stanley Hall under whom he took his Ph.D at Clark University in 1905. Under Waddell's direction, prospective teachers at UCLA received far more opportunity for practice than was the norm elsewhere, employing teaching methods in advance of those offered in the public schools. As Waddell explained, "We are consciously attempting to change the practices of public schools."[30] TC in its heyday was Waddell's model, never Chicago or Berkeley.

To the new generation, at UCLA and in the state education estab-

28. Quoted in Treacy, "Progressivism," 258.
29. Ibid., 262.
30. Waddell, quoted in Treacy, "Progressivism," 71.

lishment, however, the multitude of credentials and specializatios represented an untidy bureaucratic excess. In any event, the winds of change were moving developments in other directions. Despite Waddell's grumblings, new men and new values took over. The Teachers College, the extension of the old Normal School, was reorganized in 1939 as the UCLA School of Education. Moore, Waddell, and the other men of the old days retired. The "forward looking" at UCLA much preferred to try to match Berkeley's record in offering programs beyond elementary school teacher training and in promoting research.

By 1960, UCLA broke into the nation's top twenty doctoral-producing institutions.[31] Administrative and faculty support on the Los Angeles campus for a practical, professional program of teacher education "seemed to relax."[32] UES became more of a demonstration than a training school, as teacher training in the public schools received greater emphasis. In 1945 a committee which included Berkeley's Dean of Education, Frank Freeman, even proposed that the University Elementary School staff be selected on the basis of qualifications "required for university professorships."[33] Organizationally the schools of education at Berkeley and UCLA became increasingly alike. One impetus for this latter-day convergence was certainly the reiteration, by University administrators and Academic Senate leaders, of President Sproul's challenge delivered in his inaugural address in 1930, that research "gives a university its real reason for existence." Another was the example of leading schools of education from coast to coast. It is difficult to judge which was the more powerful influence, but they certainly worked in tandem.

Waddell supported practice and the University Elementary School out of a high regard for the progressive theory of "learning by doing." The first dean of the new School of Education at UCLA, Edwin A. Lee, possessed his own credentials as a progressive educator—even as he steered UCLA away from its past. Before coming to Los Angeles in 1940, he had something of a career as a "practical schoolman" and was a partisan of vocational education; he took his Ph.D. in 1926 at Teachers College in that still-new and suspect specialty. A graduate of Chico State Normal School, Lee taught briefly in California and New York schools and was Superintendent of San Francisco's public schools from 1933 to 1936. Yet Lee possessed even more extensive experience with schools of education—at Indiana University, Berkeley (1921–33),

31. Harmon and Soldz, *Doctorate Production,* 19.
32. Treacy, "Progressivism," 24.
33. Ibid., 288.

and Teachers College. He well knew what other leading institutions were doing and he largely opted to draw UCLA's School of Education into their orbit. Lloyd Morrisett, a graduate of Teachers College, was brought in to create a program in school administration. Another Teachers College alumnus, John Hockett, came to do for elementary education what he had had scant opportunity to do at Berkeley. Both became active in controversial efforts to reorder the relations of the Department of Education to teacher training and to UES. Under Lee's successor the Department of Training was closed in 1958. The remaining Department of Education was restructured, resembling the organization at Berkeley and other smaller schools of education.

New Approaches to Professional Education

As UCLA's School of Education matured UES became more problematic to successive administrators. Few thought it should be eliminated. For one thing they, unlike faculty, recognized the benefits of the school's prominent role in the status politics of education in the Southland. After the UES lease was cancelled by Los Angeles school officials in 1945, Dean Lee reflected on the advantage which UCLA had over USC. "There is no direct evidence that U.S.C. has had anything to do with the action of the Los Angeles Board of Education," he wrote, "but it is certain that our neighbor institution would gain immeasurably by the discontinuance of the University Elementary School. The fact that Superintendent Kersey is a U.S.C. graduate is not without significance."[34]

UCLA administrators were regularly reminded of UES influence in the whole state. "I am always able to identify graduates of the University of California at Los Angeles when I encounter them as teachers in the elementary schools of our State," Helen Heffernan told Chancellor Allen in 1954.[35] While not all elementary school teachers trained at UCLA practiced at UES, all observed lessons there and received instruction in teaching the social studies from Corinne Seeds. Until Seeds's retirement, school districts all over the state which considered themselves forward looking, invariably asked applicants from UCLA how they would "initiate and culminate" cultural units and about other pedagogical issues on which UES teachers had placed their distinctive stamp.

Yet, as early as the National Survey of the Education of Teachers,

34. Ibid., 305.
35. Ibid., 349.

in 1933, it was recommended that student teachers "obtain sufficient practice under conditions typical of those in schools in which students are likely to obtain their first teaching experience."[36] Even well-established campus practice schools were challenged on the grounds that prospective teachers should be trained in representative public schools. In 1943 Corinne Seeds complained that Lee had not scheduled observations at UES for school administrators participating in a conference on "Education for the Post-War World." She explained that UES had much to offer to "the vitality and reality of the discussion" of the conference's theme. Building on her own words, Lee's response was symptomatic of mounting dissatisfaction with campus schools, especially autonomous ones like UES. He wrote, "It is also true that each of the executives has in the classrooms in his own city programs in which 'children are living in such a way as to point the way to postwar education.' Perhaps we could add vitality and reality to our program if we visited some of these classes as well."[37]

This ill-disguised criticism of the demonstration school became a staple of faculty studies of the organization of the School of Education and its relationship to the largely independent UES. The last major committee report on UES, in 1960, reiterated the complaint that the school was something of an anachronism, widely viewed "as an experimental school which lacked proof for its program, and as a creative school whose achievements were those of master-teachership in situations unrealistic in public schools."[38]

Older members of the faculty and the UES staff perceived a growing bias against practice in the Department of Education, and noted worrisome omens. Department of Education administrators discussed with President Sproul the option of phasing out practice teaching at UES and developing it as a demonstration or experiment station. There was increasing talk in the UCLA Academic Senate about training secondary school teachers and the conduct of research, and Waddell fretted about the chronic opposition among many liberal arts professors to "anything which savors of professional training of teachers." The reorganization that created the School of Education in 1939 came about for reasons having little to do with the improvement of teacher education. Dean Lee's mandate included the need to address a universal concern of many schools of education: becoming more closely integrated with their universities.

36. *National Survey,* 3:97, "Teacher Education Curricula."

37. Quoted in Treacy, "Progressivism," 299.

38. Ibid., 331.

With UCLA now emphasizing graduate education and faculty research, the School of Education had to follow suit. In 1943 Waddell was confirmed in his worries: Lee's report to President Sproul stated that the function of a school of education is "largely graduate in character."[39] A faculty committee urged that research and experimentation be added to training and demonstration as the functions of UES. Already the education faculty had formally petitioned the regents to bring UES on campus and make it a laboratory school of the School of Education. Some of the UES-designated land was used to open a Clinic School, a research facility operated by the Department of Psychology. Committees of education faculty, sometimes augmented by friendly academicians, repeatedly asked UES to demonstrate its "wholehearted allegiance to experimentation." They proposed that the staff conduct "objective evaluation of various forms of curriculum and method," using control groups and systematic evaluation, in place of the "exploration and innovation by creative master teachers" that prevailed at UES.[40]

A committee on research for UES was appointed in 1950, but did not function despite Lee's call for linking UES and the School of Education through systematic and continuous experimentation. To capture Corinne Seed's attention, John Dewey's words were invoked: "Only the scientific aim . . . can furnish a reason for the maintenance by a university of an elementary school. It is not a normal school or a department for the training of teachers. It is not a model school. It is not intended to demonstrate any one special idea or doctrine."[41] No record exists that Seeds turned to others of Dewey's words to support *her* sense of where the sources of a science of education lay. The research lobby finally gained some victories: student teaching was restricted to one day a week and some UES teachers began to work on advanced degrees. Still, staff and parent opposition surfaced, especially to "educational manipulation" and the introduction of a "core curriculum" as alternatives to the school's distinctive activity programs. This echoed the experiences of countless other would-be laboratory schools.

In June 1954, the Committee on Educational Policy of the UCLA Academic Senate endorsed, "in principle," demonstration schools "when these schools are so conducted that they serve purposes appropriate to the University." It found Seeds's earlier-stated position inad-

39. Ibid., 273.
40. Ibid., 277–89.
41. Ibid., 333.

equate: that UES should content itself with conducting longitudinal studies of children; develop teaching methods and a curriculum based on child development and psychology; engage in "action research" and "living experimentation"; provide leadership, demonstrations, summer sessions, and otherwise meet the needs of teachers, administrators, and others concerned with education in California. In the staff's opinion, what UES most represented was the operation of a faculty of "highly trained teachers working together with common purposes and basic understandings." The UCLA committee found this statement "not a happy one"—insufficient, if not trivial.[42]

UCLA Retains Its Moorings

The first review of education as a field of study in the University of California system, done by the Academic Program Review Committee for Education, was released only in 1976. It found some things unchanged since Sproul's inaugural, such as education's "history of tensions and uneasiness with other parts of the institutions," its failure to have acquired the prestige of other professional schools and graduate departments, and a second-class status both as a profession and as an academic discipline. It echoed Sproul in speculating that "attitudes toward teaching as a profession" were a major source of the difficult situation in which schools of education found themselves.[43] Given the small combined output of teachers, the Committee recommended that such teacher education as remained in the University should be made experimental and research-based. It thought that UCLA had gone farthest in that direction with the creation of its Teacher Education Laboratory in 1969. Madeline Hunter, former UES principal, traveled widely giving workshops on teaching and learning. More of the faculty were doing theoretical or applied research conceptually connected with preservice teacher training. UCLA also surpassed Berkeley in securing extramural funds and, consistent with campus practice, it used a significant percentage of such funds for training purposes. While Berkeley's education faculty functioned as individual researchers, UCLA's adopted a corporate behavior that gave it higher visibility in

42. Ibid., 280–81, 287.

43. University of California, Academic Program Review Committee for Education, *The Study of Education: A Review of the Education Programs in the University of California* (Berkeley: Academic Planning and Program Review Board, 1976), I-2. Hereafter APPRB.

AERA and its research journals.[44] Although it aspired to national leadership as a graduate school of education and had achieved the highest ranking in education of any public university in the most recent evaluation, the Committee also found that UCLA maintained professional programs, including in-service activities, that gave it "a well-established regional role."[45]

On a campus that, while it urged research and graduate education, also recognized professional education as something like an equal partner in the enhancement of institutional reputation, UCLA's School of Education operated from a position of some strength. This was manifested by closer ties with other departments and organized research units than existed at any other major education unit in the University of California system. In the words of the Academic Program Review Committee for Education, the "catch-up" strategies pursued by the Los Angeles campus meant that, *relative to Berkeley,*

> the links between the University and the outside world were strengthened and the areas of influence extended. The education school benefited from this general policy. It has enjoyed the support of the campus administration; this is reflected in its greater autonomy and more aggressive pursuit of external support and professional functions. The relative success of the two schools in considerable parts seems to have been a matter of self-fulfilling prophecy.[46]

Another illustration of how an education school could gain or lose something important as a result of the complex interaction of campus cultures with outside events was the effective transfer of the study of higher education from Berkeley to Los Angeles during the 1970s. Berkeley was known for the nation's highest-ranking graduate program in administration in higher education. This specialization was developed by T. R. McConnell, who had taught in Minnesota's College of Education and had been dean of Minnesota's College of Science, Literature, and the Arts and then chancellor of the University of Buffalo. A Carnegie-funded research unit, not formally connected with the School of Education and employing scholars from various departments including education, the Center for the Study of Higher Edu-

44. We are indebted to C. Wayne Gordon, formerly associate dean and dean of education at UCLA for responding to a draft of our UCLA case study and answering questions about the later period. We have talked also with the other present and former UCLA faculty.

45. APPRB, VI-9.

46. Ibid., VI-12.

cation was begun in 1955 and by 1965 had evolved into a large federal research and development center. The Carnegie Commission on Higher Education (1967–74) was also headquartered in Berkeley under the leadership of Clark Kerr, formerly Berkeley chancellor and University president. The Center disappeared after the loss of an important grant, while the retirements of key education professors and the inability to secure authorizations for any new faculty left the academic program barely able to take care of those students completing their degrees.

Although UCLA had done little in the field of higher education, having only one professor in the specialization and a junior researcher recently brought from Berkeley, what its then-dean, John Goodlad, called "some rather strange and fortuitous things" occurred in the 1970s. First, Alan Cartter of New York University and the American Council on Education decided to move to southern California for purely personal reasons; his name was widely known for having launched the recent phase of reputational studies of graduate programs. Although he was involved in a Carnegie project at Berkeley, he did not wish to locate in Berkeley and have to commute to Los Angeles. When Cartter talked with Dean Goodlad, he found him both receptive and able to act; UCLA's institutional and extramural budgets substantially exceeded Berkeley's. About the same time another professor in the UCLA School of Education heard of the availability of Alexander Astin, also of the American Council on Education. With the coming of Astin and the employment of his wife, a noted researcher as a professor in the School of Education, Helen Astin, UCLA suddenly had more than a nucleus to make, in Goodlad's words, "a powerful effort in higher education to offset the sudden loss at Berkeley."

Although UCLA's education faculty, "typical of faculties generally," was only mildly interested in this coup and did not think that making so many senior appointments in higher education was consistent with the School's own development plans, the energies of the dean and chancellor carried the day. An off-campus Higher Education Research Center was brought back into the Graduate School of Education orbit, as a more integral unit.[47] Observers at Berkeley were further chagrined when a former member of its own School faculty and Center staff, Burton Clark, was also brought to UCLA from Yale. Recalling this "extraordinary set of circumstances, all coming together at one time to advance the study of higher education at UCLA," Good-

47. Goodlad was not a purist about this; his own research was housed in an off-campus center.

lad writes, "Every institution has its time and its place in the sun. That was the period for UCLA."[48] The number of faculty positions, an important indicator, certainly bore this out. UCLA's School, which was authorized to grant the Ph.D. only in 1966 when it was renamed the Graduate School of Education, had by the mid-seventies sixty-two ladder faculty compared to Berkeley's forty-one.

At the time of his retirement as the dean of UCLA's education school, John I. Goodlad described the School as having passed through two stages: the first emphasized teacher education and was a legacy of its normal school days; the second, from 1960 to 1983, focused on university-style research, using university promotion criteria to stimulate extramurally funded research and development projects. Goodlad asserted that it was now time for the School to embark on a new phase in its development: one directed toward improving policies and practices in education so as to attack "the significant problems in schools."[49] To those situated four hundred miles northward, education at UCLA seemed fortunate in both its history and its leadership.

Even during those years when the research mission was vigorously pursued and UCLA captured a steadily higher rank among schools of education, it seems to us that Dean Goodlad did not forget what a professional school is all about. Despite having earned his own Ph.D. at the University of Chicago, the most consistently "academic" institution in our ten-school study, Goodlad's career kept him com-

48. John Goodlad to James Guthrie, 5 November 1985. UCLA faculty have told their counterparts at Berkeley that there was an administrative decision made to close the Berkeley program in higher education and to relocate it in Los Angeles. President of the University of California David Saxon (then executive vice-chancellor of UCLA) was reportedly involved in the decision. Our inquiry to President Saxon was answered 29 June 1983; he wrote that he was not involved in any way. He referred our request for information to Academic Vice-President Frazer "since decisions of this sort would be under the jurisdiction of his office." We have not heard from Frazer. Our inquiry to Berkeley Chancellor Ira Michael Heyman also failed to confirm that such an administrative decision was agreed upon by the campus principals. There was, of course, precedent for such action in, for example, the 1955 decision to limit general home economics to the Santa Barbara and Davis campuses. The APPRB recommendations included the statement that Berkeley specializations that "are offered in the education school at Los Angeles might be phased out." We could not determine whether the review committee or University administrators read that to include the program in higher education.

Additional information on UCLA's faculty recruiting situation came to us through the *Executive Review,* 1977–78 (5 Dec. 1977) and *Graduate Program: Self-Review* (1 Aug. 1977), Graduate School of Education, UCLA.

49. Natalie Hall, "A Crisis in American Education," *UCLA Monthly* 13, no. 5 (1983):4, 5.

fortably close to the practitioner's world. He directed teacher education at Emory University before returning to Chicago's Center for Teacher Education. From there he went to UCLA in 1960 as professor and director of the University Elementary School, where he had the confidence of the now-retired Corinne Seeds; he kept this position after becoming dean in 1967. "Mr. Outside," Goodlad rebuilt UCLA's field connections, especially in astute and visible, if limited, collaborations with important school administrators in southern California, even while himself continuing to speak and publish about schools in ways that the women and men working in them could find pertinent.

Although there was some initial skepticism on the part of his faculty, Goodlad did not try to convert the faculty to his interests, and he proved supportive of scholarship and effective in working with his faculty in securing extramural grants; at one point the School ranked eleventh among all University of California units in extramural funding and, in 1983, had 75 percent of all research and development monies awarded to the eight schools, departments, and programs of education in the statewide University system. As a condition of assuming the deanship he received twenty-two faculty positions and used them to recruit potentially strong researchers, of basic and applied interests. Thus, while education at UCLA experienced the prevailing and endemic tensions between academic norms and professional needs it was not disoriented and defeated by them. Projecting two images, Janus-like, it prospered. Such was not the case back at Berkeley. From Berkeley's perspective the grass *was* greener at UCLA, and its own "meadow muffins" (which included perodic campus criticisms of its academic programs, curricular fragmentation, and worrisome pressures to alter the balance of Ed.D's to Ph.D's in the professional direction) seemed manageable in comparison to Berkeley's problems.

Bad News at Berkeley

In 1879 public school teachers in California, operating out of a tradition of teacher activism, expressed their desire for more professional training. They petitioned the State Superintendent of Public Instruction to draft a bill providing for a professor of pedagogics in the ten-year old state university at Berkeley. In the midst of the organizational battles we are about to describe, the one-hundredth anniversary of this event passed entirely unnoticed. Subsequent opportunities for a centennial celebration—of the regents' announcement in 1889 of the intention "to establish a course of instruction in the science and art of teaching" or of the appointment in 1892 of Elmer Ellsworth Brown as the first professor of the Science and Art of Teaching and the creation of a Department of Pedagogy—could have faced a similar fate. It became increasingly evident that an academic entity at Berkeley named "Education" might not survive to a century mark. In the tersely-stated opinion of Berkeley's Academic Senate Committee on Educational Policy in 1982, the School of Education "was clearly one case where 'disestablishment' of an academic program was a possibility, and radical restructuring probable."[50]

As president of Princeton University, Woodrow Wilson had warned that when vocational considerations enter the academy "it ceases to wear the broad and genial face of learning."[51] Many Berkeley faculty sympathized with this viewpoint and their campus accordingly reflected less of its land-grant origins than did UCLA, for example. Long-heard and long-endured references to the inappropriateness for Berkeley of a school and department of education matured in the late 1970s among active members of the Berkeley Academic Senate, particularly some in the College of Letters and Science. Nor did education have loud friends in the campus's twelve other professional schools and colleges; indeed, professors of law, engineering, environmental design, public policy, and business sat on the various committees which discussed or recommended abolishing the School of Education.

In their weakened condition, with declining enrollments and an adverse market for their graduates and expertise, education schools nationally could not contemplate with composure the possibilty of a precedent-setting disestablishment of education at a place like Berkeley. True, David Clark had predicted in 1977 that 10 percent of the nation's 1,367 education schools and colleges would, and *should* be closed. In the meantime accreditation was being denied to both credential and graduate programs in a number of institutions.[52] Following a study of America's graduate schools of education, Oxford University's Harry Judge made a similar recommendation.[53] These observers

50. University of California at Berkeley, Academic Senate Committee on Educational Policy, Annual Report, 1981–82, "Notice of the Meeting, Berkeley Division of the Academic Senate," 22 Nov. 1982, p. 35.

51. Quoted in Merle L. Borrowman, *The Liberal and the Technical in Teacher Education,* (New York: Teachers College, Columbia University, 1956), 140.

52. T. Toch, "Accrediting Body Questions Quality of Several Ed. Schools," *Education Week* 1 Sept. 1982.

53. Harry Judge, *American Graduate Schools of Education: A View from Abroad,* (New York: Ford Foundation, 1982).

usually had in mind, however, the abandonment of marginal undergraduate programs in teacher education, not the demise of nationally-ranked graduate schools of education in major research universities.

What had happened to make it conceivable that the education school might be closed at the first and most prestigious public university in the nation's largest state? Why might Berkeley—widely regarded at the best public university in the United States and the peer of the most esteemed private ones—contemplate such action? *To ask this second question is to have gone a good part of the way toward answering the first.*

Speculations about disestablishment of the School were not propelled by a financial collapse of the State, despite a taxpayers' revolt in 1978 and the economic recession of the early 1980s.[54] The savings to the University from closing Berkeley's School of Education would be delayed years in their effects and would be infinitesimally small in the total budgetary picture of a multicampus institution that had 140,000 students in 1985. Neither were the rising tides of rumor and reaction fueled by startling revelations of mismanagement, personal malfeasance, political indiscretion, or sexual misconduct.

Rather the signal event was the prolonged vacancy permitted to exist in the School's deanship. Merle Borrowman, the last "regular" dean of the School of Education, resigned in August 1977 as the delayed result of a serious vehicle accident. The campus administration allowed the School to enter one, and then another, and then still more academic years without the appointment of a regular or "permanent" dean. Between 1977 and January 1982 seven appointments were made of acting deans, in title or in fact. Notwithstanding the sorry experiences of other schools and departments of education with their cam-

54. Berkeley and UCLA had already entered a stage of "steady state" funding because of earlier regent commitments to building up the smaller campuses, including very expensive commitments to medical education. The *Revised Academic Plan, 1969–1975* (University of California at Berkeley, 1969, pp. 3, 22) opened with the note that, "Whereas previous plans have encompassed a decade of continuous and rapid expansion, the present revision deals with a transition . . . to a steady state." In 1971 the University administration transferred 110 full-time-equivalent (FTE) faculty positions from Berkeley's allotment to the newer campuses, and a staffing model was produced that encouraged the campus to make only about fifty new appointments a year. T. R. McConnell and Stewart Edelstein, *Campus Governance at Berkeley: A Study in Jurisdiction* (Berkeley: Center for Research and Development in Higher Education, University of California, 1977), 6, 13. On 25 July 1974, Dean Borrowman wrote to Provost for Professional Schools George Maslach protesting that the cuts in Education's budget were comparable only to those for the School of Criminology and Design Department; these two were subsequently closed—a bad sign for Education.

pus administrations, as we saw in earlier chapters, this situation at Berkeley appeared unprecedentedly lethal.

The Karplus Caper

During the 1979–80 academic year a search for dean was conducted by the provost for Professional Schools and Colleges. The search was badly handled, nearly invisible in all those places from which viable dean candidates would probably have come, some say "programmed to fail," and inconclusive in its results. This failed effort prompted the campus administration to turn, in the late spring of 1980, to one of the dean search-committee members as its choice: Robert Karplus, Berkeley professor of physics and associate director of the Lawrence Hall of Science. There was no consultation with the faculty of the School of Education. Unannounced and unanticipated, Karplus presented himself at Tolman Hall with the news and asked to speak with members of the faculty before making his own decision. He accepted the position, his term to begin in March 1981 after he returned from sabbatical leave. Meanwhile Karplus began extensive consultations on campus and with interested education faculty; his was, nonetheless, a personal and idiosyncratic effort.

In October 1980, Dean-designate Karplus journeyed to Sweden to accept an honorary doctorate for his contributions to research and curriculum development in elementary and secondary school science education; Stockholm University also awarded him the customary top hat and gold ring. On his return he found the chancellor's office less generous: Karplus's request for authorization to recruit up to twenty new faculty members over a five-year period (for a net gain of nine positions, considering past and projected resignations and retirements) was answered with the allocation to the School of two assistant professors, although later authorizations were not precluded. Professors of physics at Berkeley are not, however, accustomed to such rebuffs. In December, Karplus noisily resigned. As he explained to the education faculty in the best-attended School meeting in years, he believed that he had received administrative commitments to pursue a new course and to exercise leadership. As these commitments evidently were not to be honored, he would not serve. A brilliant but impatient man, unsure about the initial wisdom of his decision to shepherd the School, and without extensive experience in the byzantine politics of the Berkeley campus, Karplus had been a poor choice on the chancellor's part.

In lieu of a dean and reinvigoration by new faculty, the School reorganized itself—several times!—changing the names of its divisions, merging some and phasing out others, meanwhile attempting to fend off the campaigns of its largest division, educational psychology, to become an independent department in the School of Education or, as it later proposed, a new department in the College of Letters and Science.[55]

Studies from Outside

During the crisis period of 1976 to 1982, the School was subjected to four external "studies": one by a committee appointed by the University of California systemwide administration (APPRB), one representing the Graduate Council of the campus Academic Senate, and two appointed by the chancellor. Each of these studies was conducted by prestigious administrators or faculty. Each was time-consuming and resource-using. The School became increasingly preoccupied with supplying data, gearing up for interviews, and engaging in rebuttals. With each study it became progressively more evident that, however cooperative, informed, and articulate the School was in its response, it could do little to affect the outcome or manage the damage.

The first two of these studies were perceived as routine reviews. Each was a manifestation of the increasingly common phenomenon in contemporary American higher education of campus- or system-wide, faculty-conducted evaluations of programs, with implications for resource allocations.[56] The third review was, however, extraordinary: it was the chancellor's response to the abrupt resignation of his designated dean for education, Robert Karplus. The fourth was conducted by the chancellor's first appointment of an external acting dean, Stephen Weiner, when the School was in evident receivership.

The Eight-Campus APPRB Study. The report of the Academic Planning and Program Review Board (APPRB) was the first such effort ever undertaken to study education in the University of California system.

55. Don C. Charles, of Iowa State University, wrote a description in 1971 that could well have been of Berkeley's educational psychology division, often perceived as trying to slip westard down the corridors of Tolman Hall to join the psychology department. "Not long ago I spent some time at one of our greatest universities. In a large corridor separating two wings of the building housing the separate departments was posted a sign: 'Educational Psychology,' with an arrow pointing one way, and scribbled on the sign the words 'Real Psychology,' with the arrows pointing in the opposite direction." Charles, "Expectation vs. Reality," 32–33.

56. McConnell and Edelstein, *Campus Governance,* 48 ff.

Earl Cheit, dean of the School of Business, was chair of the review committee. Cheit held a courtesy appointment in the School of Education, taught its course on higher education finance, and was respected as an expert participant in the School's most vigorous program. The Report criticized certain elements in the Berkeley situation—such as the failure to clarify the School's mission, the isolation of Academic Senate faculty from what should be research-based programs in teacher education, and the lack of sufficient faculty mass in certain areas. The Report did not, however, strike the education faculty at the time as singling Berkeley out, or as unreasonable, or unconstructive, or threatening. Except for its small size, Berkeley's weaknesses were depressingly familiar in the universe of education schools. The dean and faculty gave a limited and, as it turned out, probably shortsighted response. Yet, given the mild reaction it got from the Berkeley Academic Senate's Committee on Educational Policy, to which it was referred—faculty committees tend to be suspicious of sytemwide academic planning and coordination efforts—the School's response did not appear inappropriate at the time. Indeed, given the campus's value system, it could well take comfort in the Committee chair's comment that the comparisons drawn between Berkeley and UCLA "were unduly influenced by Berkeley's evident weaknesses in external funding and professional and community interaction, while not sufficiently crediting the distinction of its faculty, and their scholarly work.[57]

The Berger Committee. The successor group to APPRB was the ad hoc committee appointed in mid-1976 by the dean of the Graduate Division, on behalf of the Graduate Council. Schools and departments were expected to undergo periodic evaluation of their programs of graduate education. The Berger Committee—a cognomen derived from its chairman, Stanley Berger, professor of mechanical engineering—excited little apprehension in the first phase of its work, other

57. L. M. Grossman to Vice-Chancellor I. M. Heyman (1975?), University of California at Berkeley, School of Education, Historical File. The statewide University Committee on Educational Policy (UCEP) took a harsher view, however, concluding that while the report "couches its recommendations in such diplomatic and gentle terms that the full impact of the condemnation is lost," that the university's schools and programs in education "have exhibited areas of pronounced weakness and mediocrity," and that mediocrity tends to beget mediocrity. In University of California, Committee on Educational Policy, "UCEP Response to the AAPRB Study of Education: Educational Policy Considerations" draft of March 1977, School of Education, Historical File.

than some notice given to the rumor that one member, a German-educated sociologist, held the opinion that education had absolutely no place in a university, and to the fact that another, a law professor, supported an initiative for a constitutional provision for a voucher system that would fund nonpublic schools in California.

Since the Committee required elaborate data from the School about its applicants, graduates, students, programs, and structures, it received more notice within the School, at least by administrators—who now included the first acting dean appointed after the resignation of Dean Borrowman. As the date scheduled for the completion and release of the Committee's report passed and the task lengthened through most of a second year, speculations and anxiety began to mount. By 1978 the most somnolent professor and apolitical student in education knew and wondered about the Berger Committee. For one thing, repeated questions to the provost about a search for a dean and authorization to recruit new faculty were invariably met by the assertion that all such actions awaited the Berger Committee's report. Some became conviced that powerful figures in the campus administration and Senate wished, *and expected,* that the Committee would recommend closing, or phasing out, or changing the status of the School of Education.

Released in April 1978, the Committee's report did criticize the School severely—for a proliferation of programs and the resulting fragmentation of mission; an uneven quality of student scholarship, much of it below campus standards; the lack of distinction in practice between the Ph.D. and Ed.D. degrees; and much else. The Committee did not, however, free the administration to reallocate the School's resources elsewhere. Instead, the Berger Committee and the Graduate Council's subsequent consideration of it (1978–79) endorsed recapture of lost faculty positions and recommended a nationwide search for a permanent dean. This time the response of the Department faculty was substantial, even anticipating many of the report's conclusions. It had reorganized itself into fewer units with core curricula, begun elaborate monitoring of the quality of dissertation proposals, created an office to promote grantsmanship, and launched yet another effort to differentiate the two doctoral degrees. With the release of the Committee's report it also panicked, and scuttled its largest division, Humanistic and Policy Studies. This unit was itself the product of an earlier merger that had failed to coalesce.[58] Berkeley's self-

58. Harvard created a similar grouping about the same time, despite the faculty's yearning for simpler curricula and a more homogeneous faculty and student body

confidence was too badly shaken to do much but reorganize once again.

The Smelser Commission. In no way could the School view with complacency the chancellor's formation, early in 1981, of his "Commission on Education." Created following the Karplus resignation, its stated purpose was to "diagnose and suggest policies and strategies for the future of the School of Education." The membership of the Commission was weighty and appropriately equipped for its task: Neil Smelser, chairman, professor of sociology and University Professor, actively engaged in research in education and, later, chairman of the Academic Senate; Eugene C. Lee, professor of political science, director of the Institute of Governmental Studies, author of several studies on higher education, son of Edwin Lee (onetime professor of education at Berkeley and dean of education at UCLA), and brother of the late Gordon Lee (professor at Teachers College and dean of education at the University of Washington); John Wheeler, an active Senate figure and professor of business administration who, before the present halcyon days for business schools, could surely remember the low esteem that schools of business had suffered; and a student member who bore the additional burdens of being a woman and from a racial minority.

Unwilling to add yet another review of the School, the Commission concerned itself with laying out the merits and difficulties of various strategies to deal with the consequences of administrative neglect of the School dating back to the 1950s. The possibilities discussed ranged from strengthening the School with permanent leadership and augmented resources to closing it and dispersing the tenured faculty among existing departments, schools, and support units. While it made no explicit recommendation in its May 1981 report, the reassignment of all education faculty to other departments and schools appeared to be the Commission's preferred opinion. In this event, a cross-campus group of some kind would construct and operate a teacher education program—a "solution" reminiscent of what had been tried and found wanting at Yale, Chicago, Harvard, and Duke, among others.

In contrast to the strategy to starve the School and let attrition reduce it to a state where it could be closed, consistent with the traditional view that schools of education do not belong in prestige uni-

---

and the "certain weariness [that] flows from the area's spread." Paul N. Ylvisaker, "HGSE 1977," 4–5.

versities, this proposal seemed to reflect reformist motives. It directly addressed the issue of education's low relative status and then proceeded to try to locate the academic and professional functions of education in some relationship with academic departments.[59] Nonetheless, the School would be closed. More important, as a consequence any persistence of its interests and performance of its functions would be left to chance: to idiosyncratic factors, personal whim, episodic attention, competing attractions.

"The present attitude toward campus planning at Berkeley reflects the primacy of faculty interests . . .[rather than] the desires of students or the expressed needs of the University's public constituency," a faculty member and a graduate student in the School of Education wrote together in 1977—in what seemed a bad omen for the School.[60] Following release of the Commission's report, the Budget Committee indeed recommended phasing out the School of Education and relocating its various programs in other campus units. Chancellor Ira Michael Heyman eventually rejected this advice.

If centrally placed administrators at Berkeley had not quite known their own minds about what to do with the School when the earlier reports were issued, opinion against the School had certainly consolidated by the time that the Smelser group gave its report to the chancellor. State budget deficits; the demands of business, computer science, law, and engineering faculty for augmented salaries and resources; sheer boredom with the issue of education; and longstanding prejudice against it and like units made the disestablishment of the School a popular-enough choice for the chancellor and his advisors publicly to commend the Commission. They explicitly acknowledged that the School was in grave trouble, and the Chancellor then appointed the School's first acting dean from outside the School, Stephen S. Weiner, assistant to the vice-president of the University and former associate dean of the Graduate School of Public Policy.

The Weiner Report. Weiner's proposals to the Chancellor constituted the fourth study of the School. His task was to make specific recommendations to the chancellor, and his initial proposal, presented to the faculty in October 1981, would have closed the School, and his second eliminated the Department of Education. Weiner first proposed that interdisciplinary "graduate groups" replace the School of Educa-

59. We are indebted to our colleague, Guy Benveniste, for offering this distinction between "punitive starvation" and well-meant reform.

60. McConnell and Edelstein, *Campus Governance,* 61.

tion. Education faculty would be assigned to these groups, *sans* any department affiliation, to be joined by members representing well-established departments. This was the response to the frequently heard criticism that the School lacked strong, formal cross-campus links, a charge some thought a "red herring" since strong, self-confident departments (like the Law School) are not obligated to demonstrate such ties nor to repudiate their "magnificent isolation."[61]

The proposal was fraught with obvious dangers. One was the unhappy experience at Berkeley of cross-department, cross-college, and interdisciplinary programs in competing for financial resources and sustaining the commitments of their members.[62] Another was the low status the proposed graduate-group members would suffer; it was inconceivable that programs in education could command the respectful participation of academic professors when the education faculty themselves lacked membership in that most basic building-block of the modern university: the department. Weiner's subsequent proposal—to replace the School with a "Faculty of Education," a term having no currency in the University of California—was similarly rejected by the education faculty and student body. The two ill-advised proposals of the School's latest acting dean had succeeded best in organizing the internal opposition.

The Conflict of Cultures at Berkeley

Accident and plain bad luck played a part in the crisis that Berkeley was facing. By the preceding narration of events and the comparisons made between Berkeley and UCLA, we mean to make clear that elements in an institution's traditions are also important. We do not think that the campus-level evaluations of the School of Education, which played so large a part in press reports and in subsequent reviews, were the cause of the School's parlous position by 1981. Rather, they were themselves consequences. What the chancellor's own Commis-

61. Indicative of this is the fact that, when, in 1978–79, the School of Education changed its by-laws to reduce the number of non–Education Department faculty with voting rights in the School, George Maslach, then provost for Professional Schools, congratulated the chair of the Department of Education for "finally having cut away the albatross from around the School's neck." Geraldine Clifford to Stephen S. Weiner, 19 November 1981, School of Education, University of California, Berkeley, Historical File.

62. McConnell and Edelstein, *Campus Governances*, 37–44. The experience of interdisciplinary undergraduate programs was especially unpromising. Witness the proposed creation of a department of experimental courses; seven persons were offered and rejected the chairmanship, and the project was abandoned (ibid., 39).

sion called "neglect" and "punitive starvation" of the School by campus administrators was the essential and precipitating cause of its near-extinction. This neglect was itself rooted in the fundamental contradictions of the "cultures" between which Berkeley's School of Education was trapped: the external demand for practical professional programs and the campus norms.

The anthropologist's concept of culture refers to shared patterns of thinking and behaving. Viewed thus the academic world is segmented by cultural groupings. In the modern American university departmental membership constitutes a critical cultural base; in many professional schools it is cross-disciplinary in nature. Disciplinary identification has become an important alternative basis because disciplines are "thought groups" with their reigning "thought styles."[63] Additionally, professors belong to one culture, students to another; both groups, however, may be divided into subcultures, so that, for example, professors and advanced students in the sciences may have more in common with one another than either has with faculty in the humanities or with students in the nonconformist subculture.

In an internal evaluation of teacher education programs at Berkeley made around 1969, Harold Hodgkinson wrote more broadly of the problem of "bridging the gap between the Berkeley university value system and that of the public schools and the communities which they represent."[64] In what follows we will review, in turn, elements of not two but three cultures: that of the research university, that of the professional school, and that of the field, or profession-in-practice.

Berkeley: "Excellence" and Amour-Propre

American higher education itself has been the major influence operating upon schools and colleges of education in this century. With the spectacular growth of the two post–World War II decades, university culture was confused in many institutions by the contacts of old and new groups and purposes. This was not true at Berkeley; except during the loyalty oath years, things were "in place." The pronounced

63. Tony Becher, "The Cultural View," in *Perspectives on Higher Education: Eight Disciplinary and Comparative Views,* ed. Burton R. Clark (Berkeley: University of California Press, 1984), 165–98.

64. Harold L. Hodgkinson, "Report on Elementary Internship Program," University of Calfornia at Berkeley, School of Education, Historical File, (1969?), p. 6. At the time Hodgkinson held a lecturer's appointment in the School and a research position in the Center for Research and Development in Higher Education.

features of the academic environment were two: first, a College of Letters and Science which dominated both the institution's positive self image and its politics and, second, a system of "collegial" or shared governance, using committees of the Academic Senate.[65]

Yet, not all letters and science departments enjoyed parity; like the animals in Orwell's *Animal Farm,* some were more equal than others. At Berkeley the sciences had gained a special place. The increased prestige of science that followed the United States' military and atomic achievements was very evident at Berkeley. At both the undergraduate and graduate levels enrollments of humanities majors at Berkeley were below the statewide average of the University system.[66] Epitomizing the sciences' new role in education outreach was the founding of the Lawrence Hall of Science, bearing the name of one of Berkeley's nuclear stars, Ernest O. Lawrence. Unlike the post-Sputnik curriculum projects, this was to be Berkeley's permanent, institutional contribution to strengthening precollegiate education. A science museum and research and development center in science and mathematics education and cognitive and instructional psychology, the Hall's programs and projects quickly overshadowed the instructional and research efforts in these fields in the by now starved School of Education.

Subsequent developments in electronics, the biological and cognitive sciences, and mathematics, plus public concern with the reindustrialization of America, only strengthened this prevailing culture. Scientists held key positions in the campus administration. The "hard sciences," mathematics, and engineering were also very well represented on all important faculty committees that advise the chancellor and "speak for" the faculty.[67] The ill-fated turn to physicist Robert

65. One such committee's chairman affirmed the "centrality" of arts and science departments and protected them in hard times, when programs "developed to achieve social purposes" might have to be sacrificed. University of California, Statewide Assembly of the Academic Senate, Oliver A. Johnson, "Remarks by the Chairman," *Record of the Statewide Assembly of the Academic Senate,* 26 May 1982. The response of an alert professional school dean is found in Michael L. Buckland, "Memo," University of California at Berkeley, School of Education, Historical File, 1 November 1982.

66. University of California, "Report on the Humanities Panel" (Berkeley, March 1983), Table 1: Undergraduate Major Enrollments in the Humanities at U.C. Campuses, 1976–82, and Table 3: Graduate Major Enrollments in the Humanities at U.C. Campuses, 1976–82. In contrast, UCLA was above the mean on both counts.

67. For example, three of the nine members of the 1981–82 Committee on Educational Policy that placed "disestablishment" of the School of Education in the public arena were from these areas, as were six of the eleven members who served during 1982–83 on the Committee on Budget and Interdepartmental Relations that actually recommended such action.

Karplus for dean in 1980 was one indicator of where it was thought that salvation would lie. Despite that debacle, it seemed certain that any proposed reform or revitalization of the School of Education would be judged significantly, if not exclusively, by its ability to collaborate with the Lawrence Hall of Science and to please well-placed professors in applied science and mathematics. It may be coincidental that the dean of Education finally appointed in 1983, Bernard Gifford, took his Ph.D. in biophysics, but that fact could hardly hurt the School.

Science, far more than letters, has been a man's world. But women were becoming a majority of all degree candidates in Berkeley's School of Education: in 1975 women were 49.8 percent, in 1980, 66 percent of the student body in this graduate school. This was only one of its handicaps, but old prejudices, often subconsciously held, die hard—rhetorical celebrations of the goals of affirmative action to the contrary notwithstanding. The number of tenured women on the education faculty went from one to five between 1967 and 1980. The percentages of women students and faculty were rising, of course, in most other professional schools.[68] Considering its earlier history, it is not surprising that the complement of women in the UCLA education faculty was larger: 19 percent of the ladder faculty in 1976, compared with Berkeley's 7 percent.[69] Despite the resurgence of a women's movement in academe, the Academic Senate at Berkeley remained, and was run like, a men's club.[70] The only woman in the top reaches of the campus administration, the chancellor's "kitchen cabinet," was the provost for Professional Schools and Colleges; Doris Howes Calloway was appointed in 1981, a tenacious if unsung advocate of actions to preserve and strengthen the School.

Unlike the situation at Stanford, where faculty defer to the

68. The proportions of women at Berkeley in 1980 were education, 12.2 percent; law, 12.2 percent; business administration, 6.2 percent; and engineering, 1.4 percent. University of California at Berkeley, Office of Institutional Research, "Title IX Report," n.d. (1984?).

Once a repository of women faculty, the Department of Home Economics was closed in 1957 by transfer to the Davis campus and creation of a separate Department of Nutritional Sciences. The Schools of Librarianship (established 1926) and Social Welfare (1944), where women would be expected to predominate, were as much male bastions as was Education, most women being confined to non-Senate faculty.

69. APPRB, IV-65.

70. The Academic Senate Office reported a total 1982–83 membership of 1,969. Of these 228 were women: 87 assistant professors; 113 tenured, active faculty; and 30 emerita. This was 11.2% of the Senate total. See also Committee on the Status of Women and Ethnic Minorities, Annual Report 1982–93, "Minutes of the Berkeley Division," 4 October 1983, pp. 12–16.

administration, the University of California's Academic Senate has been called probably "the most powerful such agency in the country and its important committees an oligarchy."[71] The Senate's crucial mechanism is *not* its general meetings but the Graduate Council, Committee on Educational Policy, and Committee on Budget and Interdepartmental Relations. Most Berkeley administrators are longtime members of the faculty, linked by a common set of academic preferences and prejudices. The Budget Committee advises the chancellor on all promotions, merit increases in salary, and appointments; in the 981 cases considered in 1984–85, a typical example, the chancellor decided against the Budget Committee's disposition in only six instances.[72] Since this committee also makes recommendations about faculty allocations, it undoubtedly bore major responsibility for the regular denial of resources to Education that shaped much of the School's history through the 1970s.[73] The Committee also advises the chancellor about nominees of search committees for deanships.

After his own January 1982 decision to retain Berkeley's School and to find it a dean, Chancellor Heyman again sought advice from Senate committees before launching, three months later, the search. His choice was notified in August 1982 that his nomination was going to the Budget Committee; it was December before this body, known to act quickly when it thinks necessary, completed its deliberations about the proposed new dean. The Committee recommended against the appointment. The chancellor chose to disregard this advice and Bernard Gifford was appointed dean of the School of Education. The Budget Committee was not, however, finished expressing its disapproval of the decision to retain the School of Education. In its 1984–85 Annual Report, which the chancellor attributed to "outmoded steady-state mentality,"[74] the Budget Committee stated its own sour

71. McConnell and Edelstein, *Campus Governance*, 12, 16–17.

72. University of California at Berkeley, Academic Senate Committee on Budget and Interdepartmental Relations, Annual Report, 1984–95. "Notice of the Meeting, Berkeley Division of the Academic Senate," 1 October 1985, p. 7. Chancellor Bowker had, in the 1970s, used some of his discretion, allocating new positions to some of the professional schools, not Education, despite resistance from the "basic disciplines—which in their view are the foundations of Berkeley's academic eminence." McConnell and Edelstein, *Campus Governance*, 8–9.

73. In its 1981 Annual Report, the Budget Committee asserted, without reference to any evidence, that "the School of Education does not serve its constituents well. University of California at Berkeley, Committee on Budget and Interdepartmental Relations, Annual Report, 1980–81," Notice of the Meeting, Berkeley Division of the Academic Senate," 19 October 1981, p. 20.

74. Interview with Chancellor Ira Michael Heyman, 16 October 1985.

regret that academic ("programmatic") considerations sometimes had to yield to irrelevant claims:

> We have been struck by the long-term stability of departmental FTE budgets, even when it seemed that some programs would have to be reduced to meet fiscal constraints, even when it was evident that some Campus programs only marginally approximated the Berkeley academic standard. Norms of civility and collegiality and influences of extramural groups seem to have overriden our assessments of academic quality, making it difficult to phase out weaker units or to make deliberate reductions in the size of units, even when there has been general consensus that such changes were warranted.[75]

While many universities operate through a mixed system of bureaucracy and oligarchy, Berkeley's combination is a Byzantine politics baffling to outsiders. Unfortunately for the School of Education, until recently most Education faculty were outsiders. While members were elected by their colleagues to the Representative Assembly, the Senate's general deliberative body, few were named to membership on prestigious Academic Senate committees. This was disadvantageous in at least two ways. First, School faculty lacked a voice in important committees deliberating upon the fate of their own unit, given the Berkeley tradition of not consulting with the parties most directly affected.[76] Second, Education faculty were generally not sophisticated

75. University of California at Berkeley, Academic Senate Committee on Budget and Interdepartmental Relations, Annual Report, 1984–85, p. 11.

76. To illustrate that cavalier and secretive approaches are part of the Berkeley style and not necessarily that of particular recent individual administrators, we reproduce part of the letter of resignation of the chair of the Home Economics Department, a generation ago:

> At the time I accepted the chairmanship, which, as you know, I did with great reluctance, it was with the belief that there was an opportunity to develop the potentialities this campus affords for an outstanding Department of Home Economics. There was no indication at the time that the Administration was not also looking forward to such a development. A new building had just been completed. A committee had been appointed to recommend a suitable person for the chairmanship of the Department. Another had been asked to report on the advisability of establishing a School of Home Economics. Members of the department were encouraged to propose new curricula. Yet about three months after assuming my duties I was informed for the first time that the administration entertained serious doubts as to the place of Home Economics on the Berkeley campus.

enough regarding the ways of the Academic Senate's decision-making processes and did not know how to intervene to protect themselves.

The Graduate Emphasis

While Berkeley's School of Education shared many characteristics of America's other schools and colleges of education, its differences included three interrelated characteristics: the historical prominence of graduate education, the School's concentration on teacher preparation for secondary schooling, and the absence of an undergraduate degree program leading to credentialing—something that 1,190 other institutions *did* offer in the United States in 1979, when Berkeley entered its period of greatest vulnerability.

From Pedagogy's initial decade, graduate education for research training and the preparation of school specialists, professional leaders, and college faculty competed with the function of preparing secondary school teachers for which the Department was originally created. A graduate seminar appeared in the Department's second year. This emphasis continued, despite occasional off-campus pressures to prepare more teachers. In 1955–56, for example, the School awarded more master's degrees (69) than any other school or department except engineering, and more doctorates (26) than any except physics.[77] Belatedly, in the late 1970s, the faculty formally petitioned the regents, through the chancellor's office, to be called the Graduate School of Education. It was not a propitious time to ask, however. The petition

---

> The failure to inform me at the time of my appointment that these doubts existed and the course of action of the administration during the past year indicate clearly that neither the chairman of the Department nor the staff has any share in reaching decisions on important policy changes. We have, for example, so far not seen the report on Home Economics made by the Committee on Educational Policy, nor have we had the opportunity to consider and discuss with the administration the recommendations it contains.

Jesse V. Coles to Vice-President Harry R. Wellman, 7 November 1955. There was no hint of apology in Wellman's brief acknowledgement (8 November 1955). See Maresi Nerad, "The Department of Home Economics at the University of California, Berkeley, 1916–1962" (Doctoral diss., University of California at Berkeley, 1988).

77. A decade later it had more competitors for its leadership in awarding master's degrees, but its thirty-five doctorates were second only to the combined total in chemistry and chemical engineering. University of California, Berkeley, Academic Senate, "Education at Berkeley: A Report of the Select Committee on Education," March 1966, pp. 224–25.

was neither accepted nor denied by the regents; inquiries from the School simply went unanswered, year after year.

Graduate students were important in a second way: through Berkeley's exclusive concern with training high school teachers. Because the California authorization for normal schools that would prepare elementary school teachers came in 1862, before the University of California was founded, the state's normal schools and independent colleges and universities were equal to and eager to prepare all the state's elementary school teachers.[78] The early legislation on high school teacher certification in California required a bachelor's degree from an academic department. This pushed professional courses in education into the postgraduate period.[79]

The Doctor of Education degree was also introduced early at Berkeley; in 1915, under the rubric of "Graduate in Education," and renamed the Doctor of Education in 1921. The numbers of Ed.D. and Ph.D. degrees in education awarded annually grew slowly until the 1960s when the School's output and their distribution markedly changed. The expansion and upgrading of college faculties nationally meant that thousands of college teachers sought the doctorate; many came to Berkeley which also offered, from 1955, a Ph.D. specialization in higher education. Moreover, the preparation of junior college faculty had been a Berkeley undertaking for decades; its first dean, Alexis F. Lange, was a leader of the junior college movement. The designation of junior colleges as community colleges, their separation from public school districts into community college districts, the ending of state certification requirements for faculty, and the growth of a faculty gov-

78. It was not until 1936 that Berkeley began to recommend candidates for elementary credentials to the State Department of Education, and their numbers were characteristically small. Even when Berkeley reluctantly agreed to prepare more elementary school teachers in response to the intense teacher shortages in California in the post–World War II period, students did not come to the School of Education through a Berkeley undergraduate major in education. A tiny bachelor's degree program in education, offered through the College of Letters and Science did not lead to teacher certification, and this program was entirely dropped in 1960. In the early 1950s, three to ten bachelor of arts degrees in education were awarded annually, largely to foreign students and "not related to programs leading to recommendations for teaching credentials." Dean William Brownell to Chancellor Clark Kerr, 28 April 1955. See University of California at Berkeley, School of Education, Historical File.

79. In 1961 legislation mandated a fifth-year program for both elementary and secondary school teachers, built upon a baccalaureate degree in an academic field. Thereafter the sixty-seven other teachers training institutions in the state were put in essentially the same situation that Berkeley had long occupied: offering exclusively graduate teacher education.

ernance system in this sector of higher education together made the Ph.D. or Ed.D. the new "credential" for ambitious community college faculty and administrators. By the late 1970s, doctorates in education from Berkeley were held by some 40 percent of the presidents of the state's 106 community colleges.

With its other markets and the existence of accessible state colleges, initial teacher preparation remained a small part of Berkeley's work. Characteristically, during the extreme teacher shortages of the post–World War II years, UCLA responded much more wholeheartedly than did Berkeley.[80] Even at its peak, Berkeley produced fewer teachers than its counterparts among leading state universities. In 1969–70, for example, Berkeley recommended 507 new teachers for certification to the University of Michigan's 1,480.[81] While Berkeley's modest teacher education enrollments fell in response to the dismal market for teachers and the diminished attractiveness of the occupation, doctoral enrollments grew or declined only slightly.[82] The annual ratio of awarded doctorates to teaching credentials—which was 1 to 5.3 in 1970—was 1 to 1.4 in 1980. The near-parity of doctoral work and teacher training at Berkeley is probably exceptional among those institutions that do both kinds of work.

A second important trend in doctoral work at Berkeley was the shifting balance between the Ph.D. and Ed.D. degrees.[83] In 1966, in common with the actions of most other Berkeley departments, the foreign languages requirement was eliminated for Ph.D. candidates in education. The "prestige gradient" worked perfectly. The immediate result was the rush of Ed.D. students and applicants to the Ph.D.

80. From 1948–49 to 1949–50, for example, UCLA's output of candidates for teaching credentials went from 444 to 1,367, changing its ranking among California teacher-training institutions from third to first place; Berkeley's numbers went up more modestly: from 461 to 619. UCLA operated through large lecture classes and the designation of public school personnel as "coordinators" of teacher education. University of California at Berkeley, School of Education, Historical File, President's Committee on University Programs in Education, "Report" (1950?), p. 10.

81. Richard Musemeche and Sam Adams, "The Coming Teacher Shortage," *Phi Delta Kappan* 59 (1978):691–93.

82. *The Revised Academic Plan* stated that from 724 students in 1957–58, the School of Education was projected to grow to 1,000 by 1975–76. In the doubling of advanced doctoral students in that projection, the School was expected to follow developments of the campus as a whole. University of California at Berkeley, *Revised Academic Plan,* 15, 41.

83. Between 1897 and 1965, 307 Ph.D.'s in education were awarded at Berkeley; between 1915 and 1965 the total number of Ed.D.'s was 513. School of Education, Historical File.

Whereas, in 1966 eighteen Ph.D. and fifty-two Ed.D. degrees were conferred, in 1981 the corresponding numbers were forty and three.[84] The political implications of this development were not then recognized. They proved to be threatening when the time came to make an issue of the School's relative standing on the campus in quality of graduate work. Largely uninterested in the requirements and standards of certificates and professional degrees, campus review committees and Letters and Science professors felt competent—and honorbound—to monitor Ph.D. programs and to judge dissertations in education; too often they declared the results undistinguished.[85]

The School: Adrift between Practicality and Prestige

Indifference to clients may be the norm in large bureaucratic contexts, or "among professionals who do not define themselves as client-oriented." As physicians in large health plans are given as examples of the first, academics in elite institutions, where "publish or 'perish" is the rule, illustrate the second.[86] Critics of present-day graduate schools of education contend, with justification, that they have lost their way. Under pressure, they have forgotten their essential character as training schools for education professionals because of their imitations of disciplinary departments and their chief pursuit of theoretical research. Even as more prospective teachers partook of a lengthier education, the modest pay and prestige of teaching undermined interest in preparing novices. This strengthened, in leading institutions, the emphasis upon research without consistent regard to practice.

High prestige came most predictably through rankings on national surveys, earned through zealousness in publishing one's research and in placing one's graduates in positions outside of public school classrooms. An opinion study commissioned by the regents of the Universty of California in the mid-1970s ranked Berkeley in a tie

84. This shift was also consistent with the advice of the Academic Plan Steering Committee, University of California at Berkeley, *Revised Academic Plan,* 59.

85. The by-laws and standing orders of the Board of Regents specify that the Academic Senate will authorize and supervise all courses and curricula excepting those in professional schools offering work at the graduate level only, nondegree work in University Extension, and courses in specified affiliated institutions. See McConnell and Edelstein, *Campus Governance,* 12. Courses in the Law School were exempted from review by the Senate's Committee on Courses of Instruction; those in the School of Education were not.

86. Larson, *Professionalism,* 188.

for fifth place in "faculty quality" and in fourth place in "educational attractiveness" among all education schools in the United States.[87] Comparisons among schools of education did not convince campus opinion, however, that *any* of what was being compared was "of Berkeley quality." Unlike the other graduate schools of education which, Harry Judge reports, got smiles from campus administrators when high ratings were released, Berkeley's education faculty went without such on-campus acknowledgement.

As already indicated, an alternative method of raising prestige, and one pursued increasingly by graduate schools of education in the recent period, was to hire faculty with Ph.D.'s earned in academic departments. The carrot was the unprecedented availability of federal funds for educational research. In the case of Berkeley, institutional attractions were more than sufficient. Perceptive education students at Berkeley complained, however, to the Berger Committee in 1977 that they could not hope to be hired by their own institution. What they meant was that while they were receiving Ph.D.'s in education, Berkeley's own School of Education had been hiring doctorates from academic departments: from sociology, psychology, anthropology, economics, linguistics. This fact could hardly have convinced the Committee that education schools had disciplinary or professional integrity—or much utility.

Such appointments had something to do with the utter failure of the faculty to respond altogether to the planning documents and constructive advice that came from Senate and administrative bodies in the 1960s and early 1970s. They do not explain it entirely, however, because the older faculty and the supervisors of teacher education were similarly torpid. The School was characterized by a singular absence of enlightened followership. Such habits persisted even into the years of evident crisis and partial dismemberment. As one response to external criticism of its fragmentation, a biweekly faculty research colloquium instituted in 1980 faltered and disappeared after one year. Internal indifference precluded creative discussion of important issues of professional education, leaving largely unattended the chronic problem of a faculty divided in function and status between two distinct entities: the professors "on the ladder" and the supervisors of teacher education. Had the faculty acted otherwise, on this and other vital matters, it is quite possible that subsequent investigations and

87. Alan Cartter, "The Cartter Report on the Leading Schools of Education, Law, and Business," *Change* 9, no. 2 (Feb. 1977):44–48.

administrative actions would have been prevented or moderated.[88] The *enemy within* resided in the loss of a sense of purpose, in the absence of purposeful action, in apathetic individualism. Was it greater than the *enemy without?*

Limited growth in graduate faculty during the later 1960s, the intense competition among Berkeley departments brought on by steady-state policies, and the unremitting loss of positions rationalized by declines in teacher education and the absence of a dean were particularly damaging given the unusually small size of the professorial faculty even at its peak.[89] Berkeley could never offer the comprehensive array of professional programs possible at Wisconsin, Penn State, or even Long Beach State. Thus, fewer professionals could look to Berkeley as important to their particular interests. This fact alone restricted its political base in the field. Moreover, faculty losses and changes hit the professional areas especially hard. The school administration programs were altered by retirements, by new appointments, and by realignments that progressively shifted the emphasis from school-based to theoretical and policy studies after 1968 or so. The curriculum and instruction group was weakened by deaths and resignations before it suffered the departure of key faculty to form a new language and literacy division emphasizing linguistics.

The Graduate Division faulted the School because of its students' characteristics. Their age and part-time status, the long periods elapsing before completion of the degree, and the fact that most came from the local area—all clashed with conceptions of graduate education that fit the well-funded doctoral programs in the sciences. The national trend towards "stopping out" and the preferences of some graduate business schools for mature applicants with practical experience

88. For this insight we are indebted to John Matlin who served as Assistant Director for Teacher Education during these years. See, for example, the letter of Dean Reller to the Faculty (8 Sept. 1967) concerning the wish of the graduate dean for "some conclusive action planned" on the Ed.D. and Ph.D. issue. University of California at Berkeley, School of Education, Historical File.

89. In the 1977 Ladd and Lipset survey, in which Berkeley ranked tenth in faculty distinction of all schools of education, each of five higher-ranking institutions had a faculty size above 132. In 1978 Berkeley was classified among twenty-four "R and D Centers" in education. Of these, nearly half had in excess of 160 faculty each; these included Minnesota (165) and Wisconsin (1980). Only six institutions had fewer than 80 faculty: four (Harvard, Stanford, Chicago, Pennsylvania) were in private institutions, two were public—UCLA (55 positions) and Berkeley (41). Egon Guba and David L. Clark, "Levels of R and D Productivity in Schools of Education," *Educational Researcher* 7, no. 5 (May 1978):7.

found little favor in the Graduate School at Berkeley.[90] Despite this commitment to employed professionals, the School of Education was also found guilty of not having developed or maintained sufficient and systematic ties to the profession. Certainly individual faculty had such linkages, but the School itself had few structural ties to the world of practice. Teacher unions, administrator organizations, educational policy makers, and other practitioners composed constituencies with which the School might have maintained ties. Ironically, many of these organizations had as their leaders graduates of Berkeley's School of Education. Its alumni were late in organizing, however, and badly neglected. When the School was severely threatened, most of those who had something to lose by its abolition—the discrediting of their degrees—found themselves ill informed and unprepared to assist.

Low-status groups tend to be ambivalent about their group, and try to demonstrate commitment to the norms of those higher in the stratification system. These efforts never achieved parity for education at Berkeley. Education faculty were given tenure and promoted for doing research and publishing it. But this, like the hiring of non-education-trained faculty, did not convince campus opinion leaders that the scholarship was equal to that done in cognate departments; isolation and lack of a sufficient disciplinary community were said to result inevitably in lower standards and less creative research. The emphasis that prestigious education schools gave to applied social science and research training failed to bring them honor on the campus, if Berkeley's experience is typical. Neither did it enhance the self-image and status of teachers and other school professionals, nor work to cement their loyalties to schools of education. The absence of a professional "mission" is bad enough; the absence of a professional *constituency* could prove fatal. Lacking essential support on the campus makes life miserable; lacking supporters in the education community of Alameda and surrounding counties and in the "education establishment" in Sacramento could make life unsupportable.

90. For comment on these trends see Ernest A. Lynton, "The Interdependence of Employment and Education," Alden Seminars in Higher Education, University of Massachusetts, Boston, 22 April 1982, p. 23. In fall 1986, the average age of entering graduate students ranged from 23.3 (for master's) and 23.0 (for doctoral) in Chemistry to 29.3 (for master's) and 34.8 (for doctoral) in Education. University of California at Berkeley, Graduate Division, *The Graduate* 3, no. 1 (Spring 1987):5.

Education, the Cinderella Profession

In 1913 the head of the Department of Education at Berkeley, Alexis Lange described the profession of teaching as "the Cinderella of the Professions."[91] Lange persuaded the regents to create a school of education that year but, like his successors as dean, he failed to convince the University that Cinderella "is handsomer than all of her sisters." Teaching is a mass profession, its practitioners a heterogeneous lot, its service nearly universal and mostly free. Despite the efforts and rhetoric of a century and a half education continued to be a relatively low-status field. This reflected negatively upon its professional schools, their students, programs, and faculty.[92]

Many educational faculty believed that concentration upon the higher status elements of the education profession could elevate the status of any school of education. The President's Committee on University Programs in Education wrote, around 1950, about Berkeley:

> The advantages of having as school superintendents, principals, and supervisors a large number of alumni of this institution who have had their credentials certified here are obvious. . . . The School and the University need the good will and support of public school administrators, and one of the best ways to secure this support is to see to it that a reasonable number of these administrators are alumni of this institution.[93]

But Stanford and the University of Southern California had, except in research, come "to enjoy the prestige that properly belongs to the University."[94] In 1955, only 10 percent of administrative credentials recommended to the state came from the combined campuses of the University, compared to 33 percent from the University of Southern California.[95] Other institutions had a near-monopoly in the prepara-

91. Quoted in George C. Kyte, "The Origin and Early History of Lambda Chapter of Phi Delta Kappa," University of California at Berkeley, School of Education, Historical File, March 1933.

92. Judge, *American Graduate Schools of Education,* 29 ff.

93. President's Committee Report, 2, 29.

94. University of California at Berkeley, School of Education, Dean Brownell to Sproul, 7–8.

95. Next in numbers came San Francisco State College, Stanford, and Claremont Graduate School. University of California, Liaison Committee (1955), 39.

tion and placement of the state's school administrators, through both credential and doctoral programs.[96]

In the mid-1960s, for example, now viewed as the "good years," Berkeley had three professors in school administration to Wisconsin's and Teachers College's nine apiece. While the causes may well have been multiple, the School failed to create a cadre of "schoolmen" with whom active professional collaborations could more readily have been built.

These difficulties were compounded by the reputation for campus radicalism which Berkeley earned as a result of the student-led protest movements beginning in 1964. Berkeley's reputation attracted to Education, as to other campus departments and schools, a corpus of intelligent, articulate, and passionate social critics.[97] Their presence supported the emphasis on the social science study of education but in a spirit that was disdainful and intolerant of existing public schools and of the professionals that staffed them. "Teacher bashing" was de rigueur among this new cadre of recruits to schools of education at Berkeley, Madison, or Cambridge. And, as Nathan Glazer has noted, the "deliberately antiprofessional rebel or reformer"—assigned reading in the work of Kozol, Goodman, Illich, Friedenberg—could not satisfy the "model hunger" of teachers.[98] Idealism abounded but it was directed at making revolution, at generating exposés, or, at best, at founding alternative ("free") schools. Albeit a brief phase in the School of Education's history, it offered few opportunities to build bridges to the field of practice.

There were ironies aplenty. At the same time that Arthur Jensen's classes in Tolman Hall were boycotted or disrupted because of protests against his publications on the heritability of intelligence and on racial differences in aptitude, campus administrators and other deans were fuming at another professor's "democratically run" education courses

96. Between 1920 and 1962, the production of doctorates in education was as follows: Stanford, 1,011; University of Sothern California, 724; Berkeley, 564; and UCLA (which was not authorized to grant doctorates until the 1940s), 297. Harmon and Soldz, *Doctorate Production* 20, 24.

97. Education and Criminology (closed in 1976) had higher than average numbers of minority students, as well as vocal social critics. The 16 percent of the School of Education students who were members of "minority and other disadvantaged groups" was the highest figure on the Michigan campus during its years of greatest threat. University of Michigan, School of Education, "Annual Report to the President," 7.

98. Glazer, "Schools," 362.

in which students graded themselves. In one much-muttered-about case, twenty-three Berkeley undergraduates on academic probation were credited with "A" work in education. Sanctions were imposed on the professor and the School's credibility on campus suffered further.[99]

Radical critiques of all the major institutions of American society came at a time when the School's ordinary points of contact with public education were diminishing. Teacher education enrollments peaked at Berkeley before they did nationally. Enrollments of experienced teachers in master's degree programs declined as many teachers found themselves already at the top of their district's salary scales.[100] The significant exception in School-field interactions was the Bay Area Writing Project—which conspicuously maintained its distance, attempting to minimize its connection with the School of Education.

The great political and social challenge to public education in this period was the combatting of racism and the creation of social and economic equality through the desegregation of schools. The Berkeley city schools were desegregated on the initiative of the school board, not the courts. A move widely noticed in the national press, it was met locally by appreciable white flight to the suburbs and to private schools. University faculty and staff were among both those fleeing and those staying on to try to preserve the previously high reputation of Berkeley's public schools. But those who felt forced to write tuition checks to private schools, or to battle the commute from safe suburbs, or to monitor closely their children's continued schooling in the desegregated schools could well have also blamed the nation's schools of education, however irrational that might be; there was, after all, a history of assigning blame.

In the quarter-century after 1942, the city of Berkeley gradually changed from a community dominated by "rich conservatives" to one run by "rich liberals." In the midst of this period, Bruno Bettelheim wrote about liberals who espouse racial desegration but whose high consciousness of educational advantages creates dilemmas. One response of liberal intellectuals is to favor both desegration and a toughening of academic standards and, as necessary, to exert pressure for grouping or tracking students by ability; their own children would, of

99. Theodore L. Reller, interview with Geraldine Clifford, Berkeley, 11 September, 1985.

100. The numbers of master's degrees awarded had been growing through the 1960s, in response to the large numbers of teachers trained and hired during the entire postwar period. By 1980, however, the School awarded fewer than it had in 1950. University of California at Berkeley, *Revised Academic Plan,* 168.

course, be safe from hard drugs and soft pedagogy in classes for the "gifted."[101] Berkeley's public schools, like the city, were convulsed by campaigns for and against every social and educational goal—including ability grouping. Many in the academic community, once involved in school and city affairs, had little stomach for the new-style politics of confrontation. In his seven years on the Berkeley school board, from 1975 to 1982, James Guthrie had little success in enlisting University faculty help for school district programs.

We cannot assert with certainty that University faculty members—as parents, citizens, and taxpayers—did, in fact, blame Berkeley's School of Education, or the totality of schools of education, for the disappointment they felt about the public education they knew best. The characteristics of America's schools have a larger history than is formed by a prospective teacher's brief exposure to a school of education—and social scientists, especially, must know that. But, it seems obvious that whether one's ideological preferences were of the left- or the right-wing variety, there were ample grounds for disappointment with education's performance—whether at Willard Junior High School in the city or in Tolman Hall on the University's campus.

The Instruments of Organizational Disrepair

The environmental conditions we have described served much as a nutrient through which the organizational pathologies of Berkeley's School of Education developed. The growth of pathologies was not, however, simply tolerated or permitted to run its own course. Rather, various campus administrators and Academic Senate elites occasionally intervened to hasten the active deterioration of the School. Their acts, both of commission and omission, materially helped to bring the School to the brink of "disestablishment." To conclude this case study, we recapitulate what we believe were the most important signs of disease in the institution.

A Bifurcated Faculty

UCLA avoided the problems Berkeley gained in having as a separate faculty a body of supervisors of teacher education. The "ladder fac-

101. Bruno Bettelheim, "Segregation: New Style," *School Review* 66 (1958):251–72. The breakdown of consensus in Berkeley is interestingly analyzed in Gail L. Zellman and Steven L. Schlossman, "The Berkeley Youth Wars," *Public Interest*, 84 (Summer 1986):29–41.

ulty" of the Department of Education were the professors of all ranks, invested with the protected privileges and powers conferred by membership in the Academic Senate; the Department of Education, like other departments, is a formally-constituted body of the Senate. With the closing of the University High School in Oakland in 1946, the School of Education acquired its teachers, and turned them into supervisors of teachers education; they were the second faculty. Theirs was an isolated group as only a few professors were involved directly in teacher education. Paradoxically, the supervisors might have closer working relationships with professors in other departments, working in liaison positions with subject-matter representatives and interested faculty in departments like English and Mathematics. This meant that these professors' image of the School was limited to its character as a teacher-training college—an activity in which the "real" education faculty played too little part and took scant interest.

Former department chairpersons and carefully selected teachers, the original group of supervisors and those who joined their ranks, had second-class status by their own evaluation as well as by others. As non-Senate faculty they lacked voting rights in Department meetings, although varying kinds of informal "citizenship" were periodically conferred. The supervisors were without such other faculty prerogatives as sabbatical leaves, formal tenure, and the right to teach courses outside of the teacher education "professional series" (i.e., methods courses and practice-teaching seminars). In a demonstration of its position that theirs were year-to-year appointments, the campus administration put supervisors on annual contracts. This caused prolonged resistance and culminated in grievance proceedings, held at the same time that the School was without regular leadership and beset by other problems.

Years before matters came to a head, the School's deans were bogged down in other issues surrounding this second faculty and its mission of teacher education. Outsiders to the Senate structure and the campus reward system, supervisors of teacher education were poorly positioned to share the concerns of Education's other faculty. Former Dean Theodore Reller recalls that for the first half of his deanship, during the 1960s, he received almost weekly protests from, or on behalf of, the then large supervisory faculty. Matters of salary, prerogatives, even questions of to whom invitations to faculty social events should be addressed were regularly thrown on his desk.[102]

102. Theodore L. Reller, interviews with Geraldine Clifford Berkeley, 28 August and 3 September, 1986.

Nor was the professorial faculty happy with the situation. Aside from whatever guilt or sense of injustice may have troubled its members, its leaders were party to "bitter battles" internally and with campus administrators about programs and resources. The effort to apportion some supervisory positions among graduate students, for example, was strongly resisted by the supervisors—damaging as it would be to their sense of community, professional identity, and pride-in-program.[103] For their part professors were anxious to see doctoral students receive some of the employment opportunities which departments with large undergraduate programs use to help finance doctoral study.

"The need for financial support for teacher training is apparent and easily demonstrated, while need for funds for research, for training leaders either for the schools or colleges, or for consultative service seems less pressing and can more easily be postponed."[104] In 1953, Sproul reported receiving legislative pressure to have the University satisfy more of the state's need for teachers. Because the requirements of Berkeley's teacher education programs were thought to restrict growth, and because persons denied admission to its teacher training programs nonetheless became teachers through emergency credentials, Sproul asked Dean William Brownell to consider reducing the required grade-point average for admission. The faculty was aghast and Brownell deflected Sproul by reminding him that earlier efforts to do so were opposed by the Graduate Council.[105]

The large, separately identified, state-funded budget for supervised teaching was used by the chancellor and his advisors against the Education Department. Lacking formal control over this budget, the Budget Committee restrictively wielded its advisory authority over the Department's request for additional professorial positions. It was repeatedly pointed out, for example, that supervisors could be appointed as short-term lecturers in order to staff other education courses. In 1955, there were twenty-four Senate and twenty-three su-

103. Proposed remedies were addressed in a confidential "Report on Supervised Teaching Unit, Berkeley Campus," University of California at Berkeley, School of Education, Historical File, 5 July 1966. We were unable to determine that the report was ever discussed by the faculty.

104. University of California at Berkeley, School of Education, Historical File, President's Committee on University Programs in Education, "Report," 15.

105. University of California at Berkeley, School of Education, William Brownell to Robert Gordon Sproul, 14 October 1953; University of California at Berkeley, School of Education, Historical File, President's Committee on Programs in Education, "Report," 14–15.

pervisory full-time equivalent positions (FTE); in 1965, thirty-seven professorial and forty-eight supervisory positions. Understandably, it was much easier to get supervisors, with increases in the numbers of student teachers admitted, than to convince the campus to authorize regular and permanent faculty positions. By 1970, however, the respective figures were forty-six and twenty-four; by 1983, thirty-seven and twelve. The cause was not a change in campus commitments to graduate education relative to teacher education, however. Rather, the collapse of the market for teachers as a result of the end of the baby boom affected both kinds of positions in the School. But the supervisors were far more vulnerable, as administrators and campus planners surely realized they would be.

Revolving Door Leadership

Education faculty and staff came to refer to it as the "dean-a-week" system. From 1975 to the spring of 1983 there was a total of nine "acting deans," "dean designates," and "deans." In addition, for one period in 1982 the School had no one at all with any varient of the dean title. Illness, retirement, unsuccessful search efforts, and resignation were all given by campus administrators as reasons for their inability to provide the School with solid leadership. The implication was none too subtly conveyed that the School's progressively growing weakness made it difficult to attract a leader of the calibre acceptable to the campus. The School was entrapped in what the Smelser Commission called "a family of vicious circles."

The result was a virtual crippling of the organization. It became impossible to sustain a uniform course of direction. With perfectly well-intentioned motives, each new occupant of the revolving dean's chair would chart new directions and attempt to leave a personal imprint upon the institution. In that the next yearly "dean" would have differing goals or visions, however, and feel the need to do more than "hold the phone" lest the School surely perish, priorities would be altered and the School taken in yet another direction. Under such conditions of administrative turnover it was impossible to progress toward long-range purposes, be they recruiting faculty strength in a particular academic concentration, attempting to solidify relations with professional practitioners, encouraging more extramurally-funded research, constructing an effective alumni network, or building intellectual bridges to other departments, although attempts were made in all these directions. An organization can surely focus upon several objectives simultaneously. It is unlikely to succeed, however, unless by caprice, in accomplishing any long-run purposes when goals are altered and resources reassigned on an annual basis. The example of the School of Criminology—itself beset by a succession of deans and acting deans prior to its closing—was instructive. Education was never more vulnerable. Moreover, the campus administration was also damaged, letting a bad situation get worse and adopting a style of response that bred cynicism and a certain lack of confidence in other segments of the campus community.

The Erosion of Resources

In 1975, before its major difficulties began, the School of Education had a complement of forty-six Academic Senate faculty positions, rather than the fifty-six that the campus *Revised Academic Plan* had targeted; the projected one-a-year additions had not been made.[106] Enrollments then totaled eight hundred graduate students almost evenly divided between those enrolled in fifth-year teacher credential programs (for which there were nineteen supervisors) and those seeking advanced degrees. By 1982 the faculty had dropped to thirty-seven Senate positions. Given the fact that enrollment, particularly in teacher education, had also declined by approximately three hundred students, the overall attrition rate was not alarming; faculty fell by some 30 percent and enrollments by 37 percent. This was consistent with predictions that schools of education nationally could expect to lose as much as one-third of their 1970 faculty size by 1980.[107]

One difficulty was that faculty loss was uneven and concentrated in illogical ways. For example, in a time when the nation badly needed to buttress instruction in areas related to science and technology and a shortage of mathematics and science teachers already existed, Berkeley's education faculty was permitted to function without even one active full-time specialist in mathematics education. This condition was particularly stressful given the Berkeley campus's unmatched academic reputation in mathematics and the physical sciences.

106. The faculty target assumed a 20 percent reduction in teacher education enrollments over 1965 figures, a 10 percent increase in advanced doctoral enrollments, and a 37 percent reduction in student-faculty ratio. University of California at Berkeley, *Revised Academic Plan,* 49, 59.

107. Browder, "Where Are Schools of Education Going?" 55.

Agenda Piracy

Berkeley took particular pride in individualism. Thus political science professors conducted research about the legal system; business school professors published studies about national political character; law school faculty investigated family-guaranteed income plans. There were more sociologists located outside the Department of Sociology than within it. Beyond simple academic freedom, such wide-ranging inquiry is justified on grounds that interdisciplinary study is productive; many of society's most interesting problems are to be found in the interstices between conventionally defined academic fields. Given this, it was to be expected that disciplinary scholars in other campus departments would periodically make forays into the multidisciplinary Education School's intellectual turf. The extent of such incursions over time, however, became debilitating to the School. Without sustained leadership and working with constantly eroding resources, it was powerless before the invaders. But its lack of faculty entrepreneurship was also a determining cause of this piracy of its natural agenda. By 1976, the statewide review of education programs found that Berkeley's Education School was conducting only about 12 percent of the education research that was being done on the campus, compared to UCLA's 55 percent on its campus.[108]

The ascendance of the Lawrence Hall of Science was matched almost linearly by the erosion of science and mathematics education resources in the School of Education. The Childhood and Government Project, attracting millions of dollars in outside funding from foundations such as Carnegie, Ford, and Spencer, was lodged administratively in the Law School, although most of its topics focused upon education and many of its researchers were drawn from Education. The Carnegie-funded Center for the Study of Higher Education had been established outside of the School of Education by President Clark Kerr and Professor T. R. McConnell. Whatever the advantages for encouraging interdisciplinary and cross-campus participation in research and development projects, it reinforced the impression of the School's lack of control.

108. APPRB, IV-71. A similar problem existed at Michigan. In1982, when the School of Education faced possible closure, Dean Joan Stark recommended that an Institute of Educational Research be founded at Ann Arbor "to ensure that the many other faculty working on educational problems are linked to those in the School of Education." University of Michigan, School of Education, "Annual Report to the President," 6.

These piracies of the School's agenda had at least two consequences. First, the School was increasingly faulted by the administration and representatives of the field for not having a practical research program tying it to the profession and its problems. The second was that campus officials could say, with substantial validity, that elimination of the School was of less consequence given the evidence that the campus "really cares" about education; witness all the education-related projects at Berkeley.

Reprieve and Recovery

In mid-January 1982, the chancellor announced his decision to retain and "revitalize" the School. Chancellor Heyman's statement clearly revealed that he knew and accepted as valid Harry Judge's analysis of the problems of graduate schools of education. Most, if not all that he gained from this Oxford scholar he could have learned from collegial discussions with members of the Education faculty on his own campus. It would not have been easy, however, for to have done so would have contravened a strong tradition—of disdain and disrespect on the one side and defensiveness and insecurity on the other—a tradition perhaps as old as Berkeley's sufferance of Education on campus.

Heyman's decision was undoubtedly influenced by the difficulties of locating Education faculty and programs elsewhere on the campus. It had been one thing to close the School of Criminology, where joint appointments with the Law School provided a ready mechanism for dispersing the small tenured faculty. It was an incalculably greater problem to absorb some forty tenured professors—or to break tradition and fire tenured University of California faculty, thereby raising apprehension, dissension, and unknown dangers throughout the system and, possibly, in all of the American higher education. Even to consider the possibility that six or eight Berkeley departments would be asked to take in education faculty was to galvanize and unite an opposition. The Smelser Commission's plan was clearly unworkable and some found it hard to believe that it could have been seriously offered.

Other factors involved in the chancellor's decision certainly included the political considerations which university administrators cannot ignore the way faculty committees sometimes will. As chancellor, Heyman had to deal with extramural pressures against which he had been somewhat protected in his years as the vice-chancellor. Although Chancellor Heyman told us that there was relatively little external pressure on him, either to abolish or to retain the School of

Education, it is known that alumni of the School—ironically the best organized and most active being those of the late-program in higher education—initiated a letter-writing campaign to members of the California Legislature and their professional staffs, among others.

Another political reality was the publicity being given to Stanford University President Donald Kennedy's affirmation of schools of education. In November 1981, before the Carnegie Foundation for the Advancement of Teaching, Kennedy announced his own intention to strengthen further his already top-rated School. Kennedy joined forces with Derek Bok, also on record as supporting his own school of education, in subsequently sponsoring the previously discussed Pajaro Dunes conference. Bok had recently published a book *Beyond the Ivory Tower: Social Responsibilities of the Modern University* (1982), which tried to articulate a balance between public service and academic traditions of autonomy and neutrality. These private universities appeared to be putting the state's public, land-grant institution to shame in a major public service arena.

For his part, Chancellor Heyman periodically reiterated his public statement that to close the School of Education at Berkeley would "send the wrong message" to the public about the University's concerns about education. He also told us that he did not know precisely why he had made his decision. There were rational reasons to keep the School or to close it, but the making of the decision was not all that rational, he said. Speaking of what he called an arrogant assertion of power on his part, the chancellor speculated that "perhaps it was because my mother was a teacher; I don't know."[109]

By 1982, the cumulative consequences of administrative turnover, the withdrawal of resources, the piracy of its agenda, incessant outside criticism, and deferred decision had brought the School to its organizational knees. Some professors actively negotiated early retirements and disability leaves. Others pursued positions elsewhere. Faculty productivity declined and illness and disability, internal bickering, and alienation mounted.[110] Student applications for admission plum-

109. Ira Michael Heyman, interview with the authors, 16 October 1985.

110. A study of program participants at AERA annual meetings, 1975–79, suggests as much. It ranked Berkeley in 20th place—well below its ranking on reputational studies. William H. Schubert, "Contributions to the AERA Annual Program as an Indicator of Institutional Productivity," *Educational Researcher* 8 (July–Aug. 1979):8, 13–17. Publication by Berkeley faculty in AERA journals had already declined, as well. Charles K. West, "Productivity Ratings of Institutions Based on Publication in Journals of the American Educational Research Association, 1970–1976," *Educational Researcher* 7, no. 2 (Feb. 1978): 13–14.

meted, while those already enrolled uncharacteristically hurried to complete coursework and degree requirements. Faculty were reluctant to undertake the effort necessary to plan new courses, serve on committees, or recruit new students. Self-criticism and internal dissension were becoming amost as intense as the external criticism had been. A once too-complacent institution had been effectively crippled.

On 1 April 1983 a new, long-awaited, long-despaired of dean, Bernard Gifford, appeared at Tolman Hall. Despite his ironic references to himself as an "April Fool's Joke," his administration signalled the beginning of a symbolic and real era of redemption. In 1985 the Academic Senate's Committee on Educational Policy described the situation of Berkeley's School "to be healthy, with an innovative climate."[111] Such approval was important, given the tendency of Berkeley faculty to suspect chancellor-advocated programs.[112]

Halfway through his six-year appointment, Dean Gifford had overcome the absence of an organized research unit through which to funnel large-scale and sustained research and public service efforts at the School. The number of extramural grants had gone from twenty to forty-four, representing some additional eleven million dollars in funds for research, development, and professional projects. A series of long-term, institutionalized collaborations with teachers and school administrators was begun on several fronts. Authorizations for eight new faculty positions were secured and filled, in ways that acknowledged both the still-competing claims of applied social science and of professional education. Propelled by a resumption of teacher hirings, the School's small credential programs had far more qualified applicants than they could handle, especially given the failure to recruit ladder-rank faculty in this still suspect and "dangerous" specialization. (UCLA had only one junior faculty member in teacher education in the same period.)

The Berkeley administration reopened a program in higher edu-

111. Sheldon Zedeck (Chair, Committee on Educational Policy) to Provost Doris Howes Calloway, 5 February 1985, p. 3, School of Education, Historical File. This was in notable contrast to the response of the Committee on Academic Planning to which the chancellor had referred, for comment, his decision to retain the School. Then the opinion had been that "If we were to judge the academic merits of the program of the School of Education without regard for external considerations, we would find it hard to justify continuance of the School. . . . [It] agrees that the Berkeley campus ought to make one more try to foster professional activities in education on the campus." R. E. Goodman to Chancellor Heyman, 1 March 1982, University of California at Berkeley, School of Education, Historical File.

112. McConnell and Edelstein, *Campus Governance*, 44.

cation to focus upon the community colleges, institutions being politically reexamined in their relationships to the university. The decline of the "transfer" function (preparing freshmen and sophomores for entrance to universities) and the growth of "terminal" (lower-status vocational programs, enrolling many ethnic minorities) education in the community colleges had weakened the connections between themselves and the University of California. These shifts, we would contend, had reduced the University's interest in them.[113] Now that was changing too.

As we have previously shown, early in their histories schools of education performed various services that made them attractive nuisances to universities. In the 1980s the University of California discovered anew that it had a self-interest in maintaining its own schools and departments of education. In large part this discovery was born of institutional competition. Neighboring Stanford had become a major challenger of Berkeley over the years; it, too, could claim to be "the Harvard of the West."

But this challenge might have been shrugged off had not the University also been vulnerable from its other side—in the presence of a very large, ambitious public alternative in higher education: the Cali-

113. The fastest-growing sector of higher education following World War II, by 1970 the community colleges enrolled over one-third of all students in higher education and were a similar proportion of all colleges. Their large need for teachers and administrators had been significantly met in California by the graduate program in higher education in Berkeley's School of Education and the Leadership Program at Berkeley, UCLA, and Stanford. The growth of community college vocational enrollments, however—which went from one-quarter to over one-half of their student bodies nationally between 1960 and 1975, their increasingly working-class clientele, and the virtual disappearance of their transfer role, together weakened the community of interest previously existing between community colleges and the University of California and the California State University systems. In 1972, for example, Chancellor Bowker wrote to the Budget Committee that the School of Criminology's preparation of instructors for the community colleges' programs in criminal justice, while important, were "not really a mission that needs to be handled within the framework of a major research university like Berkeley." Quoted in McConnell and Edelstein, *Campus Governance,* 50. By the mid-eighties, however, legislative inquiries about the heavy enrollments of ethnic minorities in community colleges and their very low rates of transfer to four-year institutions, the proposed revision of the California Master Plan for Higher Education, and the knowledge that impending retirements would require heavy replenishment of community college personnel combined to stimulate new interests in collaborations between community colleges and both of the State's public university systems. For an analysis of the social functions of community colleges, see Jerome Karabel, "Community Colleges and Social Stratification," *Harvard Educational Review* 42, no. 4 (Nov. 1972):521–62.

fornia State University (CSU) system. For decades, active competition existed in many states between state universities and their land-grant institutions, schools which began as primarily agricultural or engineering schools but which were diversifying and expanding to challenge the universities' preferred position.[114] Similar tensions obtained in California with the former teachers colleges.

A special study and advisory body, the California Commission on the Teaching Profession, found that the California State University system was becoming ever-more dominant in the preparation of prospective teachers: it graduated three-fourths of those being trained within the state; the private ("independent") colleges and universities contributed 20 percent; the nine campuses of the University of California together trained only 5 percent.[115] Also, as long before as 1948, the Liaison Committee had conceded that the preparation of school principals, unlike school superintendents and school research workers, is "occupational rather than of advanced graduate or professional training"; as such it could be performed by the state colleges as well as the university.[116]

Far more alarming to the University was the fact that, several

114. For an account of earlier difficulties between the University of Washington and the former agricultural college at Pullman, see Williams, "Henry Suzzallo," 57–82. The University's deposed president, Henry Suzzallo, as president of the Carnegie Foundation for the Advancement of Teaching, sponsored a master plan for higher education in California that would have placed all higher institutions under the regents of the University of California, with a State Educational Planning and Coordinating Council composed of regents and State Board of Education members. Such a body was created in 1933 but with little power to control growth or allocate functions in California public higher education. See Stadtman, *University of California,* 263.

115. The figures are for those enrolled in teacher training programs during the 1982–83 academic year. Murphy, "Teacher Preparation in California," 27.

116. University of California, Liaison Committee (1948), 48. The Donohoe Act, passed by the legislature in 1960, created the *Master Plan for Higher Education in California.* It represented, in good part, the wish of the University of California to see a clear differentiation in function and privileges maintained between it, the state colleges, and the junior (community) colleges. The University was declared the "primary state-supported academic agency for research," given sole authority in public higher education to award the doctoral degree in all fields of learning. Its instructional authorization also included preparation for the teaching profession—the historic domain of the normal schools and state colleges. The University did relatively little of this, however. Only some 8 percent of California's newly credentialled teachers in the early 1970s, the peak period in numbers prepared, studied at the University; over 60 percent were graduates of the State Universities and Colleges system, the successor to the individual state teachers colleges, and the large remainder were trained in forty-two private institutions. The State also received many teachers who migrated to California. Murphy, "Teacher Preparation," 27.

times since 1960, the California State University administration had also launched efforts to change the California "Master Plan" for Higher Education—which gave the University of California a monopoly on research and the award of doctoral degrees.[117] Joint-doctorates between UC and CSU campuses were authorized in 1960 as a limited concession to its pressures to become a second *full* university system; a few such programs were created, most in the field of education. The University of California had not opposed adding the name "university" to the other system's title, perhaps recognizing the legislature's intent to confer status on it in lieu of commitments of resources and authority.[118] To do more, however, would be to divert resources from the University and other state-funded programs and agencies.

When Chancellor Heyman was deliberating the closing of Berkeley's School in 1981, surely among the most alarming prophecies he received came from Professor Emeritus T. R. McConnell who had developed the doctoral program in higher education at Berkeley. Should the ability of Berkeley to produce doctorates in education be effectively curtailed as a result of disbanding its School of Education, McConnell warned, "The state universities in this area—and ultimately in the entire state—will inaugurate a campaign to amend the Master Plan so that they can offer doctoral degrees in education and, very soon, in other fields."[119] He also reminded his readers that the chairman of the National Commission on Excellence in Education had called the chancellor about proposals to close the School. McConnell queried, "Can't you imagine that the Commission might use the virtual elimination of the U.C. School of Education as an unfortunate example of University abandonment of educational leadership?" The Commission chairman, University of Utah President David Pierpont Gardner, was himself a 1966 graduate of the doctoral program in higher education in Berkeley's School of Education. David Gardner was also named, not long after, President of the University of California—and, in a supreme irony, professor in the School of Education at Berkeley.

Late in 1985, the CSU Board of Trustees indeed concluded that

117. On the provisions of the Master Plan and the tensions emerging early between the sectors of public higher education see Falk, *Development,* 190–207.

118. Trow, "Analysis of Status," 139.

119. T. R. McConnell to Acting Dean Stephen S. Weiner, 15 October 1981. Copies were sent to University President David Saxon, Chancellor I. M. Heyman, Provost Doris H. Calloway, and Education Department Chair James Guthrie. Quoted by permission of T. R. McConnell.

"the verifiable need and demand for additional doctoral programs in the field of education at public California universities had been demonstrated." It resolved that its representatives work with appropriate State authorities "to offer an independent doctoral degree in education," and in other professional doctoral programs when the need was demonstrated and the resources available.[120] Clearly the education doctorate had to be perceived as the opening wedge, a tactic to be strenuously resisted. This threat to the University's monopoly in doctoral education, and the research function traditionally coupled with it, was resisted, just as sixty years earlier, the University had stood up to challenges to its prerogatives in awarding bachelor's degrees. Both assaults came from the same source: teacher training institutions that were determined to become more. That Berkeley did retain its School of Education strengthened the University's position in its successful attempts to blunt the aspirations of the California State University system to offer doctoral degrees.[121]

Conclusion

The efforts made by UCLA campus administrators, academic faculty, and professors in the School of Education in the 1950s to bring the successful and popular educational "experiment" in the form of the University Elementary School into conformity with a reigning research paradigm bear a striking resemblance to a development at Berkeley a quarter-century later. The similarities lie in the spirit animating the two events and in the status positions of the principal antagonists. The Berkeley target for legitimation and reform was the Bay Area Writing Project (BAWP). Begun by James Gray, a supervisor of teacher education possessing well-established ties with English teachers in the state—something like Seeds's ties with working professionals—the Project proceeded from the observation that some teachers were indeed successful in teaching writing to their students. Further,

120. California State University, Board of Trustees, "The Mission of the California State University, Agenda Item 1, November 12–13, 1985, and Attachments." In February 1987 the Master Plan Commission recommended to the California Post Secondary Commission and the Legislature that the CSU doctoral proposal be rejected; the fourteen such programs in education already in existence in the University and private institutions were declared adequate to meeting California's forseeable needs.

121. Subsequently, the staff of the California Postsecondary Education Commission also recommended against CSU's request for authority to offer doctorates in education.

it was believed that with University and colleague assistance these teachers could develop their understanding of why they were successful and could teach others to be successful. The Project flourished, receiving funds from foundations, the state, and the federal government, expanded into the California and National Writing Projects, and then spread to other nations. A California Mathematics Project was built on the model and also funded by the state legislature. Teachers became and remained enthusiastic about this participant-centered approach, and about the dignity they gained from institutional faith in teachers-teaching-teachers.

As BAWP gained adherants and attention, however, administrators were being urged to "reign it in"—i.e., bring it into closer association with the School of Education's administration, faculty, and programs. The possibility that its identification with the School was so limited precisely because the School itself had long since pushed any kind of teacher education to the margins was not much considered; the "blame" for its isolation lay with BAWP and its empiricism. The same pressures figured in the UCLA-UES relationship. In neither instance was there much evidence that academics (inside or outside of their schools of education) were expected to *learn from* these successful experiments in practice, in revising their own programs; only the reverse was expected. Hence, it was urged that conventional research be conducted on the effects of BAWP workshops and summer seminars, and that theory be developed to undergird the Project. Otherwise, it was stated, BAWP would remain a questionable activity for the University of California, unable to confer credit on the School except, perhaps, as a peripheral public service contribution somewhat analogous to University Extension.

In its struggles with the University, the CSU trustees stated that "opportunities for study at the University of California are limited—programs are small and research-oriented and not particularly designed for practitioners." How would the University and its graduate schools of education handle this new challenge to the University's monopoly on doctoral education, given the primacy of univesity-defined research and its historically limited commitment to the education of professionals in education? How would other universities with a similar ethos respond to pressures, within and without higher education, to take affirmative action in working with elementary and secondary schools and their staffs in new ways?

One potential set of answers lay in the 1984 report of the University-Wide Program Review Committee for Education, appointed late in 1983 by the University's new president, David Gardner.[122] The Committee assumed that the University would never usurp the California State University's role in preparing the majority of the state's teachers. It is, however, obligated to improve the attractiveness of the teaching profession through its own careful preparation of teachers and in giving leadership to broad-based efforts in that direction. This conclusion was consistent with the manifesto issued by the Pajaro Dunes participants. Despite the current low involvement of ladder faculty in teacher education—around 5 percent even at UCLA—the Committee recommended that present and future faculty be drawn into at least part-time participation in teacher education. It noted the presence of scholars and scientists in schools of education whose work is devoted to *basic* research, with implications for education "but not exclusively the domain of schools of education," such as studies of the brain and cognition. The Committee recommended however, that "the employment, promotion, and reward of professors of education be based on criteria recognizing the distinctively educational character of their scholarly work and professional contributions." The rationale for this advice, the Committee argued, resides in the warrant of professional schools: "A small handful of professors of education pursuing such basic inquiry is a condition to be cherished and cultivated but it does not add up to adequate justification for the maintenance of schools of education, any more than it adds up to adequate justification for schools of medicine, law, business, engineering, architecture, or agriculture."[123]

Schools of education must, then, remember that they *are* professional schools and act accordingly. But, so must their universities support these actions and concentrate their energies to improve schooling upon and through their schools of education. To do otherwise is to

122. University of California, University-Wide Program Review Committee for Education, "The Role of the University of California in Precollegiate Education," October 1984. The membership of the Committee was Eugene H. Cota-Robles, (biology, Santa Cruz), Philip C. Curtis (mathematics, UCLA), Eugene C. Lee (political science, Berkeley, and member of the aforementioned "Smelser Commission"), Elliot W. Eisner (Stanford School of Education), and John Goodlad, chair.

123. Ibid., 21. To the recommendation, the Berkeley Committee on Educational Policy, however, took some exception. It thought that those "concerning promotion criteria should be viewed cautiously. The language of the existing promotion criteria seems adequate to us. Furthermore, we wonder if it is sensible to reconsider the type of appointment for work of this type, rather than inducing ladder-rank faculty to pursue it through special criteria." Committee on Educational Policy to Provost Doris Calloway, 5 February 1985, p. 5, School of Education, Historical File.

scatter their efforts and undermine, once again, the legitimacy of these agencies.[124] Concerted and continual efforts are necessary to counter the strong general tendency of higher education—especially in prestigious and nationally- or internationally-oriented universities—to offer technical services largely through individual initiative and entrepreneurship rather than through systematic mechanisms and institutional elements that are integral to university life.[125]

124. Old habits die hard. Staff in the President's Office at the University of California, for example, drafted proposals for long-term efforts in educational research and professional training during 1985–86. It did so without coordination, or even consultation, with the four deans of the University's schools of education. Bernard R. Gifford to Doris H. Calloway, 27 June 1986, School of Education, Historical File.

125. Ernest A. Lynton, "The Economic Impact of Higher Education: Review Essay," *Journal of Higher Education* 54, no. 6 (Nov.–Dec. 1983):696, 707.

4 Conclusion

Eight Places of Action and Places of Analysis: Advice for Schools of Education

The teacher training institution really has two tasks—to teach students a subject and at the same time to teach them how to teach it. This requires twice the intelligence, twice the training, twice the time, twice the strength, twice the ability and twice the resources that it requires to teach a subject in total oblivion of the students who are to be taught by the prospective teachers. . . . The education of the taxpayer and the philanthropist to the full comprehension of this achievement, so vital for the fundamentals of our democracy, is the task of the educational leaders of this continent.

Bruce R. Payne, 1930

We can imagine few endeavors that are more urgent and worthy than the improvement of the knowledge of the educational process and the application of that knowledge to that process.

Neil J. Smelser, 1981

Some would say that neither university schools of education nor the public schools to which they are conceptually and historically linked have a future in the twenty-first century. First, it is argued, education schools have no *content:* the academic departments "own" the only substantial knowledge which future teachers require. Second, education schools have no *function* except that of keeping bright people from teaching: practitioners have both professional experience and sufficient earned degrees to provide pedagogical knowledge and supervise induction of teacher trainees.[1] As for public schools, it is reasoned that they have outlived their usefulness except as custodial institutions serving the poor and the listless. Thus, the former dean of Rut-

We owe the language of our chapter title to William Taylor, "The Crisis of Confidence in Teacher Education: An International Perspective," *Oxford Review of Education* 9, no. 1 (1983): 48.

1. Borrowman, "About Professors of Education," 59.

gers University's Graduate School of Education concludes that most of the nation's future social, business, industrial, and governmental leaders are already products of either private or quasi-private (suburban) schools. "Their education depends to a significant degree on intellectual and cultural stimulation and motivation and role modeling provided by their families and friends and then on the quality of the postsecondary institutions they attend."[2]

The proposition that subject-matter "mastery" (as it is now acquired) is sufficient to empower one with the knowledge of either what or how to teach is so well contradicted in everyday experience that we must reject it. Nor is it evident that practitioners in any field today can, unassisted, select, socialize, and equip their replacements by an apprenticeship system. To expect them to do so and also to advance the knowledge base of their practice is to require so massive a restructuring of the profession as to render it impracticable. As for the future of the public schools, they *do* require a substantial improvement in order to recapture the trust, patronage, and loyalty of the American middle classes. Such a reform was argued for and pursued in the mid-nineteenth century on these same grounds, and with conspicuous success. The twenty-first century counterpart of that movement may have already begun—and some of the nation's graduate schools of education have regained a measure of vigor and legitimacy in the process.

At all levels teaching is remarkably labor intensive, and no technologies on the horizon suggest any immediate change. Thus, improving schooling equates mainly to recruiting, training, and retaining masterful teachers and restructuring the systems in which they work so as to stimulate excellence in their performance. It also means preparing school administrators who can collaborate more effectively with teachers in improving instruction. To prepare such professionals—practitioner-scholars at the best—means improving schools of education, and that is the focus of this concluding chapter.

Good and strong schools of education do exist. Some, far too few in our observations, enjoy clear institutional commitment to their labors. On balance, however, our historical descriptions and case analyses demonstrate that they are vulnerable institutions. As a committee of faculty from Stanford and three campuses of the University of California concluded in 1984, "Education schools have been unable either to establish the degree of academic prestige enjoyed by schools

2. Schwebel, "Clash of Cultures," 6.

such as law and medicine or to obtain a perception of indispensability on the part of the education profession."[3]

Their legitimacy is repeatedly challenged because of pedagogy's weak technological underpinnings. They have had to cope as "feminine" agencies in a masculine-dominated world. Consequently they have been like the mammals in the age of the dinosaurs—small, quiet, nocturnal omnivores, coming out after 4:10 P.M. to forage and ruffle their fur a little, reflecting a few rays of the vanishing sun.

Victimized by the American disease of "status anxiety," schools of education have been tracking in circles. One presumed route to higher regard was to encourage abandonment of the classroom. Rather than bend their talents to helping teachers gain skills and build structures that would professionalize teaching, the most nationally visible professors of education constructed their own careers without much reference to that most important and challenging task of professional education: creating the effective and influential teacher. Another well-worn path that brought them far short of their destination was to be as academic as possible. The usual and unexpected reward was repudiation by other academics on the grounds that such work could only rarely be as worthy as the same work done in disciplinary departments.

In tracing the evolution of education schools in the United States, we have described the characteristics of the best-known institutions and asserted their influence on the much larger universe of schools, colleges, and departments of education. We explained their strategies in coping with their positions within prestigious research universities. We have, perhaps at excessive length, chronicled the factors that appear to shake their authority and periodically jeopardize their survival.

Our methods for assessing these topics have been those of social scientists: the historian and the policy analyst. While we do not contend that history only repeats itself, we do believe that present-day decision makers are advantaged by knowing this past.[4] To this end we have reconstructed developmental histories and made case compari-

3. "Ironically, even the instructional and evaluative practices of professors of education are not conspicuously guided by the fruits of educational research." University of California University-Wide Program Review Committee for Education, "The Role of the University of California in Precollegiate Education," October 1984, pp. 3, 22. (Hereafter, University of California Committee.)

4. Richard E. Neustadt and Ernest R. May, *Thinking in Time: The Uses of History for Decision Makers,* (New York: Free Press, 1986).

sons of a sample of schools of education. These techniques, while far from controlling for exogenous variables, do permit an identification of common features and an analysis of variation.

Now we alter our focus to present our views about how schools of education might reform themselves to serve better both the education profession and the nation's welfare. From our historical and contemporary institutional analyses, we (1) distill what we believe are the fundamental problems troubling education schools, (2) analyze the success and failures of their various organizational strategies, and (3) present an agenda of strategic and tactical advice for pursuing a more productive future.

Fundamental Problems

The difficulties besetting schools of education include those endemic to American culture, and there is little that schools of education as institutions can do to alleviate the situation. This is not meant as an apologia. As we conclude below, the basic strategies that schools of education have used to confront their difficulties have often been flawed. Nevertheless, it should be acknowledged that not all the problems are of their own making, nor can schools of education eliminate them, even with help. Some may be realities to be endured rather than problems awaiting solution.

Intellectual Ambivalence

In chapter 1 we referred to the ambivalence that Americans exhibit regarding matters of the intellect. Education policy generally, and public schools in particular, suffer the results of mixed emotions. On the one hand, the nation has increased the resources allocated to schools fivefold over the last half century. Yet on the other, the blame for almost every one of the nation's major social and political crises—be they domestic or international—is laid at the schoolhouse door. Schooling is seen as both the problem and the solution. While educated persons are esteemed, they are also better respected if neither their brains nor their schooling are flaunted. And if intellect is to be admired, a practical payoff is also expected.

Educators are admired in that almost every successful person recalls an influential teacher. But when it comes to that great American index of social status, income, few members of the public contend that teachers deserve to be paid as highly as physicians, attorneys, financiers, professional athletes, and entertainers. The places where teachers are trained, schools of education, are the crystalline embodiment of society's mixed view. And universities have contributed to this situation. As Donald Kennedy, president of Stanford University, told the audience celebrating the seventy-fifth anniversary of the Carnegie Foundation for the Advancement of Teaching in November 1981, "Only if the best institutions care about schools and their own schools of education will the public think that they are worth caring about; and nothing could be more clearly the business of America's academic leaders."[5]

Weak Technology

The knowledge base in modern medicine is said to double every seven years or so, posing dilemmas for medical educators. Education knowledge grows slowly, and practice changes hardly at all. As Larry Cuban has demonstrated, a 1937 teacher would not be shocked upon entering an American elementary or secondary school classroom in 1987. Certainly, the architecture of the school and the attire (and behavior?) of its inhabitants would be different, along with certain alterations in "mood." Fundamental components of instruction have, however, generally remained the same. Teachers still lecture and explain, students still listen (or pretend to), take notes, use workbooks, and do written assignments and (perhaps) homework. Now and then this routine is enlivened by use of a film or videotape. Increasingly, students have access to computers, both in school and at home, apparently used primarily for drill and practice. However, the attempt to alter instruction dramatically by means of electronics has not yet been made.

Not only has instruction remained labor intensive and stylistically familiar, it carries no mystique of hard won, esoteric professional prowess. An unusually able classroom teacher may put forth the performing energy and creativity of a Laurence Olivier or Sarah Bernhardt, and do it day after day. To the unknowing public it all appears simple. Physicians and scientists display their shiny, "high-tech" tools and communicate in a baffling argot. Laypersons realize fully that they could not readily step up to an operating table, jetliner flight panel, or nuclear power plant control console and be anything less than hopelessly confused. Nevertheless, many people believe they could step into a public school classroom tomorrow and perform credibly, as well perhaps as the assigned teacher. They have, after all, had on average

5. Stanford University, Donald Kennedy, "Advancing Knowledge," *Campus Report* 14, no. 10 (Dec. 1981), 14.

more than twelve years of watching teachers teach; and the more articulate critics of teachers and schools possess appreciably more experience than this, as students or as teachers themselves.

In reality, teaching large numbers of students how to read, interpreting complicated diagnostic test results to parents, or participating in the legal swamp of a "fair hearing" for a handicapped student requires training and experience for success. Nonetheless, the public perception that education is technologically weak—when stacked up against occupations such as surgery, engineering, and architecture—coupled with the belief that almost anyone can do it, reinforces the low status of the field.

A Feminized Occupation

Women are two-thirds of the nation's teachers, 80 percent of those in elementary schools. Educational administration, a male preserve for much of this century, may now be succumbing to the first signs of feminization. Throughout the preceding chapters we have compared teaching with the male-dominated fields, but closer analogies can be drawn with such other female-intensive occupations as nursing and social work. Immersed in an often unconsciously held sociology of occupations that "takes the lives of men as the norm," academics have failed to take women students and women professionals seriously.[6]

Growing numbers of women in conventional male fields such as law, medicine, and engineering, may someday alter public perceptions. Nevertheless, traditionally feminized occupations are not accorded equal social status and resources with male undertakings. This condition also contributes to the fundamental lack of status of education schools. As Adeline Levine suspected in 1968, MAT and nursing programs set in scholarly universities "may well be the ignored stepchildren in the university family. For the social researcher, the situa-

6. Linda Darling-Hammond criticized the Carnegie plan for imposing "a standard male model of professionalism" at a conference of researchers and educators in Washington, D.C., in December 1986. See also Sari Knopp Biklen, "Can Elementary Schoolteaching be a Career? A Search for New Ways of Understanding Women's Work," *Issues in Education* 3, no. 3 (Winter 1985):217. See also Jill McCalla Vickers, "Memoirs of an Ontological Exile: The Methodological Rebellions of Feminist Research" in *Feminism in Canada,* ed. Geraldine Finn and Angela Miles (Montreal: Black Rose Books, 1982), 27–46.

Jeanne Chall has observed that both women and practitioners are overlooked when professors of education identify leaders in American education. See Chall, "Restoring Dignity and Self-Worth to the Teacher," 170–74.

tion affords a fascinating topic. For the nursing and teaching professions, and particularly for the universities it should provide a challenge."[7] It should indeed!

A Muddled Mission

Status deprivation is woven deeply into the larger cultural, social, and economic fabric of the United States. Through concerted effort, schools of education might assist in ameliorating such conditions; they could themselves be less sexist institutions. But the problem is too encompassing for even the entire education establishment to solve. Especially as they have only compounded the problem by the befuddled and often detached manner in which they have conventionally defined and pursued their rightful mission. After eighty years or more of existence, the education professiorate should no longer be allowed the luxury of its "identity crisis," of its separation of academic training from clinical applications.

Major medical, business, law, and engineering schools all conduct research. Moreover, the greater the prestige of the campus on which they are located, the more likely these schools are to be affected by the primary orientation of their universities toward the conduct of research. Nevertheless, there is little question that their first objective remains preparing cadres of their respective professionals: physicians, business leaders, attorneys, and engineers. These institutions regard the maintenance of linkages to their professional organizations and practitioners as crucial to their health and welfare. Imagine, if you can, a medical or law school that consciously eschewed preparing practitioners for their often mundane duties; that decided to alter its charter so as to deemphasize its practical mission; or that deliberately sought to dampen or sever its ties with hospitals or the legal system. There may well be research institutes that indulge in such cleavages, places which consider that *all* their "customers" are other academics, but these are not *professional schools*.

The analogous scenarios for schools of education are not hypothetical situations, bizarre exceptions to conventional practice. Schools of education in research universities have exhibited embarrassing confusion and insecurity regarding their fundamental purpose. At various historic points they have sought security in chameleonlike efforts to take on the coloration of whatever academically acceptable undertaking was available to them. Stanford University virtually aban-

7. Levine, "Marital and Occupational Plans of Women," 72.

doned professional preparation, to build its school of education into one of the nation's finest behavioral and social science research institutes. When a new dean attempted to reorient the school prominently toward local schools and practitioner interests, the commitment of resources, time, and energies to this difficult task undermined faculty confidence and he was replaced by another individual even if not another ideology. Berkeley sought refuge during its leanest years in the almost single-minded pursuit of academic research and in efforts to ape the departments in the campus's dominating College of Letters and Science. The University of Chicago flirted twice with professional school status, but retreated, with undisguised relief, into the safety of that university's sanctioned pursuit of pure knowledge. Harvard's Graduate School of Education furnishes the most notorious example of "muddled mission," but that distinction may be partly a function of the fact that Harvard's is one of the few education schools having a history written with candor.

An argument could be made that unless the above-mentioned schools of education (and others known to the reader) had tried to find an acceptable campus niche, they would not be in existence today. After all, some historically prominent schools and departments of education simply disappeared. Johns Hopkins's was one, Duke's another, Yale's a third. Institutional demise is possible. So, the question might be asked, Would America be better off without any school or department of education, even if tainted by survivalism, at Chicago, Harvard, Stanford, Michigan, or Berkeley?

Relative to the potential professional contributions that powerful campuses such as these, and others, *could* have made to education, it is not clear to us that their mere survival is justified. The most obvious and beneficial outcome of their continued existence is that they have preserved resources—primarily buildings, faculty positions, and a tenuous connection with public education—that under visionary leadership and vigilant followership, in their schools and on their campuses, can be turned to more productive endeavors.

Our question is put differently by a state-wide committee appointed by David Pierpont Gardner, chairman of the National Commission on Excellence in Education, shortly after his selection as president of the University of California, "What kind of research, what kind of inquiry, justifies the maintenance of several dozen faculty members in major graduate schools of education where the commitment to professional programs for teachers and administrators is low and where time is devoted primarily to the scholarly activities of professors and graduate students?"[8] Its answer is also ours. Moreover, to the extent that the historic survival of unproductively focused schools of education, by virtue of their presence on major campuses, also distorted the missions of dozens of other less renowned teacher preparation colleges, then American education might have been better off if these elite education schools had joined the dinosaurs in extinction.

There are major schools of education which, though by no means pristinely professional, have maintained—in image or in fact—an alignment with the profession *and* survived. UCLA and Teachers College consistently have exhibited noticeable linkages to practicing educators. Michigan State University has undergone a daring and imaginative revitalization during the 1980s which, if sustained, also justifies its inclusion among model professional schools. Each of these three schools has oriented a clearly *visible* portion of its research, dissemination, or training activities to issues important to the field. Each opened various channels to practitioners for reporting, interpreting, and applying their work.

Each has, of course, periodically fallen prey to one or another fad or pressure. For example, during the 1960s both UCLA and Teachers College made unalloyed behavioral and social science faculty appointments, and gained reputational points in the process of pursuing "detached empiricism." In 1981, a Teachers College committee recommended that Ed.D. dissertations should follow "a rigorous research mode with structured hypotheses that are to be tested through the application of discipline-based analytical methods."[9] Nevertheless, each institution also retained a connection with and enjoys the loyalty of professional educators. Teachers College has done this by virtue of its size and "remembered self," as well as by new ventures. UCLA did so by a campus administration alert to the schooling needs of a vast metropolis and by an administrative style that permitted academic honors to be garnered by an entrepreneurial faculty while the dean and a few associates got the institution's name into the newspapers by conducting research on professional issues. (His successor announced, in 1986, the formation of *three* centers aimed at "helping teachers in the trenches."[10]) Michigan State has allocated major fac-

8. University of California Committee, 20.

9. Teachers College, Ed.D. Committee, "The Doctor of Education Program," 1971, p. 11.

10. Lewis C. Solomon, "Helping Teachers in the Trenches," *Education* [UCLA], 4, no. 1 (Spring 1986): 4–5.

ulty resources toward understanding and improving teaching in the most practical and applied manner. Many of its faculty and administrators have played a leading role in the cause of professionalizing teaching.

The fact that, in all of these institutions, there may have been more rhetoric than substance to their professional reachings out, and more praise than was deserved, suggests that even images of responsiveness matter to the hungry community of practitioners. It is heartening that one of these schools of education is private and the other two are public, and that two began as purely teacher training schools.

Dysfunctional Coping Strategies

In coping with their multifaceted and chronic status deprivation, schools of education on research-oriented campuses have pursued three survival strategies: (1) interdisciplinary appeasement, (2) academic intensification, and (3) a search for social science legitimacy. These are prototypical classifications. In reality, campuses have pursued mixtures and variations of each. These strategic categories are neither all encompassing nor mutually exclusive. Nevertheless, they provide a framework within which to examine what have been essentially defensive undertakings, aimed at organizational survival in a skeptical to hostile academic environment.

Interdisciplinary Appeasement

Schools of education have repeatedly accommodated themselves to other disciplines and campus departments. The focus of accommodation differed depending upon the prestige structure on a particular campus and the time period in question. The mechanisms of appeasement are many. The more typical tactics include joint faculty appointments and joint faculty recruitment and selection committees.

Joint Faculty Appointments. In recent years deans have tried to stretch the mantle of prestige and legitimacy from a high-status department over a school of education by the sharing of a faculty member. Joint faculty appointments between education and anthropology, sociology, economics, history, and psychology departments are the most common examples. In a few instances appointments have also been made between education and the sciences or foreign languages, and even between education and such formerly unlikely departments as English, linguistics, or classics.

The professed justification for multidepartment faculty appointments is at least twofold. First, education is alleged to be a rather hollow intellectual vessel which can be filled only by injecting knowledge generated in "real" disciplines. Hence, it follows that an individual steeped in a cognate field has more of substance to bring to education that one specializing in education itself. Second, it is argued that individuals are the best interdisciplinary bridges. Study groups and multidisciplinary training programs can be used, but they require cooperative activities which prove difficult to coordinate and sustain. A joint faculty appointment reduces such complexity.

That joint appointments are problematic is clear to any awake academic. If the faculty member is recruited to the joint position from a doctoral program in the cognate field, he or she has likely been well socialized to the academic and status norms of the particular discipline. Consequently, most social and behavioral scientists "almost invariably assume that there is less than meets the eye when they study educational events."[11]

When academic positions are in short supply, individuals will accept a dual appointment. As time passes, however, the prestige and larger intellectual community of the cognate department appears increasingly attractive. Additionally, in order to gain promotion, the joint appointee must satisfy the norms of both camps. Peers in the cognate field are unlikely to approve of a great deal of applied research and professional publication. Almost inevitably, the initially pliable joint appointee is seduced back into the status ambit of the cognate field and lost to education. While we agree with Donald Kennedy that education is a proper subject for investigation by social scientists, we also concur with Donna Kerr: "far more is at issue than finding new uses for the foundering social sciences."[12]

When joint appointments fail, the loss may not be limited to personal interest and research energy. There is often a more tangible deficit in transfer of the partial position in education to the mother discipline. University administrators, cognizant of the handicaps borne by education faculty, take pity and restore the misguided scholar fully to the rightful academic home. Education thus finds itself having its

11. J. Myron Atkin, "A New Evaluator Perspective for Professors of Education," in *The Professor of Education: An Assessment of Conditions,* ed. Ayres Bagley (Papers of the meeting of the Society of Professors of Education, University of Minnesota, College of Education, 1975), 83.

12. Donna H. Kerr, "Teaching Competence and Teacher Education in the United States," *Teachers College Record* 81, no. 3 (Spring 1983): 545.

low status confirmed while being deprived of a partial faculty position. Schools of education might better concentrate their joint appointments on well-regarded, established scholars who can relish the challenge and surmount, personally, the status and institutional obstacles.

Joint Recruitment. Another policy is to invite faculty from academic fields to participate in the recruitment and selection of education faculty. It is virtually inconceivable that a university department of physics or history would invite an education professor to participate in decisions regarding a professorial appointment or permit them to exercise a veto. It is hard to imagine a law school inviting outsiders to this most crucial activity. However, status-deprived schools of education routinely invite such invasive participation.

Professional pride aside, under the best of circumstances such external participation provides education schools with an objective and expert assessment of a faculty candidate's disciplinary qualifications. Under the worst of circumstances, it serves only to reinforce their lack of power. "They cannot even be relied upon to select qualified faculty if left to their own devices" is the unspoken conclusion. In some instances joint selection provides an opening for an outside department to make an appointment of an individual in whom it has an interest but for whom it has no position; this has sometimes stemmed from antinepotism regulations or departmental unwillingness to employ a married couple. In effect, the outside department acquires services and, perhaps, loyalties for which the school of education pays the price.

Academic Intensification

An even more widely practiced strategy has been to adopt the scholarly orientation of more prestigious undertakings on their campuses. This takes two major forms. One is the students' pursuit of the academic Ph.D. degree, rather than the professional doctorate. The second is the faculty's patterning their activities after academic research styles rather than involving themselves with the concerns of the practitioner.

Academic Degrees. Like engineering and chemistry schools and earlier science departments, many graduate schools of education on research campuses concentrate heavily on the now-traditional doctor of philosophy degree rather than on their own advanced professional degrees. In hierarchical terms, though certainly not in either academic or public prestige, the Doctor of Education ranks with the Doctor of Medicine (M.D.), Doctor of Dentistry (D.D.S.), and Doctor of Jurisprudence (J.D.). Neither the Ed.D. nor any of the above-listed professional degrees is hierarchically the equivalent of the Ph.D. degree, however.

In the United States the Ph.D. was introduced during the nineteenth century.[13] On research-oriented campuses, it remains the preferred emblem of academic standing. It is typically viewed as the property of the entire university, jealously guarded by the graduate school. To be able to offer the Ph.D. is thought to enhance the status of a school of education. To have a Ph.D. program cancelled, as happened at Michigan, is considered a devastating rebuff.

As evidence of doctoral-level achievement, a Ph.D. candidate is typically required to take an oral examination and to submit a dissertation based on original research. Most universities require that at least one faculty member of both the oral examination and dissertation committees be from outside the doctoral candidate's department or school. Education school doctoral candidates are subject to these same procedures. "Outside" faculty on doctoral committees represent the interests of the university, as opposed to those of the candidate's department, upholding disciplinary canons, research quality, and scholarly rigor. Such persons can be of legitimate academic assistance to the candidate in the conducting of research and in preparing for qualifying examinations. They can bring a refreshing alternative perspective to both a research problem and to the framing of examination questions, thus moderating parochialism within university disciplines. Moreover, because the student's concerns are the focal point of this cross-disciplinary faculty interaction, such joint committee undertakings are often of the highest professional nature. On balance, whether it be for education or any other university component, joint Ph.D. committees appear highly justified when academic degrees are involved. What then is the problem?

The problem is that many schools of education in their understandable wish to acquire the trappings of prestigious academic departments have virtually abandoned professional degrees to concentrate on awarding Ph.D.'s. If the impetus has come from their students, they have weakly acceded. In the process they have often rejected applied research of potential value to professional practitioners. It is

13. The definitive study of the transformation of leading American colleges into Ph.D.-hungry universities remains Laurence Veysey, *The Emergence of the American University* (Chicago: University of Chicago Press, 1965).

as if medical schools forewent M.D.'s and law schools J.D.'s in order to concentrate upon the preparation of academic researchers with Ph.D.'s.

The Doctor of Philosophy dissertation is required to be theoretically based and to advance knowledge. It must be grounded in the theoretical and research literature of an academic discipline. In order to meet scholarly standards, Ph.D. students with a practical problem that they wish to study are compelled to find some theory through which to frame the issues. We must acknowledge, of course, a long list of irrelevant, silly, superficial, or contorted Ed.D. dissertations. Our point, however, is that orienting a school of education toward the doctor of philosophy does not guarantee either good scholarship, higher regard from academic departments on campus, or more useful contributions to the field. Indeed, it sometimes has the opposite effect.

We laud the work of researchers interested in the field of education. There are literally scores of Ph.D. researchers who have made magnificent contributions to our understanding of, for example, the social and economic evolution and performance of schools. We hope there will be institutional mechanisms developed to assist an expanding stream of scholarly researchers interested in schooling, education, human learning, and instruction. Like that of many other observers, our concern is with the unproductive constraining of prospective educators by the pursuit of advanced doctoral research of little utility to them or to the field. By feeling they must focus their training and dissertations on topics that fit Ph.D. standards, many students have squandered their time, university resources, and an opportunity to gain more appropriate professional preparation. They and the world would be better served if they sought a true professional degree, the Ed.D., with research and practicum experiences geared to practical situations. The Ph.D. degree could then be reserved for those truly desiring a research career, while Ed.D. programs would establish high standards for those who go out into the community. John W. Gardner asserted that a society that did not value both philosophers and plumbers would find itself in a situation where neither its theories nor its pipes held water.[14] The same might be said of professional education. Ironically, the over-emphasis on ideas, the Ph.D., and the relative neglect of pipes, the Ed.D., have accompanied the weakening of schools of education as professional schools.

14. John W. Gardner, *Excellence: Can We Be Equal and Excellent, Too?* (New York: Harper & Co., 1961).

Aside from its inappropriate and wasteful nature, has the orientation of education doctoral students to the Ph.D. enhanced the *academic* status of the field? Are schools of education on prestigious campuses which award the Ph.D. more secure and held in higher regard than those on campuses restricted to the M.A. or Ed.D.? A moment's reflection gives the answer: "No." Supporting testimony could probably be obtained from education faculty at formerly Ph.D.-granting schools and departments of education such as Duke, Yale, and Michigan. We know that there are education professors who believe that the restriction of most doctorates to Ed.D.'s at Harvard and Columbia is a factor that prevents their education schools from standing at the very top of national ratings. We think, however, that other explanations can also be adduced.

Faculty Research. If promotions and merit salary increases are controlled by committees comprised of powerful members of academic departments, then education faculty quickly come to understand which research and publication efforts "count" and which do not. During the years of UCLA's rise to prominence as a nationally ranked graduate school of education, the faculty perceived that the wish of administrators and influential faculty to overtake Berkeley meant that they must tend unfailingly to getting published in respected, i.e., academic, refereed journals. For those who wished both to work with basic theories from the social and behavioral sciences *and* to develop more effective instructional techniques, the "window of opportunity" seemed narrow at times.

The result of this ethos is that education faculty veer away from professionally demanding activities and toward those understood and hence rewarded in academic departments. The tactic may work, and does, for individual faculty; many career rewards and rapid promotions are the proof. Seldom, however, will an education faculty member be genuinely acknowledged on the campus for having conducted an outstanding piece of research; the shadow of relative status deprivation prevents it in most cases. Accolades and public honors are typically reserved for faculty in the most prestigious fields.

A virtually exclusive academic research agenda in education forges a double-edged sword of disregard and disappointment. On the one side, the absence of faculty research focused on problems of professional practice alienates practitioners from schools of education. When pursued in a school of education a scholarly paper such as "Gentlemen's Athletics at Oxford between 1880 and 1890"—an actual topic not of our creation—raises questions. Academics wonder why it is not the product of a department of history or, perhaps, sociology. Its irrelevance to their day-to-day world causes teachers, principals, and superintendents to ask why public funds support schools of education and educational research institutes.

The Route of Social Science Legitimacy

The appointment of social scientists as faculty members is, we have argued, another strategic accommodation practiced by status-anxious education schools. A general lack of school experience on the part of such faculty has done little to endear them to alumni or practitioners. Nor have the recommended post-doctoral appointments appeared, which could have been used to acquire first-hand knowledge of the professional culture and its concerns. Nevertheless, on at least one dimension, these social science appointments appear to have been successful.

The decades of the 1960s and 1970s mark a high point in the history of educational research. More exciting research paradigms, reports, and findings were produced in this period than during any previously comparable time span—except, perhaps, when Edward L. Thorndike and John Dewey were pursuing their divergent paths. The recent period is one of remarkable creativity. The relationship between school resources and student outcomes was explored with new intensity. Intrastate school finance patterns were mapped in a sophisticated fashion and artful new legal theories were designed to guide resource equalization throughout the states. Cost-benefit analysis was at last applied to instructional processes with the hope of devising policy and guidelines for practice. Imaginative strategies were developed for evaluating the outcomes of many federally sponsored compensatory education programs. Fundamentally different theoretical and methodological perspectives appeared in schools of education. New research reporting journals were initiated and additional education–social science research organizations were formed. Membership in the American Educational Research Association skyrocketed.

Sheldon White has wondered if researchers in disciplinary departments, schools of education, contract firms, and the labs and centers are being linked with school practitioners in "an overarching enterprise that begins and ends in educational practice." If so, "all share an enterprise that is concerned not with making research a commodity, or with making data a commodity, or with discovering 'the facts,' but with putting together intellectual instruments by which educators can think about what they do to make it better."[15] Would that educational research yet deserved such a nimbus!

The infusion of social science and social scientists into education schools had, unfortunately, less unifying and practice-sensitive consequences. The education school curriculum in advanced degree programs did reflect social science disciplinary and research interests. Courses in the politics, economics, sociology, and anthropology of education appeared in catalogues and bulletins. As a part of the program in a cognate department, such courses easily could be, and sometimes were taught in education schools by individuals holding a Ph.D. in the disciplinary field, who were generally innocent of any direct professional experience in schools. Texts and reading materials were drawn from the cognate field and expanded the range of reading and discussion for education students in often exciting ways.

There were costs as well as benefits, however. These offerings contributed to a further fragmentation of the curriculum as they were usually not coordinated with existing courses. Thus, students found a cafeteria-like array of social science subject-matter areas with few integrative course offerings; disciplinary specialization made developing and teaching such courses unattractive and the other members of the faculty were intimidated or insufficiently sensitive to curricular considerations. As a consequence, students were encouraged to become "expert" in one or two of the social science specialities, but not pressed to apply their content. There were few, *and decreasing,* efforts to build a common core of knowledge useful to practitioners.

Whereas medical schools were forced to select from the growing range of scientific knowledge potentially useful for a physician to know and weave that into a generally uniform and remarkably stable set of curricular arrangements taken by medical students prior to specializing, education schools were permitting their doctoral candidates to specialize almost from the outset. There was seldom a first-year common education school curriculum as required by most law schools. Nathan Glazer has characterized the curriculum of the schools of the "minor professions" as so insecure that "radical revolutions" were fomented every decade or so.[16]

Educational psychologists pursued one curriculum, educational

15. Sheldon White, "Federal Programs in Educational Research: Responses," *Harvard Educational Review,* 52, no. 4 (Nov. 1982):555–56.

16. Glazer, "Schools," 351.

historians another, school administrators yet another. An administrator in training might come to know a great deal about economics, politics, and organizational sociology, but little regarding the basis of disputes about methods of reading instruction, or testing programs, or the burning issues in the mathematics curriculum. An educational psychologist might be able to act virtually the same way as a clinical psychologist in private practice, but have little exposure to such professionally relevant matters as the consequence of collective bargaining for school finance or the interactions of racial desegregation policy and tracking programs. Intense subject specialization also reinforced the academic research emphasis and the misguided pursuit of the doctor of philosophy degree discussed above.

At the height of the social science movement in education schools, Nathan Glazer wrote:

> This replacement of experienced members of the profession for which students are training by members of academic disciplines undoubtedly brings into the school and into the training of students more sophisticated knowledge. It is rather more questionable whether this is the most useful knowledge for the intended occupation. *It is certainly unquestionable, however, that it will add to the prestige of the school and advance the prestige of the profession if scholars from established disciplines can be induced to join the staff and participate in the training.* [Emphasis added.][17]

Glazer's assertion is consistent with the views of education school deans and those who advised them, and with the conventional wisdom of the time. It may not, however, be a historically warrantable conclusion. *Did* such new appointments bring added prestige? If so was it a temporary benefit until the novelty wore off and the incumbents began to be tagged as "educationists?" For example, Stanford's School of Education became a virtual *Who's Who* of social scientists in the 1970s. Other academics on the campus probably nodded their heads approvingly upon hearing that a famous cultural anthropologist was leaving Harvard to join the education school at a handsome salary. This individual and others like him may have attracted a nucleus of first-rate social science doctoral students. Teacher trainees and administrative credential candidates, however, seldom if ever saw him as an instructor, local and regional education practitioners never heard

17. Ibid.

of him unless they had read one of his books in their undergraduate days, and his research bore only the most tangential relationship to education. This is a strange and expensive kind of prestige. It is as if the National Football League Tampa Bay Buccaneers decided to enhance their reputation by adding baseball Hall of Fame outfielder Willie Mays to their roster. It might make headlines, but it was unlikely to make touchdowns and win games.

Much of the growth in social science faculty appointments occurred shortly before and during the steep decline in the 1970s in public school enrollments and the slackening demand for new teachers. It is not possible, therefore, to make a valid assessment of whether this strategy would eventually have added to the status of schools of education had the resource base and demand for graduates remained stable. What can be said is that it did little to forestall the threats which began to develop in the late 1960s. These were among the most perilous times in the history of schools of education, and neither all the kings' men nor all the social scientists could put schools of education back together again.

Proposed Reforms

The strategies of appeasement and accommodation described above generally failed. Despite a decades-long ameliorative posture, education schools found themselves in as great a jeopardy during the 1970s and early 1980s as at any point in their histories. In their attempts to compensate for their status-deprived condition, education schools have legitimated, not repudiated, it.

We think that the only successful strategy is to identify a correct professional purpose which will strengthen American education, then align education school activities in a manner consistent with that course of action. Continual attempts to compensate, supplicate, and accommodate higher status opinion on university campuses waste time and siphon energy from the more important task of preparing teachers and other professional educators in the most effective and professionally enhancing fashion possible. Are there any guides into this future? In 1986 two provocative, potentially far-reaching reports were distributed regarding teachers and teaching training. In educational policy circles they came to be known as the Carnegie report and the Holmes Group report. Time will tell if they are "merely the latest skirmish in a war that has gone on for centuries" about teachers and their preparation.[18] In what follows we seek to relate their principal features to our thesis.

The Carnegie Report

The more sweeping and far-sighted of the two, *A Nation Prepared: Teachers for the Twenty-first Century,* was issued by the Task Force on Teaching as a Profession sponsored by the Carnegie Forum on Education and the Economy. This 135-page report undertook a comprehensive analysis of teaching and teachers in the United States in the context of international economic competition. It offered an eight-point reform agenda that reaches deeply into the manner in which schools are organized and managed and teachers recruited and trained. The report was released in May 1986 with an unusually effective media campaign. The composition of the panel's membership assisted greatly in attracting public and professional attention. The report's signers included high-level business, government, foundation, and media executives, as well as the California chief state school officer and the heads of the American Federation of Teachers and the National Education Association. Its analysis of teaching in the United States and its comprehensive recommendations underscored points which teachers and teacher leaders had been making ever more insistently, since the school reform movement coalesced in 1983.

The Carnegie report directed three of its core recommendations to areas affecting teacher education and schools of education. The report urged that teachers not be admitted to professional preparation programs until they have completed a baccalaureate program in an arts or science subject-matter area. If this idea were pursued fully, all schools of education in the nation would, in effect, become graduate-level institutions.

The Carnegie report also recommended the establishment of a National Board for Professional Teaching Standards that would have regional and state representatives. The Board and its components would be made up primarily of practicing teachers, would be responsible for specifying what effective instructors need to learn in their preparation programs, and would oversee development and administration of procedures to assess whether or not prospective teachers met such standards. Periodic recertification was recommended as a

18. Lawrence A. Cremin, Preface to *Teacher Education in America: A Documentary History,* ed. Merle L. Borrowman (New York: Teachers College, Press, 1965), vii.

way to ensure that teachers would maintain currency in the substantive advances of their subject-matter and pedagogical fields.

The report further recommended that schools of education offer a professionally oriented master of teaching degree. Acquiring this degree would necessitate both internships and residencies in schools, as well as acquisition of systematic knowledge regarding learning, and instruction. The report acknowledges that schools of education cannot easily implement changes such as these by themselves. A spectrum of additional reforms must take place, such as elevating teacher salaries, establishing a two-tier professional career ladder, eliminating emergency credentials and other backdoor methods for becoming teachers, and creating schoolwide instructional performance incentives. These reforms were declared essential in order to render teaching a sufficiently attractive career that individuals would make the greater commitment required to become teachers; in the absence of such changes, existing economic and psychic returns do not justify the necessary added investment. We think the Carnegie report exhibits a proper understanding of the interconnected nature of America's educational problems.

In some ways the outstanding feature of the Carnegie report is the unprecedented recognition it gives to the qualities and experiences of teachers. The "accumulated knowledge of exceptional teachers" would be central to the process of setting professional standards. Board-certified teachers would determine most of the membership of the National Board.

Why should the public be willing to grant teachers recognition and authority, and elevate their salaries, without a concomitant guarantee of more effective teaching? Similarly, why should an able individual plan to enter teaching without the prospect of advancement and professional compensation? Why should a school of education alter its curriculum and entry standards, and subject itself to the risk of declining admissions, if the state does not correspondingly elevate teacher credential requirements and eliminate the backdoor entry to instructional positions? If the report is flawed, the weaknesses are to be found at those points where the proposals have to be translated into practical policy.

Where does one break this policy circle? Seemingly, for anything to happen, everything must happen at once. This is not, however, necessary; there are ways to invade this loop. For example, phasing out emergency credentials while simultaneously elevating licensing requirements could expand education school enrollments. Increased enrollments could provide these schools with the added resources they need to begin to revise their curricula and upgrade their faculties. This would be a good first step, and one whose costs are within bounds.

Higher teacher salaries and a phased-in professional career ladder would seem to be another natural policy package. Higher salaries are justified in the eyes of policy makers only if there is a commensurate increase in teacher quality. Hence, higher salaries need to be initiated at the same time as career ladders to demonstrate the connection between money and quality. Also, career ladders make it possible for teachers to aspire to higher pay, but it is not a guarantee of higher pay for every teacher. Hence, higher salaries can be a manageable added expense for a state. Whatever the logical attractions of these proposals, however, they will not be adopted readily by state policy makers. To the Carnegie Forum's credit, it has retained staff to assist states in developing implementation details.

The Holmes Group Report

Published almost simultaneously with the Carnegie Report, *Tomorrow's Teachers: A Report of the Holmes Group* concentrates on teacher training and the role of higher education in creating a three-tier teacher career ladder. Like the Carnegie report, the Holmes Group report recognizes schools of education as suffering from the status deprivation plaguing almost all of America's education system. Its recommendations, though restricted primarily to education school reforms, fully acknowledges the necessity for systemwide change.

The association bears the name of Henry W. Holmes, dean of the Harvard Graduate School of Education from 1920 to 1940, and includes deans of the nation's largest and most well-regarded schools of education. With financial assistance from several philanthropic foundations, the Holmes group met repeatedly throughout the mid-1980s and fabricated an extensive agenda of reform proposals for education schools and teacher preparation. Prime among these is the recommendation that a professional career ladder be established for teachers that, in effect, would prevent advancement to tenure of any individual who does not have a full understanding of a subject-matter field and a fifth-year of graduate preparation in pedagogy. The three tiers recommended would be Instructors (college graduates with little or no professional training), Professional Teachers (having a master's degree in teaching), and Career Professional Teachers (typically with a doctorate or equivalent from a graduate school of education).

The Holmes Group's recommendations endorse the long-heard and occasionally practiced proposition that undergraduates hoping to become teachers should major in disciplines which are the core subjects of the schools' curriculum. In order to render such a change more practicable, they describe the alterations necessary in America's liberal arts curriculum, at the same time reinforcing other complaints that undergraduate curricula have become increasingly fragmented and unjustifiably specialized. The Group proposes sponsoring a national conference on the role of the liberal arts in teacher education. The plea is for a restructuring of liberal arts and sciences majors such that an undergraduate could come to understand the fundamental structure of knowledge in those major subject-matter fields. In an echo of turn-of-the-century discussions, the Holmes Group argues that the teaching in liberal arts courses should be improved so that the instructors themselves are models for their students and understand the pedagogy connected with their field of study.

Institutions with professional teacher training programs are admonished to assess and reform their curricula so that they no longer offer "sprawling and often scattered courses of study." Also, "generic" methods courses are to be abolished and replaced by instruction in the pedagogical principles specific to the subject matter at hand. In these recommendations, the Holmes Group acknowledges the balkanization which has also occurred in education school offerings, particularly in response to the social science movement and the laissez-faire approach associated with the student protest movement on American campuses.[19]

Researchers increasingly insist that the appropriate manner and format for teaching, for example, mathematics are different from the way in which students should be taught reading or writing. Hence, the pedagogical reforms advocated by the Holmes Group stress developing understanding of the inherent architecture of the various fields of knowledge and the necessity to reflect this structure in the manner and sequence in which material is presented to learners. Like the Carnegie Forum, the Holmes Group assumes that a body of coherent, scientific knowledge now exists on teaching and learning. Assertions to this effect, however, are not documented.

The Holmes Group also advocates a spectrum of exchanges between professional schools of education and schools in which teachers instruct. This is presented as a two-way exchange with universities making "better use of expert teachers in the education of other teach-

19. Alan Bloom, *The Closing of the American Mind* (New York: Simon & Schuster, 1987).

ers."[20] School of education faculty would appear in schools not only to conduct research but also to interact with career teachers and cooperate better in supervising teacher trainees. Schools are seen as an opportunity to apply educational research, linking it to practice in much the same manner as teaching hospitals do for the medical field—a concept that was prominent in the rhetoric of the earliest university schools of education and sometimes practiced in the better normal schools. In no sense, however, is the impression conveyed that teachers are equal partners. A tone of historically familiar condescension toward teachers in general may be read in various places in the report.[21] As the Group's proposals endorse graduate schools of education and give them a role in shaping teaching and teachers that they have often evaded before, critics have faulted the Group for being both self-serving and hypocritical.

The Holmes Group had attracted more than one hundred member teacher-education institutions by 1988. Each member institution pledged itself to implement the reform agenda. A number of major universities, however, such as the University of North Carolina, chose not to join. A major point of controversy is the proposed abolition of undergraduate courses and majors in education. Such changes would reduce the budgets of many institutions and appear threatening as a consequence. There is also the perception that elementary school teacher preparation is slighted or its requirements misunderstood in the Holmes Group's reform agenda for teacher education and certification.

Going Beyond the Reports

We regard both the Carnegie and Holmes Group reports as thoughtful efforts to render American education and teaching more effective. We propose, however, additional steps, ones that address more directly our central interest in the location of schools of education between academic and professional constituencies. The reforms they advocate, and with which we are in some agreement, are not likely to occur unless several further actions are taken. Neither of the reports sufficiently acknowledges the fundamental historic dynamics of education schools in elite research universities. The reforms being advocated will require, to borrow and underscore the Holmes Group's words, "*un-*

20. The Holmes Group, *Tomorrow's Teachers,* 4.
21. William R. Johnson, "Empowering Practitioners," 221–40.

precedented cooperation across departmental and disciplinary lines within universities."[22] Given the preference of university schools and departments "to operate within real or imagined jurisdictional boundaries rather than to sanctify commonalities with joint participation," the incentives to stimulate such unknown cooperation are simply not present.[23]

Members of the Holmes group must have known with more firsthand intensity than any other individuals the pain and discouragement of seeking intracampus collaboration in educational research and teacher preparation. Their lack of attention to the manner in which cooperation could be induced is an important oversight. Perhaps they thought higher salaries for teachers would elevate education's campus status much in the manner affecting business and engineering schools in the early 1980s, when a resurgence in American trust in the private sector changed the attitudes of many college students. This, in turn, forced administrators and faculty leaders, however grudgingly, to appropriate resources, if not to allocate status, to these long-suspect units. Market demand even overcame the effects of the increase of women students in undergraduate business and MBA programs.

The ability of teaching to attract again some of the brightest students in America's colleges and universities is essential. Unless this happens it is feared that elite universities will be sorely tempted to leave all teacher education to other colleges and universities, further damaging teaching's intellectual, economic, and social status. Potential earnings are implicated, although they are not the only incentives in choosing teaching as a career. Another is the presence or absence of social approval. Certainly, in time, if salaries were elevated significantly such that teaching was more highly regarded by the overall public, then chemistry and classics professors might consent to praise their students' choice to teach and demonstrate support by cooperating with the school of education on their campuses. Sufficient economic incentives are, however, likely to be a long time in coming. This might occur at approximately the same time that mean teacher sala-

22. Holmes Group, *Tomorrow's Teachers,* 18.

23. Henry Levin, in Mayhew et al., *Educational Leadership,* 50. Levin proposes three conditions that promote programs across departmental lines: (1) a common interest in developing programs in areas not serviced; (2) the possibility of substantial cost savings or program enhancement by sharing student and faculty resources; (3) financial incentives from university or extramural sources.

ries in the United States approximate $50,000 annually in terms of 1988 purchasing power; in 1985, they averaged less than half that amount.[24]

Mechanisms must be identified which can motivate change more rapidly. What is needed is one or more levers which will induce academic departments to pay productive attention to teacher preparation because not to do so would jeopardize something they care about a great deal, something causing them to risk their status by cooperating with schools of education. We believe that several such levers exist. These levers depend primarily upon the undergraduate enrollments that support graduate instruction and faculty research. If joint action on the part of education schools, possibly operating through the Holmes Group, in close cooperation with a National Teaching Professional Standards Board, began to restrict education entry to holders of bachelor degrees who possess more coherent liberal arts undergraduate majors than now prevail at most colleges, then even prestigious departments might have to pay attention to the nature of their liberal arts curriculum. Disciplinary faculty may never truly come to regard schools of education highly—as they have never come to regard business, city planning, and engineering schools highly, and still retain grave doubts about law and medical schools. Such regard is irrelevant. Schools of education do not require campus regard; they do, whether or not they admit it, need sufficient professional and public regard to survive. Some other problems, not all, will solve themselves following attainment of that objective.

In the next section we illustrate the changes schools of education need to make in order to enhance their professional and public regard and reach their ultimate objective: to improve their effectiveness in preparing professional teachers and other education leaders. This is surely not the only possible menu of useful changes; nor it is a menu which may prove appropriate for all time and all institutions. However, we believe it is a useful means of elevating and concentrating their focus.

The Whale's Tail: Strategies for Reform

In the course of obtaining information and verifying perceptions for the case analyses contained in the preceding chapter, we interviewed

24. The figure is an estimate produced by the National Education Association. See National Center for Education Statistics, *The Condition of Education, 1985,* (Washington, D.C.: National Center for Education Statistics, 1985).

the chancellor of the University of California at Berkeley, Ira Michael Heyman. After we had discussed numerous factual components of his decision to revitalize Berkeley's graduate school of education, Heyman stated that *"If you want people to think you are a whale, then you should act like a whale."* What his remark captured was that schools of education, through their self-perceptions and self-fulfilling actions, masochistically invited much of the status deprivation they have experienced. By believing themselves to be higher education's second-class citizens, they have acted accordingly, further tarnishing their image.

Full revitalization will depend crucially upon several factors, among them a purging of self-demeaning attitudes. We are not so naïve, we hope, as to believe that the chronically displayed low academic status, scholarly self-doubt, and professional confusion from which schools of education have suffered throughout this century, and which their predecessor institutions had in even larger measure, will disappear through creation of a Madison Avenue–style new "image." We concur with Heyman, however, at least to the degree that "If you want people to believe you are a whale, one of the things you had better do is start acting like a whale." Here are our prescriptions for new "WHALES." They should occasion no surprise given our earlier analyses.

Reorient the Profession in Fundamental Ways

The major mission of schools of education should be the enhancement of education through the preparation of educators, the study of the educative process, and the study of schooling as a social institution. As John Best has observed, the challenge before schools of education is quite different from that confronting the specialist in politics in a department of political science; concerned with building the discipline, he or she is under no obligation to train county clerks, city managers, and state legislators, and to improve their performance by conducting research directed toward that end.[25] In order to accomplish *their* charter, however, schools of education must take the profession of education, not academia, as their main point of reference. It is not sufficient to say that the greatest strength of schools of education is that they are the only places available to look at fundamental issues

25. John Best, "Death and Taxes and Politics of Education: The State of the Field of Educational Studies in Relation to Policy Making in Education" (Presidential Address, American Educational Studies Association, Washington D.C., 2 Nov. 1978).

from a variety of disciplinary perspectives. They have been doing so for more than half a century without appreciable effect on professional practice.[26] It is time for many institutions to shift their gears.

We are not advocating a severence of ties with colleges and universities. The Holmes Group report rightly asserts that no major occupational undertaking has achieved professional status without institutional linkage to higher education. Moreover, an enormous amount of ignorance and misconception remains about such central educational matters as instruction, learning, the structures within which they take place, how teachers acquire knowledge, and the place of schooling in society.[27] These matters will continue to require systematic research of a kind best conducted in universities—although that is not the only kind of research which education schools should foster. Thus, maintaining the link to higher education is important. This should be, however, *the secondary relationship in determining the essential character of education schools.* Their prime orientation should be to educate practitioners, and education faculty must be made more cognizant of the technical or experiential culture of schooling for that to happen.[28] To require less is to continue to frustrate both research and training activities. We think it sound policy that faculty appointments in education redress the imbalance that exists on many graduate school faculties by including substantial professional criteria in the guidelines and processes of faculty appraisal.[29] This appraisal should cover both appointment and promotion decisions.

In redirecting themselves to the profession they should serve, schools of education should evaluate the productive activities and

26. Or consider the observation that "Teachers, after nearly forty years of the study of education in universities, were still not professionals at all." See Powell, "University Schools of Education," 13.

27. An example of the kind of inquiry that has recently entered the literature is Michael Huberman's "What Knowledge Is of Most Worth to Teachers? A Knowledge-Use Perspective," *Teaching and Teacher Education* 1, no. 3 (1985): 251–62.

28. Accumulating evidence underscores this point: "Significant improvement in the learning of children and youth requires simultaneous focus on both those who work in schools and the school circumstances within which teaching and learning proceed." See University of California Committee, 26.

29. This is the position of the above-cited committee, chaired by John Goodlad: "We recommend that the employment, promotion, and rewards for professors of education be based on criteria recognizing the distinctively educational character of their scholarly work and professional contributions." It should be noted that this was one of the recommendations of the Committee to which the Academic Senate Committee on Educational Policy at Berkeley reacted with caution. Ibid., 11, 23.

outlook of other professional schools such as engineering, architecture, medicine, and law. This does not mean, however, that we are determined that schools of education should help teachers to reach some sociologically defined nirvana called "true profession" to replace its labels of "semi-profession" and "women's profession." Static and universal criteria of professionalism are experiential untruths; they are not based upon the histories of professional communities of interest. Today's teacher or school administrator has not been evenly advanced over his or her predecessor according to traditional but static concepts of professionalization. The increasingly rule-bound practice of teaching is "deprofessionalizing," for example, but progressively more professionals of all kinds labor in bureaucratic organizations. Today's physician is unlike today's attorney in historically determined and interesting ways; neither one can be, however, a role model for teachers nor do their divergent histories furnish a dependable guide on "how to professionalize."

Nor does the reorientation of schools of education to the education profession—rather than to the academic profession—suggest that professors of education must become traveling medicine men, concocting and hawking nostrums for the relief of the many debilitating ailments encountered in teaching and managing schools. As one of our informants cogently phrased it, schools can always generate more problems than we education professors can solve, or can solve in the time before practitioners get bored with a particular issue or are distracted by another urgent matter. Yet, as difficult (and dangerous) as such concessions to responsiveness may be, it is probably simpler than pursuing the twin processes we think are crucial; one, the development of mutual understanding and tolerance of the necessary and desirable differences in the natural instincts of the professor and the practitioner, and, two, the patient enlargement of the area of their shared concern and collaborations.

As we have made clear in earlier chapters, professional schools are not mere auxiliaries to their professions. They must be both independent and critical on important dimensions. We need institutional mechanisms to compound the "complimentary interests and insights" of professors and practitioners, for one cannot "overstate the propensity of speculative minds to lose all perception of reality nor the tendency of practitioners to lose their perception of possibility."[30]

Schools of education would be irresponsible if they pandered to the prejudices of the profession as they do to those of the academy. To

30. Borrowman, "About Professors of Education," 60.

apply a distinction developed by David R. Olson, researchers traditionally deal in "texts" (written, formalized, logical, context-free language) while practitioners deal in "utterances" (oral, interpersonal, and context-rich language).[31] These are artifacts of different cultures, and that fact and its implications need recognition by both parties. The pursuit of basic research in education, something that will be done only in universities, appears to create or perceive problems where there were none to be seen, while ignoring the opportunities to "retire" those that are making teachers' and administrators' daily experiences problematic and often unproductive.[32] But the possibility of working upon *both* "discovered problems" and "presented problems" is enhanced when researchers and practitioners are partners in asking questions and determining priorities in the labor of constructing answers.[33] In so doing, school professionals, teachers' organizations, and even whole school faculties will work with professional school faculties in ways *not* characteristic of the relations of law and medical schools to individual physicians and lawyers, bar associations, and medical societies.[34]

This will not be easy. As William R. Johnson notes, "Research universities will not readily relinquish the view that educational research rather than practitioner wisdom will be the chief transforming agent of the public school."[35] A professional school's responsibility is to work with practitioners in ways that enrich their wisdom. It cannot be done simply by top-down methods, however well intended. Thus,

31. David. R. Olson, "From Utterance to Text," *Harvard Educational Review* 47, no. 3 (August 1977): 257–81.

32. Another way of stating this is that "The university's engagement with the enigmatic rather than the apparent, the ultimate rather than the immediate, the fundamental rather than the pragmatic, renders it liable to the charge that it is not doing anything useful or practical"; J. W. Getzels, "Paradigm and Practice: On the Impact of Basic Research in Education," *Impact of Research on Education: Some Case Studies,* ed. Patrick W. Suppes (Washington, D.C.: National Academy of Education, 1978), 506, 508.

33. Arthur Powell points out that an additional difficulty is the questionable assumption that authoritative knowledge for education rests on research alone. "Unlike some other fields, education has not learned how to codify, preserve, and transmit the lore of successful experience." In Powell, "University Schools of Education," 20.

34. See, however, the plan of the Department of Electrical Engineering and Computer Science at the Massachusetts Institute of Technology, which called for "lifelong cooperative education" with engineering and managerial professionals. Cited in Ernest A. Lynton, "The Nature of the College and General Education: Questions in an Age of High Technology," Alden Seminar in Higher Education, 20 January 1983, (University of Massachusetts, Boston), 20.

35. William R. Johnson, "Empowering Practitioners," 240.

even if it were possible, we do not advocate the mindless aping of other professional schools. No one of them meets completely the criteria necessary for a renaissance in education. For example, many engineering and business schools have become estranged from the manufacturing and commercial sectors of the American economy, although sometimes for good reason. Business school graduates have allowed many industries to deteriorate because of overtechnical or inappropriate financial training at the expense of intense knowledge of manufacturing and general societal understanding. Medical schools are faulted for their failures in teaching concepts related to public health and prevention of illness, the treatment of female and aging patients, the health and medical needs of many underserved groups, and, indeed, for allowing a diminished concern with patients as subjects rather than as the objects of medical science. Engineering schools, it is said, lack clinical experiences and their graduates are sometimes incompetent in their first jobs.[36] Law schools only reluctantly rely upon the application of either scientific or social scientific findings to advance legal knowledge, and ethical issues in legal practice have not been accorded the weight that many lawyers and laymen think essential.

Schools of education will have to evolve their own professional amalgam, but there are some constructive elements for them to consider. The productive connection to the field of many law schools, the emphasis given to the practical application of research results found in many medical schools, and the high standards for preparing graduates characteristic of many engineering schools are all potential features in a new professional blend for education schools. "Medical schools and law schools offer unabashedly practical training; they are not distinct disciplines but crafts based on applied science," writes Michael Katz. "Their honesty of purpose, coupled with the competence and the high social standing of their graduates, creates respectability within universities."[37] If that last attribute is not available to the schools of education, the first two are decidedly within its reach.

In one way, at least, the school, college, or department of education should be like the medical school: the majority of the faculty should be qualified and engaged in the training of beginning profes-

36. For a representative sample of such criticisms, see Fred M. Hechinger, "Business Schools Criticized," *New York Times,* 13 April 1982; David E. Sanger, "Harvard Business School at 75," *New York Times,* 5 March 1984; "Why Engineering Deans Worry a Lot," *Fortune* 105, no. 1 (11 Jan. 1982): 84–90.

37. Katz, "From Theory to Survey," 331.

sionals. This activity need not be unproductive of benefits to one's research agenda. If it is true, as we think it is, that "field-generated inquiries are at least as likely as discipline-generated inquiries to advance the base of knowledge relevant to both the field of study and educational practice," competent researchers should not suffer unduly and educational advance will profit; schools of education could become more like schools of agriculture: places of programmatic research "designed to 'swarm all over a problem.'"[38] That is, after all, the *raison d'être* of schools of education. This may be an especially propitious time for professional school teacher-researchers also to recall their social mission, as other disciplines are questioning traditional research paradigms, making interdisciplinary forays, involving practitioners in research and "flocking to the real world" for phenomena to investigate.[39] What, then, are the tactical elements of such a reorientation?

Advocate National Professional Standards. We think the Carnegie Forum proposal for national professional standards is connected to the reform of education schools as a group. By adopting the general strategy we espouse, as well as the individual tactics we are about to describe, particular schools may escape the present vale of deprived status, but the elevation of education schools as a genre would be aided by the development of a national board capable of appraising individual capability and issuing a professional certificate. National standards, if set sufficiently high so as not to function as the lowest common denominator to which participants can agree, could upgrade the curricula of all schools of education. By defining, with teachers, the minimum of education-related knowledge, skills, and techniques that teachers must master in order to obtain a nationally acknowledged professional certificate, the National Professional Standards Board could exercise enormous leverage. This would require incorporating knowledge of practice in which practitioners *believe.* Individual schools of education would have little choice but to alter their offerings, requirements, and instructional performance. Although campus-wide bodies to set policies and requirement in the area of teacher education have commonly dissolved in the past as academicians lost interest, the mechanism of board certification could keep the pressure

38. University of California Committee, 21–23.

39. See the special issue of *Chronicle of Higher Education* 31, no. 1 (4 Sept. 1985), esp. 11–14, 18.

on academic departments to develop strong major programs for those who would teach.

In promulgating the possible advantages of a National Professional Teacher Standards Board, we assume that the major mechanism upon which it would depend is individual *candidate appraisal,* not program approval. The assessment must be of both the candidate's subject-matter knowledge and ability to perform as a teacher. If national certification comes to rest upon a candidate's completion of a prescribed set of courses at accredited teacher training institutions, the new system could prove to be a national repetition of the pathetically inadequate state mechanism presently used for licensing teachers. Individual appraisal assuredly will necessitate written examinations in order to assess subject-matter knowledge and information regarding important pedagogical principles in areas such as testing, human development, and classroom management. In addition, national appraisal boards should rely upon costly but justifiable assessment formats such as oral interview panels, role playing, case analysis, videotaped simulations, and other kinds of professional problem-solving exercises. Requiring that a candidate successfully complete an accredited fifth year teacher training program could serve as a prerequisite for taking a national professional standards board examination, but formal preparation should not, by itself, substitute for individual appraisal of professional competence.

Abandon the Undergraduate Major. In 1975, David Clark and Gerald Marker argued convincingly, we think, that "until *no* institutions offer teacher education at the undergraduate level, *all* institutions will offer teacher education at that level. And this feature of the present institution of teacher education is at the root of many of the most serious problems in the field."[40]

Ending teacher education as an undergraduate major is a step toward enhancing the profession, although not sufficient in itself as the case of California, where there are no such majors, demonstrates. There are at least three unhappy consequences to continuing to permit undergraduates to declare education as a major. First, it encourages academic departments to crowd the professional curriculum to the interstices between general education and subject-matter preparation. Second, courses in pedagogy and student teaching at the undergraduate level crowd out important subject-matter content that all teachers need, including those preparing for elementary school ca-

40. Clark and Marker, "Institutionalization," 85.

reers. Third, undergraduate education on most campuses lacks the priority and resources available to graduate students. It "justifies" limited personal commitments, low investment in teacher education and schooling by universities and society, and the consequent earnings and bureaucratic arrangements that push all but the most stubbornly dedicated teachers out of the field or into lacklustre performance.[41]

Some institutions will refuse to abandon undergraduate majors in education. They will be subjected to intense budgetary pressures to maintain the status quo. Reducing the number of education courses, and concentrating the remainder of pedagogical requirements at the graduate level may trigger a reduction in faculty positions in schools of education. This certainly will provoke resistance. Certain institutions, including some of elite status, will prefer to allow liberal arts majors to complete a truncated professional program and acquire certification, they and their students not expecting teaching to lead to lifelong careers in education. This is a kind of "Peace Corps" volunteerism that we, too, find inimical to teacher professionalism but which is recognized in the Holmes Group's "instructor" classification.[42]

Many state legislatures will oppose the expense involved in transforming the bulk of education training to a graduate degree. They will hear that increasing the amount of time required to prepare for teaching will penalize children of the poor and of those families new to higher education who have short-range views on investment in education. Political pressures will be especially intense during times of teacher shortages. Escalating certification requirements will be taken as an effort to raise the price of labor and restrict opportunity; political opposition will be triggered as a consequence. There are valid fears that unless teachers' earnings rise appreciably, the quantity and quality of teachers will be reduced by the greater investment required in preparing to teach.[43]

There is little pressure that can be brought against teacher training institutions that continue to offer undergraduate education ma-

41. See the discussion of "eased entry" into teaching in Lortie, *Schoolteacher,* esp. 17–19.

42. Alan R. Tom, "The Holmes Report: Sophisticated Analysis, Simplistic Solutions," *Journal of Teacher Education* 37, no. 4 (July–Aug. 1986):45.

43. On the basis of their study, Sedlak and Schlossman conclude that graduate level instruction, teacher testing, and other innovations designed to raise the qualifications of teachers are *not,* "by themselves, likely to significantly diminish the attractions of the profession to potentially desirable recruits." Sedlak and Schlossman, *Who Will Teach* ix; on salaries, see p. 36.

jors. Organizations such as the Holmes Group may refuse membership to these institutions, but the short-run outcome of such a sanction is dubious. Most of the likely recalcitrant institutions are either supported by legislatively derived enrollment formulas or by student tuition. In either case, their need for funding may overcome their wish to achieve whatever status Holmes Group membership confers.

National organizations such as NCATE are likely to be internally fragmented by these proposals and, therefore, unable to exercise leadership on the issue. For these reasons, crucial leverage on the issue may have to come from a source such as a National Professional Standards Board. Only by having to prepare teaching candidates to meet a high national standard can strangleholds at the state and institutional levels be broken.

Assist in the Effort to Reform Undergraduate Liberal Education. In a review of several major books and reports on the 1980s' school reform movement, Hilton Smith noted their collective refusal to acknowledge anti-intellectualism in the American character. He claims that the nation's colleges and universities contribute to this by their own teaching: "Perhaps it makes us all a bit uncomfortable to realize that demeaning attitudes toward students and intellectualist postures by university faculty members, coupled with huge doses of didactic instruction, reinforce popular attitudes of suspicion towards learning as a worthy pursuit on its own right."[44] There were four national reports during the early 1980s on undergraduate education. In the research universities there was private agreement, at least, with the charge that undergraduate education was the perennial stepchild of the family.

Because an effective general education for undergraduates is so central to the foundation of preparing effective teachers there is need to stress the oft-made point that present undergraduate education is inadequate. This criticism is a companion to the requirement that undergraduates who wish to teach declare an academic subject-matter major and minor, in order to obtain the broad foundation of knowledge and specific control over subject matter on which the professional preparation of teachers should rest.

There is much merit in Willis Hawley's observation that schools of education have an obligation "to engage undergraduates early and provide them with the support and experiences that many young people need to sustain their idealism and reinforce their dispositions

44. Hilton Smith, "Contemporary Studies of American Schooling," *Educational Studies* 16, no. 1 (Spring 1985): 13.

to serve others through teaching."[45] Accordingly, and as a part of the improvement of undergraduate education, we propose that schools, colleges, and departments of education, alone or in concert with disciplinary departments, develop courses in educational studies and human learning and development as a desirable part of a liberal education. Indeed, other professional schools should consider the contributions that their fields may make to reformulations of undergraduate education. In the eighteenth-century university, educators like Yale's president Ezra Stiles appreciated the cultural value of legal studies and its role in "forming Civilians."[46] To widen recognition of this possibility may also mean going part of the way toward eliminating invidious distinctions between the "liberal" and the "technical" in higher education that have long nourished unreason in academe. As useful as such professionally oriented undergraduate courses should be, we wish to make clear that they should be few in number and should *not* comprise an education undergraduate major.

Reject the Doctor of Philosophy as a Graduate Degree in Education. The great majority of schools of education do not engage in doctoral work. For those that do, their advanced graduate study in education should be directed toward a professional doctorate, the Ed.D. degree. Ph.D. standards are established and controlled by academic department faculty interests. The intellectual standards they have appropriately imposed on their own students, preparing for careers as scholars or scientists in a limited specialization within a single discipline, are patently inappropriate for individuals in training for professional roles. Moreover, few candidates will have the disciplinary preparation to do sophisticated enough studies to match those done in the cognate graduate departments—nor should most be required to gain that competence.[47] Graduate schools of education, to the degree to which they offer the doctorate, should concentrate on preparing professional leaders. This preparation should certainly encompass knowledge of and appreciation for academic research. It should not, however, be oriented primarily toward academic inquiry. We agree, then, with those university administrators who are seeking to reduce

45. Willis D. Hawley, "A Critical Analysis of the Holmes Group's Proposals for Reforming Teacher Education," *Journal of Teacher Education* 37, no. 4 (July–Aug. 1986):50.

46. Noted in Johnson, *Schooled Lawyers,* 21.

47. In the academic areas themselves, the Ph.D. thesis is being criticized as "irrelevant to subsequent responsibility and performance." See Cremin, *Education,* 21.

the number of professional practice students in the Ph.D. program, which is basically a research degree, while increasing their number in the Ed.D. program.[48] The fact that this awareness has been forced upon university administrators by competitive forces does not invalidate the distinction.

The evidence clearly shows that, "a program that offers both doctoral degrees ensures that students will opt for the Ph.D. degree despite the fact that it does not represent the best preparation for professional roles."[49] The proper advanced graduate degree for professionals in education is the Ed.D. It should be the analogue of the J.D., the *juris doctor* degree awarded to law students. If advanced degree students in education desire to conduct academic research, they should certainly be encouraged to acquire the added skills and to pursue such a line of endeavor. This occurs with medical doctors and lawyers. Both believe themselves free to conduct academic research while possessing only their professional degrees.

In instances where a research career cuts across academic and professional fields, such as psychology and education or economics and education, then the individuals should be enrolled in a Ph.D. program operated jointly by education and the relevant disciplinary department; in effect, the Ph.D. in education *should be* a joint academic degree. The number of enrollees in such joint programs might be more numerous than the number of law students jointly seeking Ph.D.'s in economics or medical students seeking Ph.D.'s in physiology because education is a more encompassing and universal social institution. But the numbers should be determined by function and not by prestige. The functionally appropriate vehicle for professional educators is the doctor of education degree.

Tactical Reminders for Schools of Education

In addition to the four strategic changes mentioned above—adherence to national professional standards, concentration on graduate professional preparation, building upon revised and strengthened under-

48. Hallie Masler and Charles E. Young, "Tackling the Tough Questions," *UCLA Monthly* 17, no. 1 (Sept.–Oct. 1986): 7. The majority of schools offering both doctoral degrees have most of their students in Ph.D. programs despite their intentions to pursue nonacademic professional careers. See B. L. Schneider, "Ed.D. and Ph.D. Programs: An Issue of Distinction," Council of Graduate Schools in the United States, *Communicator* 7 (1984): 1–2.

49. Lewis B. Mayhew et al., *Educational Leadership,* 38. The Stanford experience with the two degrees has been the general one.

graduate liberal arts and subject-matter major requirements, and a focus on the professional doctorate—there are several important tactical points to keep in mind that will secure for schools of education a productive role and useful niche in higher education.

Specifically, we must strive to ensure the following five conditions: (1) a clear sense of organizational purpose, (2) strong leadership and competent followership, (3) effective external relationships with professional education organizations, (4) high levels of productivity, and (5) an effective alignment between organizational purposes and organizational structure. We developed tactical points from our experience and our observations on the schools we have discussed. Those readers who may not have been convinced by the foregoing "grand strategies," may still find some profit in considering these tactics.

Maintaining a Sense of Purpose. Schools of education are generally noteworthy for their fragmented sense of mission. Their agenda includes preparing an elite of education leaders; establishing research projects that relate education with the social and behavioral sciences; analyzing educational policy issues; devising and criticizing the content of public school curricula; preparing teachers, administrators, and other education personnel; and catering to the panoply of such education-related occupations as counseling, adult education, early childhood education, nursing education, and training in nonschool settings. It is unlikely that many schools of education can accomplish all these ends and do justice to their constituents and clients. Some focus upon specific objectives is necessary if for no other reason than resources are always finite. "Each step along the way, each replacement of a retiring faculty member, each commitment of dollars, must be guided by a clear, shared image of the path chosen to be followed."[50]

Beyond resources, concentration is probably necessary in order to project clearly to important officials and the public what an organization stands for and is attempting to accomplish. Having a well-specified sense of purpose clarifies judgments and provides a base against which to assess progress. It is essential for schools of education to improve their *own* knowledge of "what they are about."[51] To do so

50. University of California Committee, 25.

51. In 1983 an advertisement was circulated for the position of chair of the Department of Educational Studies at Washington University in Saint Louis. The mission of this department was clearly stated: "In its research and educational efforts, the reorganized department will emphasize the liberal study of educational institutions, the

enables a school of education better to define itself and, if necessary, protect itself from the ravages of unfriendly incursions, to specify its role on a larger campus, and to discourage other units from appropriating projects which rightly belong in education—resisting the piracy of its agenda to which we earlier referred.

Building Sustained Leadership and Enlightened Followership. The early 1980s was marked by an infusion of initiative in addressing educational issues by the presidents of several major universities. Some of the activities of Donald Kennedy, Derek Bok, and Ira Michael Heyman have been discussed and their influence traced. Hannah Gray, of the University of Chicago, made a major effort to secure funding from the Amoco Foundation for the School Mathematics Project. Not since James B. Conant has one seen such visible leadership exercised by university presidents. However providential this was, it should not be expected to continue. Sustained leadership must come from those in schools of education themselves.

Obviously, if there were a choice, good is better than bad leadership. Weak leadership is almost never to be desired, but there is a worse condition, the revolving administration on which we commented in chapter 7. Consequently, faculty, staff, and students must ensure that a leader be selected in keeping with appropriate procedures of the institution. On whether the leader should be selected from "inside" or "outside," be old or young, a successful practitioner or professionally oriented scholar, and so on, for a long list of conventionally posed questions, we do not have a position; the correct answers to such questions will differ from institution to institution and time to time. We wish to underscore, however, the absolute necessity of having a leader—*and having an effective voice in the selection of that leader.* The more dire the outside threat, the stronger the leader should be and the more the faculty may have to cede, however temporarily, some of its own authority. That this is a difficult choice for entrepreneurial and almost anarchistic academics to consider is well understood. Whatever the circumstances, leadership and an informed and alert followership are the sine qua non of healthy organizations, able to secure and protect their purpose.

---

social and intellectual processes that they undertake, and the environmental forces that affect them. Professional preparation will be de-emphasized." Although this is not the institutional choice we advocate, the faculty and the institutions should be commended for making a decision and articulating it publicly. This strikes us as an essential undertaking against which to monitor subsequent actions.

Improving External Relations. Strong friends outside of the school represent potentially powerful supporters during inevitable times of stress. Harry Judge has observed that long-time denizens of education schools learn to relegate much of the ritually recited criticism of them to "the status of cosmic noise." It is, however, important, he reminds us, to be ready and able to distinguish between "noise" and "signal."[52]

Many education schools lack strong or systematic ties either to other campus entities or professional field of education, including their own alumni. But, general and specialized teacher organizations, administrators' associations, policy makers at various levels, and other practitioners are essential constituencies with which schools of education must maintain working relationships. While even major schools of education are unlike major university law and business schools in expecting that their individual graduates will be prominent in state legislatures and on university boards of trustees, they do possess organizational power and resources; collective economic and political strength do obtain in the world of education.

In some cases, Teachers College has been one, attempts have been made to broaden the constituency of schools of education, and thus to enlarge their mission. In 1981, UCLA announced the opening of a new research program through a Laboratory in School and Community Education. Besides collaboration with school districts and community colleges, other educational resources in the community were to be drawn into UCLA's orbit: libraries, museums, business, and the media. As valuable as this broadening may be, a more generally sound approach, also present in this example, is the intent to improve the design of research and dissemination of its results as a way of cementing the new bridges being built.

Maintaining Productivity. As with most other pieces of advice, the one about to be described is substantially easier to advocate than to achieve. Nonetheless, another dimension of effort necessary to preserve an organization is continued attention to professional productivity. In times of greatest peril, declines in faculty productivity often accompany the inevitable problem of plummeting morale.[53] Only

52. Harry Judge, "Research, Practice, Institutions: An Explanatory Note," *Oxford Review of Education* 9, no. 1 (1983): 5–8.

53. We cannot say this absolutely because few summary records were kept previously regarding such matters as faculty publications, social science citation index reports, and national honors. Our strong impression as the individuals who served as chair of the Department of Education of the University of California at Berkeley from

those faculty equipped with the most powerful of internal gyroscopes are able to maintain a balanced and cohesive line of research when the organizational battering starts. The slump in productivity contributes, however, to an academic unit's downward spiraling. Fewer publications are taken as added evidence of the ineffectual nature of the faculty and of the need to consider altering or eliminating the school altogether. Campus-wide prejudices are strengthened.

Organizational Alignment. "No American university has successfully melded first-rate scholarship in education with a continuing and constructive engagement with the problem of schools. This is the challenge that we should accept during this decade."[54] Although we have sometimes found ourselves in disagreement with former Berkeley Acting Dean Stephen Weiner, on this dimension we nevertheless endorse both his observation and his conclusion.

It has been said of professional schools that they are places for behavioral and social scientists "who prefer to work within the context of a problem rather than within a single discipline."[55] This characterization challenges education schools to be places that facilitate problem-oriented cooperation. Some of the ostensibly most successful schools of education, like many academic departments, have been mere "holding companies" for entrepreneurial individuals, but we are arguing that such "success" has been purchased at excessive price.

There are few firm answers regarding the internal organizational structures of education schools. Internal units, whether they be called departments, divisions, or whatever, should, of course, be established along lines of functional specialization. It is crucial, however, that their number and authority encourage interaction among colleagues rather than promote or permit parochialism, insularity, and self-regard. The exchange of ideas across subspecialities must be encouraged, not impeded. Equally important, internal structure should reflect the purposes of the organization and should discourage formation of internal status hierarchies or castes of academic untouchables.

In the case study of Berkeley's school of education, we described

---

1977 through 1983 is, however, that overall faculty efforts on dimensions such as innovation, research, consulting, participating in professional activities, and public service were lower than had been the case a decade previously.

54. University of California at Berkeley, School of Education, Stephen S. Weiner, "Message from the Dean," *Update* (Spring 1982), 7.

55. Sizer and Powell, "Changing Conceptions," 71.

the deleterious effects of having teacher education staff separated from the main body of the academic faculty. Such an arrangement allows professors to concentrate upon their scholarly endeavors and to divorce themselves from professional responsibilities involving training and supervision; it serves the function of putting distance between academically ambitious faculty and those interested in the practical facets of teacher training. Whatever the advantage for individuals, such a practice unfairly deprives professionals in training from contact with those faculty who most control the character and destiny of the organization. Exempting these persons from participation in professional education at its most crucial juncture means, in the words of David Dill, that "the overall quality of mind and effort brought to research on teaching and the training of teachers will continue to diminish."[56] Education schools *must* engage in systematic inquiry but they must also integrate that inquiry in all their training programs. Knowledge must be tested by practitioners. To borrow from Theodore Roszak, information is not knowledge, for knowledge is created when individual minds draw on individual experience, discern the significant, and make value judgments.[57] Educational research has been dealing with information more than knowledge. Only when inquiring minds are engaged in teacher education can we reasonably expect that teachers will be similarly disposed.

The removal of professional training from the consciousness of the most powerful of the faculty also contributes to the status-deprived nature of teacher preparation. An internal organizational apartheid is fueled with all its corresponding hard feelings and personal resentments, while a negative message about responsibility to the profession is communicated to those outside of the school.

Conclusion

By the mid-1980s American education was on the upbeat side in one of its cyclical swings in and out of public favor. Opinion poll results revealed added confidence in public schools. Their enrollments were increasing. Financial resources had almost regained the ground lost during the economic instability of the 1970s and early 1980s. Teacher salaries were beginning to climb. It was once again an exciting time to be connected with American public education. Public officials recog-

56. David D. Dill, "New Strategies for Schools of Education Ought to Include Schools of Teaching," *Chronicle of Higher Education* 27, no. 9 (18 Jan. 1984): 80.

57. Theodore Roszak, *The Cult of Information* (New York: Pantheon, 1986).

nized this, and competed with one another to be the friends of education.[58]

This new-found excitement, however transitory, could be expected to seep into the nation's thirteen hundred schools and departments of education and teacher training programs—just as the earlier depression in public school affairs redounded in education school circles. Virtually from their inception, education schools have acted like flowers turned toward other suns. In an effort to gain social prestige, academic acceptance, scholarly recognition, and security of resources, they periodically have taken on the coloration of social science departments, research centers, management institutes, and consulting agencies. What passed for cachet and fashion in intellectual and scholarly realms outside of pedagogical circles was often imported by schools of education in hopes of attracting similar attention.

Only in exceptional instances has this copy-cat strategy proved successful. Despite widespread efforts to appear more scholarly, more research oriented, more attuned to academic trends, and more intellectually rigorous, American education schools have seldom secured a comfortable place in their own college or university campus's pecking order. We remain convinced that schools of education, like most other professional schools, cannot best the disciplinary departments at their own game. Nor should they think that game is worth the candle. Such a strategy, successful or not, fails to gain the respect of practicing public school educators and public officials, or earn the high regard of the general public. Moreover, repeated efforts to adapt to higher education's prestige systems have impeded the ability of education schools to contribute to the efficacy of the education professions and improve the quality of teaching in the United States.

Trying to mediate between the relatively insular culture of academe and the wide-open world of public education, schools of education have been troubled places for most of their histories. It is Harry Judge's conclusion that university schools of education cannot and should not expect to be comfortable places; it is hard to quarrel with that conclusion.[59] A perceptive and fair-minded student of American educational history, David Tyack, tells us these tensions are often creative in their effects. It may indeed sometimes be so, but we see it otherwise: as being predominantly unproductive and defeating. We, therefore, recommend that schools of education, backed by their uni-

58. The National Governors Association, *A Time for Results: 1991 Report on Education* (Washington, D.C.: N.G.A. Center for Policy Research, 1986).

59. Judge, "Research, Practice, Institutions," 6–7.

versities, make hard choices and cast their lot with their natural constituency. Despite the dominant emphasis in the literature on reform of professional education, which is that "more and more intense relationships between professional schools and other units of the university" be developed, we have argued otherwise.[60] It is to the field that education schools must first put out their hands.

Making this decision would not end academic criticism to be sure; it would, indeed, raise some among those who were formerly silent, especially among social and behavioral scientists. Some would say that schools of education, in so doing, have succumbed to the narrow vocationalism so popular among the "me first" generation, and that their choice merely confirms (if such were really necessary!) what has been said all along: that professional schools do not belong on university campuses. Stanford's former dean, J. Myron Atkin, told the Stanford University Senate in 1981, that "as far as status and reputation are concerned, if there is an error to be made in overly orienting a school toward one or the other, it seems far preferable to err on the side of theory and research. Institutions that have done so rank highest consistently in the surveys. But perhaps we should not assume that the kinds of decisions made in the past serve us best for the future."[61]

Both the observation and its coda are warranted. What the chancellor at Berkeley said about his education school, then, must be made true even on campuses less excellent and self-confident: "An excellent and self-confident university . . . can proudly have within its midst an ebullient and productive faculty group seeking in appropriate ways to confront the serious problems of education in America."[62] We believe it is time for education schools to face their historic failures boldly, to divest themselves of false pretenses to being miniature models of social science institutes or liberal arts departments. To acknowledge their need to become professional schools and align themselves with their natural constituency of practicing educators is to contribute more intensely than they have at any time in this century to the building of a profession of education in the United States.

For their part, the colleges and universities which maintain schools, colleges, and departments of education would be well advised

60. Mayhew et al., *Educational Leadership,* 49.

61. Stanford University, School of Education, J. Myron Atkin, "Report to the Stanford University Senate," 5.

62. University of California at Berkeley, Ira Michael Heyman, Memo on the School of Education addressed to Academic Senate committees, 13 January 1982, p. 4.

to look beyond their traditionally narrow self-interest in elementary and secondary education as primarily a means for affecting the quality of incoming freshmen. The society's heavy investment in higher education is based, as it should be, upon expectations of a responsibility to contribute to the common welfare. Both liberal and professional education need to engage in, as their shared concern, "the unfinished business in the outlying society."[63] Citizens of the United States of America are not yet ready to concede that education remains anything less than *the American secular religion.* A half-century ago George Counts urged the National Education Association to promote the preparation of teachers of high qualifications because, "perhaps the school, staffed by such teachers, might make somewhat easier the truly difficult road to the future."[64] We cannot but believe that schools will continue to be deeply implicated in this society's deepest needs and most elevated hopes. That, from our present perspective, the road into the future looks no easier means that education schools have ample work before them.

63. Elting E. Morison, "The New Liberal Arts," an occasional paper of the Sloan Foundation, 1981, cited in Lynton, "Reexamining the Role of the University," 23.

64. George S. Counts, "Presentday Reasons for Requiring a Longer Period of Pre-Service Preparation for Teachers," National Education Association, *Addresses and Proceedings,* vol. 73 (Washington, D.C.: NEA, 1935).

References

Alexander, Carter. "Aims of Departments of Education in Colleges and Universities." School Review Monographs, no. 6, pp. 2–6. Chicago: University of Chicago Press, 1915.

Alonso, William. "The Unplanned Paths of Planning Schools." *Public Interest* 82 (Winter 1986): 58–71.

American Association of Colleges for Teacher Education. *The Doctorate in Education.* 2 vols. Washington, D.C.: AACTE, 1960.

———. *Teacher Education Policy in the States: A Fifth-State Survey.* Washington, D.C.: AACTE, 1986.

American Council on Education. "Professional Education." *American Universities and Colleges,* 12th ed., 37–116. New York: Walter de Gruyter, 1983.

American Teacher: Restructuring the Teaching Profession. New York: Metropolitan Life Insurance Co., 1986.

Atkin, J. Myron. "Institutional Self-Evaluation Versus National Professional Accreditation—or Back to the Normal School?" *Educational Researcher* 7, no. 10 (Nov. 1978): 3–7.

———. Interview with Geraldine Clifford, 15 April 1986, Stanford University.

———. "A New Evaluator Perspective for Professors of Education." In *The Professor of Education: An Assessment of Conditions,* 81–84. Papers of the meeting of the Society of Professors of Education, edited by Ayres Bagley. Oct. 1975, College of Education, University of Minnesota.

———. "Research Styles in Science Education." *Journal of Research in Science Teaching* 5 (1967–68): 338–45.

Atkin, J. Myron, and E. R. House. "The Federal Role in Curriculum Development, 1950–80." *Educational Evaluation and Policy Analysis* 3 (1981): 5–36.

REFERENCES

Auerbach, Jerrold S. "Enmity and Amity: Law Teachers and Practitioners, 1900–1922." *Perspectives in American History* 5 (1971): 551–601.

Bagley, William C. "The University School of Education, a Source of Educational Leadership." In *The Changing Educational World, 1905–1930,* edited by Alvin C. Eurich. Minneapolis: University of Minnesota Press, 1931.

Bailyn, Bernard. *Education in the Forming of American Society.* Chapel Hill: University of North Carolina Press, 1960.

Baker, Curtis O. *Earned Degrees Conferred: An Examination of Recent Trends.* Washington, D.C.: National Center for Education Statistics, 1981.

Balderston, Frederick E. "Academic Program Review and the Determination of University Priorities." *International Journal of Institutional Management in Higher Education* 9, no. 3 (Nov. 1985): 237–48.

Baldwin, Bird T. "Practice Schools in University Departments of Education." *Journal of Educational Psychology* 2 (1911): 459–63.

Bardeen, C. W. "Why Teaching Repels Men." *Educational Review* 35 (April 1908): 351–58.

Barr, Robert D. "School of Education Mergers: Institutional Survival or Administrative Madness?" *Journal of Teacher Education* 36, no. 4 (July–Aug. 1985): 50–54.

Becher, Tony. "The Cultural View." In *Perspectives on Higher Education: Eight Disciplinary and Comparative Views,* edited by Burton R. Clark, 165–98. Berkeley: University of California Press, 1984.

Beck, Robert H. *Beyond Pedagogy: A History of the University of Minnesota College of Education.* St. Paul, Minn.: North Central Publishing Co., 1980

Beckett, John. "Dean Hopes to See Reorganization in Education School's Review." *Ann Arbor News,* 6 Jan. 1983.

———. "Recommended Cuts in Education School Hard to Take, Dean Says." *Ann Arbor News,* 29 May 1983.

Best, John H. "Death and Taxes and Politics of Education: The State of the Field of Educational Studies in Relation to Policy Making in Education." Presidential address, American Educational Studies Association, 2 Nov. 1978, Washington, D.C.

Bettelheim, Bruno. "Segregation: New Style." *School Review* 66 (1958): 251–72.

Biklen, Sari Knopp. "Can Elementary Schoolteaching Be a Career? A Search for New Ways of Understanding Women's Work." *Issues in Education* 3, no. 3 (Winter 1985): 215–31.

Bigelow, Karl W. "Moving Ahead in Teacher Education." *American Association of Colleges for Teacher Education Tenth Yearbook,* 13–25. Oneonta, N.Y.: AACTE, 1957.

Billington, Ray Allen. *Frederick Jackson Turner: Historian, Scholar, Teacher.* New York: Oxford University Press, 1973.

Blau, Peter M., and Rebecca Z. Margulies. "The Reputation of American Professional Schools." *Change* 6 (1973–74): 42–47.

Bledstein, Burton J. *The Culture of "Professionalism": The Middle Class and the Development of Higher Education in America.* New York: W. W. Norton, 1976.

Bloom, Allan. *The Closing of the American Mind.* New York: Simon & Schuster, 1987.

Bok, Derek. "The President's Report, 1985–86, Harvard University." Cambridge, Mass.: Harvard University, April 1987.

Bolton, Frederick E. "Curricula in University Departments of Education." *School and Society* 2, no. 50 (11 Dec. 1915): 829–41.

Bonney, James K. "A Profile of the Harvard Graduate School of Education: A Report Compiled for Professor Harry Judge's Study of American Graduate Schools of Education." Feb. 1981. By permission of Professor Judge, Oxford University.

Bonser, Frederick G. "Curriculum-Making in Laboratory or Experimental Schools." In *Curriculum-Making: Past and Present,* 353–62. 26th Yearbook of the National Society for the Study of Education, part 1, edited by Guy M. Whipple. Bloomington, Ill.: Public School Publishing Co., 1927.

Borrowman, Merle L. "About Professors of Education." In *The Professor of Education: An Assessment of Conditions,* edited by Ayres Bagley, 55–60. Papers of the meeting of the Society of Professors of Education, Oct. 1975, College of Education, University of Minnesota, 1975.

———. *The Liberal and the Technical in Teacher Education.* New York: Teachers College, Columbia University, 1956.

Borrowman, Merle L., ed. *Teacher Education in America: A Documentary History.* New York: Teachers College Press, 1965.

Bowen, Howard R. *The Cost of Higher Education: How Much Do Colleges and Universities Spend per Student and How Much Should They Spend?* San Francisco: Jossey-Bass, 1980.

Brandt, H. C. B. "How Far Should Our Teaching and Textbooks Have a Scientific Basis?" *Transactions of the Modern Language Association of America, 1884–5,* 1:57–64. Baltimore: MLA, 1886.

Brauner, Charles J. *American Educational Theory.* Englewood Cliffs, N.J.: Prentice-Hall, 1964.

Brickell, Henry M. "State Organization for Educational Change: A Case Study and a Proposal." In *Innovation in Education,* edited by Matthew B. Miles, 493–531. New York: Teachers College, Columbia University, 1964.

Brickman, William W. "Power Conflicts and Crises in Teacher Education: Some Historical and International Perspectives." In *Responding to the Power Crisis in Teacher Education,* edited by Ayres Bagley, 1–28. Washington, D.C.: Society of Professors of Education, 1971.

Brophy, Jere E., and Thomas L. Good. "Teacher Behavior and Student

Achievement." In *Handbook of Research on Teaching,* 3d ed., edited by Merlin C. Wittrock, 570–602. New York: Macmillan, 1986.

Browder, L. H. "Where Are Schools of Education Going?" *Journal of Teacher Education* 29 (1978): 52–56.

Brown, Elmer Ellsworth. "The Development of Education as a University Subject." *Teachers College Record* 24, no. 3 (May 1923): 190–96.

Brown, Lawrence D., and J. Marlowe Slater. *The Doctorate in Education.* 2 vols. Washington, D.C.: American Association of Colleges for Teacher Education, 1960.

Brownson, William E., and Joseph J. Schwab. "American Science Textbooks and Their Authors, 1915 and 1955." *School Review* 71, no. 2 (Summer 1963): 170–80.

Brubacher, John, et al. *The Department of Education at Yale University, 1891–1958.* New Haven, Conn., 1960.

Brumberg, Joan Jacobs, and Nancy Tomes. "Women in the Professions: A Research Agenda for American Historians." *Reviews in American History* 10, no. 1 (June 1982): 275–96.

Buckland, Michael L. "Memo." University of California at Berkeley, School of Education, Historical File, 1 Nov. 1982.

Bureau of Labor Statistics. *Occupational Outlook Handbook, 1984–1985 Edition.* Washington, D.C.: U.S. Department of Labor, 1984.

Burrage, Michael. "Practitioners, Professors, and the State in France, the USA, and England." In *Education for the Professions: Quis Custodiet . . . ?* edited by Sinclair Goodlad, 26–38. Guilford, England: Society for Research into Higher Education/NFER-Nelson, 1984.

Burstall, Sara A. *Impressions of American Education in 1908.* London: Longmans Green, 1909.

Bush, Robert N., and Peter Enemark. "Control and Responsibility in Teacher Education." In *Teacher Education,* 165–294. 74th Yearbook of the National Society for the Study of Education, part 2, edited by Kevin Ryan. Chicago: University of Chicago Press, 1975.

Butts, R. Freeman. Letter to Geraldine Clifford, 25 Aug. 1986.

———. Interview with Geraldine Clifford, 15 April 1986.

———. "Reflections on Forty Years in the Foundations Department at Teachers College." Paper prepared for 1975 Alumni Day, 11 April 1975.

California State University. Board of Trustees. "The Mission of the California State University, Agenda Item 1, 12–13 November 1985 and Attachments."

Caplow, Theodore. *The Sociology of Work.* Minneapolis: University of Minnesota Press, 1954.

Caplow, Theodore, and Reece J. McGee. *The Academic Marketplace.* New York: Science Editions, 1961.

Carnegie Foundation for the Advancement of Teaching. "Future Teachers: Will There Be Enough Good Ones?" *Change* 18, no. 5 (Sept.–Oct. 1986): 27–30.

Carnegie Task Force on Teaching as a Profession. *A Nation Prepared: Teachers for the Twenty-first Century.* New York: Carnegie Forum on Education and the Economy, May 1986.

Carter, Susan B. "Academic Women Revisited: An Empirical Study of Changing Patterns of Women's Employment as College and University Faculty, 1890–1963." *Journal of Social History* 14, no. 4 (Summer 1981): 675–99.

Cartter, Alan. "The Cartter Report on the Leading Schools of Education, Law, and Business." *Change* 9, no. 2 (Feb. 1977): 44–48.

Chall, Jeanne S. "Restoring Dignity and Self-Worth to the Teacher." *Phi Delta Kappan* 57, no. 3 (Nov. 1975): 170–74.

Chambers, Clark A. "Women in the Creation of the Profession of Social Work." *Social Service Review* 60, no. 1 (March 1986): 1–33.

Charles, Don C. "Expectation vs. Reality: Behavioral Science Response to Teacher Education Demand." In *Responding to the Power Crisis in Teacher Education,* 29–46. Major papers and abstracts of the 1971 conference in Chicago, edited by Ayres Bagley. Washington, D.C.: Society of Professors of Education, 1971.

Chase, Francis S. "Can Teachers Be Scholars or Pupils Students?" Speech given in Oklahoma City, 23 Oct. 1958. Courtesy of Professor William Pattison, Department of Education, University of Chicago.

Chase, Francis S., and Harold A. Anderson, eds. *The High School in a New Era.* Chicago: University of Chicago Press, 1958.

Clark, Burton R. "The High School and the University: What Went Wrong in America," Part 1. *Phi Delta Kappan* 66, no. 6 (Feb. 1985): 391–97.

Clark, David L. "The Real World of the Teacher-Educator: A Look to the Future." 18th Charles L. Hunt Lecture. *Yearbook 1977,* 1:1–23. Washington, D.C.: American Association of Colleges for Teacher Education, 1977.

Clark, David L., and Egon G. Guba. *A Study of Teacher Education Institutions as Innovators, Knowledge Producers, and Change Agents.* National Institute of Education Project, no. 4-0752, n.d.

Clark, David L., and Gerald Marker. "The Institutionalization of Teacher Education." In *Teacher Education,* 53–86. 74th Yearbook of the National Society for the Study of Education, part 2, edited by Kevin Ryan. Chicago: University of Chicago Press, 1975.

Clifford, Geraldine Jonçich. "'A Hopeless Tangle of Tormenting Questions': History, Gender, and Education." Paper presented at the annual meeting of the American Educational Research Association, April 1986, San Francisco.

———. "The Impact of Technology on Education in the United States." In *Technology, the Economy and Society: The American Experience,* edited by Stuart Bruchey and Joel Colton, 251–77. New York: Columbia University Press, 1987.

———. "'Shaking Dangerous Questions from the Crease'": Gender and American Higher Education." *Feminist Issues* 3, no. 2 (Fall 1983): 3–62.

———. "A Sisyphean Task! Historical Perspectives on the Relations of Reading and Writing Instruction." Technical Paper, no. 7. Center for the Study of Writing, University of California at Berkeley, and Carnegie-Mellon University, Pittsburgh, 1987.

Clifford, Geraldine Jonçich, ed. *Lone Voyagers: Academic Women in American Coeducational Universities, 1869–1937.* New York: Feminist Press, 1988.

[Clifford,] Geraldine Jonçich. *The Sane Positivist: A Biography of Edward L. Thorndike.* Middletown, Conn.: Wesleyan University Press, 1968.

———. "Scientists and the Schools of the 19th Century: The Case of American Physicists." *American Quarterly* 18 (Winter 1966): 667–85.

Coley, Richard J., and Margaret E. Thorpe. *A Look at the MAT Model of Teacher Education and Its Graduates: Lessons for Today.* Final report, sponsored by the Ford Foundation. Princeton, N.J.: Division of Education Policy Research and Services, Educational Testing Service, Dec. 1985.

Commager, Henry Steele. *The American Mind.* New Haven, Conn.: Yale University Press, 1950.

Committee on the Status of Women and Ethnic Minorities. Annual Report, 1982–83. Minutes of the Berkeley Division, University of California, Berkeley, 4 Oct. 1983.

Committee Q. "Required Courses in Education." *Bulletin of the American Association of University Professors* 9, no. 3 (March 1933): 173–200.

Conant, James B. *The Education of American Teachers.* New York: McGraw-Hill, 1963.

———. *My Several Lives: Memoirs of a Social Inventor.* New York: Harper & Row, 1970.

Cornbleth, Catherine. "Ritual and Rationality in Teacher Education Reform." *Educational Researcher* 15, no. 4 (April 1986): 5–14.

Corwin, Ronald G. "The New Teaching Profession." In *Teacher Education,* 230–64. 74th Yearbook of the National Society for the Study of Education, part 2, edited by Kevin Ryan. Chicago: University of Chicago Press, 1975.

Counelis, James Steve. "The Professoriate in the Discipline of Education." *To Be a Phoenix: The Education Professoriate,* 1–29. Bloomington, Ind.: Phi Delta Kappa, 1969.

Counts, George S. "Presentday Reasons for Requiring a Longer Period of Pre-Service Preparation for Teachers." *National Education Association Addresses and Proceedings,* vol. 73. Washington, D.C.: NEA, 1935.

———. "What Is a School of Education?" *Teachers College Record* 30, no. 7 (April 1929): 647–55.

Courtis, Stuart A. "Curriculum-Construction at Detroit." In *Curriculum-Making, Past and Present,* 189–206. 26th Yearbook of the National Society for the Study of Education, part 1, edited by Guy M. Whipple. Bloomington, Ill.: Public School Publishing Co., 1927.

Creager, J. O. "The Professional Guidance of Students in Schools of Education in State Universities." *Educational Administration and Supervision* 13, no. 3 (March 1927): 192–99.

Cremin, Lawrence A. "The Education of the Educating Professions." 19th Charles W. Hunt Lecture. American Association of Colleges for Teacher Education, Chicago, 21 Feb. 1978.

———. Preface. In *Teacher Education in America: A Documentary History,* edited by Merle L. Borrowman. New York: Teachers College Press, 1965.

———. "The Problematics of Education in the 1980s: Some Reflections on the Oxford Workshop." *Oxford Review of Education* 9, no. 1 (1983): 9–20.

———. *The Transformation of the School: Progressivism in American Education, 1876–1957.* New York: Knopf, 1961.

———. *The Wonderful World of Ellwood Patterson Cubberley: An Essay on the Historiography of American Education.* New York: Teachers College Press, 1965.

Cremin, Lawrence A., David A. Shannon, and Mary Evelyn Townsend. *A History of Teachers College, Columbia University.* New York: Columbia University Press, 1954.

Creutz, Alan. "From College Teacher to University Scholar: The Evolution and Professionalization of Academics at the University of Michigan, 1841–1900." Doctoral diss., University of Michigan, 1981.

Cronbach, Lee, and Patrick Suppes, eds. *Research for Tomorrow's Schools.* New York: Macmillan, 1969.

Cuban, Larry. *How Teachers Taught: Constancy and Change in American Classrooms, 1890–1980.* New York: Longman, 1984.

Cubberley, Ellwood P. "The College of Education and the Superintendent of Schools." *School and Society* 17, no. 438 (19 May 1923) 538–45.

Darling-Hammond, Linda. "Teacher Supply and Demand: A Structural Perspective." Paper presented at the annual meeting of the American Educational Research Association, April 1986, San Francisco.

Depencier, Ida B. "The History of the Laboratory Schools, University of Chicago, 1896–1957." Chicago, 1957.

Dewey, John. "The Relation of Theory to Practice in Education" (1904). Reprinted in *Teacher Education in America: A Documentary History,* edited by Merle L. Borrowman. New York: Teachers College Press, 1965.

Dill, David D. "New Strategies for Schools of Education Ought to Include Schools of Teaching." *Chronicle of Higher Education* 27, no. 9 (18 Jan. 1984): 80.

Dolan, W. Patrick. *The Ranking Game: The Power of the Academic Elite.* Evaluation of Higher Education Committee of the Study Commission on Undergraduate Education and the Education of Teachers. Lincoln: University of Nebraska, 1976.

Dubbert, Joe L. "Progressivism and the Masculinity Crisis." In *The American Man,* edited by Elizabeth H. Pleck and Joseph H. Pleck, 303–19. Englewood Cliffs, N.J.: Prentice-Hall, 1980.

Ducharme, Edward R., and Russell M. Agne. "The Education Professoriate: A Research-Based Perspective." *Journal of Teacher Education* 33, no. 6 (Nov.–Dec. 1982): 30–36.

Dunn, John. "Bureau of School Services Cuts Bringing Howls from around State." *Ann Arbor News,* 22 April, 1983.

Eash, Maurice. "Educational Research Productivity of Institutions of Higher Education." *American Educational Research Journal* 20, no. 1 (Spring 1983): 5–12.

Elliott, Edward C. "Cooperative Research within the Field of Education." In *Research within the Field of Education, Its Organization and Encouragement. School Review* Monographs, no. 1, pp. 57–59. Papers presented at the Society of College Teachers of Education, 23–24 Feb. 1911, Mobile, Ala.

Ellis, A. Caswell. "Preliminary Report on Committee W, on Status of Women in College and University Faculties." *Bulletin of the American Association of University Professors* 7, no. 62 (Oct. 1921): 21–32.

Ellis, Samuel R. "The Social Status of the American Teacher." *School and Society* 31, no. 785 (11 Jan. 1930): 47–50.

Elsbree, Willard S. *The American Teacher: Evolution of a Profession in a Democracy.* New York: American Book Co., 1939.

Etzioni, Amitai, ed. *The Semi-Professions in America.* New York: Free Press, 1969.

Falk, Charles J. *The Development and Organization of Education in California.* New York: Harcourt, Brace, & World, 1968.

Feistritzer, C. Emily. *The Making of a Teacher: A Report on Teacher Education and Certification.* Washington, D.C.: National Center for Educational Information, 1984.

Feldman, Saul D. *Escape from the Doll's House: Women in Graduate and Professional School Education.* Report for the Carnegie Commission on Higher Education. New York: McGraw-Hill, 1974.

Ferris, James, and Donald Winkler. "Compensation and the Supply of Teachers." Paper prepared for the California Commission on the Teaching Profession, April 1985, Sacramento.

Filene, Peter. *Him, Her, Self: Sex Roles in Modern America.* New York: Harcourt, Brace, Jovanovich, 1974.

Findlay, J. J. "The Problem of Professional Training: Recent Movements in Germany and England." *School Review* 1, no. 5 (May 1893): 281–90.

Finkelstein, Barbara. "Servants, Critics, Skeptics: The Place of Foundations Faculties in Professional Education." *Teacher Education Quarterly* (California Council on the Education of Teachers) 11, no. 2 (Spring 1984): 14–21.

Flexner, Abraham. *Funds and Foundations.* New York: Harper & Row, 1952.

———. *Universities: American, English, German.* New York: Oxford University Press, 1930.

Flexner, Abraham, and Frank B. Bachman. *Public Education in Maryland: A Report to the Maryland Educational Survey Commission.* New York: General Education Board, 1916.

Florio, David H. "Research and the Politics of Education." *Educational Forum* 42 (May 1978): 490–501.

Ford, Boris. "Schools of Education and Social Work." In *The Idea of a New University: An Experiment in Sussex,* 2d ed., edited by David Daiches, 135–52. London: Deutsch, 1970.

Freedman, Sara, Jane Jackson, and Katherine Boles. "The Effects of the Institutional Structures of Schools on Teachers." Boston Women's Teachers' Group, Final report, National Institute of Education G-81-0031, 1 Sept. 1982.

Freeman, Frank N. *Practices of American Universities in Granting Higher Degrees in Education.* 19th Yearbook of the National Society of College Teachers of Education. Chicago: University of Chicago Press, 1931.

Fuller, Wayne E. *The Old Country School: The Story of Rural Education in the Middle West.* Chicago: University of Chicago Press, 1982.

Gage, N. L., and Philip H. Winne, "Performance-Based Teacher Education." In *Teacher Education,* 146–72. 74th Yearbook of the National Society for the Study of Education, part 2, edited by Kevin Ryan. Chicago: University of Chicago Press, 1975.

Gardner, David P. *The California Oath Controversy.* Berkeley: University of California Press, 1967.

Gardner, John W. *Excellence: Can We Be Equal and Excellent, Too?* New York: Harper & Co., 1961.

Gates, Max. Education School Budget Axed—But not Enrollment." *Ann Arbor News,* 16 Sept. 1983.

Gerbner, George. "Teacher Image and the Hidden Curriculum." *American Scholar* 42, no. 1 (Winter 1972–73): 66–92.

Getzels, J. W. "Paradigm and Practice: On the Impact of Basic Research in Education." In *Impact of Research on Education: Some Case Studies,* edited by Patrick W. Suppes, 477–521. Washington, D.C.: National Academy of Education, 1978.

Gevinson, Steven. "What Happened to the 'Master of Arts' in Teaching and the Graduate School of Education?" Seminar paper, University of Chicago Department of Education, 12 Dec. 1984.

Gifford, Bernard R. "Prestige and Education: The Missing Link in School Reform." *Review of Education* 10, no. 3 (Summer 1984): 186–98.

———. "Teacher Competency Testing and Its Effects on Minorities: Reflection and Recommendations." In *Educational Standards, Testing, and Access.* Proceedings of the 1984 ETS Invitational Conference. Princeton, N.J.: Educational Testing Service, 1985.

Gifford, Bernard R., and Trish Stoddart, "Teacher Education: Rhetoric or Real Reform?" In *Education on Trial: Strategies for the Future,* edited by William J. Johnston, 177–97. San Francisco: Institute for Contemporary Studies, 1985.

Glazer, Nathan. "The Schools of the Minor Professions." *Minerva* 12, no. 3 (July 1974): 346–64.

Good, H. G. *The Rise of the College of Education of the Ohio State University.* Columbus: Ohio State University Press, 1960.

Goodenow, Ronald K., and Robert Cowen. "The American School of Education and the Third World in the Twentieth Century: Teachers College and Africa, 1920–1950." *History of Education* 15, no. 4 (1986): 271–89.

Goodlad, John. "Report of the University-Wide Program Review Committee for Education." University of California, Oct. 1984.

Goodlad, Sinclair, ed. *Education for the Professions: Quis custodiet . . . ?* Guilford, England: Society for Research into Higher Education/NFER-Nelson, 1984.

Gordon, Margaret, and Clark Kerr. "University Behavior and Policies: Where Are the Women and Why?" In *The Higher Education of Women: Essays in Honor of Rosemary Park,* edited by Helen S. Astin and Werner Z. Hirsch. New York: Praeger, 1978.

Graham, Hugh. "The Rise and Progress of the College of Education of the University of Minnesota." *School and Society* 31, no. 798 (12 April 1930): 510–13.

Graham, Hugh Davis. *The Uncertain Triumph: Federal Education Policy in the Kennedy and Johnson Years.* Chapel Hill: University of North Carolina Press, 1984.

Graham, Patricia Albjerg. "Memorandum to the Faculty." Harvard Graduate School of Education, 1985.

Grant, W. Vance, and Thomas D. Snyder. *Digest of Educational Statistics, 1983–84.* Washington, D.C.: National Center for Educational Statistics, 1984.

Graybeal, William S. "Status and Trends in Public School Teacher Supply and Demand." *Journal of Teacher Education* 25 (Summer 1974): 200–209.

Guba, Egon G., and David L. Clark. "Levels of R and D Productivity in Schools of Education." *Educational Researcher* 7, no. 5 (May 1978): 3–9.

Guthrie, James W. "The Educational Policy Consequences of Economic Instability: The Emerging Political Economy of American Education." *Educational Evaluation and Policy Analysis* 7, no. 4 (Winter 1986): 319–32.

———. "Social Science, Accountability, and the Political Economy of School Productivity." In *Indeterminacy in Education,* edited by John E. McDermott, 253–308. Berkeley: McCutchan, 1976.

Haberman, Martin. "Licensing Teachers: Lessons from Other Professions." *Phi Delta Kappan* 67, no. 10 (June 1986): 719–22.

———. "Perspectives on Tomorrow's Teacher Education." In *Teacher Education,* 310–20. 74th Yearbook of the National Society for the Study of Education, part 2, edited by Kevin Ryan. Chicago: University of Chicago Press, 1975.

Hall, Natalie. "A Crisis in American Education." *UCLA Monthly* 13, no. 5 (1983).

Harmon, Lindsey R., and Herbert Soldz. *Doctorate Production in United States Universities, 1920–1962, with Baccalaureate Origins of Doctorates in Science, Arts, and Professions.* Publication no. 1142. Washington, D.C.: National Academy of Sciences–National Research Council, 1963.

Harrisberger, Lee. "Curricula and Teaching Methods in Engineering Education." In *Education for the Professions: Quis Custodiet . . . ?* edited by Sinclair Goodlad, 133–40. Guilford, England: Society for Research into Higher Education/NFER-Nelson, 1984.
Hart, Albert Bushnell. "The Teacher as a Professional Expert." *School Review* 1, no. 1 (Jan. 1883): 4–14.
Hartwell, Edward H. "Discussion" [in response to Leonard P. Ayres, "Measuring Processes through Educational Results"]. *School Review* 20 (May 1912): 314–17.
Harvard Committee. *The Graduate Study of Education.* Cambridge: Harvard University Press, 1966.
"The Harvard Graduate School of Education." *School and Society* 11, no. 267 (7 Feb. 1920): 166–67.
Hatry, Harry P., and John M. Greiner. *Teacher Incentive Plans.* Washington, D.C.: Urban Institute Press, 1985.
Havighurst, Robert J. "Who Goes to College and Why?" In *Recent Research and Development and Their Implications for Teacher Education,* 103–13. 13th Yearbook of the American Association of Colleges for Teacher Education. Washington, D.C.: AACTE, 1960.
Hawkins, Hugh. *Between Harvard and America: The Educational Leadership of Charles W. Eliot.* New York: Oxford University Press, 1972.
Hawley, Willis D. "A Critical Analysis of the Holmes Group's Proposals for Reforming Teacher Education." *Journal of Teacher Education* 37, no. 4 (July–Aug. 1986).
Hazlett, J. Stephen. "Education Professors: The Centennial of an Identity Crisis." Paper presented at the annual meeting of the American Educational Research Association, April 1986, San Francisco.
Hechinger, Fred M. "Business Schools Criticized." *New York Times,* 13 April 1982.
———. "Colleges Reaching Out to Aid Public Schools." *New York Times,* 14 Dec. 1982.
———. "Three Years of Lessons." *New York Times,* 29 Jan. 1985.
Herbst, Jurgen. "Nineteenth-Century Normal Schools in the United States: A Fresh Look." *History of Education* 9, no. 3 (1980): 219–27.
———. "Professionalization in Public Education, 1890–1920: The American High School Teacher." In *Bildungsbürgertum im 19. Jahrhundert,* vol. 1, *Bildungssystem und Professionalisierung in internationalen Vergleichen,* edited by Werner Conze and Jürgen Kocka, 495–528. Stuttgart: Klett-Cotta, 1985.
Heyman, Ira Michael. Interview with the authors, University of California at Berkeley, 16 October 1985.
Higgins, H. Stephen. "The Rating of Selected Fields of Doctoral Study in the Graduate Schools of Education." Doctoral diss., Columbia University, 1968.
Hildenbrand, Suzanne. "Ambiguous Authority and Aborted Ambition: Gender,

Professionalism, and the Rise and Fall of the Welfare State." *Library Trends* 34, no. 2 (Fall 1985): 185–98.

Hill, Henry H. "Preparing Teachers for the High School of the Future." In *The High School in a New Era,* edited by Francis S. Chase and Harold A. Anderson, 249–60. Chicago: University of Chicago Press, 1958.

Hill, Thomas. "Remarks on the Study of Didactics in Colleges." *American Journal of Education* 15, no. 38 (March 1865): 177–79.

Hinsdale, Burke A. "Pedagogical Chairs in Colleges and Universities." Pamphlets on Higher Education, no. 2. Syracuse: C. W. Bardeen, 1889.

———. "The Training of Teachers." Monographs on Education in the United States, no. 8, 3–49. Albany, N.Y.: J. B. Lyon Co., 1899.

Hodgkinson, Harold L. *Institutions in Transition: A Study of Change in Higher Education.* Berkeley: Carnegie Commission on Higher Education, 1970.

———. "Report on Elementary Internship Program." University of California at Berkeley, School of Education, Historical File, n.d. [1969?].

Hofstadter, Richard. *Anti-Intellectualism in American Life.* New York: Random House, 1962.

Holmes Group. *Tomorrow's Teachers: A Report of the Holmes Group.* East Lansing, Mich.: Holmes Group, 1986.

Horn, Ernest, and Maude McBroom. "Curriculum-Making in the University Elementary School of the State University of Iowa." In *Curriculum-Making: Past and Present,* 291–96. 26th Yearbook of the National Society for the Study of Education, part 1, edited by Guy M. Whipple. Bloomington, Ill.: Public School Publishing Co., 1927.

Hronek, Pamela C. "Women and Normal Schools: Tempe Normal, A Case Study, 1885–1925." Doctoral diss., Arizona State University, 1985.

Huberman, Michael. "Recipes for Busy Kitchens: A Situational Analysis of Routine Knowledge Use in Schools." *Knowledge: Creation, Diffusion, Utilization* 4, no. 4 (June 1983): 478–510.

———. "What Knowledge Is of Most Worth to Teachers? A Knowledge-Use Perspective." *Teaching and Teacher Education* 1, no. 3 (1985): 251–62.

Hughes, Raymond M. "Report of the Committee on Graduate Instruction." *Educational Record* 15, no. 2 (April 1934): 193–234.

Húsen, Torsten. "Research and Policymaking in Education: An International Perspective." *Educational Researcher* 13, no. 2 (Feb. 1984): 5–11.

Inman, Virginia. "Certification of Teachers Lacking Courses in Education Stirs Battles in Several States." *Wall Street Journal,* 5 Jan. 1984.

Jackson, Philip W. "Divided We Stand: The Internal Organization of the Education Professoriate." In *The Professor of Education: An Assessment of Conditions,* 61–70. Papers of the meeting of the Society of Professors of Education, edited by Ayres Bagley. College of Education, University of Minnesota, October 1975.

———. "Facing Our Ignorance." *Teachers College Record* 88, no. 3 (Spring 1987): 384–89.

Jencks, Christopher, and David Riesman. *The Academic Revolution.* Garden City, N.Y.: Doubleday, 1968.

Jenkins, William A. "Changing Patterns in Teacher Education." In *The Teaching of English,* 260–81. 76th Yearbook of the National Society for the Study of Education, part 1, edited by James R. Squire. Chicago: University of Chicago Press, 1977.

Jerrolds, Bob W. *Reading Reflections: The History of the International Reading Association.* Newark, Del.: International Reading Association, 1977.

Johanningmeier, Erwin V., and Henry C. Johnson, Jr. "The Education Professoriate: A Historical Consideration of Its Work and Growth." In *The Professor of Education: An Assessment of Conditions,* 1–18. Papers of the meeting of the Society of Professors of Education, edited by Ayres Bagley. College of Education, University of Minnesota, Oct. 1975.

Johnson, Henry C., Jr., and Erwin V. Johanningmeier. *Teachers for the Prairie: The University of Illinois and the Schools, 1868–1945.* Urbana: University of Illinois Press, 1972.

Johnson, Terry. "Professionalism: Occupation or Ideology?" In *Education for the Professions: Quis custodiet . . . ?* edited by Sinclair Goodlad, 17–25. Guildford, England: Society for Research into Higher Education/NFER-Nelson, 1984.

Johnson, William R. "Education and Professional Life Styles: Law and Medicine in the Nineteenth Century." *History of Education Quarterly* 14, no. 2 (Summer 1974): 185–207.

———. "Empowering Practitioners: Holmes, Carnegie, and the Lessons of History." *History of Education Quarterly* 27, no. 2 (Summer 1987):221–40.

———. *Schooled Lawyers: A Study in the Clash of Professional Cultures.* New York: New York University Press, 1978.

Jonçich, Geraldine. *The Sane Positivist: A Biography of Edward L. Thorndike.* Middletown, Conn.: Wesleyan University Press, 1968.

———. "Scientists and the Schools of the Nineteenth Century: The Case of American Physicists." *American Quarterly* 18 (Winter 1966): 667–85.

Judd, Charles Hubbard. "The Department of Education in American Universities." *School Review* 17, no. 9 (Nov. 1909): 593–608.

———. "Teachers Colleges as Centers of Progressive Education." *Proceedings of the National Education Association.* Washington, D.C.: National Education Association, 1929.

Judge, Harry. *American Graduate Schools of Education: A View from Abroad.* New York: Ford Foundation, 1982.

———. "Research, Practice, Institutions: An Explanatory Note." *Oxford Review of Education* 9, no. 1 (1983): 5–8.

Kaiser, Jeffrey S. "Pessimistic Optimism in an Era of Slowed Growth: An Administrator's View." *Educational Perspectives* 14 (Dec. 1975): 10–13.

Kalman, Laura. *Legal Realism at Yale, 1927–1960.* Chapel Hill: University of North Carolina Press, 1986.

Karabel, Jerome. "Community Colleges and Social Stratification." *Harvard Educational Review* 42, no. 4 (Nov. 1972): 521–62.

Katz, Michael B. "From Theory to Survey in Graduate Schools of Education." *Journal of Higher Education* 37, no. 6 (June 1966): 325–34.

Kemper, Richard E., and John N. Mangieri. "America's Future Teaching Force." *Phi Delta Kappan* 68, no. 5 (Jan. 1987): 393–95.

Kennelly, Karen, C. S. J. "Mary Molloy, Women's College Founder." In *Women of Minnesota: Selected Biographical Essays,* edited by Barbara Stuhler and Gretchen Kreuter. St. Paul: Minnesota Historical Society Press, 1977.

Kerr, Donna H. "Teaching Competence and Teacher Education in the United States." *Teachers College Record* 81, no. 3 (Spring 1983): 525–52.

Kimpton, Lawrence A. "The University and the High School." In *The High School in a New Era,* edited by Francis S. Chase and Harold A. Anderson. Chicago: University of Chicago Press, 1958.

Koerner, James D. *The Miseducation of American Teachers.* Boston: Houghton Mifflin, 1963.

Koppich, Julia, and William Gerritz. *The California Teacher.* Analysis of a survey conducted by Louis Harris Associates for Metropolitan Life Insurance Co., New York. Berkeley: Policy Analysis for California Education, 1986.

Kroc, Richard J. "Using Citation Analysis to Assess Scholarly Productivity." *Educational Researcher* 13, no. 6 (July 1984): 17–22.

Kyte, George C. "Education in the University of California at Berkeley, 1892–1965." University of California at Berkeley, Education-Psychology Library, 1965.

———. "The Origin and Early History of Lambda Chapter of Phi Delta Kappa." School of Education, University of California at Berkeley, Historical File, March 1933.

Labaree, David F. "Proletarianizing the High School Teacher." Paper presented at the annual meeting of the American Educational Research Association, April 1986, San Francisco.

Lanier, Judith E., and Judith W. Little. "Research on Teacher Education." In *Handbook of Research on Teaching,* 3d ed., edited by Merlin C. Wittrock, 527–69. New York: Macmillan, 1986.

Larson, Margali Sarfatti. *The Rise of Professionalism: A Sociological Analysis.* Berkeley: University of California Press, 1977.

Lazerson, Marvin. "If All the World Were Chicago: American Education in the Twentieth Century." *History of Education Quarterly* 24, no. 2 (Summer 1984): 165–79.

Levine, Adeline Gordon. "Marital and Occupational Plans of Women in Professional Schools: Law, Medicine, Nursing, and Teaching." Doctoral diss., Yale University, 1968.

Linder, Roscoe G. *An Evaluation of the Courses in Education of a State Teachers College by Teachers in Service.* Contributions to Education no. 664. New York: Teachers College, 1935.

Lonn, Ella. "Academic Status of Women on University Faculties." *Journal of*

American Association of University Women 17, no. 1 (Jan.–March 1924): 5–11.

Lortie, Dan C. "From Laymen to Lawmen: Law Schools, Careers, and Professional Socialization." *Harvard Educational Review* 29, no. 4 (Fall 1959): 252–369.

———. *Schoolteacher: A Sociological Study.* Chicago: University of Chicago Press, 1975.

Lucas, Christopher J. "Teacher Education and Its Governance." *Educational Forum* 42 (May 1978): 469–82.

Ludmerer, Kenneth. *Learning to Heal: The Development of American Medical Education.* New York: Basic Books, 1985.

Lykes, Richard Wayne. *Higher Education and the United States Office of Education (1867–1953).* Washington, D.C.: U.S. Office of Education, 1975.

Lynton, Ernest A. "The Economic Impact of Higher Education: Review Essay." *Journal of Higher Education* 54, no. 6 (Nov.–Dec. 1983): 693–708.

———. "The Interdependence of Employment and Education." Alden Seminars in Higher Education, University of Massachusetts, Boston, 22 April 1982.

———. "The Once and Future University: Reviving an American Tradition." 1984–85 Distinguished Lecture Series, University of Massachusetts, Boston, 29 April 1985.

———. "The Nature of the College and General Education: Questions in an Age of High Technology." Alden Seminars in Higher Education, University of Massachusetts, Boston, 20 Jan. 1983.

———. "Reexamining the Role of the University." *Change* 15, no. 7 (Oct. 1983): 19–23, 53.

———. "Universities in Crisis." Paper prepared for the Directorate of Social Affairs, Manpower and Education, Organization for Economic Cooperation and Development; Center for Studies in Policy and Public Interest, University of Massachusetts, Boston, n.d.

Lyons, Gene. "Why Teachers Can't Teach." *Texas Monthly* 7 (Sept. 1979): 122 ff.

Margulies, Rebecca Zames, and Peter M. Blau. "The Pecking Order of the Elite: America's Leading Professional Schools." *Change* 5, no. 9 (Nov. 1973): 21–27.

Masler, Hallie, and Charles E. Young. "Tackling the Tough Questions." *UCLA Monthly* 17, no. 1 (Sept.–Oct. 1986).

Mason, Ward. *The Beginning Teacher: Status and Career Orientations.* Washington, D.C.: U.S. Government Printing Office, 1961.

Mathis, B. Claude. "The Teaching School—An Old Model in a New Context." *Journal of Teacher Education* 29 (May–June 1978): 9–13.

Mattingly, Paul H. "Academia and Professional School Careers, 1840–1900." *Teachers College Record* 83, no. 2 (Winter 1981): 219–33.

Mayhew, Lewis B. *Changing Practices in Education for the Professions.* Atlanta: Southern Regional Education Board, 1971.

———. *Graduate and Professional Education, 1980: A Survey of Institutional Plans.* New York: McGraw-Hill, 1970.

Mayhew, Lewis B. and [Stanford University] Committee on Administration and Policy Analysis. *Educational Leadership and Declining Enrollments.* Berkeley: McCutchan, 1974.

Mayo, Amory Dwight. *Southern Women in the Recent Educational Movement in the South, 1892,* edited by Dan T. Carter and Amy Friedlander. Baton Rouge: Louisiana State University Press, 1978.

McArthur, John. *The First Five Years of Teaching.* Educational Research and Development Committee, report no. 30. Canberra: Australian Government Publishing Service, 1981.

McCartney, James L. "The Financing of Sociological Research: Trends and Consequences." In *The Phenomenon of Sociology: A Reader in the Sociology of Sociology,* edited by Edward Tiryakian, 384–97. New York: Appleton-Century-Crofts, 1971.

McConnell, T. R. Letter to Stephen S. Weiner 15 October 1981. Quoted by permission of T. R. McConnell.

McConnell, T. R., G. Lester Anderson, and Pauline Hunter. "The University and Public Education." In *Education for the Professions,* 281–301. 61st Yearbook of the National Society for the Study of Education, part 2, edited by N. B. Henry. Chicago: University of Chicago Press, 1962.

McConnell, T. R., and Stewart Edelstein. *Campus Governance at Berkeley: A Study in Jurisdictions.* Berkeley: Center for Research and Development in Higher Education, University of California, 1977.

McDonnell, Lorraine M. "NEA Priorities and Their Impact on Teacher Education." *1977 Yearbook of the American Association of Colleges for Teacher Education,* 51–68. Washington, D.C.: AACTE, 1977.

Meckel, Henry C. "Research on Teaching Composition and Literature." In *Handbook of Research on Teaching,* edited by Nat L. Gage, 966–1006. Chicago: Rand McNally, 1963.

Melchiori, Gerlinda S. "Smaller and Better: The University of Michigan." *Research in Higher Education* 16, no. 1 (1982): 55–69

Melosh, Barbara. *"The Physician's Hand": Work, Culture, and Conflict in American Nursing.* Philadelphia: Temple University Press, 1982.

Menchik, Mark David, et al., *Fiscal Restraints in Local Government: A Summary of Research Findings.* Santa Monica: Rand Corp., 1982.

Messerli, Jonathan. *Horace Mann, A Biography.* New York: Knopf, 1972.

Michigan State University. Institute for Research on Teaching. *IRT Communication Quarterly* 9, no. 1 (Fall 1986).

Mitzel, Harold E. "Increasing the Impact of Theory and Research on Programs of Instruction." *Journal of Teacher Education* 28 (Nov.–Dec. 1977): 15–20.

Monroe, Paul. "Co-operative Research in Education." In *Research within the Field of Education, Its Organization and Encouragement. School Review* Monographs, no. 1, 14–32. Papers presented at the Society of College Teachers of Education, 23–25 Feb. 1911, Mobile, Ala.

Movrich, Ronald. "Before the Gates of Excellence: Abraham Flexner and Education, 1866–1918." Doctoral diss., University of California at Berkeley, 1981.

Mulcaster, Richard. "Positions" (1581). In *Essays on Educational Reformers,* edited by Robert H. Quick. London: Longmans, Green, 1888.

Murphy, Monica. "Teacher Preparation in California: A Status Report." Prepared for the California Commission on the Teaching Profession, Sacramento, April 1985.

Musemeche, Richard, and Sam Adams. "The Coming Teacher Shortage." *Phi Delta Kappan* 59, no. 10 (June 1978): 691–93.

Nash, Paul. "The Humanistic Foundations of Education." *Teacher Education Quarterly* (California Council on the Education of Teachers) 11, no. 2 (Spring 1984): 53–59.

National Center for Education Statistics. *The Condition of Education, 1985.* Washington, D.C.: National Center for Education Statistics, 1985.

———. *Projections of Educational Statistics to 1990–91.* Washington, D.C.: U.S. Department of Education, 1982.

National Commission on Excellence in Education. *A Nation at Risk.* Washington, D.C.: U.S. Government Printing Office, 1983.

National Education Association. *Status of the American Public School Teacher,* 1985–86. Washington, D.C.: National Education Association, 1987.

National Governors' Association. *A Time for Results: 1991 Report on Education,* Washington, D.C.: N.G.A. Center for Policy Research, 1986.

National Survey of the Education of Teachers. *Bulletin,* 1933, no. 10 (6 vols.) Washington, D.C.: U.S. Office of Education, 1935.

Nerad, Maresi. "The Department of Home Economics at the University of California, Berkeley, 1916–1962." Doctoral diss., University of California at Berkeley, 1988.

Neustadt, Richard E., and Ernest R. May. *Thinking in Time: The Uses of History for Decision Makers.* New York: Free Press, 1986.

Newlon, Jesse H. *Educational Administration as Social Policy.* New York: Scribner's Sons, 1934.

Niebuhr, H. Richard. *The Social Sources of Denominationalism.* New York: World Publishers, 1929.

Niebuhr, H. Richard, Daniel Day Williams, and James M. Gustafson. *The Advancement of Theological Education.* New York: Harper & Bros., 1957.

Odden, Allan R. "School Finance, 1983–1987." Paper presented at the annual meeting of the American Educational Research Association, April 1987, Washington, D.C.

Ognibene, Richard. "Promoting Change in Catholic Education, 1940–1965." Paper presented at the annual meeting of the American Educational Research Association, April 1985, Chicago.

O'Leary, Timothy F. *An Inquiry into the General Purposes, Functions, and Organization of Selected University Schools of Education.* Washington, D.C.: Catholic University Press, 1941.

Olin, Helen. *The Women of a State University.* New York: G. P. Putnam's Sons, 1909.

Olson, David R. "From Utterance to Text." *Harvard Educational Review* 47, no. 3 (Aug. 1977): 257–81.

Olson, Lynn. "Study Examines 'Appeal' of Teaching." *Education Week* 6, no. 17 (21 Jan. 1987): 5.

"The Organization of the Cincinnati Association of Public School Teachers," *School and Society* 11, no. 272 (13 March 1920): 326–27.

Ornstein, Alan C. *Education and Social Inquiry.* Itasca, Ill.: Peacock, 1978.

Park, Joe. "Value Conflict, Rights, and Teacher Education." In *Responding to the Power Crisis in Teacher Education,* edited by Ayres Bagley, 47–63. Major papers and abstracts of the 1971 conference in Chicago. Washington, D.C.: Society of Professors of Education.

Pattison, William. University of Chicago. Telephone interview with Geraldine Clifford, 23 April 1986.

Payne, Bruce R. "Difficulties in the Integration of Subject Matter and Method in Teachers Colleges." *School and Society* 31, no. 808 (21 June 1930): 821–27.

Pease, G. R. "A Graduate Student Criticism of the College of Education." *School and Society* 28, no. 724 (10 Nov. 1928): 577–79.

Perkin, Harold. "The Historical Perspective." In *Perspectives on Higher Education: Eight Disciplinary and Comparative Views,* edited by Burton R. Clark, 17–55. Berkeley: University of California Press, 1984.

Peterson, Paul E. *The Politics of School Reform, 1870–1940.* Chicago: University of Chicago Press, 1985.

Phelps, C. L. "What Is a Teachers College?" *School and Society* 31, no. 789 (8 Feb. 1930): 183–85.

Pillet, Roger A. "MAT-5 Quarter Program." University of Chicago, Graduate School of Education, Fall 1969.

Pollard, Lucille A. *Women on College and University Faculties: A Historical Survey and a Study of Their Present Academic Status.* New York: Arno Press, 1977.

Powell, Arthur G. "Speculations on the Early Impact of Schools of Education on Educational Psychology." *History of Education Quarterly* 11, no. 4 (Winter 1971): 406–12.

———. *The Uncertain Profession: Harvard and the Search for Educational Authority.* Cambridge: Harvard University Press, 1980.

———. "University Schools of Education in the Twentieth Century." *Peabody Journal of Education* 54, no. 1 (Oct. 1976): 3–20.

Quick, Robert H. *Essays on Educational Reformers.* New York: Appleton, 1890.

"Quotations: Women in the Harvard Graduate School of Education," *School and Society* 11 (16 Oct. 1920): 348–49.

Ravitch, Diane. *The Troubled Crusade: American Education, 1945–1980.* New York: Basic Books, 1983.

Reller, Theodore L. "Report on Supervised Teaching Unit, Berkeley Campus," University of California at Berkeley, School of Education, 5 July 1966.

———. "A Survey of the Requirements for the Degree of Doctor of Education." *School and Society* 39, no. 1008 (21 April 1934): 516–20.

———. "Teacher Education in the School of Education: A Position Paper." University of California at Berkeley, School of Education, Nov. 1968.

———. Interviews with Geraldine Clifford, Berkeley, California, 11 Sept. 1985, 28 Aug. 1986, 3 Sept. 1986.

Reynolds, O. Edgar. *The Social and Economic Status of College Students.* Teachers College Contributions to Education, no. 272. New York: Teachers College, Columbia University, 1927.

Roemer, Robert E., and Marian L. Martinello. "Divisions in the Education Professoriate and the Future of Professional Education." *Educational Studies* 13, no. 2 (Summer 1982): 203–23.

Rossiter, Margaret. *Women Scientists in America: Struggles and Strategies to 1940.* Baltimore: Johns Hopkins University Press, 1982.

———. "'Women's Work' in Science, 1880–1910." *Isis* 71 (1980): 381–98.

Roszak, Theodore. *The Cult of Information.* New York: Pantheon, 1986.

Rothman, Robert. "More College Freshmen Note Interest in Teaching Career." *Education Week* 6, no. 6 (14 Jan. 1987): 12.

Ruediger, William C. *The Present Status of Education as a Science: The Principles of Education. School Review* Monographs, no. 2. Chicago: University of Chicago Press, 1912.

Rugg, Harold. "Curriculum-Making in Laboratory Schools." In *Curriculum-Making: Past and Present,* 83–112. 26th Yearbook of the National Society for the Study of Education, part 1, edited by Guy M. Whipple. Bloomington, Ill.: Public School Publishing Co., 1927.

Russell, James Earl. "Further Development of the School of Education." *School and Society* 17, no. 438 (19 May 1923): 533–38.

Sanger, David E. "Harvard Business School at 75." *New York Times,* 5 March 1984.

Sarason, Seymour B. *The Culture of the School and the Problem of Change* 2d ed. Boston: Allyn & Bacon, 1982.

———. *Schooling in America: Scapegoat and Salvation.* New York: Free Press, 1983.

Schlechty, Phillip C., and Victor S. Vance. "Recruitment, Selection, and Retention: The Shape of the Teaching Force." *Elementary School Journal* 83, no. 4 (1983): 469–87.

Schlossman, Steven, and Michael Sedlak. "The Age of Autonomy in American Management Education" (draft report). Santa Monica, Calif.: Graduate Management Admission Council, 1985.

Schneider, B. L. "Ed.D. and Ph.D. Programs: An Issue of Distinction." Council of Graduate Schools in the United States. *Communicator* 7 (1984): 1–2.

Schubert, William H. "Contributions to the AERA Annual Program as an Indicator of Institutional Productivity." *Educational Researcher* 8, no. 17 (July–Aug. 1979): 13–17.

Schwebel, Milton. "The Clash of Cultures in Academe: The University and the Education Faculty." *Journal of Teacher Education* 36, no. 4 (July–Aug. 1985): 2–7.

Scully, M. G. "The Well-Known Universities Lead in Rating of Faculties' Reputations." *Chronicle of Higher Education* 17, no. 18 (1979): 6–7.

Sears, Jesse Brundage. *An Autobiography.* Palo Alto, 1959.

Sears, Jesse Brundage, and Adin D. Henderson. *Cubberley of Stanford.* Stanford, Calif.: Stanford University Press, 1957.

Sedlak, Michael, and Steven Schlossman. *Who Will Teach? Historical Perspectives on the Changing Appeal of Teaching as a Profession.* Santa Monica, Calif.: Rand Corp., 1986.

Sizer, Theodore. "On Myopia: A Complaint from Down Below." *Daedalus* 103, no. 4 (Fall 1974): 333–39.

Sizer, Theodore R., and Arthur G. Powell. "Changing Conceptions of the Professor of Education." In *To Be a Phoenix: The Education Professoriate,* edited by James Steve Counelis. Bloomington, Ind.: Phi Delta Kappa, 1969.

Slater, Frances, ed. *The Quality Controllers: A Critique of the White Paper "Teaching Quality."* London: Institute of Education, University of London, 1985.

Slosson, Edwin E. *Great American Universities.* New York: Macmillan, 1910.

Smith, B. Othanel. *A Design for a School of Pedagogy.* Washington, D.C.: U.S. Department of Education, 1980.

Smith, Dora V. *Instruction in English.* Bureau of Education Bulletin, no. 17. Washington, D.C.: U.S. Government Printing Office, 1933.

Smith, Hilton. "Contemporary Studies of American Schooling." *Educational Studies* 16, no. 1 (Spring 1985): 1–14.

Smith, Marshall. "Stanford School of Education Budget Presentation Outline." 19 Dec. 1986.

Smith, Nila Banton. *American Reading Instruction.* Newark, Del.: International Reading Association, 1934, 1965.

Solomon, Barbara Miller. *In the Company of Educated Women: A History of Women and Higher Education in America.* New Haven, Conn.: Yale University Press, 1985.

Solomon, Lewis C. "Helping Teachers in the Trenches." *Education* 4, no. 1 (Spring 1986).

Spaulding, Frank E. "Dr. Spaulding's Letter of Resignation from the Superintendency of the Cleveland Schools." *School and Society* 11, no. 266 (31 Jan. 1920): 13–34.

Spillane, Robert R. "Agenda for 1986: The Profession of Teaching." Paper prepared for the National Governor's Association Task Force on Teaching, 12 Dec. 1985.

Stadtman, Verne A. *The University of California, 1868–1968.* New York: McGraw-Hill, 1970.

Stanford University. Donald Kennedy. "Advancing Knowledge." Campus Report 14, no. 10 (Nov.–Dec. 1981).

Stanford University. School of Education. J. Myron Atkin. "Report to the Stanford University Senate," 8 Jan. 1981.

Stark, Joan S. University of Michigan School of Education. "Annual Report to the President of the University." *Innovator* 14, no. 3 (Dec. 1982).

Stern, David S. "Compensation for Teachers." *Review of Research in Education* 13 (1986): 285–316.

Stevens, Robert B. "The American Law School." *Perspectives in American History* 5 (1971): 403–548.

———. *Law School: Legal Education in America from the 1850s to the 1980s.* Chapel Hill: University of North Carolina Press, 1983.

Stone, James C. *Breakthrough in Teacher Education.* San Francisco: Jossey-Bass, 1970.

Strober, Myra H., and Audri Gordon Lanford. "The Percentage of Women in Public School Teaching: Cross-Sectional Analysis, 1850–1880." School of Education, Stanford University, Institute for Research on Educational Finance and Governance, program report 84-B11, Nov. 1984.

Strum, Harvey. "Discrimination at Syracuse University." *History of Higher Education Annual* 4 (1984): 101–22.

Swygert, Michael, and Nathanial E. Gozansky. "Senior Law Faculty Publication Study: Comparisons of Law School Productivity." *Journal of Legal Education* 35 (1985): 373–94.

Sykes, Gary. "Contradictions, Ironies, and Promises Unfulfilled: A Contemporary Account of the Status of Teaching." *Phi Delta Kappan* 65, no. 2 (Oct. 1983): 87–93.

Talbot, Marion. *The Education of Women.* Chicago: University of Chicago Press, 1910.

———. *More Than Lore: Reminiscences.* Chicago: University of Chicago Press, 1936.

Taylor, Alex. "Why Women Managers Are Bailing Out." *Fortune* 114, no. 4 (18 Aug. 1986): 16–23.

Taylor, William. "The Crisis of Confidence in Teacher Education: An International Perspective." *Oxford Review of Education* 9, no. 1 (1983): 39–49.

Teachers College, Columbia University. Ed.D. Committee. "The Doctor of Education Program." 1971.

Toch, T. "Accrediting Body Questions Quality of Several Ed. Schools." *Education Week* 1, no. 42 (1 Sept. 1982): 4.

Tom, Alan R. "The Holmes Report: Sophisticated Analysis, Simplistic Solutions." *Journal of Teacher Education* 37, no. 4 (July–Aug. 1986): 44–46.

Treacy, Robert E. "Progressivism and Corinne Seeds: UCLA and the University Elementary School." Doctoral diss., University of Wisconsin, 1972.

Trent, William T. "Equity Considerations in Higher Education: Race and Sex

Differences in Degree Attainment and Major Field from 1976 through 1981." *American Journal of Education* 92, no. 3 (May 1984): 280–305.

Trow, Martin A. "The American Academic Department as a Context for Learning." *Studies in Higher Education* 1, no. 1 (March 1976): 11–22.

———. "The Analysis of Status." In *Perspectives on Higher Education: Eight Disciplinary and Comparative Views,* edited by Burton R. Clark, 132–64. Berkeley: University of California Press, 1984.

Tyack, David. *The One Best System: A History of American Urban Education.* Cambridge, Mass.: Harvard University Press, 1974.

Tyack, David, and Elisabeth Hansot. *Managers of Virtue: Public School Leadership in America, 1820–1980.* New York: Basic Books, 1982.

U.S. Department of Labor. *Job Horizons for College Women.* Bulletin 288 (rev.). Washington, D.C.: U.S. Government Printing Office, 1967.

University of California. Benjamin I. Wheeler, "President's Biennial Report, 1899–1900."

University of California. Inaugural Address of Robert Gordon Sproul as President of the University, 22 Oct. 1930. Bancroft Library, University of California at Berkeley.

University of California. Liaison Committee of the Regents of the University and the California State Board of Education. "A Report of a Survey of the Needs of California in Higher Education." 1 March 1948.

———. "A Restudy of the Needs of California in Higher Education: A Digest." Berkeley, 1955.

University of California. "Report of the Humanities Panel." Berkeley, March 1983.

———. "Report of the President's Committee on Programs in Education." Typescript, n.d. [1950?]. Historical Files, Graduate School of Education.

———. Academic Program Review Committee for Education. "The Study of Education: A Review of the Education Programs in the University of California." Berkeley: Academic Planning and Program Review Board, 1976.

———. University-Wide Program Review Committee for Education. "The Role of the University of California in Precollegiate Education." Oct. 1984.

———. Statewide Assembly of the Academic Senate. Oliver A. Johnson, "Remarks by the Chairman." Record of the Statewide Assembly of the Academic Senate, 2–5. 26 May 1982.

———. University Committee on Educational Policy. "UCEP Response to the APPRB Study of Education: Educational Policy Considerations" (draft), March 1977. School of Education, Historical File.

University of California, Berkeley. Academic Senate. "Education at Berkeley: A Report of the Select Committee on Education," March 1966.

University of California, Berkeley. Academic Senate Committee on Budget And Interdepartmental Relations. Annual Report, 1980–81. "Notice of the Meeting, Berkeley Division of the Academic Senate," 18–22. 19 Oct. 1981.

———. Annual Report, 1981–82. “Notice of the Meeting, Berkeley Division of the Academic Senate,” 7–11. 22 Nov. 1982.
———. Annual Report, 1984–85. “Notice of the Meeting, Berkeley Division of the Academic Senate,” 7–18. 1 Oct. 1985.
University of California, Berkeley. Academic Senate Committee on Educational Policy, Annual Report, 1981–82. “Notice of the Meeting, Berkeley Division of the Academic Senate,” 28–41. 22 Nov. 1982.
University of California, Berkeley. Capital Campaign. “Builders of Berkeley.” Draft manuscript, 1986.
University of California, Berkeley. “Chancellor Looks at Budget Cuts' Impact on Berkeley,” *Monday Paper* 7, no. 7 (3 Nov. 1978).
———. “Revised Academic Plan, 1969–1975,” 1969.
———. Ira Michael Heyman. Memo on the School of Education addressed to Academic Senate committees, 13 Jan. 1982.
———. Neil J. Smelser et al. “Report of the Commission on Education,” May 1981.
———. Graduate Division, *The Graduate* 3, no. 1 (Spring 1987): 1–6.
———. Eunice L. Burns to Robert B. Ruddell, 7 May 1979. Graduate School of Education, Historical File.
———. Office of Institutional Research. “Title IX Report,” 1984.
———. Office of the Dean, School of Education, Historical File.
———. School of Education. William A. Brownell to R. G. Sproul, 14 Oct. 1953.
———. School of Education. “Report on Supervised Teaching Unit, Berkeley Campus,” 5 July 1966.
———. School of Education. Update (Spring 1982).
———. Graduate School of Education. James W. Guthrie, “Annual Report of the Chairman of the Department of Education,” 1982.
University of California, Los Angeles. Alumni Association. *UCLA Monthly* 17, no. 1 (Sept.–Oct. 1986).
———. Graduate School of Education. “Helping Teachers in the Trenches: A New Direction for GSE.” *Education* 4, no. 1 (Spring 1986): 4–5.
———. Graduate School of Education. “Executive Review, 1977–1978,” 5 Dec. 1977.
———. Graduate School of Education. “Graduate Program: Self-Review,” 1 Aug. 1977.
University of Chicago. “Report and Recommendations Concerning a Graduate School of Education,” 5 March 1958.
———. “Report of the Committee to Examine the University's Resources and Future Commitments in Education,” 16 May 1975.
———. Council of the University Senate. “Minutes” for 11 March 1958 and 15 April 1958.
University of Chicago, Department of Education. “Report of the Committee on the Merger of the Graduate School of Education and the Department of Education,” 6 Nov. 1975.
———. *Friends* (newsletter), October 1977.

———. *Education News.*
———. "Minutes of the Meetings of the Faculty of the Department of Education."
———. "Report on Master's Degree Programs for the Preparation of Secondary School and Junior College Teachers," 6 April 1959.
University of Chicago, Graduate School of Education. Minutes of the Council of the Graduate School of Education, 12 May 1964.
———. "Minutes of the Meeting of the Graduate School of Education Faculty."
University of Michigan. Associates in the Social Foundations of Education. Notes and Abstracts in American and International Education, nos. 61, 62, and 63.
———. School of Education, Wilbur E. Cohen. "Report to the President." *Innovator* 10 (39 Nov. 1978).
University of Minnesota. College of Education. *Points* (newsletter) 11, no. 7 (15 March 1983).
Veysey, Laurence. *The Emergence of the American University.* Chicago: University of Chicago Press, 1965.
Vickers, Jill McCalla. "Memoirs of an Ontological Exile: The Methodological Rebellions of Feminist Research." In *Feminism in Canada,* edited by Geraldine Finn and Angela Miles. Montreal: Black Rose Books, 1982.
Vogel, Robert. "Teachers' Colleges Shift Their Focus to Related Fields," *New York Times,* 11 Nov. 1979.
Walberg, Herbert J. "University Distinction in Educational Research: An Exploratory Study." *Educational Researcher* 1, no. 1 (Jan. 1972): 15–16.
Walsh, Mary Roth. *Doctors Wanted, No Women Need Apply: Sexual Barriers in the Medical Profession, 1835–1975.* New Haven: Yale University Press, 1977.
Walton, Henry. "Overview of Themes in Medical Education." In *Education for the Professions: Quis custodiet . . . ?* edited by Sinclair Goodlad, 41–55. Guilford, England: Society for Research into Higher Education/NFER-Helson, 1984.
Ward, Dwayne. "Labor Market Adjustments in Elementary and Secondary Teaching: The Reaction to the 'Teacher Surplus.'" *Teachers College Record* 77, no. 2 (Dec. 1975): 189–218.
Warren, Donald. "Learning from Experience: History and Teacher Education." *Educational Researcher* 14, no. 10 (Dec. 1985): 5–12.
Wasserman, Jeff. "Normal Schools and the Educational Hierarchy, 1860–1890." *Journal of the Midwest History of Education Society* 7 (1979): 1–22.
Watanabe, June. "UH's Dean of Education Quits in Policy Dispute," *Honolulu Star-Bulletin,* 4 May 1984.
Watts, Doyle. "Can Campus-Based Preservice Teacher Education Survive?" *Journal of Teacher Education* 31, no. 1 (Jan.–Feb. 1982): 50–53.
Webster, David S. "America's Highest Ranked Graduate Schools, 1925–1982." *Change* 15, no. 4 (May–June 1983): 14–24.
———. "The Bureau of Education's Suppressed Rating of Colleges, 1911–

1912." *History of Education Quarterly* 24, no. 4 (Winter 1984): 499–511.

Wechsler, Harold S. "The Primary Journal for Secondary Education, 1893–1938: Part 1 of a History of *School Review.*" *American Journal of Education* 88, no. 1 (Nov. 1979): 83–106.

———. "From Practice to Theory: A History of *School Review,*" Part 2. *American Journal of Education* 88, no. 2 (Feb. 1980): 216–44.

Weidman, Carla Sue, and John C. Weidman. "Professors of Education: Some Social and Occupational Characteristics." In *The Professor of Education: An Assessment of Conditions,* Papers of the meeting of the Society of Professors of Education, edited by Ayres Bagley. University of Minnesota, Oct. 1975.

Weis, Lois. "Progress but No Parity: Women in Higher Education." *Academe* 71, no. 6 (Nov.–Dec. 1985): 29–33.

Wesley, Edgar B. *NEA: The First Hundred Years; The Building of a Teaching Profession.* New York: Harper & Bros., 1957.

West, Charles K. "Productivity Ratings of Institutions Based on Publication in the Journals of the American Educational Research Association, 1970–1976." *Educational Researcher* 7, no. 2 (Feb. 1978): 13–14.

White, Sheldon. "Federal Programs in Educational Research: Responses." *Harvard Educational Review* 52, no. 4 (Nov. 1982): 552–56.

White, Stephen. "Why Journalism Schools?" *Public Interest,* no. 82 (Winter 1986): 39–57.

White, Woodie T. "The Decline of the Classroom and the Chicago Study of Education, 1909–1929." *American Journal of Education* 90, no. 2 (Feb. 1982): 145–74.

"Why Engineering Deans Worry a Lot." *Fortune* 105, no. 1 (11 Jan. 1982): 84–90.

Wiebe, Robert. *The Search for Order, 1877–1920.* New York: Hill & Wang, 1967.

Williams, Donald T. "Henry Suzzallo and the University of a Thousand Years." *History of Higher Education Annual* 5 (1985): 57–82.

Williamson, Obed Jalmar. *Provisions for General Theory Courses in the Professional Preparation of Teachers.* Contributions to Education, no. 684. New York: Teachers College, 1936.

Willis, Margaret. *The Guinea Pigs after Twenty Years: A Follow-up Study of the Class of 1938 of the University School, Ohio State.* Columbus: Ohio State University Press, 1961.

Wilson, Ann Jarvella. "Knowledge for Teachers: The Origins of the National Teacher Examination Program." Paper presented at the annual meeting of the American Educational Research Association, April 1985, Chicago.

Wilson, Kenneth L., and Eui Hang Shin. "Reassessing the Discrimination against Women in Higher Education." *American Educational Research Journal* 20, no. 4 (Winter 1983): 529–51.

Woodring, Paul. "The Development of Teacher Education." In *Teacher Education,* 74th Yearbook of the National Society for the Study of Education, part 2, edited by Kevin Ryan, 1–24. Chicago: University of Chicago Press, 1975.

———. "The Ford Foundation and Teacher Education." *Teachers College Record* 62, no. 3 (Dec. 1960): 224–31.

———. *Investment in Innovation: An Historical Appraisal of the Fund for the Advancement of Education.* Boston: Little, Brown, 1970.

———. *New Directions in Teacher Education.* New York: Fund for the Advancement of Education, 1957.

Woods, Ralph H., recorder. "Public Participation in Teacher Education." In American Association of Colleges for Teacher Education, *Ninth Yearbook,* 45–52. Oneonta, N.Y.: AACTE, 1956.

Yarger, Sam J., and Bruce R. Joyce. "Going beyond the Data: Reconstructing Teacher Education." *Journal of Teacher Education* 28 (Nov.–Dec. 1977): 21–25.

Ylvisaker, Paul N. "HGSE 1977: Another Stage of Growth." Harvard University, Harvard Graduate School of Education.

Zellman, Gail L., and Steven L. Schlossman. "The Berkeley Youth Wars." *Public Interest* 84 (Summer 1986): 29–41.

Zimmerman, Joan Grace. "College Culture in the Midwest, 1890–1930." Doctoral diss., University of Virginia, 1978.

Index

All page numbers followed by "t" denote tables.